THE MYSTERY OF COURAGE

THE MYSTERY OF COURAGE

WILLIAM IAN MILLER

HARVARD UNIVERSITY PRESS

Cambridge, Massachusetts, and London, England

Third printing, 2002

Printed in the United States of America

First Harvard University Press paperback edition, 2002

Library of Congress Cataloging-in-Publication Data
Miller, William Ian, 1946–
The mystery of courage / William Ian Miller.
p.   cm.
Includes bibliographical references and index.
ISBN 0-674-00307-1 (cloth)
ISBN 0-674-00826-X (pbk.)

BF575.C8 M55 2000
179'.6—dc21   00-029559

For my father, Norman Miller,
who fought in the Pacific, 1943–1945

CONTENTS

Preface

THIS BOOK is a meditation on courage, but it didn't start out that way. My original intention was to focus on cowardice, especially the petty cowardices of daily life, those occasions on which we try to satisfy ourselves that it was our politeness and tact that kept us silent in the face of offensiveness rather than our fear of making an enemy or a scene. Had that book been written, it would have been mostly about the words we should have said but feared to say (and the craven words we did say); in short, it would have been an anatomy of a modern-day lickspittle. I thought such a book would fit rather nicely in a misanthropic series preceded by my writings on humiliation and disgust. Of course I would have had to discuss courage, but as an absence, as a glorious and admonishing phantom whose chief effect was to render us miserable by our inability to measure up, except in pathetic vengeful fantasies which we had neither means nor intention of carrying out. But courage could not be so rudely constrained. It laid siege to my initial intentions and succeeded in breaching them with ease. No wonder cowardice gave way; that's what cowardice always does.

Cowardice, however, still must play a major role in this book. In courage's story it is the vice and temptation to be resisted. And given the elusive psychology of courage it is often the case that the surer knowledge of our cowardice will give us some access to the uncertain knowledge of our courage. So often our experience of courage must be cobbled together by negative inference from those miserable moments in which we wished we had it and found it wanting. But we are not without resources to get at courage, even though it must in the end remain a mystery. There is no shortage of relevant matter to examine, given that humanity has been passionately recording tales of courage since the invention of writing. Nor does courage have just one genre, but finds itself equally at home in philosophy, in history, in imaginative literature—whether epic, romance, comedy, or tragedy—or in the memoirs and letters of soldiers and prisoners caught up in an experience that taxes them in ways they never imagined possible.

All scholarly books require by convention a craven gesture right at the start, a desperate effort to plead the limits of expertise and knowledge to ward off figurative beatings anticipated down the road. The philosophers have claimed courage as their turf, and I am not a philosopher. I cannot avoid them, nor do I want to; in many ways Aristotle and Aquinas organize this book. But I do not have the special tools of a philosopher for one, and then my particular sensibility points me in other directions. I draw heavily on soldiers' memoirs. I suspect I will be blamed for this as privileging a particular set of voices at the expense of others. But in fact this is not a book about soldiers or about war, it is about courage, which means that inmates of death camps, martyrs, other quiet sufferers, even you at times, all figure in these pages. It is just that the soldiers, at least those who wrote the memoirs I draw on, feel obliged more than most to try to come to terms with courage. A book on courage must grant them their authority, not only because of the particular horrors they endured, but because they thought so hard about their experiences in terms of courage and cowardice.

I OWE A LARGE DEBT to those scholars who have written on soldiers' experiences. It was they who introduced me to the memoir literature; they consistently demonstrated an eye for the interesting and an uncanny talent for drawing the best from the memoirs and letters. I name them here because their influence on this book goes beyond the citations to them in the notes: John Keegan, Richard Holmes, John Ellis, Paul Fussell, Gerald Linderman, James McPherson, Samuel Hynes, Joanna Bourke, and Denis Winter.

Closer to home, and more directly, I owe a special debt of gratitude to Anne Coughlin and Don Herzog, both of whom gave me more of their time than I ever meant to ask. My fears about inadequately repaying them remind me of a story of Egil Skallagrímsson, a Viking of the tenth century and something of a berserk. Egil once received a gift of such value that he despaired of making adequate recompense. So he rode out intending to kill the man who had made the gift, though he soon thought better of it and decided instead to compose a poem in his honor. I am blessed with neither poetic nor murderous talents, so this tale of Egil will have to suffice for recompense, though I do count myself blessed with such friends. Add, too, Carol Clover and Phoebe Ellsworth, with whom I always consult. Others have suggested helpful bibliography or told me apt tales: Omri Ben-Shahar, Paul Dresch, Peter Edwards, Jon Elster, Rick Hills, Orit Kamir, Ronald Mann, Martha Nussbaum, Brian Simpson, Mark West, and J. J. White. Yale Kamisar, a gifted storyteller, treated me to his Korean War adventures in the best mock-heroic style. My students during the past three years made points that have found their way into this book: special mention is due Gloria Claro, Angela Hilt, Katie Kalahar, Cynthia Rusic, Aaron Singer, and Greg Walker. Finally, thanks to Kathy Koehler, my wife, who not only greatly preferred the subject of this book to that of my last one, but who also reads everything I write in its earliest drafts, in the stages, that is, when I would be too ashamed to let anyone else see it, and what she says goes, goes.

Ann Arbor
May 2000

LACHES: For I fancy that I do know the nature of courage; but, somehow or other, she has slipped away from me, and I cannot get hold of her and tell her nature.

PLATO

It is hard to be brave. It is hard to know what bravery *is*.

TIM O'BRIEN, *If I Die in a Combat Zone*

I

Introduction: The Good Coward

ROBERT J. BURDETTE enlisted in the 47th Illinois
Regiment in 1862. He was eighteen. He was soon a Vicksburg veteran, and
later a journalist, humorist, friend of Mark Twain, and successful Baptist
preacher. He published his memoir of the Civil War, a collection of dis-
crete episodes and portraits, late in his life. One chapter, titled "The Coward," is a portrait of a man who earned an indelible place in Burdette's
memory:[1]

> I remember a coward whom I knew in the army. A good coward.
> In all other respects, a good soldier. A pleasant looking man . . .
> A manly voice; an intelligent mind. A cheery comrade; rather
> quiet. Never shirked a duty in camp or on the march. Neat in his
> dress; excellent in drill. Gun and accouterments always bright
> and clean. In scant-ration times, always ready to divide what was
> left in his haversack or canteen, taking the smaller portion for
> himself.

The man was, in short, a model of decency and good intention. But "This
man was a coward."

He knew it. He was ashamed of it. He tried to overcome his cowardice. The regiment never went into battle that he didn't start
in with his company. If his number brought him into the front
rank, there he stood . . . He made all the preparations of an experienced, "first-class fighting man" who intended to volunteer
when a forlorn hope was called for some desperate duty, on
which only picked men would be taken.

The coward's reputation was known to the others, "his weakness and
his good points." His "comrades stood by him and helped him" as they
readied to attack. Men of every rank seemed to take an interest in him,
encouraging him, and presumably assuring themselves by assuring him.
The sergeant eyed him; his nearest comrade poked him with his elbow and
told him to "play the man." The lieutenant nodded encouragement; the
captain whispered encouragement in his ear. Then came the order to
advance. "And just as we were ready to dash forward like dogs of war the
man nearest the coward stopped, choked, coughed up a stream of blood
and fell sidewise. And the coward ran away . . . Sometimes shame kept him
away from the regiment for a day or two, or even three. But he always came
back with a wild excuse for his disappearance which we all knew, himself
included, was a foolish lie, and resumed his duties."

At first the men resented him and his pathetic excuses, but by degrees
their attitude changed. This coward was never punished, though Burdette
had witnessed men formally drummed out for cowardice. Back then,
Burdette, "being a young soldier when [he] joined the regiment," used to
wonder why the coward was treated so leniently. The other soldiers, perhaps not quite so young or whose experience made them more willing to
pardon, understood then, it seems, what it took years for Burdette to come
to understand (or rather to find enough charity to relax his earlier standards): that categories like coward are not so easy to fathom. Cowards may
come in so many varieties and with such different moral quality that a unitary concept can never be sufficiently refined to get the moral call right:
"But whereas in the fierce old days I wondered why the colonel didn't
court-martial the coward for running away, I now wonder if the man was a
coward, after all!"[2]

Burdette is not about to deny the reality of cowardice. There are real
cowards, but their defining trait is that they "all ran away before the battle,
when they didn't have to run":

They played sick the day before. They fell out of the marching ranks when we began to double quick. They stopped at the fence when the regiment suddenly deployed into line to tie up a shoe that was already so knotted they couldn't untie it. They got details in the hospitals in St. Louis and Cincinnati and northern cities months before. There were scores of ways of keeping out of battle without actually suffering the charge of cowardice. And some there were who ran away on the way in, who got so far across the brook they could hear the distant batteries and the nearer skirmishers. But this man went in every time.

So much hinges on the "every time." This man tries again and again. His comrades do not consider his efforts a charade. He means to do his duty, wants to, tries to, but can't succeed. Yet one can imagine the "every time" providing the basis for a broadly comic tale too. Sure, this man went in every time, but he also ran away every time. Burdette hints that that is one way this story could be told; he even makes small feints in the comic direction early on. But once he doubts whether the coward is even properly to be called a coward, comic possibility disappears. The doubt threatens to unravel some of Burdette's understanding of the moral order, for his sense of mystery cannot be contained. Not only might the coward be no coward, it just might be that he was brave, braver than the rest:

> With what beating of heart, and straining of nerves, shortness of breath, and strenuous calling of all the reserves of resolution and will-power, God knew, and the colonel half guessed. A braver man, up to that point than any of the rest of us . . .
>
> The coward served through the war, and when the regiment marched home to welcome and honors, I think one of the bravest men that went with them was the coward. I know he was beaten in every fight he went into, but he went in. And he fought. And such fighting! Much we knew about it, we laughing, shouting, devil-may-care schoolboys playing with firearms!
>
> What is a coward, anyhow? Cravens, and dastards, and poltroons, we know at sight. But who are the cowards? And how do we distinguish them from the heroes? How does God tell?

Even God, it seems, must be baffled by the mystery of cowardice and courage. "How does God tell?" is not a rhetorical question that concedes

that God knows the answer. Not at all. And it would also be wrong to read
Burdette as posing a simple theory that courage or cowardice is solely an
issue of inner struggle and proper intention. Good intentions and agoniz-
ing inner struggles, as far as Burdette knows, also characterize those men
who got hospital details in St. Louis and Cincinnati. But he is not about to
embark on a sympathetic reconstruction of the psychic turmoil of shirkers
and malingerers, for they, to his mind, don't deserve his time or his pity.
Acts matter. Burdette demands evidence that this coward did some serious
work toward the proper goal before he will undertake a moral reevaluation
of a man he had probably once treated meanly. The man's try must be
wholehearted by some objective standard, not that kind of "nice try" that
can barely be uttered without contempt unless to encourage a child.[3]

A good coward's acts must involve undertaking real risk, a genuine
exposure to being killed. It matters greatly that the man next to the coward
stopped a bullet, just as it matters that that did not deter the coward from
overcoming his inner demons to line up for the next battle, though flee he
would yet again. It also matters that the good coward suffers his shame. It is
not for him to declare himself "good" on the basis of giving it a good try.
That grace is only for others to grant, should they be so inclined. We are
not yet dealing with self-esteem in the comical American style of the last
decades of the twentieth century.

But it is Burdette's own confusion, his befuddlement as to what true
courage and true cowardice are, that makes this story so moving. One suspects his uncertainty about bravery is an atonement he feels he owes the
coward. There is more than just a hint that Burdette treated the poor man
contemptuously longer than those who were quicker than Burdette to see
this man's virtue. He wanted the book thrown at him, for the young Burdette had no doubts that bravery and cowardice were simple matters and
this miscreant should have been punished. His penance, now, takes the
form of a meditation on courage and cowardice, on admitting their mystery
and confessing their unfathomability, a mystery that even God, he suspects, cannot solve.

NOT ALL ARE worshipful in the face of courage and
its mysteriousness. Some comfortable souls see it as a lowbrow virtue, if it is
even to be considered a virtue. Courage is all too martial and masculine,
too low-class for some present tastes. It also is rather promiscuous in that
we are obliged to grant it to some nefarious actors as well as to noble ones,

to scourges of humanity as well as to benefactors, to enemies as often as to friends.[4] With good reason courage's detractors can cite any number of times when calls to courage have been calls for injustice, calls to plunder, rape, and murder, calls to die for dubious reasons. Siegfried Sassoon, whose comfortableness ended with his war experience and whose consistent heroics under fire are well documented, thus speaks of the "exploitation of courage" and sees that exploitation as "the essential tragedy" of the Great War.[5]

The earliest discussions of courage, however, unambivalently place it either first among virtues or no lower than third among the four cardinal virtues that include also prudence, justice, and temperance. Construed narrowly as the capacity to face death in feud or war, courage was frankly granted to be necessary to defending self, family, and one's own against external threat, and thus absolutely crucial to securing the space in which other virtues could develop. In this role courage might also be seen as the spiny protective side of caring and concern for others.[6] Construed more broadly as fortitude, it denoted "a certain firmness of mind," a necessary component of virtue in general;[7] in this guise it provided the will and dedication that kept prudence, temperance, and other more tranquil virtues' noses to the grindstone when the going got rough. In Samuel Johnson's formulation: "Sir, you know courage is reckoned the greatest of all virtues; because, unless a man has that virtue, he has no security for preserving any other."[8]

Even courage's detractors concede its necessity; but they would prefer we begrudge it its place rather than thrill, as we so often do, to tales of courage.[9] They would wish to remind us that courageous characters have often not been displeased to see arise the terrible circumstances that provide them the opportunity to exercise and display their virtue. They fear that courageous people may seek to foster the very conditions that make courage necessary. We could imagine the courageous, like those pyromaniacal volunteer firemen who pop up in the news frequently enough to be an identifiable type, going about fanning "courage fires" so they can courageously put them out.

But whether you hate or love it, no one seems very successful at devising a definition or a theory of courage that doesn't raise as many problems as it solves. Some impose so rigorous a standard that Homeric heroes have a hard time qualifying; others are so absurdly soft on admission to the club that just about anyone who sticks to a diet qualifies. There are nonetheless easy cases about which almost everyone will agree, but even the doers of self-evidently grand deeds often turn out not to be as certain as the observers handing out the praise that they deserve the accolade. A good number of soldiers who write memoirs feel obliged to discuss courage and commit themselves to some view of it so that they can judge whether they had whatever it was; and they do not agree among themselves. Moral philosophers and theologians likewise have grappled with it, and they too do not agree. Socrates, in Plato's dialogue devoted to courage—*Laches*—makes his typically frustrating attacks on the reasonable definitions proposed by his interlocutors—Laches and Nicias—but in the end he gives up and postpones the question to confront it again in the *Republic* and elsewhere, where he still speaks obscurely about it.[10] Aristotle's crucially central discussion of courage has driven modern commentators either to various forms of despair or to analytic virtuosity in attempts to give it coherence.[11] Aquinas makes the most valiant and sustained effort, but he ends up solving the courage problem by dissolving it into a solution of patience and sufferance, virtues, if virtues they be, that do not strike us as being as psychologically problematic as courage, even if as morally troublesome.

The main difficulty, though hardly the only one of consequence, is establishing a psychology of courage. It is clearly intimately connected with fear, but how? Does true courage mean possessing a fearless character, being a person who "don't scare worth a damn," as one soldier said of Ulysses S. Grant;[12] or does it require achieving a state of fearlessness by overcoming fear so as to send it packing by whatever feat of consciousness or narcotic that can do the trick? Or does overcoming fear mean never quite getting rid of it, but just putting it in its proper place so that it doesn't get in the way of duty? Or does it mean being gripped by fear, feeling its inescapable oppressiveness, its temptations for flight and surrender, yet still managing to perform well in spite of it? Some suggest that courage has no psychology; they argue it is a "privative" state characterized only by the absence of a certain motive. The coward is thus moved to act by fear; the courageous person simply lacks this motivation.[13] Others evidence their despair at discovering courage's psychology by claiming courage to be a description of deeds, not a special set of motives or a trait of character; in their view calling the people who do courageous deeds courageous is merely a loose, though harmless, way of talking.

There is much more to courage's frustrating complexity than the elusiveness of its relation to fear. Real courage, whatever it is, is mimicked by states that, after reflection or consultation with our betters, we hesitate finally to declare perfect or true courage. These are the cases, roughly, in which courage seems uncomfortably annexed to and potentially annulled by sometime bad things like rashness, stupidity, stubbornness, self-deception, madness, criminality, pitilessness, fury, hardness, cruelty; or middling things like pride and fear of disgrace; or more comfortably annexed to good things like skill and experience that also, arguably, undo the possibility of courage by making fearful things routine matters and thus not so fearful at all.

With an elusive psychology if it even has one, and a propensity to be confused with close facsimiles of itself, even with its opposite, as Burdette came to understand, courage is no easy virtue to get a grip on. Like other virtues, it resists being fixed in stone, defined so as to foreclose any possibility that it may change, expand or contract, with changes in ideology or material conditions. All virtues have histories and sociologies. But courage and its corresponding vice, cowardice, are more at the mercy of social and cultural context than some of the simpler virtues and vices. Temperance, for example, can be reduced to a grammar of easy rules of thumb: don't have more than x drinks, don't eat until you get sick or fat, don't fornicate with more than one loved one and then not too much. Courage cannot be so reduced. The courage of aggression, the courage of offense, for instance, makes very different behavioral and psychological demands from the courage of defense; storming a wall requires a different kind of mustering of will and guts than enduring interrogation in an Argentinean prison or internment in a gulag or death camp. There is a courage of dishing it out and a courage of taking it. Not all that infrequently the same action can with justice be described as an example of courage or of cowardice: thus suicide and the problem of the good coward. And cowardice, which as an initial matter seems easier to get a grip on than courage, suffers from courage's complexity. What is the status of retreat? Of surrender? Of trickery and cunning? Of guerrilla warfare? Of politeness and good manners, tolerance and prudence?

If courage, for some, has had its reputation tarnished by the moral compromises it makes and its occasional vulgarity, that does not keep us from thrilling to tales of it. Courage is the stuff of good stories. In fact, so good is courage at occupying the ground of the interesting and the gripping that I would hazard the claim that it is the most frequent theme of all world literature. Only love gives it a run, and the course of true love never quite succeeds in separating itself from courage, moral courage as when desire focuses on socially unacceptable objects, but physical courage also. One so often has to fight to gain one's love, and then there are issues of sacrifice for and protection of the loved one once secured (such anyway are the common themes of romance).

The true miracle is that courage makes for better stories than its corresponding vice. By necessary implication and often by explicit presentation, cowardice figures in any story of courage as the temptation to be overcome, but cowardice takes a back seat to its opposing virtue in its ability to grab attention. Quite a contrast with other virtues; it is undeniable that most vices are better material for gripping attention than their corresponding virtues. Vices, after all, have their seductive side; that is why they are vices. To be fair, virtues like loyalty and justice drive narratives that hold us as much in their grip as their corresponding vices. But then loyalty derives no small part of its narrative force from making demands on one's capacity for courage (like courage, it is a gray virtue, equally serviceable for both good and bad causes). And justice tends to generate good stories only when it is operating in the corrective mode, that is, when it makes demands on courage to undertake the risky business of revenge, of paying back what is owed, of punishing wrong, of reasserting one's honor and dignity. In its distributive mode, justice makes for narratives little more interesting than do the other two cardinal virtues, temperance and prudence. Whereas stories of corrective justice entertain the warrior as well as the worrier, stories of distributive justice tend to entertain broadly only when sentimentalized; its genre is melodrama. Without treacle distributive justice seems to provide themes entertaining only to the specially cultivated sensibilities of theologians, clergy, moral philosophers, and an occasional political theorist.

In spite of courage's primitiveness, of its obvious suitability to a rough-and-tumble life of little amenity, despite Herculean efforts to cultivate a taste for Merchant-Ivory films and talk courage down, most men and no small number of women would, if they had their druthers, choose to be known first for courage than for any other virtue. With courage secured the other virtues will take care of themselves, and besides, if they don't, no one will push you around. You will escape the misery of self-loathing for cowardice and its attendant fantasies of revenge, that is—and here is a theme that will recur as one of the central issues of this book—if you are capable of recognizing your own courage and have confidence in its summonability.

Courage has that special enigmatic something. Let Samuel Johnson articulate the claim for martial courage's charisma:[14]

> We talked of war. JOHNSON. "Every man thinks meanly of himself for not having been a soldier, or not having been at sea." BOSWELL. "Lord Mansfield does not." JOHNSON. "Sir, if Lord Mansfield were in a company of General Officers and Admirals who have been in service, he would shrink; he'd wish to creep under the table . . . No, Sir; were Socrates and Charles the Twelfth of Sweden both present in any company, and Socrates to say, 'follow me, and hear a lecture on philosophy;' and Charles, laying his hand on his sword, to say, 'follow me, and dethrone the Czar;' a man would be ashamed to follow Socrates. Sir, the impression is universal; yet it is strange."

Mansfield, by the way, is dear to law professors. He is known as "the father of commercial law" and hence, if a hero, a hero of prudence for people of prudence. That, I suspect, is Boswell's reason for bringing him up, not to suggest Mansfield's inferiority (Mansfield, born a Scot, was on that basis alone eligible for Boswell's solicitude) but rather to test Johnson against this example of a man of parts who distinctly does not prefer the martial to the mercantile, let alone to the philosophical. Johnson is adamant, as is his wont: even the great Mansfield would be ashamed to assert the primacy of his virtues over those of Charles.

Courage has a special cachet; people care about it desperately. They compete for it and want to be known for having it. Courage still ranks people morally (and in honor-based societies it ranks them socially and politically). The courageous are not only objects of admiration and awe; they are also objects of gratitude. Courage is one of the few virtues that polities feel it advantageous to recognize officially. Prizes, praises, and medals breed envy among those eligible and not-so-eligible who are passed over, and anxiety, at times, among those charged with conferring official recognition.[15] Disgruntlement, anger, distrust, and cynicism over the award of medals and honors is a commonplace of military memoirs. Indeed this is the fillip that launches the *Iliad in media res*. The Greeks made fighting over prizes for valor and mistrusting the bases for which they were awarded as much a signature of Greekness as we have come to believe philosophizing and sodomizing to have been. The image passed on to future ages is of Ajax so aggrieved when Achilles' armor was awarded to Odysseus that he went crazy and eventually, by one account, committed suicide.

People care so much about courage, are so jealous of it, that we should be just a little suspicious that self-interest may infect even the driest of theories about it, even those of the gravest moral philosophers. There is thus a special politics of courage. For example, more than one philosopher argues, admittedly not without some basis, that courage is intimately bound up with reason and deliberation.[16] They claim either that courageous action requires practical wisdom in some form, or they claim that proper courage should serve reason by keeping us acting rationally when fear would divert us.[17] However, when men for whom reason itself, employing it and manipulating it, is the means by which they achieve authority, thus define courage, might there not be something self-serving infecting the process?[18] Is there not some basis for suspecting a bias in their theories of courage when it grants philosophers more courageous possibility than warriors? Sometimes the attempts are so patently self-serving as to prompt mirth. When Cicero, second to no one in self-congratulation, "the vainest man in the world" according to Montaigne, claims that "the courageous deeds of civilians are not inferior to those of soldiers," he is not about to offend most readers of this book, but when he boasts to his child that his own service to the republic provides the proof, we should, if we could, greet him with catcalls.[19] Nor does his argument go along the lines one might suspect: that given the assassination rate for Roman politicians there is a high risk of mortality in politics, so that it takes real guts to play the game. Instead he argues the general proposition, not indefensible despite his self-interest, that courageous politicians keep their reason and judgment operating coolly in crisis and are less inclined to favor the rashness that aggressive honor often entails.

Unmatched, though, is Plato's claim that philosophers are the most truly courageous of people, ostensibly because they do not fear death but actually desire the "separation of soul from body," whereas those conventional men of courage, warriors for instance, "face death . . . through fear of something worse," such as dishonor and disgrace.[20] True courage as a kind of *tedium vitae*? A bored contempt for and impatience with life? Not only does Plato put this argument in the mouth of Socrates, a truly courageous person if ever there was one, but he has Socrates, when he is making it, sitting in prison awaiting death, not at some drunken symposium. Plato thus bullies us with piety, for who would laugh at Socrates then? Not all abstract discussions of courage and cowardice are this self-serving, but such is the nature of courage and cowardice that they must always have a politics to them. Too much is at stake in who qualifies. And courage aids and abets this unsavory politicization of itself because, by virtue of its mysteriousness, it is able to support so many plausible competing versions of itself.

Courage and cowardice have a rich political and social history. They have inevitably been part of the ideologies that justify and maintain hierarchies of men over women, of rich men over poor men:

> That which in mean men we entitle patience
> Is pale cold cowardice in noble breasts.[21]

By a very common and widespread ideology that informed early stratified societies the free must be brave since only the brave could be free. Your very lack of freedom was proof of your cowardly blood or the bad blood of your ancestors, who had arranged by their martial failure to ensure the servitude of their descendants.[22] The ancient Greeks and medieval Catalonians agreed with the Vikings on this matter; the higher in the social order, the greater the sum of your ancestors' courage, the greater your courageous capacity. Only in very recent times have we begun to invert our presumptions on this score, even though the old association of ideas dies hard ("o'er the land of the free and the home of the brave"). Liberal democratic ideals undid the complacency with which such cant could be maintained. In the new social and economic order the chief vice of the lowly was no longer cringing servile cowardice, but laziness and drunken or drugged intemperance. Yet no sooner are the blinders of the high removed as to the manifest toughness of the lower orders than courage loses some of its unquestioned worthiness. Despite courage's power to generate good stories, it suffers for its ineffable vulgarity, the steroid virtue of professional wrestlers.

The new nervous politics of courage inverts courage's ancient place in the social hierarchy. It is more an attribute of the classes feared by the high than of their own. Once the upper classes became lawyers and insurance executives rather than military officers, gave up dueling for golf, courage, though still a virtue, became insensate and dim, the domain of the lowly. Might it be the case that once the high lost their ideological monopoly on courage they decided to debase its coin? Courage is thus now held to be what it takes to invest in a Silicon Valley start-up or to vote no on a manifestly weak tenure file.

In this way the high's debasement of rare courage converges with another current that seeks to characterize courage so as to make it readily available to those who were denied it by aristocratic ideology. Contemporary gender, sexual, and ethnic politics argues that all are entitled to their stories of courage, that no one is to be denied the virtue simply for having been relegated to powerlessness. It is even suggested that being invisible to or disfavored by the dominant ideology is itself a form of courage. As we will see, this move is not so new; Nietzsche complained that Christianity used a similar strategy against warrior values. The politics of identity is thus participating in an ancient battle—whose beginnings are as old as, even older than, the Stoics—as to whether courage is best manifested in aggression or in enduring aggression, in victory or in defeat, in the charge or in stolid sufferance and endurance. But the modern movement has gone farther to "dephysicalize" courage (if I may coin such an ugly word), by using it loosely to congratulate anyone who by his own estimation undertakes some struggle for self-realization. Some of these struggles may indeed involve something like courage, but that will depend on the amount of real pain endured and real dangers faced. Merely being all you can be need hardly involve courage; more likely it is a less glorious matter of plain hard work.

Yet courage retains its gritty allure. The core of courage's ancient tale is attack and defense against the Other, other men to be exact. The core is about the fear of violent death, pain, and mutilation, the fear of being killed and at times, too, the fear of having to kill. From that core courage expands and we will follow its various emanations outward. The core is not all that restrictive; within it there is space for the courage of endurance as well as for the courage of attack and aggression. Even a kernel of courage as self-realization is present at the ancient core, but only a kernel, for self-realization in honor societies was about proving oneself in battle and feud; in those cultures self-realization was inseparable from acquiring and displaying the courage of confrontation, attack, and defense. Proving one's courage was *the* rite of passage, and the only way to pass the test was to overcome dangers that were, first and foremost, physical ones. The point is simply that no theory of courage can ignore war or the experience of fighting, without being hollow at its core.

With courage, then, and its story come war and strife. War seems to generate in some soldiers a philosophical temperament, a desire to describe and understand their extreme experience, to put it in writing. Not a few of these writings reveal a genuine literary talent, some demonstrate literary genius, sometimes with little (apparent) consciousness of having it. One suspects that in many cases, but for their war experiences, these men would never have been tempted to put pen to paper. The superb memoirs of Abner Small and Eugene B. Sledge are examples. One cannot help but suspect too that the horror, excitement, and pity of war did more than draw forth dormant genius; rather, by some strange alchemical quintessencing, they formed it. The greatest reward for me in researching this book was acquainting myself with this rich, powerful, and worthy literature. Courage compels us to defer to the likes of Robert Burdette, Abner Small, John Dooley (Civil War), Frederic Manning, the pseudonymous Mark VII (the western front), E. B. Sledge (World War II, Pacific theater), Philip Caputo, James McDonough, and Tim O'Brien (Vietnam), among others, no less respectfully than to Plato, Aristotle, Aquinas, and their modern commentators. On this issue, these men, private soldiers or low-ranking officers, give nothing away to those greatest of thinkers.[23]

With courage comes embedded a theory of manhood. In a significant number of cultures, as chastity was to women, so courage was to men: the virtue at the center of their gendered identity, in each case very constraining and sometimes lethal. Courage and notions of manhood were inseparable, the very word for courage in many languages deriving from the word for man. Courage made the man; cowardice unmanned him, got him called a woman. These understandings are under stress now, but they have always been under stress of one sort or another for thousands of years, as the legacy of Medea, the Amazons, and various shieldmaidens from the Viking north, from fifteenth-century France, and from early twentieth-century Albania bears witness.[24] So in some attenuated sense much of this book is about men confronting the anxiety of their defining virtue. Women's problem, broadly speaking, is that male anxiety about courage has important consequences for its ideological availability to women. This is no easy problem and merits more explicit attention than the chapter I devote to it.

Taking my cue from Burdette, this book is best understood as an extended meditation on a theme. I doubt too that I will be able to avoid the politics that comes embedded with courage, for I agree with Johnson. One cares too much about courage, about having it, about not having it, to see exactly what it is independently of one's desire to have a chance at it. My title, borrowed in its sense from a Civil War soldier, already warns that I have no single theory, for none I have seen, nor none I can come up with will work. But there are roughly zones, as Robert Frost so perfectly says. Though the zones I map out will be too narrow to please all, they are not so narrow that I have left myself and thus you completely out in the cold either. So follow me, no, not to dethrone czars, that's too risky, but to search for courage.

2

Aristodemus, or Cowardice Redeemed

IF ANYONE, surely the Spartans should have had a straightforward understanding of courage. They were tough, stolid, non-complaining, not given to being overly theoretical or philosophical in the Athenian style. Sparta should thus be a good place to go to test whether some of the conceptual difficulty I am claiming inheres less in courage and cowardice themselves than in the propensity of academics, philosophers, and people of cowardly dispositions to find difficulties everywhere.

Herodotus (7.229–232) recounts the story of a certain Aristodemus who, along with one other member of the Spartan Three Hundred, did not fight to the death at Thermopylae. Leonidas, the Spartan king and battle leader, sends Aristodemus and another soldier, Eurytus, to nearby Alpeni to recover from acute eye inflammations. There, getting word that the Three Hundred have been surrounded by a Persian force, Aristodemus and Eurytus quarrel. Eurytus opts for returning to their war band and orders his servant to lead him back to the battle site where he joins the fray and gets killed; Aristodemus, "finding his heart failed him," stays behind. Eurytus, Herodotus notes, makes Aristodemus look bad. "Now if only Aristodemus had been involved—if he alone had returned sick to Sparta—or if they had both gone back together, I do not think that the Spartans would have been angry; but as one was killed and the other took advantage of the excuse, which was open to both of them, to save his skin, they could hardly help being very angry indeed with Aristodemus." Aristodemus returns in disgrace. He gets cursed with the generic nickname, Trembler, that the Spartans conferred on cowards, and no one will speak to him or give him a light to start his fire. But they do not kill him, preferring evidently to treat him just as Plato's *Laws* say a coward should be treated: the coward is to be kept alive, given, in effect, just what he wanted, "a pitiful clinging to life" so that he can endure his infamy as long as possible (12.944e).

Herodotus suggests that Aristodemus could have avoided being a pariah without dying at Thermopylae if he had not been paired with someone who felt the call of duty more keenly. Aristodemus was also the victim of some bad moral luck beyond the misfortune of having made a sorry contrast to Eurytus. True, his heart failed him, but it failed in a way it might not have had he never been given a viable excuse for not fighting. Suppose that Aristodemus had not had an eye infection, that Leonidas had never, as a result, sent him to the rear to recuperate. He would no more have run than the others did. If nothing else, peer pressure would have preserved his honor. Now put him back in the situation he was in, just he and Eurytus, neither, in their commander's opinion, fit to fight. There is no indication that either Aristodemus and Eurytus were feigning illness or that Leonidas sent them to Alpeni to shame them as malingerers. Their eyes were bad and even over the short spaces separating combatants in fifth-century B.C.E. battles, it is better to see than not to. He and Eurytus learn that the Persians have trapped their comrades. Those comrades have no choice except how to die; he and Eurytus, however, have a real choice between life and death, for they are sick, have been excused, and are not trapped. Their choice offers them a temptation that the others do not have to face.

There is also an inertia problem. It is much easier to fight when you have accepted that that is what is going to happen; it is quite another thing to be relieved—in the double sense of being officially excused and in experiencing a psychological release from fears of impending doom—and then have to struggle to reassemble the will to fight. The battle will come to the Three Hundred, like it or not. Aristodemus, however, has to remuster the will to seek out trouble he could reasonably avoid.

Yet Herodotus adds a detail to suggest that Aristodemus might have been no better off had he been alone, without Eurytus. For there was another member of the Three Hundred, Pantites by name, who also survived. He had been ordered to take a message to Thessaly and through no fault of his own missed the battle. He returned to Sparta and "found himself in such disgrace that he killed himself."[1] Pantites' sensitivity to matters of honor and shame suggest that in certain settings surviving is socially and morally risky business, no matter how good your reason. The survivor's guilt may not just be an internally generated compensation to his dead comrades for their having died in his stead; the fact of surviving, when so few others did, raises suspicions about all excuses that grant life and that attempt to justify one's special good fortune. We might find ourselves being blamed for happenstance, for our good luck as much as for our bad. Pantites, no doubt, thought he saw in the eyes of those who had lost their sons, fathers, husbands, or brothers at Thermopylae looks that would kill when they looked at him.

Two books earlier in his *Histories* (5.87), Herodotus tells a story relevant to Pantites' plight. A hapless Athenian force sent to punish the Aeginetans was either destroyed by an earthquake (the Athenian version) or wiped out by the Aeginetans (the Aeginetan version), but for one survivor. When the survivor returned to Athens and reported the disaster, "the wives of the other men who had gone with him to Aegina, in grief and anger that he alone should have escaped, crowded round him and thrust the brooches, which they used for fastening their dresses, into his flesh, each one, as she struck, asking him where her husband was." And thus he perished, his good luck turning out to be his bad luck. He was blamed not only for surviving when his comrades hadn't, but for bearing the bad tidings as well. In rougher times, and even today, it takes a certain cast of mind—call it courage or insensibility—or just plain bad luck to be a messenger of ill news.

Pantites had too exquisite a sense of shame. Herodotus readily envisages Aristodemus returning to Sparta without disgrace, if only he had not had the misfortune of being shown up by Eurytus, his more punctiliously honorable companion. Aristodemus had a worthy excuse; his eyes really were bad. Why else would Leonidas have excused him? Some kinds of surviving are excusable if the circumstances are right, circumstances such as Aristodemus would have had but for the zealousness of his companion. Nor did the sole survivor of the Aeginetan expedition return to Athens expecting to have to live his life in shame, let alone to be brooched to death. The women got out of hand and the Athenian men, undoubtedly a little nervous themselves, quickly responded by passing a law requiring the women to exchange Dorian for Ionian fashion, the latter dispensing with the need for lethal brooches.

Still, the sole survivor is in a rather ambiguous position. Surviving raises suspicions about his courage, envy for his luck, and vague nagging doubts that his survival is in some unfathomable way part of the causal mechanism that produced the death of the others. If the sole survivor was to be granted any excuse it was a grudging one, allowing him another chance to perform with unambiguous propriety when the next opportunity arose; that appears, though, to be as good as an excuse could get. There was some doubt that lingered, some suspicion about the substance of his good fortune. Just imagine if he came home a second time from a general debacle. But at a later date, in the unrelenting misery and horror of trench warfare on the western front in World War I, continued good luck under constant stress was less culpable than one-shot good luck in acute, but localized, misfortune like Thermopylae. Robert Graves can thus write of the "fellowship of 'only survivors'" and report that they had "great reputations . . . 'See that fellow? That's Jock Miller. Out from the start and hasn't got it yet.'"[2]

Herodotus leaves Aristodemus, miserable, cold, and contemptible after Thermopylae, with the observation that he would make amends at the battle of Plataea a year and two books later. There is no doubt in Herodotus' mind that at Plataea "much the greatest courage was shown . . . by Aristodemus—the man who had suffered the disgrace of being the sole survivor of the Three Hundred at Thermopylae." But all are not of Herodotus' view. It is a man named Posidonius—remember his name—who gets the prize:

> However, when after the battle, the question of who had most distinguished himself was discussed, the Spartans present decided that Aristodemus had, indeed, fought magnificently, but that he had done so merely to retrieve his lost honor, rushing forward with the fury of a madman[3] in his desire to be killed before his comrades' eyes; Posidonius, on the contrary, without any wish to be killed, had fought bravely, and was on that account the better man. It may, of course, have been envy which made them say this; in any case, the men I mentioned [two other Spartans along with Posidonius] all received public honors except Aristodemus—Aristodemus got nothing, because he deliberately courted death for the reason already explained. (9.71)

Putting aside for the moment any suggestion of bad faith in the reasons the Spartans offer for denying Aristodemus his glory, can we extract a partial Spartan theory of courage from this? The theory would distinguish what one might call a semblance of courage that is a mad fury from the more deliberate and true courage of someone who fights with a full awareness that he has something to lose that he would prefer to preserve if that could be accomplished without undermining his desire to perform courageously. A distinction is drawn between a willingness to *risk* death in battle and a desire to *seek* death in battle. Maybe too we could extract from this tale the view that to the Spartans, courage was not a matter of heedless fearlessness, but either a proper overcoming of fear properly felt, or acting bravely in the presence of a proper awareness of the risks and stakes, which awareness may well be experienced as fear. Posidonius, it is alleged, feared death, at least to the extent that he distinctly preferred not to suffer it, and performed well, incurring great risk to life and limb. Aristodemus' deliberate courting of death to reclaim lost honor doesn't move these crusty Spartans.

In judging Aristodemus so harshly, these Spartans seem to anticipate in some ways that good Athenian, Aristotle, whom they precede by a century. To the extent that Aristodemus is "insensate" he is no different from those dim Celts, who, according to Aristotle, were afraid of nothing, not even earthquakes or floods.[4] The Celts carry fearlessness too far, not fearing things that it is crazy not to fear. Or by another view, since it is not quite clear just what mental state the Spartans were attributing to Aristodemus, his behavior is not so much insensate as too passionate, a matter of fury. Aristotle's scheme distinguishes between inhuman insensibility, on one hand, which is an inappropriate fearlessness characteristic of Celts, and, on the other, the fury of a wounded beast—spirit or mettle—which is a semblance of courage, approximating it but lacking the perfection of reason, fine motive, and principle; it is heedless raw feeling, not "deliberate choice and purpose."[5]

But Aristodemus is not furious like a wounded animal, nor is he insensate like the Celt; he feels his shame as an exquisite torture not to be borne. His fury does not lose sight of his purpose, which is to go out in some semblance of glory, because he is not shameless, because he desperately wants to erase the taint of cowardice that has deprived him of moral and social standing among his people. Neither animal, nor insensible like a stone (or Celt): human, all too human. And all the more disturbing for that.

Aristodemus may have nothing more to lose than a life he no longer cares for, but he still hopes to regain some part of the honor he lost at Thermopylae. Though in one sense he is despairing to the point of irrationality, it is hardly the case that he is not pursuing what he believes to be a reasonable way of redeeming himself. Aristotle, citing Homeric example, is more than willing to admit that the properly courageous might get into a zone when they fight and be possessed by what the Norsemen would later call "battle spirit." Aristodemus' madness, then, is not his battle fury, but his desire to die rather than use that fury to feel sword-, spear-, and stoneproof so as better to advance the group's agenda and, yes, to get home that evening if he could so arrange it honorably.

The Spartans admit that Aristodemus "had, indeed, fought magnificently." But they fault him in three respects that differentiate him from Posidonius. He wants to die, whereas Posidonius wants to live; he fights to regain lost personal honor, whereas Posidonius fights for the polis, his quest for honor subordinated to and dependent on the success of the group; and thus Aristodemus rushes forward with the fury of a madman, while, presumably, Posidonius, consistent with his merging of his own interests with the group's, achieves his successes without abandoning his position in the phalanx's shield wall, even though, as it turned out, his actions were of less avail than Aristodemus'.[6]

To the extent that the Greek style of phalanx fighting allowed for any individual charges in the berserk style, it was apparently not an option that the Spartans liked to use. Daring offense was more the Athenian way; offense by slow, controlled, and relentless push of the shield wall was the Spartan way: discipline, not fury, even when they assumed the offensive. The Spartans, notes Montaigne with admiration, made use of flutes as they approached the enemy "to calm [their valor] in war lest it cast itself into rashness and frenzy, whereas all other peoples normally employ shrill sounds and powerful voices to stir and inflame the hearts of their warriors."[7] The Spartans do in fact indicate their displeasure with Aristodemus for rushing forward and leaving the line.[8] His own risk seeking imposed greater risks on his fellows by opening a gap in the line of shields. But that is not the reason they give to justify denying him the prize; they focus on the imperfection of his desires.

Regaining lost honor is hardly a motive that is strange even to us and would have made perfect sense in the toughminded honor-based societies of ancient Greece. Can the difference between the desires, the mental states, of Aristodemus and Posidonius, especially when all the Spartans can know about either's inner state was deduced primarily from the way each fought, justify the disparity in their treatment? In the Spartan judgment Aristodemus fought *as if* he did not care to live. But he did live, and perhaps there was something about his fighting style that made that outcome reasonably possible if not probable. Why not assume that Aristodemus was aware of this? He would have known that the berserk style worked well for Homeric heroes like Achilles, Diomedes, and Ajax; he did not choose to ensure his death by hanging himself as the overly sensitive Pantites did. Aristodemus figures he must atone for his once having cared too much to live by now not caring as much as he should, but his actions are not without reason. To Herodotus' taste and mine too, he did it up just right.

But something, obviously, is fishy here, and Herodotus suspects it. It is clear to him that Aristodemus was by far the most courageous that day, and surely his theories of courage are not likely to be that different from the Spartans'. One senses that Aristodemus is being subjected to special rules. Herodotus suggests that envy had something to do with Aristodemus not getting first place, not getting any mention at all, in fact, except the reasons proffered for denying him mention. But isn't it precisely the case that Aristodemus was beneath envy? No Spartan, even after Plataea, would exchange his position for Aristodemus'. Aristodemus, they admit, had fought magnificently, but because it was Aristodemus it didn't count. That is what it means to be a person who has lost his moral and social standing in a community. He is a dead man with an embarrassingly alive body. He suffered a kind of civil death at Thermopylae. So contemptible is Aristodemus that his good deeds do not count, precisely because they are *his* good deeds; he is cursed with an inverse Midas touch—what he touches turns to lead.

The reasons, then, the Spartans give for not awarding Aristodemus may not be proffered in perfect good faith. Communal contempt for Aristodemus seems to be biasing the abstract articulation of the proper psychology of courage. Aristodemus, they allege, wished to die, and that desire makes his fighting something less than courageous because, evidently, it was three parts pathology. The inner state of the winner, Posidonius, was reasonable and manifestly sane. He had something to lose, appreciated its value, properly cared not to lose it, and risked all to fight very well, to do his duty and even then some. This sounds reasonable to us; positions similar to this are articulated by Aristotle, Aquinas, and a significant number of other philosophers who have undertaken to define courage. Why though do the Spartans even bother to justify not giving an award to such a contemptible man? Had this been the *Iliad* and Aristodemus named Thersites, no one would feel obliged to address the merits of his claim; they would treat him to derision and blows or ignore him as invisible.[9] Argument *ad hominem* would have been sufficient. Something about Aristodemus' actions embarrasses them sufficiently to put them to giving reasons.

Thersites was unambiguously of low status. Aristodemus had once been a member of the select Three Hundred, who had failed to live up to that special position. His deeds were not as easily ignored as those of someone who had been of no account to begin with. He had been one of them. And so, in spite of his shameful behavior at Thermopylae, to deny him honor at Plataea requires reasons. The reasons look like good reasons, entirely plausible ones, as I said, that place reason itself at the core of courage. The reasons also do not have the look of having been invented for the occasion. People who discussed the mysteries of courage, as one would guess people in warrior cultures were wont to do, would have heard it all before. It would have been circulated as a reasoned view of what courage was—incurring risk of death in battle for right reasons with a full awareness of what was at stake and a desire, if it could be so arranged, to come home alive.

Herodotus, however, is not convinced by the reasons given. Aristodemus had just dealt death like a Homeric hero. That may have given some cause for blame once individualized styles of fighting gave way to the disciplined phalanx style. But the Homeric values remained robust, and individuals within the phalanx felt their individual honor to be on the line just as the heroes of old had.[10] How could Aristodemus' deeds not be courageous? What did not caring to live have to do with it?[11] Had not Leonidas chosen a suicidal strategy for himself and the Three Hundred? According to Herodotus' story, Leonidas had no wish to return home either. He could have abandoned the position, but in order to achieve the glory of dying within the terms of an oracle that prophesied that only the death of a Spartan king could stem the Persian tide and "combined with his wish to lay up for the Spartans a treasure of fame in which no other city should share" he chose to resist to the death. The Three Hundred stepped to battle "knowing that they were going to their deaths" (7.223). The Spartans, I have already suggested, have a good answer to these points: it is one thing to seek death to secure Sparta's honor and safety and another to seek it for purely personal reasons, even though these reasons may also be justifiable, such as reclaiming lost honor.[12]

Yet had the Spartans been better disposed toward Aristodemus the reclamation of his own lost honor would not have prevented recognizing his merit, especially since, as it turned out, it was Sparta who was the beneficiary of his glorious deeds against the Persians. Plutarch, writing considerably later, says that in his view the Spartan "men of old seemed to regard courage not as fearlessness, but as fear of censure and terror of disgrace."[13] This is a theory of courage as shame-driven, one that honorably qualifies Aristodemus in its terms, even though his courage at Plataea is not to prevent disgrace but to recover from it. Fear of shame, of disgrace, is a compelling motive of courageous action. Aristotle, however, thought shame a less than perfect motive of courage, more accurately a semblance of courage than proper courage. As we shall discuss later in greater detail, Aristotle wants to make true courage more than just a balancing of two kinds of fear, one of death, the other of disgrace.[14] He wants courage to flow from a disposition properly cultivated to produce courageous deeds for the sake of the virtue. This is hardly an undisputed view of courage, and for all we know Posidonius did not qualify under it either.

Theories of courage aside, although no one would have wished to be Aristodemus, there are few who would not have wished to have done what he did that day. That's the substance of the envy; but there is also chagrin that such a despised person should accomplish such grand action. The cosmic order botched it. And Aristodemus botched it again too, not by having the wrong inner state to accompany his grand action, but by not dying as he meant to and as his fellows would have wished. Dying grandly would have solved Aristodemus' own problem and the Spartans' "Aristodemus problem"; perhaps they would have then been more willing to forget and forgive his prior failure. His coming back alive a second time makes for an embarrassing situation. What in the world are they to do with him now?

Aristodemus' case thus exemplifies the politics of courage. The jealous competition for courage, it may be suspected, biases the Spartan definition of true courage. They are not giving detached views, but a view for the nonce, articulated to help enforce certain status differentiations that they feel needed to be asserted in Aristodemus' case. But, as I said, it is not as if they invented that view of courage just to cheat Aristodemus of his just award; that view of courage was available to be used; it was already in the air. What they did not own up to, though, was the hefty portion of their own heroic tradition that would have construed Aristodemus' battle fury as admirable and enviable, if only it had not been Aristodemus who had shown it. Courage can still be found in unreason, in fearlessness born of despair, for despair could just as well lead to cowardly inaction. It takes a certain kind of virtue to turn one's despair to good ends.

RECONSIDER POSIDONIUS, the winner of the first prize for courage. He fought well, very well. But he also held something back. He was not a berserk; nor, apparently, did he go berserk (that is, he was not a specially recognized type of warrior who was supposed to fight in the battle-crazed style of the Norse berserks, the amoks of the Malay peninsula, or the crazy-dogs-wishing-to-die of the Plains Indians; notice, by the way, how English never generates English terms for this type of crazed warrior but borrows them from other languages: going to Old Norse for *berserkr*, to Malay for *amok*, to Arabic for *assassin*, or to Hindi for *thug*). There is a problem for courage in certain settings, battle being only the most ready example, and that is the problem of holding something in reserve, of the troubled contention of prudence and tactic against the urgings of the ecstatic model of courageous energy. It is prudent to hold something in reserve. Armies do not commit all their troops in the first assault; some are held in reserve from the level of division all the way down to company and platoon. It would be purest folly to do otherwise. The problem here, however, lies not in holding some of a group in reserve, but in how much of himself an individual committed to the attack is allowed to hold in reserve, for down that path cowardice lies. If 85 percent of a combat division is playing some kind of reserve or support role, the 15 percent committed to action cannot in turn hold the same ratios of reserve to action as obtain at the level of the division, or we would end up with the absurdity of the actual force applied to the enemy approaching zero at the sharp end. Each individual in that final 15 percent, clearly, has to give something more than 15 percent himself; he is not allowed to hold nearly as much of himself in reserve as the commander is allowed at the level of division, brigade, or battalion.[15]

In battle the prudence that qualifies as a virtue is not the prudence of each individual figuring out the wisest course for himself to pursue, but the prudence of strategy and tactic at the level of the group—the division, the army, the nation. What is prudence for the group often demands that the individuals who make up the group forgo more personalized prudence and opt instead for duty, heroism, honor, and glory, which provide them some kind of moral compensation for having the misfortune of being sacrificed for the greater good. Individualized prudence, we suspect, is too easily used to provide a serviceable gloss for cowardice.

But we do not want each individual to give 100 percent either, except in the most desperate of circumstances. Posidonius held more in reserve than Aristodemus. He wanted to live if he could while still honorably discharging his duty; he may even have wanted to do better than that, for he was a type who thought of himself as in that class of warrior who could reasonably compete for the top prize. Yet, he did not go berserk but, in the manner of that mantra of interviewed athletes, "stayed within himself." Even Aristodemus, who did go berserk, must have doubted that he really had given his all, for he lived when he had intended to die. Was it just luck or the sheer force of his fury that kept him alive? Or did he too make choices that would keep him alive longer so as to do more damage? He must have, for he could hardly expect to regain his lost honor by whooping and running forward only to be pierced through the heart before he had killed a single Persian. Berserk as he was he still had a purpose that required some prudential considerations. He wished to kill a lot of enemy in a world of no machine guns or grenades, when killing required intense expenditures of human muscular energy usually at arm's length or no less than stone's throw from the target, rather than in intermittent small movements of a finger on a trigger or a hand pulling a lanyard. He had to stay alive for some length of time to carry out his plan. The odds were against him, so much so that some might call his behavior suicidal, but fixing to die is not always suicide, though it may be suicidal. Still, he had a plan, and it required holding something in reserve part of the time. That does not mean, however, that he held reserves at the level people recognized Posidonius did. But there is that niggling doubt Aristodemus must have had in the aftermath that he really hadn't been quite willing to die, otherwise he would have managed it.

It is of some interest that the men Leonidas handpicked for the Three Hundred were "all fathers of living sons," which was not just happenstance but evidently a necessary qualification (7.205). That meant they all were respectable, that their shame, if they behaved shamefully, would be visited on people they loved who survived them. Leonidas was thus, in effect, holding the sons of the Three Hundred as moral hostages to secure the verve of his troops. But it also meant that they had someone to come home to. This minor detail points to a grim irony in the motivation of the Three Hundred: be willing to fight to the death because you have someone you want to come home to who will be ashamed to see you if you don't fight to the death. We don't know that Posidonius had a living son, but Aristodemus clearly did or he wouldn't have been chosen for the Three Hundred. If it was just fear for his own life and not also his desire to see his son, one might wonder why after Thermopylae he returned to Sparta, where he must have known he would be seen as beneath contempt. He thought he could bear it; he had misjudged; he didn't want to come back a second time.

What if Posidonius, while fighting, was experiencing fear of the sort that cowards and anxious wrecks know so well? That is, he had not overcome his fear in the least, yet performed well in its spite, hating himself perhaps for feeling it, for being nauseous, for doubting his bowels and bladder, for wanting to run and cower and beg for quarter. And simultaneously, because he knew he was doing well, he may have experienced moments of exultation and a growing sense of a nervous kind of relief, a feeling that luck might be with him that day, that he was doing quite well indeed, that he was not going to shame himself, even though he was scared, really scared. But there is still a catch. At the end of the day, if he was going to win the prize and if his consciousness was as I have just described, he would also have managed not to let others notice his fear. He would not have involuntarily evacuated bowels or bladder; he would not have paled or shivered; his voice would not have quavered, nor his tongue have cleaved to the roof of his mouth. He was not Posidonius the Trembler.

To recite this litany of fear symptoms, though, is to make the case for just how unlikely it was that this was Posidonius' inner state. The roil on the inside would surely have given telltale signs on the outside; and some of his competitive and envious comrades would not have failed to notice, even in the midst of the fray, because all were envious of each other's success, careful to note bases for undermining a competitor's claim to glory. If he was so well able to control the mayhem his consuming fear sought to wreak on his body, letting no signs of the inner turmoil humiliate himself before others, then, by that fact alone, we might guess with the others that he was not operating in spite of presently felt fear; rather, he had overcome it. In any event, were he so able to fake it, who is to say that such peerless faking is not courage itself?

THE SPARTANS LEAVE us not much better off than we started. Courage is still a psychological mystery. But hero or coward, Aristodemus manages something quite remarkable. He is remembered by name, not exactly as he would have liked, but then not so unfavorably either. Part of being remembered is luck, some good luck this time to go with his bad moral luck, which was no small reason he had the good luck to be remembered. Luck got his tale into writing; more luck made that writer Herodotus, who in turn had the luck to have been good enough in his own time that enough people copied his writings so that some of them had the luck to survive to the present, where, by luck (and by merit), he is counted good enough to be read still. But Aristodemus' story interested Herodotus because Herodotus had an uncanny talent for noticing the genuinely interesting. Had Aristodemus just been a coward he would most likely have been forgotten; had he just done his duty, even done it with heroic excess, and died at Thermopylae, he also in all likelihood would have been forgotten (only five or six of the Three Hundred have been further singled out by name). Aristodemus is interesting because he was neither shameless, nor a constitutional coward nor constitutionally courageous, but equally capable of cowardice and sublime heroism, swinging wildly between extremes. I also suspect the story is more interesting because the cravenness preceded the heroism, not because such moral regeneration and resurrection makes for the kind of treacly triumphs so many are addicted to, but because the politics of honor and shame, and more precisely the politics of courage, botch the ending, fail to give credit where credit was due, making it a frustrating but compelling tale of injustice.

How indelible is an act of cowardice (or courage for that matter)? What is its decay rate? How long must one wait, how much must one show to rehabilitate his reputation, if ever? To what extent does a reputation for courage survive individual acts of cowardice? Is one to be tormented for a lifetime like Lord Jim, or does one get the benefit of the more practical doctrine that those who run might fight again very well the next day, with all bygones pardoned as bygones? But Aristodemus already has a nickname, and nicknames have a habit of sticking. It might be that no matter what Aristodemus did in the future, no matter how brave, he would always be "Trembler." Nor can we imagine that Burdette's good coward took any solace in his title, though Burdette meant to bestow it generously. It might be that the best Aristodemus could hope for was that people would eventually come to understand his nickname as an ironic description of someone everyone had come to recognize and respect as one tough hombre.

WE LEAVE SPARTA now for the Athens of Socrates, Plato, and Aristotle; but this Athens will be mediated through the eyes of soldiers writing mostly in the past one hundred years; it will also shift focus from awards and competition, public and external matters, to inner experience.

3

Tim O'Brien and Laches

MORAL PHILOSOPHERS and soldiers share an interest in theorizing courage, in trying to figure out just what it is. The former come to it by profession because it is the kind of issue that they are expected to tackle. The latter have it thrust upon them by having to measure up to it in their own eyes and in the eyes of others judging them. Even nonmartial nonphilosophical sorts can hardly avoid self-assessments and assessments by others that force them to wonder about what Abner Small, a Civil War soldier, referred to as "the mystery of bravery."[1]

At least one well-known philosopher, Socrates, was also a soldier of note[2] and so fearless looking that even while retreating along with the general rout of the Athenian force at Delium (424 B.C.E.) the enemy would not dare approach him. As Plato has Alcibiades, an eyewitness, tell it in the *Symposium* (221b),

> I noticed for one thing how much cooler he was than Laches, and for another how . . . he was walking with the same "lofty strut and sideways glance" that he goes about with here in Athens. His "sideways glance" was just as unconcerned whether he was looking at his own friends or at the enemy, and you could

see from half a mile away that if you tackled *him* you'd get as good as you gave—with the result that he and Laches both got clean away.

Thanks to Plato, Socrates was one of very few common soldiers whose experience of battle was considered worthy of being recorded in any form until the age when armies were conscripted and conscripts were also largely literate. Thus direct evidence of common soldiers' views of courage begin to appear only during the Napoleonic wars and in considerable number from the time of the American Civil War. But when they do appear we are treated to some stunning performances.

Take Tim O'Brien, a conscripted infantryman, literate and self-consciously so, who served in Vietnam in 1969–70. In war O'Brien found his theme, and that theme was courage, a desperate seeking of it in himself and others, even if he was not quite sure what he was looking for or how to recognize it when he found it. O'Brien is not quite the typical Vietnam War soldier; he was meant for graduate school and in fact ended up there, at Harvard no less, *after* serving a tour of intense combat duty, not as a strategy to avoid serving it. As a kid, he tells us, he read not only the Hardy Boys but also Plato "and enough Aristotle to make [him] prefer Plato."[3] As a college student, he canvassed for Eugene McCarthy; he was the very type who usually managed somehow—by letters from hastily consulted psychiatrists, by fleeing to Canada, by parental pull with the local draft board, by getting the right information about flunking physicals, by doing alternative service, by getting into the National Guard—to avoid that war. O'Brien's memoir of the war, *If I Die in a Combat Zone*, appeared in 1973. In it, Socrates and Plato, even Aristotle, have their roles, important ones at that; it is Socrates who accompanies him "through basic training as [his] friend" (53). And once under fire in Vietnam O'Brien seeks them out for help in understanding courage, and Socrates, especially, again comes to his aid to assist in the production of O'Brien's rightly admired memoir.

Johansen

O'Brien offers a sustained essay on courage in a chapter titled "Wise Endurance." The title comes from the Platonic dialogue *Laches*, named after the same Laches, a notable Athenian general, whom Socrates accompanied in retreat at Delium. The essay begins with a worshipful meditation on O'Brien's brave captain. Captain Johansen is a "living hero," one who has the attributes of the heroes of fiction, the ones, that is, unlike Achilles, who are without warts. O'Brien believes in the virtue of courage; he is not so disillusioned by the war as to think courage is itself a sham, a false value, and so he is relieved to find "that human beings sometimes embody valor, that they do not always dissolve at the end of a book or movie reel" (145).

What, then, are the particular attributes that make Johansen the perfect exemplar? O'Brien struggles with this, for to determine these attributes is to get a bead on something that tends to fade to black in the defining; the fear is that courage partakes of too much circumstance and contingency ever to be fixable. O'Brien makes several attempts to get a fix on Johansen, to determine what it is that makes him the figure of courage. He floats a theory, he digresses, he comes back, he circles in, he rejects, he gets ironical, then moody about his own inability to measure up to Johansen's standard. He finally ends up arguing for a courage of making do, a kind of minor-league courage, but courage nonetheless, whose less stringent demands he can plausibly meet.

He studies his captain who lies sleeping, "only a shadow rolled in a poncho" and he wonders late in the chapter, in a kind of summing up, what it is "about him that makes him a real hero." First, "he was blond. Heroes somehow are blond in the ideal" (144). The tone is not ironical; it is a bit uncertain, thus the "somehow," but there is likely to be a feeling of greater certainty on surface matters of the heroic, its looks, than on its substance. It somehow matters that our heroes look like heroes, that they have the style of courage. Start then with what is an indisputable matter of perception: Johansen was blond. O'Brien surely does not intend to have us dismiss his discussion as irrevocably shallow in its easy and vaguely ironical recourse to a once thriving racialist myth. The point is that the heroic comes packaged in a limited number of ways, and though there may be competing traditions that prefer one way to another, the tradition of blondness is one that holds more than Tim O'Brien in its grip. He might even have colored Johansen's hair for the role. *If I Die in a Combat Zone* carries something like a limitation of liability in its front matter: "Names and physical characteristics of persons depicted in this book have been changed." Johansen was not Johansen's name. Did the requisite of blondness pull the Nordic name in its wake? To O'Brien's credit he does not forge a Viking ancestry for Johansen,[4] nor does he, literate though he is, connect him to Nietzsche, who also colored heroes blond. The associations he does make are less ominous: Alan Ladd's Shane. Blond means movie stars, and both blondness and stardom are objects of desire for mere dark-haired mortals, and thus rare and distant and difficult to attain. Johansen, himself, threatens to fade away in his blondness; in this scene he dissolves into shadow, asleep in his poncho, ghostlike, blond, but as realized an action hero as is humanly possible.

The Greeks, too, wanted courage to walk, talk, and look a certain way. Socrates cultivated a certain way of walking, a certain way of looking askance, of letting others know he was cut in the mold of a man of courage. Johansen was more than blond; he also had scars received from auto racing, and he had won medals, although, as O'Brien knows, medals may mark one as a beneficiary of a medals spoils system more than as a distinguished soldier. The difference with Johansen's medals is that O'Brien could verify the actions that earned them.

Johansen does not just look the type; to O'Brien he *is* the type. He meets O'Brien's conditions of bravery, or, more precisely, it is through his assessment of Johansen that he starts to articulate his own theory of courage. The chapter starts with a picture of Johansen watching his soldiers drinking their beer at the end of the day after having dug themselves in. He was "separated from his soldiers by a deadfall canyon of character and temperament" (134). That great divide does not prevent him from addressing O'Brien: "'I'd rather be brave,' he suddenly said to me. 'I'd rather be brave than almost anything. How does that strike you?'" As we shall see, it is this brief bland statement of a commonplace preference that will raise Johansen to the purest embodiment of courage in O'Brien's theory of the virtue. He is self-conscious in his bravery; concerned and worried about it; it is this hint of anxiety that separates him from those oafs of action who so disgusted Dostoyevsky's Underground Man and O'Brien himself.[5]

A month earlier Johansen had charged a Viet Cong soldier, killing him at "chest-to-chest" range, "first throwing a grenade, then running flat out across a paddy, up to the Viet Cong's ditch, then shooting him to death." This was Johansen showing the "steady, blood-headed intensity of Sir Lancelot" (135). There are two features of this image of courage: the individualization of the combat and the charge. Individualized combat died in favor of drill and mass movements of men against other amassed men. Groups were what charged. Then group charges—though still favored by the Japanese and Russians as late as World War II and by the Iranians in the 1980s—mostly passed away because the chances of success were severely diminished as muskets gave way to rifles, which gave way to repeating rifles, which then metamorphosed into Gatling and Lewis guns. Though outmoded and often downright stupid, the charge "is the first thing to think about when thinking about courage. People who do it are remembered as brave, win or lose. They are heroes, forever. It seems like courage, the charge."[6] This is the image of an active courage, offensive rather than defensive, taking it to the enemy rather than letting him take it to you.

Johansen, however, knows not "seems." O'Brien, though certain of his captain's courage, is suspicious of the charge, as too pat, too easy. Not easy in the doing, but too simple to capture the evasive essence of courage. The charge turns out to be a kind of seeming, almost too obvious, and perhaps somewhat suspiciously self-glorifying or despairing or stupid, or just too well-worn, a dated story not able to capture the courage of modern battle, where suffering rather than making suffer is how one's mettle is tested. The point though is that Johansen is courageous for all time; he makes it in the old style and more, for the allure of the old style does not die; it survives to mock the present by its failure to measure up to the stark grandness of the past. But where does that leave O'Brien? Despite his suspicions of the old style, it still provides a ready standard that he fears he can never measure up to; mightn't there be a courage that holds some possibility for the likes of him?

Out in the field, "at a place east of My Lai," there was a different kind of seeming: "bullets seemed aimed straight at you" (136). There are thus two kinds of bullets: some minuscule percentage that were indeed aimed at you, and the rest, some unfathomably large number that *seemed* aimed at you. Is it terror that makes one believe all bullets have your name on them, or does the belief come first and generate terror? Is such a belief of your own special targetedness a sign of a cowardly disposition? The thought has been entertained:

> . . . 'tis a general cowardice that shakes,
> The nerves of confidence, he that hides treasure
> Imagines every one thinks of that place
> When 'tis a thing least minded . . .[7]

O'Brien describes himself writhing under fire as if awakening in the midst of a heart transplant, "the old heart out, the new one poised somewhere unseen in the enemy's hands." Heroism seems beyond reach; one merely hopes not to crack up or collapse in cowardice. He whimpers, and in contrast to the minds in unseen bodies directing those bullets he is deprived of all intention, "the soul gone . . . no thought." He tells Johansen he wished he had behaved better, more bravely. Johansen tries to reassure him: "You're a sensitive guy, like I said. Some guys are just numb to death" (137). He recognizes that O'Brien runs a double risk that the other guys don't; he carries the radio with the antenna sticking up, and his position is right next to Johansen who, as an officer, *is* a prime target. That antenna makes O'Brien more than a random target.

O'Brien is hard on himself, but he also does some very subtle special pleading on his own behalf. To whom, after all, among the grunts did Johansen, separated from his soldiers by a deadfall canyon of character, confess his anxieties about his own bravery? Is Johansen recognizing in O'Brien, by singling him out from the other side of the divide, at least the possibility of courage? Or is Johansen, paragon that he is, taking on himself O'Brien's anxieties about O'Brien's own lack of bravery, by making it appear that he shares the same anxiety, brave though he knows he appears to be to the young private? No wonder these men will fight for Johansen. Whatever Johansen's purpose, O'Brien feels he owes him because Johansen was kind to him, because he recognized and understood him.

Wise Endurance

These are but preliminaries. O'Brien is ready now to stake his position. Courage, he says, must be "wise courage." "It's acting wisely, acting wisely when fear would have a man act otherwise. It is the endurance of the soul in spite of fear—wisely" (137). Wise endurance of the soul. This is Laches' view with some Socratic refinement. Does this mean that courage can dispense with the charge? Can it now shift from offense to defense?

The dialogue *Laches* begins with two fathers of young sons discussing whether it would be advisable for the boys to be tutored in the art of fighting in armor.[8] They consult Laches and his fellow general Nicias, who in turn seeks the advice of Socrates, who directs the discussion to courage. He solicits definitions of courage from Laches and then Nicias, who do creditable jobs only to have their offerings taken apart by Socrates before whom they fold their intellectual tents too quickly, as much in deference to Socrates' reputation as a soldier as to his reputation as a dialectician. Says

Laches to Socrates: "So high is the opinion which I have entertained of you ever since the day on which you were my companion in danger, and gave proof of your valor such as only the man of merit can give. Therefore, say whatever you like, and do not mind about the difference of our ages."[9]

Socrates offers no definition of his own, and in the end, with some ironical posturing, he confesses himself defeated by the project. Yet, while admitting the intellectual difficulty of understanding exactly what courage is, this man, so powerful in self-command, knows he's got it. He cannot resist self-flattery when attributions of courage are involved: "Laches, . . . anyone would say that we had courage who saw us in action, but not, I imagine, he who heard us talking about courage just now" (193e). Even in this kind of good-old-boy self-proclamation of courage, however, one must put the identification of it in the mouths of hypothetical observers—"*anyone* would say . . . who saw us"—and also grant it to Laches, one's comrade-in-arms. This allows for some compliance with the relevant modesty norms, but it also is an admission that the determination of courage cannot be trusted to the self-assessment of the actor. External arbiters of action and demeanor must be called to witness. The discussion with Nicias fares no better: "Then, Nicias," says Socrates, "we have not discovered what courage is."[10] The dialogue peters out amidst gossipy conversation about possible tutors for the boys.

But O'Brien is drawn to Socrates' exchange with Laches. When first asked by Socrates to offer a definition of courage, Laches proposes, "He is a man of courage who does not run away, but remains at his post and fights against the enemy" (190e). Socrates will accept that such a man is courageous but, being rather excessively literal, claims it to be too narrow. Consider, he says, the Scythians (whom no one ever wishes to mess with) who fight by flying, feinting, and then pursuing; they run away. Laches evidently was thinking solely in terms of the Greek phalanx, where holding place in line is crucial, and Socrates is not willing to understand him more generally to intend any kind of sticking it out in combat whatever the style of fighting.

Socrates asks Laches to think more broadly. Can he come up with the quality that is common not just to those courageous in war, but also to those who are courageous in disease, in perils at sea, poverty, politics, and not only "courageous against pain or fear, but mighty to contend against desire and pleasure" (191d)? This is a very expansive view of courage, much more expansive than Laches' first definition was narrow. This is the view of courage as a necessary part of all virtue in resisting temptations and weaknesses of will, anticipating our willingness to make courage available to dieters. O'Brien then quotes from *Laches* (192b–d):

SOCRATES: What is that common quality which is called courage, and which includes all the various uses of the term when applied both to pleasure and pain, and in all the cases to which I was just now referring?

LACHES: I should say that courage is a sort of endurance of the soul . . .

SOCRATES: . . . yet I cannot say that every kind of endurance is, in my opinion, to be deemed courage. Hear my reason. I am sure, Laches, that you would consider courage to be a very noble quality . . . And you would say that a wise endurance is also good and noble . . . But what would you say of a foolish endurance? Is not that, on the other hand, evil and hurtful?

LACHES: True . . .

SOCRATES: Then, according to you, only the wise endurance is courage?

LACHES: It seems so.

O'Brien stops quoting here; but Socrates goes on to reject the revised formulation.

Whom, Socrates asks, do we think braver—the man who wisely calculates and thus understands correctly that he is up against inferior men arrayed in inferior numbers, the man who has wisely acquired greater skill in the use of his weapons, who wisely planned his strategy, or "would you say . . . that he or some man in the opposing army who is in the opposite circumstance to these and yet endures and remains at his post is the braver?" In other words, who is braver, the big tough guy in top shape who has a black belt in karate or the pear-shaped accountant who stands his ground against him? Enduring when the odds are in your favor strikes us and Laches as making fewer demands on courage than enduring when the odds are against you even though it was your own wisdom and skill that created the favorable odds.

No wonder O'Brien truncated the Platonic text before Socrates so quickly killed off "wise endurance" by making "wise" refer only to those moves we make to lower our exposure to risk, not to wisdom as O'Brien understands it. O'Brien still suspects there is possibility in the wise-endurance formulation, and he is not so quick to give up on it. He will test it out, and though the testing quickly leads him to self-pity, to bitter and pained self-doubt, in the end he sticks to a modified version of it. It is not as if his task is made any easier by hitting on wise endurance as the common attribute of all courage. Wisdom is hardly less opaque than courage: "What, then, under the dispassionate moon of Vietnam, in the birdless, insectless silence," he asks, "what, then, is wise endurance?" (138).

The question should prepare us for something more passionate than a purely analytical exposition. He knows he has endured. He suffered through basic training with its boorishly loathsome drill sergeants and the other trainees who all seemed next of kin to the sergeants in their vulgarity and brutality. He endured the talk of drag races and twin-cammed engines (40). (His disgust for the lower classes was harder for him to endure than the physical rigors of drill.)[11] Most important to O'Brien, and an obsession in his corpus of writing, is that he endured war and the military because his nerve failed him when he wanted to desert during training and head to Canada. He sees himself as too cowardly to resist the inertia of small-town and familial expectations.[12] Endurance then becomes for him not the substance of his courage, but the proof of his cowardice: "Was my apparent courage in enduring merely a well-disguised cowardice?" (139). He answers yes.

There is something vaguely self-congratulatory and not even vaguely self-indulgent in such self-blame. Only a soldier can get away with it, indeed only one who actually was at the sharp end, in the thick of things. Imagine a kid who fled to Canada or who joined the National Guard or who took enough drugs of a certain kind to flunk his induction physical who claimed he was courageous by so doing. Because O'Brien fought, because he endured bullets, filth, carnage, and terror and dished some of the same back, he has the moral authority to claim cowardice for choosing this option rather than one that offered physical safety. There is an irreducible asymmetry here. A person may in fact feel himself a moral coward for not running away, may in fact be one, but one cannot feel brave for running away from physical danger no matter how great the moral claim that sends one running, unless that running also leads to danger of a mostly physical kind. There will always be a doubt that one's morals were operating too much in one's interest to be trusted for their virtue when they get one out of a fray whose wages are death.

Endurance threatens to shift meaning for O'Brien. It is no longer enduring danger and the misery of combat and army life: it is enduring your own moral inadequacy, not just on the big issue of the justifiability of this particularly awful war he finds himself in, but in all the moral tests that war imposes. He tells of some Vietnamese boys herding cows near a village in a free-fire zone. Some men in his company fire at the boys and cows. One cow stands her ground: "bullets struck its flanks, exploding globs of flesh," and the cow just stood there, looking away, not moving. "I did not shoot, but I did endure, without protest, except to ask the man in front of me why he was shooting and smiling" (139). This is grim, making Socrates' assaults on the inadequacy of endurance as the summa of courage look like kid's stuff. This is endurance as failure of nerve in humans and lack of enough nerves in cows, which should have been spared.

Endurance is also about mines and minefields, suffering the constant anxiety and terror about the risk of merely taking the next step. As one soldier, a nineteen-year-old, with eight months in the field and with uncanny insight, put it: "It's more than the fear of death that chews on your mind . . . It's an absurd combination of certainty and uncertainty: the certainty that you're walking in mine fields, walking past the things day after day; the uncertainty of your every movement, of which way to shift your weight or where to sit down" (127). Endurance means negotiating a nightmare world in which the most basic features of physical space cannot be relied on. Gravity itself is dangerous; the earth may not support your next step, the tree next to you cannot be leaned against, its branches pushed aside.[13]

O'Brien wonders, bitterly, whether there can be wisdom in such a world and what its content would be. He proceeds this way: Soldiering in war, he says, makes a "fellow think about courage, makes a man wonder what it is and if he has it" (140). This thinking about it is good, and in his view a requisite of courage. Although one should not be obsessed with courage, there is a "sublime and profound concern" about bravery and "hence about cowardice" that one should strive for. For O'Brien,

> men must *know* what they do is courageous, they must *know* it is right, and that kind of knowledge is wisdom and nothing else. Which is why I know few brave men. Either they are stupid and do not know what is right. Or they know what is right and cannot bring themselves to do it. Or they know what is right and do

it, but do not feel and understand the fear that must be overcome. It takes a special man. Courage is more than the charge.
(141)

Self-consciousness, knowledge, and self-knowledge are crucial to his theory of courage; courage must know itself as courage; that is wisdom.[14] How
ultimately Socratic and how ultimately unsatisfying. O'Brien is trying to
rescue courage from rashness, from suicide rushes, from stupidity and
insensibility; but might it not be that consciousness of a certain kind,
Hamlet's kind, may be just as much an obstacle to true courage as less self-
conscious kinds of action?

Might it be that for courage to be imaginable for O'Brien, it must be
imaginable as an experience for someone with his self-querying sensibility?
Otherwise, he thinks, the experience of courage must be forever opaque to
him. When you and I indulge ourselves in daydreams of being Michael Jor-
dan, we do not wish to lose our consciousness of ourselves in the process.
We want to be ourselves when we are he, with our inner life intact but with
his physical skills and social position, just as the commercial, wisely, had it:
be *like* Mike, not *be* Mike. So, in like vein, O'Brien means to save courage
as a moral and psychic possibility for the wise, for the sensitive, for the fearful; he does not want courage if courage means the inner life of the dim and
dull. But how is courage to know itself? Does it happen by epiphany at just
the moment when knowledge and action and affective state come
together? Must he engage in actions that the culture recognizes as prima
facie courageous? Like charges? But then any kid who charges meets the
condition, and that is just what O'Brien will not accept.

He does not seem to be demanding that the courageous have the sensibility of Hamlet, always indulging self-accusations of cowardice. He does
not give us Hamlet; he gives us Johansen. That means we should not press
him too much on just one statement—"men must *know* what they do is
courageous"—and instead read him as he means to be read. The condition
of wisdom is met when a person shows proper *concern* about bravery, when
he worries about its conditions, when he wonders if he makes it, when he
cares enough about it to wonder exactly what it is. The demand to be thus
philosophical and self-doubting and self-knowing is not all that rigorous.
Johansen makes it by letting down his guard for one small instant before
one of his men: "I'd rather be brave than almost anything." Is this all that

wisdom means? It seems so, not just because of what got said, but because of who said it and to whom (it matters for the measure of sincerity of the statement that a captain made it privately to a private). O'Brien has seen Johansen act; he knows that his captain did brave things. There is such a strong presumption in favor of Johansen having the proper understanding and self-understanding. Any indication that his bravery wasn't merely automatic, that he, even he, wasn't sure he met the conditions of courage, would suffice.

It is almost as if proper wisdom regarding courage is had by respecting the mystery of courage, which respect involves, more than anything else, proper manifestations of bafflement as to its psychology. There is a politics in this: O'Brien means to deny courage to the thug, to the guy looking for a fight, to the dullard who just isn't bothered much by moral questions, and give it, or give its possibility, to the troubled self-doubter, to the person who wonders where he stands in the moral order. Captain Johansen, it should be noted, capable of suicidal charges, does not deny his pleasure in being posted to the rear (140).

Nagging him throughout is the question of the proper ends of courage: thus "[men] must know [what they do] is right." What is the possibility for courage in a wrong war? Since O'Brien takes his inability to walk away from that war as his grand cowardice, he has left himself in a muddle as to his own courageous possibility within it. But not too much of a muddle: the larger justifiability of the war is one thing; dealing with mines, bullets, shelling, wounds, death, is another, and in that world one's capacity for courage is tested continually. Doesn't it still take courage to rescue the wounded or to be shot at in a wrong war? Isn't it right to kill someone who is about to kill your friends and you? One sees grand action and grand men, even in Vietnam: "So Captain Johansen helped to mitigate and melt the silliness showing the grace and poise a man can have under the worst of circumstances, a wrong war. We clung to him" (145). The wrongness of the war perversely enhances Johansen's achievement.

For O'Brien the courageous soldier must be conscious of more than his courage. He must also "feel and understand the fear that must be overcome." Why should the fear have to be understood, and what does it mean to understand it? Isn't feeling it enough? One is in a minefield, being shot at; what is there to understand about the fear? Does he mean that by some Socratic-like magic the understanding is the overcoming, or, at the very least, the understanding enables the overcoming? It is something less grand, I think. The thrust of all O'Brien's writing, here and in other works, is that fear, however understood, is never got rid of; you are never not scared out of your wits. If you do well, it is because you have learned to "understand the fear" to the extent that you and it reach an accommodation in which your fear agrees to let you do what you have to do. And those, presumably, who neither feel fear nor understand it are either too stupid or too crazy to qualify properly for courage.

Showing Proper Concern

O'Brien keeps a contemptuous distance from most of his fellow soldiers. He is frustrated by their way of talking about death, by their joking about it, by their euphemizing it; admissions of fear had to be accompanied with dismissive shrugs and grins that "took the meaning out of courage" (142). The language for being wise did not exist. O'Brien wants high seriousness, a certain *gravitas* that his fellow grunts won't indulge. He is wrong, I think, about courage requiring it. True, most virtues only suffer from the comedic; they demand pious tones, and have a bit of pretentiousness about them that begs for deflation. Courage is different. Unlike the other cardinal and theological virtues, which continually demand stultifying piety, courage thrives in certain restricted comedic veins. In some cultural settings the heroic style demands insouciance or the grim mordancy of gallows humor, whether this functions as a way of steeling oneself against one's own fears or, as is often the case, as a way of instilling fear in others, as when you joke in the face of their deaths: "Go ahead, make my day."

O'Brien is wrong; the joking does not undo courage, but undertakes instead to mock all temptations that would undermine courage, such as life itself. His is a disagreement over the style, not the meaning, of courage. To be sure, not all styles of courage demand joking in the face of death, but it is a style of ancient pedigree, one that in its ultimate effect was not self-effacing at all but the most sublime assertion of grand character and one's special place in the moral order. Thus the frequent association of the virtue of magnanimity with courage.[15]

O'Brien is in no laughing mood, and as a result he becomes rather ungenerous, too restrictive, as to whom he grants true courage: "Most soldiers in Alpha Company did not think about human courage" (141). They just wanted out. But then there is the case of Doc, the medic. Doc does brave things, but resolutely refuses to give any evidence he thinks about the meaning of courage or his own role in it:

> "You don't talk about being a hero, with a star pinned on your shirt and feeling all puffed up." The soldier couldn't understand when I asked him about the day he ran from his foxhole, through enemy fire, to wrap useless cloth around a dying soldier's chest. "I reacted, I guess. I just did it."
> "Did it seem the right thing to do?"
> "No," Doc said. "Not right, not wrong either."
> "Did you think you might be shot?"
> "Yes. I guess I did. Maybe not. When someone hollers for the medic, if you're a medic you run toward the shout. That's it, I guess."
> "But isn't there the feeling you might *die?*"
> Doc had his legs crossed and was leaning over a can of C rations. He seemed intent on them. "No. I won't die over here." He laughed. "Maybe I'll never die. I just wondered why I didn't feel anything hit me. Something should have hit me, there was so much firing. I sort of ran over, waiting for a kind of blast or punch in the back. My back always feels most exposed." (142)

Doc will not theorize his act of courage, even when asked leading questions to coax him to do so. Not self-conscious enough, Doc's courage, in O'Brien's view, lacks the wisdom that is needed to perfect it. Doc talks, instead, about instinct and luck, reflex, automatism, and magic, not about virtue or fear or doubt; someone hollers for a medic, and he runs to the call, through fire and brimstone if need be.

O'Brien reads Doc as dim, a soldier who "just couldn't understand" his questions. Doc may well be incapable of talking about courage in the way that O'Brien's theory demands. He may just be a simple man, not given to self-reflection or much self-doubting, that hazard of self-reflection. But couldn't O'Brien be misreading Doc? Take Doc's intimations of immortality ("Maybe I'll never die"). Put aside the question of the degree of seriousness that informs this kind of magic talk. Doc makes clear that, though looking back he can joke about being bullet-proof, he manifestly did not feel the least bit bullet-proof the time he ran out to comfort a dying man without cover in heavy fire. He expected to die. He waited for the punch in the back. Who can blame him for talking the language of magical immortality after surviving that?

Why not assume that Doc is more modest than stupid? Even if not among the brightest, why not credit his knowledge of death's proximity and the luckiness of escaping it? He gives every indication of feeling awkward talking about his bravery. "I just reacted" is the language of modesty. As Doc says right from the start, "You don't talk about being a hero." Isn't this exactly the proper way to talk about actions that everyone knows were courageous? How to be self-effacing in this setting without making the self-effacement ring false is no easy matter. Doc carries it off. Had he said, "I was only doing my duty," when everyone else knew the circumstances had relocated duty somewhere above and beyond the call of duty, the modesty would ring false or he would seem a prig.[16] Doc's "When someone hollers for the medic, if you're a medic you run toward the shout. That's it, I guess" finds just the right way of substituting instinct for duty that represents a most competent fulfillment of modesty's proper claim.

His modesty, however, may not be modesty about the greatness of his achievement, but modesty about having any special insight into it. Doc may just be rendered inarticulate by courage like so many other courageous people, which may only be more evidence that courage is a psychological mystery. As one of the better recent philosophical writers on courage has noted, "Modesty aside, the courageous themselves standardly cannot find what the world calls courage among their enabling dispositions . . . The courageous generally say that they were able to do what they did because they saw that it had to be done."[17] One estimable soldier concurs. William Tecumseh Sherman claimed that "the most courageous men are generally unconscious of possessing the quality."[18] And in Sherman's view it behooves those who are conscious of their courage not to be too open about it or risk having it mistrusted as so much fakery. Doc, then, is no less courageous even if it is not modesty but lack of self-consciousness of his own bravery that makes him unable to formulate what drove him to risk life and limb to minister to a dying man. Even if he "just reacted," was it not courage that made him do so? We want to distinguish between those medics, the courageous ones, who just react and those who don't just react, but who delay, deliberate, and thus waste precious seconds and miss opportunities to soothe and salve that Doc doesn't miss.

Doc and some of the other guys may also have been putting the cerebral, serious, and slightly pretentious O'Brien on, repaying some of the contempt for them they may have detected in his questions. Might not O'Brien be exacting the revenge of the educated, the anxious, the self-conscious, on the uncomplex, sanguine, and not-overly-given to worry? Is this the resentment of the brainy college kid desperately trying to fathom his fear in the cerebral style that suits him by rejecting the ways of talking that manage fear for the less sophisticated? O'Brien is playing at the politics of courage as the Spartans did in Aristodemus' case, by denying courage to those whom one disfavors. For if Doc is not brave, who is?—that is unless, like O'Brien, we really do believe Doc is too stupid to know the risk he ran aiding the stricken soldier. I see nothing in Doc's conversation that hints he did not understand the risk.[19] Even if Doc did not appreciate the risk, we would want to know whether he achieved that blessed vacuity by virtue of stupidity or by training himself up to courage by developing the capacity to tune out the sense of danger when duty demanded. Doc reveals certain shortcomings in O'Brien's theory.[20]

O'Brien wants a certain style of talking about courage, and it is not all that hard to fake it to satisfy his conditions. Had Doc said, "I have always tried to be brave but I feel so much fear that I doubt I am," would that have changed the selfless nature of his deeds? Would Doc be more courageous if he expressed anguish about his warrant for giving aid to the dying in the thick of things? Do Doc's deeds require any commentary at all beyond the mere recitation of them? Could his courage be any more perfected by answering questions that only embarrassed him? Yet there is a point to O'Brien's suspicion of those who go beyond modestly denying that they acted courageously by professing not to understand their actions at all. To attempt to understand courage—or, more properly, to confess to others some desire to understand—is to go a long way toward committing oneself to a proper respect for the virtue. Once, for instance, Johansen says that he worries about being brave, it becomes that much more difficult (or costly) for him not to be. This is true even if Johansen were to be faking his concern. By professing ignorance about his courage, Doc may be understood to be leaving himself an out for the next time; he preserves wiggle room for himself to be, if not a coward, at least not courageous either.

But if this is O'Brien's concern, it is still ungenerous to Doc. Doc's prior deeds and present reputation, no less than any words he may have uttered, work to commit him to courage the next time the demand is made on him. So one wonders whether O'Brien in writing up Doc's story doesn't mean to expose a certain pretentiousness in his own philosophizing about courage.

It might be so, for within pages, struggling desperately to establish his own courageous possibility, he in effect junks the theory that went before when he confronts his own performance.

Doing Well on Average

The great divide that separates the model of courage represented by Johansen from his own performance in the field sinks O'Brien into the slough of despond: "It is more difficult, however, to think of yourself . . . as the eternal Hector, dying gallantly. It is impossible. That's the problem. It's sad when you learn you're not much of a hero" (146). Maybe the problem lies with the bipolarity of notions like hero and coward. Some days O'Brien finds himself cowering, writhing insensibly under bullets; other days he does okay. That he sometimes does okay leads him to float a more tolerant theory: "It is more likely that men act cowardly and, at other times, act with courage, each in different measure, each with varying consistency. *The men who do well on the average, perhaps with one moment of glory, those men are brave*" (146; emphasis added). This is a big concession to the non-heroic, but he is not willing to dispense with the heroic entirely. He still wants one moment of glory in the grand style, just one.

But that too is too high a standard; he concludes powerfully thus:

> The easy aphorisms hold no hope for the middle man, the man who wants to try but has already died more than once, squirming under bullets, going through the act of death and coming through embarrassingly alive. The bullets stop. As in slow motion, physical things gleam. Noise dissolves. You tentatively peek up, wondering if it is the end. Then you look at the other men, reading your own caved-in belly deep in their eyes. The fright dies the same way novocaine wears off in the dentist's chair. You promise, almost moving your lips, to do better next time; that by itself is a kind of courage. (147)

This is the substance of wise endurance as O'Brien comes to reformulate it downward so that it is available for soldiers, average people, who must endure mines, booby traps, and being sniped at for a year. Endurance is now the promise to do better the next time.[21] The promise itself embodies the proper attitude toward the virtue, representing the desire to accord one's behavior to it, but it also contains the grim awareness that succeeding is not always possible, for each promise is undertaken in the dust of present failure.

And where is the wisdom in that? The wisdom is no longer about risk calculation, the understanding of proper ends properly pursued; it is about accepting one's less-than-heroic limits and doing the best that is reasonably possible given the circumstances. This kind of wise endurance means that some acts will be cowardly, but it accepts that you will not be a coward if you resolve to do better the next time and then in fact do better enough next times to show a proper respect for the virtue. This is something more than Burdette's good coward, who is all good intention and serious preparatory action, but runs away every time. He has no actions that will raise his average performance. Under O'Brien's theory averaging is a privilege: you do not get the benefit of it unless you actually come through sometimes, and when you don't you must still follow up with the proper resolve to do better the next time. Even that might not help you. What if, as the Spartans did with Aristodemus' performance at Thermopylae, one of your failures is assigned a value of negative infinity?

We might see O'Brien, in darkly comic fashion, to be revising Aristotle's doctrine of the mean to the more insistent demands of modern warfare. Rather than holding each action to the strict requirement of avoiding the vices of excess and vices of insufficiency, O'Brien lets the mean be achieved by averaging performance across a multitude of actions. Thus reformulated do we even have a theory of courage? Or just a theory of muddling through? But muddling through is also a kind of courage given the appalling setting in which it is demanded, day in and day out, not just once in a blue moon.

4

Courageous Disposition

TIM O'BRIEN enlists Plato and Socrates to help him solve his problems with courage, the intellectual ones that tax him in trying to articulate a theory of courage, and the moral and physical ones of just managing under fire. In the end he despairs and settles for a theory of average performance with the resolve to raise the average by doing better next time. If Socrates first led him to understand courage to be a matter of knowledge and self-knowledge, then so what? How does such knowledge help you *do* courageous deeds? O'Brien, for all his torturing self-consciousness, got little help, and types like Doc didn't seem to need Socrates' assistance. Aristotle, too, is dissatisfied with what he sees as Socrates making courage a matter of knowledge.[1] For him courage is primarily a disposition to be cultivated. The problem is less to know courage than to train for it.

Aristotle's Virtuous Disposition

Aristotle on courage is a pit of quicksand, frustratingly implausible in some ways. But it is he, not Plato or Socrates, who rightly sets the terms for later philosophical discussions of courage. Except, perhaps, for Aquinas' intricate account, which significantly transforms Aristotle's, there is none more important.

Most of us have the rough intuition that virtue involves warring against and defeating temptation. Virtue has got to be hard in the doing—being courageous in spite of one's fear, managing to say no to the allure of cheesecake, whiskey, and other enticements of the flesh. It is about over-coming and self-mastery. Aristotle, however, disagrees. Those people who triumph over bad desires show great self-control, but they are inferior to those who are not tempted to vice in the first place, whose desires are also virtuous. Virtue, for Aristotle, is about a perfect matching of action and a particular emotion. The person of self-control has the action right, but not the emotion; his fundamental desires are still bad. For Aristotle, "a man who abstains from bodily pleasures and enjoys the very fact of so doing is temperate; if he finds it irksome he is licentious. Again, the man who faces danger gladly, or at least without distress, is brave; the one who feels distressed is a coward."[2] This view of virtue is harsh and runs counter to some of our ready intuitions about virtue and courage in particular. Aris-totle, though, is not consistently this ungenerous to people of self-control; in fact, it is not at all clear that in his own discussion of courage he doesn't vacillate; if the courageous man is not insensibly fearless like the Celt and must fear appropriately, how is he to manage such fear without self-control figuring into it?[3]

The person of self-control might not hold the highest rank, but he ranks higher in excellence of character than those people who lack self-control, who are weak-willed. They not only do not get the emotion right, they also don't act right, yet they still wish they could. Some part of their inner being, their sense of shame, laments both their lack of self-control and their improper desires. These weak-willed souls are in turn of superior moral stature to those who desire wrongly, act wrongly, and want to act precisely as they do. These are the truly licentious.[4] We have not yet hit rock bottom; the licentious are still operating in the world of vice and virtue, that is, they still count as human. They thus rank above the brute, a type "commonest among the non-Greek races," although Aristotle con-cedes that the term is often applied to extremely licentious people. Brutes "have a taste for raw meat," human raw meat at times, occasionally satisfied by serving up their children for the tribal feast; they also bite their nails.[5] They lack the degree of civilization and refinement necessary to have their behaviors qualify as delicious and exquisite vices. The brutes contrast not with the virtuous but with the gods, who, not being human, likewise do not play in the world of virtue and vice, "for a god has no virtue or vice anymore than the brute has."[6]

True virtue, then, the perfect matching of emotion and action, demands cultivating a virtuous disposition; it is more than doing the right deed; it is doing it as the expression of a disposition cultivated to do virtue, doing virtuous deeds for their own sake.[7] Aristotle recognizes that we talk a slightly different game, that an act will be called courageous if it is such as a courageous person would do. It is not clear, though, that he would concede this to be any more than a fashion of speaking, for if the act is to be properly virtuous in Aristotle's scheme, it must flow from a disposition to do that kind of act. But one cultivates the disposition by doing individual acts that meet the description of the virtue. We end up courageous by doing courageous deeds so that we end up disposed to be courageous when the crunch comes: "It is by habituating ourselves to make light of alarming situations and to face them that we become brave, and it is when we have become brave that we shall be most able to face an alarming situation."[8]

Virtue comes to look like a habit—a good one to be sure, but a habit. But where is the virtue in that? If, as noted earlier in discussing *Laches*, we perceive the person who is skilled in combat to be manifesting less courage than the person with no skill who sticks it out nonetheless (Aristotle endorses this view, finding skill in martial endeavors to be more a semblance of courage than perfect courage), then can't we find in the training that leads to a courageous disposition a kind of psychic skill that undoes somewhat the uncanny grandness of the courageous act when that act is done by someone who is not habituated to act that way? It is the difference between the courage of old army professionalism and that of volunteer citizen brigades, both admirable, but one to be expected as part of a tough job and true to type, the other representing a kind of triumph of the will against type.

Aristotle's virtue, however, is more than just a hard-wired habit requiring no mobilization of inner resources once the disposition is acquired. It still means having the right feelings "at the right times on the right grounds towards the right people for the right motive and in the right way."[9] In Aristotle's scheme this takes judgment, or what is usually rendered "practical wisdom."[10] I am a bit suspicious about the alacrity with which so much recent philosophy latches onto this Aristotelian warrant to recruit courage to the camp of reason and deliberation.[11] It looks like another case of defining courage so as to make it more readily available for one's own class than for certain disfavored others. Doc, remember, did not deliberate. In any event it is not clear just what judgments practical wisdom is supposed to make on courage's behalf. Are they readily available to any socially competent person as rules of thumb or as well-attested cultural scripts? How much judgment does it take to know to stay in line in the phalanx, to hit the enemy instead of your fellow soldier, and to do that in battle and not at some other time? Aristotelian practical wisdom is too lofty to deal with such gritty matters. And if wisdom is meant to be applied before the encounter to determine whether it is worth it to proceed or how to plan the action, there remains the problem of the psychic resources you must bring to bear to carry out your wise strategies.

Most courageous action will not require much practical wisdom; practical wisdom may discern what goal to pursue, what the best way of getting it done is, but the courage is in the doing. For the poor foot soldier, courage usually means following an order. He is told to charge; the courage is not in thinking about how to do it. There are indeed some settings in which it will take something like practical wisdom to make tough calls as in emergencies, in which keeping one's wits is everything, or when one is giving orders and must also see to their implementation under circumstances demanding courage, as in a constantly evolving tactical situation. Even here the wisdom brought to bear is less deliberative than desperate attempts to marshal any practical sense one can in the midst of fear and confusion.[12]

A virtuous disposition, according to Aristotle, is acquired by doing the very deeds that you will be able to do once you are so disposed. It must be hard at first and require rigorous training and shaming. Undoubtedly, too, some people are by their natures already more disposed than others to acquire a courageous disposition. Free citizens are understood to be born to the possibility and necessity of acquiring it, as against those for whom courage is by definition not a social possibility: slaves and women.[13] But within that class of males from which the city draws its hoplites some will have a greater likelihood of having what it takes than others.

Courage comes more easily to some, fresh out of the womb.[14] Our tendencies toward fearfulness and fearlessness seem to be partly inherited. Consider the rat. Like humans, rats defecate when they are scared. If rats that defecate a lot when frightened are bred with each other, and those more stolid types that defecate less are bred with their ilk, within ten generations two distinct strains emerge: a strain of nervous wrecks and a strain of very hard-to-scare rats. The experiments were conducted so as to exclude all explanations but the genetic.[15] Let the reader draw what conclusion he or she wishes regarding the martial versus peaceful natures of whole cultures: but genetics can't even begin to account for the transition of ferocious Vikings into modern Scandinavian social democrats, or the transition of diasporan Jews into Israeli paratroopers. Yet within each culture it is hard to deny our children's varying propensities for fearfulness, how some seem born to a courageous disposition, while others must be cajoled, threatened, exhorted before they manage to be so disposed, and yet others, irrevocably uncourageous, never get there, try as they might. It is also the case that those who are unable to cultivate a courageous disposition both envy and contemn those born to be courageous. The grounds for envy are obvious, the grounds for contempt involve a self-serving suspicion that the cost of being a member of the strain that does not feel the urge to defecate when in danger may be not only constipation but also stupidity and a dull inner life.

Aristotle's dispositional view of courage seems at first glance to undercut one of our most popular narratives of moral education: the adolescent-coming-of-age story in which the weakling of little or no courage redeems himself by triumphing in the face of danger. No one-shot redemptions in Aristotle. But the genre itself is quite clearly in Aristotle's camp. The proper sense of an ending in these stories draws only partly on the revenge that gets taken at the end, for as any student of honor culture knows, revenge is not an ending but a new challenge that the other side has to answer. Closure in this coming-of-age story depends rather on our believing that from now on our hero will be disposed as an Aristotelian man of courage; no backing down the next time or any time thereafter; he has now become, via training and education, properly disposed to be courageous whenever occasion demands. Doing it once at the end of the story does not singly create the disposition; it serves as the sign that the hero has acquired that disposition, molded himself into a person of courage. The educational process itself takes up the bulk of narrative time in these stories; they are more about training than about revenge. One can see what Aristotle is getting at: he wants someone who can be relied on from the start, not someone who gives others little cause for hope, but only an occasion for pleasant surprise.

There are two matters that I wish to pursue in more detail regarding Aristotle's notion of a disposition for courage. Call the first the problem of a disposition's generality or scope; the second, the problem of a disposition's durability or life expectancy, that is, whether it can be expected to grow stronger over time or to wear itself out from demands made upon it. Start with the disposition's scope. Aristotle, unlike Socrates in *Laches*, does not construe courage broadly. For him it is most properly about facing death, and then in the noblest setting, which he believes is war, "where the danger is greatest and most glorious . . . so in the strict sense of the word the courageous man will be one who is fearless in the face of an honorable death . . . and it is in war that such situations chiefly occur."[16] He does expect that the courageous person will also "be fearless on the sea or in outbreaks of a disease,"[17] but in these settings there is little place for glorious death because the goal is not as noble and so courage proper is not really at stake. Since "the nature of any given thing is determined by its end,"[18] the purest courage is about behavior in battle on behalf of the polis.

Montaigne and other moralists, especially those of a stoical bent, support an expansive view of courage, making it pretty much coterminous with all grounds that prompt fear; they thus demand the cultivation of a disposition with no holes in it, no idiosyncratic weak spots. They note with disapproval that people's courage is not uniformly available to them in all settings in which it can do useful service. They take those lapses as signs of inconstancy, another lamentable failure of a foolish and weak humanity, not a reason to reconceptualize the proper scope of the virtue. Montaigne takes a very hard line:

> A man who is truly brave will always be brave on all occasions. If a man's valor were habitual and not a sudden outburst it would make him equally resolute in all eventualities: as much alone as with his comrades, as much in the tilt-yard as on the battlefield; for, despite what they say, there is not one valor for the town and another for the country . . . If he cannot bear slander but is resolute in poverty; if he cannot bear a barber-surgeon's lancet but is unyielding against the swords of his adversaries, then it is not the man who deserves praise but the deed.[19]

Few indeed can meet this rigorous standard—not even Alexander the Great, who, though absolutely fearless in battle, is chided by Montaigne for being excessively anxious about plots against his life from within his own ranks, to say nothing of those Homeric heroes who trembled every time they heard thunder. In Montaigne's view those people who are not courageous without exception are not themselves courageous, just erratic souls who every once in a while get it together to do a praiseworthy deed. Most of us cowardly souls would gladly settle for doing an occasional deed that impresses others, and it is clear from Montaigne's own account that the general view in his time was more relaxed too.

Even if we follow Aristotle and narrowly limit courage's scope to facing death in war, we still are confronted with Montaigne's problem. War itself offers all kinds of very particular ways of dying or suffering pain, some of which people find easier to face than others. One may be courageously disposed in the face of one kind of battle death but not in another. In pre-industrial battle the ways of dying were not all that varied: one got bludgeoned, hacked, trampled, or pierced. Nor do we have memoirs or other texts that discuss whether one preferred to die by club or ax, spear or arrow. There is some aristocratic concern about the disgracefulness of death by arrow to the extent that it meant dying at the hands of a low-ranking archer; otherwise, with the exception of Beowulf wondering what it may be like to be eaten, the question does not make it into the written record.

These things change when new weaponry allows for varying forms of death, which coincides nicely with the era in which soldiers start to write memoirs so that we have a window open to the specificity of their fears. Which weapon you prefer to die by emerges as a leitmotif in memoirs from twentieth-century wars, with roots already discernible in the American Civil War. The men even note the irrationality of obsessing on the issue given the instantaneousness of death in any event. Thus Frederic Manning:

> Whether a man be killed by a rifle-bullet though the brain, or blown into fragments by a high-explosive shell, may seem a matter of indifference to the conscientious objector, or to any other equally well-placed observer, who in point of fact is probably right; but to the poor fool who is a candidate for posthumous honors, and necessarily takes a more directly interested view, it is a question of importance . . . Death, of course, like chastity, admits of no degree; a man is dead or not dead, and a man is just as dead by one means as by another; but it is infinitely more horrible and revolting to see a man shattered and eviscerated, than to see him shot.[20]

Rifles versus Artillery:
The Particularity of Courageous Dispositions

Although there are more than a few accounts of people who cannot bear the idea of dying by incineration in a tank who would gladly exchange that possibility for death by artillery or rifle,[21] the main focus in the memoirs is about the relative fear of dying by artillery shell or by rifle bullet. The issue merits a fuller discussion, for it drags the question of courageous disposition out of airy abstraction back down to earth, vividly showing what the stakes are. A disposition to be courageous might really be an assemblage of many dispositions much more specifically honed, biologically, psychologically, historically, and sociologically. Scary things frighten in different ways, even when the end is the same amount of pain or death. "There is no such person as the soldier who is dauntless under all conditions of combat," writes military theorist General S. L. A. Marshall.[22]

First there is the terror of unfamiliar weaponry, where novelty itself provides much of the fear. "So great is our horror of death," says David Hume in his essay on suicide, "that when it presents itself under any form, besides that to which a man has endeavored to reconcile his imagination, it acquires new terrors, and overcomes his feeble courage."[23] Even when courage is not so feeble this is the case. Writes one Confederate officer: "It is very curious how soldiers become so familiar with one kind of danger, to which they have been exposed, as to disregard it almost entirely, and yet become demoralized when danger in a new form presents itself." They got used to musketry, even field artillery, "but when they came under fire from the big guns on the gun boats below Richmond in 1862 they became nervous at seeing large trees cut off clean and whirled bottom upwards. To this they became accustomed. Then the mortar shells came . . ."[24]

World War I revealed that novelty was only one small part of the terror, for many found there was no getting used to shelling from mortars and big guns in the same way one got used to rifle fire. It was the noise that did some in. Siegfried Sassoon tells of Jenkins, "a good officer before and afterwards," who stayed crouched in a corner of a dugout after an artillery bombardment had ceased, unable to lead his men forward: "He was an example of the paralyzing effect which such an experience could have on a nervous system sensitive to noise."[25] Says one character in Ford Madox Ford's *Parade's End:* "Damn it all . . . don't think I'm afraid of a little shrapnel . . . It's, damn it, it's the beastly row. Why isn't one a beastly girl and privileged to shriek?"[26] For others it was a sense of unfairness. The consistently insightful pseudonymous memoir of Mark VII (the literary critic Max Plowman) speaks of the feeling of futility that being shelled in the trenches produced. One "poor scared fellow" who "had just come out of trenches where most of his companions had been killed by shelling . . . said, 'Why this isn't war at all. It's bloody murder!' "[27] Unfair it was, not only in the quantity of killing, but in its quality too. Others, like William Manchester (World War II), felt about artillerymen as both Greeks and Trojans did of Paris sitting back and firing his arrows from behind the melee: "There is something grotesque and outrageous about a man safely behind fortifications, miles away, pulling a lanyard and killing other men who cannot see, let alone reach him."[28]

There was another aspect of the noise of shelling; it was not just the sound of the explosion that was unbearable; it was that you could hear the shells coming (and often see them too) and do nothing about it. The apprehension of waiting for each one to hit, one after another, day in and day out, broke many men. You could hear rifle bullets whizzing *by*, but you did not hear them *coming*. In the debate as to whether bullets or artillery shells are worse we thus pit those who fear more the ominousness of impending doom against those who can't bear surprise and suddenness, the thought that something as momentous as the transition from being to nonbeing could occur without warning.

For others it was a sense that shelling was random and that the randomness engendered a world of unworldly disorder, terror, and hopelessness; shells turned the world upside down, making it rain earth.[29] You didn't have to be caged in a Great War trench to be tortured by artillery. Marine private E. B. Sledge records his experience under bombardment during the landing at Peleliu in 1944 as he desperately tried to find cover in a shallow crater carved out by a shell in the hard coral:

> The heavy mortar barrage went on without slackening. I thought it would never stop . . . If any orders were passed along, or if anyone yelled for a corpsman, I never heard it in all the noise. It was as though I was out there on the battlefield all by myself, utterly forlorn and helpless in a tempest of violent explosions . . . I learned a new sensation: utter and absolute helplessness.[30]

It could be worse, as when, for instance, the shells that had rendered you utterly forlorn and helpless turned out to qualify as "friendly": "To be killed by the enemy was bad enough; that was a real possibility I had prepared myself for. But to be killed by mistake by my own comrades was something I found hard to accept."[31] There seems here to be an implicit bargain that courage can be rightly demanded against the enemy, but is it courage to die in a farce? Aristotle, recall, made courage a matter of noble death in war for the polis; the assumption was that death was to be dealt by the enemy, nobly, not by one's own in a comedy of errors and arrows. If such a death was not quite meaningless it could surely not rank even as high as Aristotle's low-prestige deaths by shipwreck or disease, both of which lack the element of farce.

Sledge finds the fiendish whistle of approaching shells unbearable. Like the character in Ford's novel he must "fight back a wild, inexorable urge to scream, to sob, and to cry." The shelling thus threatens emasculation in more ways than the obvious one; it turns men, sobbing and shrieking, into "beastly girls" who by ideology have acquired the "privilege" of screaming. Unlike the character in Ford's novel, Sledge does not make women the scapegoat for his misery. He hates shelling because it threatens his sanity, his humanity more than his manhood; he can never quite believe his mind has not been shattered irrevocably when it at last subsides; he expects his sanity to go in a snap, but for him the break will come less dramatically, as a slow wasting away by degrees:

> To be under heavy shell fire was to me by far the most terrifying of combat experiences. Each time it left me feeling more forlorn and helpless, more fatalistic, and with less confidence that I could escape the dreadful law of averages that inexorably reduced our numbers. Fear is many-faceted and has many subtle nuances, but the terror and desperation endured under heavy shelling are by far the most unbearable.[32]

If fear has many faces with many subtle nuances, does it generate specific courages and cowardices to match? Sledge is willing to go much further than Aristotle on this point toward answering yes, and it is hard to deny the authority of his experiences.

To Sledge death by bullet is a consummation to be preferred, if not to be wished, to death by shell: "To be killed by a bullet seemed so clean and surgical. But shells would not only tear and rip the body, they tortured one's mind almost beyond the brink of sanity. After each shell I was wrung out, limp and exhausted."[33] Not just sensitive souls like Sledge felt this way.[34]

William Manchester takes vengeful delight in the tearful collapse during shellfire of a strutting, bullying sergeant, known to be fearlessly heroic in the face of rifle fire.[35] Sledge reminds us also what shells do to the body. Bullets kill but still leave a body looking like one, still classifiably a body, still obviously having belonged to a human. Not so shells; when they hit a person he can simply cease to be, leaving no trace but some dampness, goo, and fragments which metamorphose into shrapnel that maim and wound his former buddies.[36] So much courage is metaphorized and vernacularized in images of body parts, soft tissue at that, not bones; courage is blood, guts, nerve, balls, heart. The artillery shell mocks the corporeal diction of courage, by thus exposing it as nothing but metaphor; bullets, presumably of the nonexpanding sort, were more mannerly.

Who could possibly think death by small arms worse? But such opinion is well represented. The randomness of shelling, which unmanned so many, was just what made it acceptable to others, Robert Graves (World War I) for instance: "The gunner, I knew, fired not at people but at map-references—crossroads, or likely artillery positions . . . Even when an observation officer in an aeroplane or captive balloon or on a church spire directed the gun, it seemed random somehow." What made rifle fire unbearable was precisely its nonrandomness, its specificity. Bullets were aimed, aimed at *you*. Again Graves: "A rifle bullet, even when fired blindly, always seemed purposely aimed. And whereas we could usually hear a shell approaching, and take some sort of cover, the rifle bullet gave no warning. So, though we learned not to duck to a rifle bullet because, once heard, it must have missed, it gave us a worse feeling of danger."[37] Graves is one of the few, evidently, who could overcome the instinctual flinch when hearing a bullet whiz by. The tenacity of this reflex, even though totally irrational for the reasons Graves gives, becomes another commonplace of military memoirs.[38]

Robert Crisp (World War II), shocked to find himself so completely frightened by being shot at, is also of Graves's party: "These bullets were aimed at me. They were meant to kill me personally. No careless indiscriminacy about them. Bombs in the night were quite different."[39] And Tietjens in *Parade's End*:

> It is no doubt terrible to you to have large numbers of your comrades instantaneously annihilated by the explosion of some huge engine, but huge engines are blind and thus accidental; a slow,

> regular picking off of the men beside you is evidence that human terribleness that is not blind or accidental is cold-bloodedly and unshakably turning its attention to a spot very near you. It may very shortly turn its attention to yourself. (582)

Some just find the intentionality of rifle fire perplexing. What, asks Philip Caputo (Vietnam), did I ever do to him that he should be trying to kill me?[40] Strange how some are undone by indiscriminacy, others by focused intentionality. Each party—antiartillery, antirifle—takes turns at making the other look courageous. Does mechanized modern war, by offering weapons that kill in varied ways, introduce a more equitable redistribution of courageous possibility, where earlier it had been completely engrossed ideologically by aristocrats? Courage is not, it turns out, just about the mastery of the fear of death, but about different masteries of different fears of different kinds of deaths.

None of the reasons given for terror or relief as between bullets and exploding shells are surprising; they all seem, though superficially contradictory, completely just and plausible, since most of us would be equally terrified to be fired upon by a rifle or to find ourselves in the general area of exploding shells. There are surprises though. Tietjens offers another reason for artillery being easier to bear than rifle fire:

> Of course, it is disagreeable when artillery is bracketing across your line: a shell falls a hundred yards in front of you, another a hundred yards behind you; the next will be half-way between, and you are half-way between. The waiting wrings your soul; but it does not induce panic or the desire to run—at any rate to nearly the same extent. Where, in any event, could you run to? But from coldly and mechanically advancing and firing troops you *can* run. (582)

Artillery saves you from cowardly flight, lowers your chances of disgracing yourself, by giving you no way out. What depressing humor. Aristotle's hoplites had their own horrors, but they were not of this magnitude. Spear and sword were just about it. A unitary disposition of courage able to meet whatever demands battle makes was thus easier to contemplate. But Aristotle recognized that people have different talents for keeping their cool: "some people who are cowardly in the perils of war are liberal with their money and face the loss of it with equanimity."[41] The sagas, too, recognized that a hero, like Grettir, fearless in battle against men and monsters, could be terrified of the dark, while another great warrior, Gisli, could fear his obsessive bad dreams. Courage, it seems, has always been understood to encompass more capacities than any one man who had not given himself over entirely to stoical passivity or psychopathology could ever possess.

The Half-Life of Courageous Dispositions

Pre-industrial weaponry was tied to the limits of human muscular power. A spear could be thrown only so far. Even force multipliers like catapults and bows needed significant amounts of human muscle power to be cocked or drawn. This is part of the reason that the duration of pre-industrial battles was measured in hours, and it was a rare one that was resumed the next day; when people got tired the battle stopped. When missiles can be launched by trigger or lanyard, not only does the battlefield get bigger, but the battles go on longer and longer. Could it be that the human capacity for courage is ineffably tied to the limits of our bodily powers, not just our spiritual and moral powers? Could it be that the internal clock or the half-life of the disposition for courage runs to the beat of human musculature? For one kind of courage this seems true: the courage of the charge, the courage of aggression and attack; but the courage of endurance, the courage of defense, the courage to persevere, marches to a different beat, demands different rhythms making for slower psychic tunes.

The horrors of trench warfare of the Great War, anticipated by the ever-lengthening battles of the last year of the American Civil War, produced behaviors embarrassing to the easy assumption that practice makes perfect in matters of courage. How did one explain the nervous collapse of men who had good combat records with shell shock in World War I, combat fatigue in World War II, post-traumatic stress disorder in Vietnam, all exhibiting roughly the same symptoms though the names for the phenomenon changed, as experts intruded new, more pretentious jargon?[42]

Start with an image from the incomparable Wilfred Owen:

> Where once an hour a bullet missed its aim
> And misses teased the hunger of his brain.
> His eyes grew old with wincing, and his hand
> Reckless with ague. Courage leaked, as sand
> From the best sand-bags after years of rain . . .[43]

Men, their moral capacities at least, are compared to sandbags, just as their corpses in a crunch were put to use as sandbags to mend parapets and trench walls.[44] The leaking sand from the sandbag suggests the time-marking sand of an hourglass—one, however, that cannot be restored to perfect usefulness merely by turning it on end. The disposition for courage, courageous capacity, comes with a life expectancy attached. Even war-loving warriors in the old style like Ernst Jünger (German, World War I) subscribed to this view: "The notion that a soldier becomes hardier and bolder as war proceeds is mistaken. What he gains in the science and art of attacking his enemy he loses in strength of nerve."[45] Says a British private soldier (World War II):

> We thought we should get used to things, we thought that expe-
> rience under shell fire would harden our indifference to it . . . I
> thought I had some imagination. But it didn't show me how we
> should become increasingly less used to it; how experience of
> shell fire saps your indifference to it . . . how the time would
> come when the first shell to land even remotely near us during
> an attack would blow our courage to smithereens.[46]

Aristotle, too, accepts a version of the view that courageous possibility decays over time; in his *Rhetoric* he adopts the ancient anthropology that makes rashness and courage the lot of youth, and timorousness and cow-ardice the attendants of old age.[47] In his scheme time takes its toll simply by being time; no cumulation of unendurable horrors is necessary. Once you are old Father William don't even think about courage; you needn't apply.

Robert Graves, who loves the irony of reducing the heroic to probabil-ity, to odds and statistics, comes up with the following timetable for the useful life of an officer, which turns out to anticipate uncannily the results of empirical studies undertaken in World War II. For the first three weeks the fresh subaltern was too inexperienced to be of much use. By three to four weeks "he was at his best, unless he happened to have any particular bad shock or sequence of shocks." Then started the decay as neurasthenia developed. He was still of use at six months, "but by nine or ten, unless he had been given a few weeks' rest on a technical course, or in hospital, he usually became a drag on the other company officers. After a year or fifteen months he was often worse than useless."[48] Of interest too is that World War I evidence revealed that officers withered away differently from the men; the former had typically neurasthenic disorders, twitching, nightmares, insomnia; the latter generated physical hysterical symptoms such as paralysis of limbs or blindness.[49] But both officers and men withered away.

One World War II study found that a soldier had, by most generous computation, a useful life of 200–240 days of combat, at which point he became "so overly cautious and jittery that he was ineffective and demoralizing to the newer men."[50] Another study, sampling troops during the intense fighting in Normandy in 1944, found their maximum period of efficiency occurred between 12 and 30 days, after which it decayed rapidly through stages of hyperreactivity to complete emotional exhaustion ending in a vegetative state by day 60.[51] The "two-thousand-year stare," the GIs called it. Only 2 percent, it was found, did not succumb, and although no one personality type dominated in this small group, "aggressive psychopathic personalities, who were poorly disciplined before combat, stand out."[52] British soldiers were believed to last longer because they were rotated in and out of the front lines on a regular basis, with 4 days' rest for each 12 in the line;[53] the Americans, in contrast, were notorious for not relieving men for sometimes as long as 40 days and more. By the time of the Vietnam War, in a grudging concession to these studies, the Americans limited a combat tour to a year.

It is not just the drain of time; there is another aspect to the process of courage depletion. Courage seems to lose its magic. People expect great things from courage; its force is supposed to change the world, to yield results. Could it be that it made no difference how courageous you or your troops were, that little hinged on men's characters at all, but rather on which polity had the most men and machines to expend? We do not have to wait until the horrors of twentieth-century war to hear these suspicions expressed. Robert Burdette observed that in the Civil War the winner had to pay as much for winning as "the loser pays for his losses."[54] And imagine the despair of the Confederate soldier who wins battle after battle but sees it all come to a grand expense of spirit and blood: "Our victories seem to settle nothing; to bring us no nearer the end of the war. It is only so many killed and wounded, leaving the work of blood to go on with renewed vigor."[55] One problem with the implicit narrative of courageous action is that courage is supposed to bring about a climax, to effect some kind of resolution. War had got too big for courage and the courageous disposition. New, less flattering images of diminishment, exhaustion, depletion, and decay become part of a new narrative of courage.

For Owen, courage was sand seeping from a sandbag with its hourglass associations. For another soldier courage "diminished imperceptibly . . . as a chord on a piano once struck grows steadily weaker and can never behave otherwise."[56] Lord Moran, in *The Anatomy of Courage*, coins images of credit, capital, and bankruptcy:

> A man's courage is his capital and he is always spending. The call on the bank may be only the daily drain of the front line or it may be a sudden draft which threatens to close the account. His will is perhaps almost destroyed by intensive shelling, by heavy bombing, or by a bloody battle, or it is gradually used up by monotony, by exposure, by the loss of the support of stauncher spirits on whom he has come to depend, by physical exhaustion, by a wrong attitude to danger, to casualties, to war, to death itself.[57]

The point is that those who qualify as good Aristotelian men of virtue—those who have cultivated a disposition for courage so that their courageous deeds are properly motivated, not just accidents—have only a fixed sum to spend.

Theories of courage had to be readjusted in light of the demands that modern warfare makes on the soldier. In premodern warfare battles were short, and apart from disease there was little danger between rare battles. Moral reserves could be replenished. The conditions of hoplite battle allowed for a view of courageous possibility in which disposition-talk made sense. Courage was the courage of attack, marching out to meet the enemy, or not breaking and running when attacked. Night fell or one side had quit the field earlier, often within an hour, a trophy was set up, a truce was established to gather in the corpses for proper burial, and there was an end to it, until next spring. Courage got exercised nicely; deposits were made to the account. Indeed, the ancients had long campaigns too and suffered hunger, cold, homesickness, and disease, but then we read of massive desertions and collapsed morale. Says Alexander the Great in a passage that moved David Hume by its sublimity: " 'Go!' cries [Alexander] to his soldiers, when they refused to follow him to the Indies, 'go tell your countrymen, that you left Alexander completing the conquest of the world.' "[58] But the miseries of campaigning did not change the ancient view that, except for what old age did to courage, courage was inexhaustible to those properly disposed.

It may not be much comfort to the poor soldier to know that if he is lucky enough to live, he may do so at the expense of his sanity. The idea that cracking up isn't a form of cowardice dies hard, and even when it dies there is no honor in being considered mentally ill.[59] Those who think that the removal of what were once moral matters to the domain of medicine and psychiatry will substitute compassion for blame underestimate the tenacity of our impulses for blame and self-blame. But for us others there is some comfort in knowing that even most of the toughest, roughest, hardest are expected to crack in the end, unless they are psychotic to begin with. So for us it happens at day 30, for them at day 60, or 240 or whenever; but we are all democratically united in our limited possibility. The notion that courage was an exhaustible resource spoke to a specific problem in a particular environment; it evidenced a new politics of courage. The trenches revealed that the expectations for courage derived from epic could not be met, though various genres in pop culture are still committed to the ancient view. But the old heroic ideal dies hard; when soldiers perform in that genre they win Medals of Honor, Victoria Crosses, Pour le Mérites, and when they don't the new imagery of depletable courage comes to some small kind of rescue.

Aristotle made good sense in hoplite war; he still makes excellent sense for the demands peace makes on our courage.[60] Remember that these images of finite and scarce courage were meant to capture the limits of courageous possibility not just under fire, but under incessant fire. It is the relentlessness that excuses:

> It was the reasoned crisis of his soul
> Against more days of inescapable thrall,
> Against infrangibly wired and blind trench wall
> Curtained with fire, roofed in with creeping fire,
> Slow grazing fire, that would not burn him whole
> But kept him for death's promises and scoff
> And life's half-promising, and both their riling.[61]

This reasoned crisis led the soldier in Owen's poem to kiss the muzzle of his own rifle, to commit suicide, the only form of self-inflicted wound a broken soldier still desperately committed to the old norms of honor would allow himself, no ignoble shooting himself in the hand or foot.

By the time Tim O'Brien was writing, the bank-account model had become general.[62] Everyone talked in its terms. The U. S. Army, shifting to the year-in-country rule for Vietnam, bowed to its demands. O'Brien gives us his own accounting of the costs and benefits of the metaphor, one that he seems to accept. First the upside: "Courage, I seemed to think, comes to us in finite quantities, like an inheritance, and by being frugal and stashing it away and letting it earn interest, we steadily increase our moral capital in preparation for that day when the account must be drawn down." The vision is of saving up for the big purchase, the grand heroic action of youthful fantasy, that "in a moral emergency" he would "behave like the heroes of [his] youth."[63] This is quite an expansion of the bank-account model of courage beyond Lord Moran's formulation. O'Brien contemplates the fund growing; Moran saw only depletion. O'Brien sees the image as funding heroic fantasy; Moran sees it only as a deflation of that fantasy.

But O'Brien is compulsively probing about courage and his own share in it. He sees a serious downside to images of economizing on scarce courage: "It was a comforting theory. It dispensed with all those bothersome little acts of daily courage; it offered hope and grace to the repetitive coward; it justified the past while amortizing the future."[64] The theory might still be right as a descriptive matter, but if it led people to economize on their courage, to save it up, it was a theory whose moral costs might outweigh its benefits. Rather than excuse the mental and moral collapse of people asked to give more than should ever have been demanded of them, it becomes an excuse to give little if anything at all.

O'Brien, almost perversely uncharitable to himself, ends up years later seeing the virtue in Aristotle's commitment to training up a disposition for courage by doing courageous deeds. The nth time may be difficult because your fund of courage is running down, but the first time may still be the hardest. He tells of a girl in his fourth-grade class whom he adores. She is dying of a brain tumor and wears a scarf to school to cover her shaved head. One boy tries to rip it off her and eventually succeeds. Tim, miserable and confused, watches the girl's misery and does nothing: "I should've stepped in: fourth grade is no excuse. Besides, it doesn't get easier with time, and twelve years later, when Vietnam presented much harder choices, some practice at being brave might've helped a little."[65]

O'Brien accepts the constraints of finite courageous possibility, but he refuses to let it serve as an excuse to avoid the hard work of training and predisposing oneself for courage as Aristotle would recommend. His modest revision of Aristotle, in which a courageous disposition is measured by averaging performances coupled with a vow to do better next time, updates a theory designed for hoplite warfare to make it more suitable to the trenches of the western front, the *bocage* of Normandy, or the jungles of Vietnam. In any event O'Brien is so much more plausible in his theory of courage than those philosophical discussions that fail to distinguish between courage on isolated and one-shot bases and courage under conditions of unrelenting demands on the virtue. The attempts to finesse the problem by recourse to "dispositions," which once in place take care of everything, don't solve the matter. The Great War proved that.

Finally, if there is a defensible difference between something called physical courage and something called moral courage, then it comes down in part to this: physical courage decays under the intense and relentless demands of combat while moral courage needs its daily constitutional; it grows by the doing of deeds that require its mobilization. Standing up for what we think is right is not easy, but it may well get easier if we cultivate the habit of doing so. But the comparison is not quite apt, for we can structure our lives so that the occasions demanding moral courage march to the rhythms of hoplite warfare; they do not fire their shells into our lives each day, each night, as we huddle in a trench, at least in a way that forces us to sit up and notice, unless we have the misfortune to live in one of those nightmarish regimes that so characterize the history of the twentieth century.

5

Courage and Scarcity

IF IT WERE EASY to get massive compliance with the demands a virtue makes, we might suspect—or should suspect, given the ample justifications humanity gives to the misanthrope—that our sights are set too low, that we have merely defined our expectations downward so that they coincide with what we are and what we do. What if virtuous dispositions were not scarce, if nearly everyone had cultivated one? Would that cheapen the coin of the virtue? Imagine a polity so successful at training its soldiers to be courageous that it gets almost 100 percent compliance with a norm of death before dishonor; they will not surrender or let themselves be taken prisoner. Imagine, in other words, something resembling the Japanese performance in World War II. Surrender was explicitly forbidden: The Japanese field service code reminded the soldier to "meet the expectations of your family and home community by making effort upon effort, always mindful of the honor of your name. If alive, do not suffer the disgrace of becoming a prisoner; in death, do not leave behind a name soiled by misdeeds."[1]

And people obeyed, not just soldiers but civilians too. In the defense of Saipan, for instance, 41,244 soldiers died out of a total strength of 43,682, not to mention mass suicides among the civilian population.[2] Those few who surrendered had not only to face the risk all surrenderers have to face—getting an offer of surrender accepted without getting shot in the process—but also to contrive it so that their fellow soldiers would not shoot them in the back as they came forward to give themselves up.[3] Yamauchi Takeo is rebuked by two of his subordinates, a mere "farmer and a city man who'd only graduated from elementary school," because he suggests that they give themselves up after their regiment has been reduced to fewer than 200 from an initial strength of 3,500: "Squad leader, you're talking like a traitor. Behave like a military man!" His men eventually abandon him in disgust, and he ends up in a cave with several other soldiers from a different unit. The Americans broadcast promises of food and water if they surrender, but Yamauchi fears "that if I surrendered within sight of our own men during daylight, I might be shot in the back." It takes him another three days to extricate himself from his fellow soldiers so that he can give himself up with only the Americans to fear. His fears of being shot in the back were not unfounded. A young student nurse on Okinawa reports seeing an American boat offering her and her desperate group assistance if they would surrender:

> I shuddered. I was completely exposed. Suddenly, a Japanese soldier climbed down the cliff. A Japanese soldier raising his hands in surrender? Impossible! Traitor! We'd been taught, and firmly believed that we . . . must never fall into the hands of the enemy. Despite that, a Japanese soldier was walking right into the sea. Another soldier, crouching behind a rock near us, shot him. The sea water was dyed red. Thus I saw Japanese murdering Japanese for the first time.[4]

When an enemy is courageous in roughly the same degree as we are, we often concede them their courage and admire them, however grudgingly, for it. But when they are willing to face death in numbers and on occasions beyond our ability to fathom, then we change the valence of their valor and call it fanaticism (especially if the Other is Eastern or Middle Eastern or even Christian if they are a little too confidently committed to a belief in eternal reward for falling in battle). If they are German then we discount their courage somewhat for their excessive discipline and obedience to authority. Hard and tough, traits often highly correlated with something like courage, but just not quite right. In American self-loathing about Vietnam we came to be no more charitable to ourselves than to the enemy when conventionally courageous deeds came in quantities too excessive to be seemly. Such excessiveness led journalist Michael Herr to wonder whether ostensibly grand suicidal action isn't rather a form of desertion: "How many times did somebody have to run in front of a machine gun before it became an act of cowardice?"[5]

There are good reasons to be suspicious of the bias and interest that affect our assessments of enemy courage. But there may be some small justice to our reluctance to accord our adversary praise for what we judge to be an excessively produced virtue. Can't a case be made that it is more courageous for an American soldier to charge a Japanese pillbox than for a Japanese soldier to charge an American one? Might it not be easier for them to do such deeds because their culture, for whatever reasons, is more adept than ours at socializing its members along such lines? Certain belief systems may just be too good at getting people to prefer the promise of eternal bliss to present life, or to prefer death to the threat of a life of irredeemable shame.

It is true that we are willing to award Medals of Honor or Victoria Crosses to much of the same behavior that we dismiss as fanaticism when done by Japanese, or that the Spartans dismissed as unseemly when done by Aristodemus.[6] The Medal of Honor citation for gunnery sergeant William Walsh describes behavior akin to a one-man banzai attack: he "fearlessly charged . . . against the Japanese entrenched on the ridge above him, utterly oblivious to the unrelenting fury of hostile automatic weapons fire and hand-grenades employed with fanatic desperation to smash his daring assault."[7] Walsh was fearless, oblivious to being shot at, and daring; the Japanese whom he was thus attacking resisted with "fanatic desperation," the "fanatic" being little more than an empty modifier routinely employed against the Japanese even when it does not fit their behavior. Walsh's fearlessness is admirable. Nor does it matter all that much to us whether Walsh came to his fearlessness by the fortune of having been born not to scare easily, or by an act of will in overcoming his fear, or by "losing it" in desperation or rage; indeed, it may not matter to us in the least whether he is in fact fearless as far as his inner state goes. What matters to us is not only that Walsh's behavior is commendable but that it is rare and rather lonely, a *one-man* banzai assault.

This time the Americans are on the defensive against a Japanese assault:

> In the early morning hours Sgt. McGill, with a squad of eight
> men, occupied a revetment which bore the brunt of a furious at-

tack by approximately two hundred drinkcrazed enemy troops . . .
All members of the squad were killed or wounded except Sgt.
McGill and another man, whom he ordered to return to the next
revetment. Courageously resolved to hold his position at all
cost, he fired his weapon until it ceased to function. Then, with
the enemy only five yards away, he charged from his foxhole in
the face of certain death and clubbed the enemy with his rifle
in hand-to-hand combat until he was killed. At dawn 105 enemy dead were found around his position. Sgt. McGill's intrepid
stand was an inspiration to his comrades and a decisive factor in
the defeat of a fanatical enemy.[8]

McGill's feat is extraordinary and rather Japanese-like: fight to the death
and go down taking as many of the enemy with you as you possibly can.
The Japanese are more than fanatical in this account, they are also
"drinkcrazed." Even their rum rations seem to work better than Western
ones. But if fanatical why the drink, unless their fanaticism does not come
as easily as we want to believe?

Germans are also called fanatical in Medal of Honor citations, but at
about one-third the Japanese rate. They got the benefit of looking like
model 1944 Americans, while that same racism underwrites the simultane-
ous loathing contempt and awed demonization of the Japanese.[9] Yet one
wonders. Consider those 105 dead Japanese surrounding Sergeant McGill,
those implausible action-adventure movie numbers. The numbers may
well have been inflated for purposes of getting McGill his medal, but even
if he killed only half that many there is reason to find the Japanese behavior something other than courageous. Fanatical? Drinkcrazed? Foolhardy?
Stupid? Sad? But those are our judgments. What did *they* think it took to
die in heaps? Loyalty, obedience, courage? Just doing their duty? Doing
duty does not dispense with the demand for courage. Surely the kamikaze
pilot felt it a special privilege to die in a lonely suicidal mission, but these
men? Duty or not, there were just too many of them willing to die to take
out one man to make it virtuous.

I do not know enough about Japanese culture to construct their views
of courage; as should be clear, I am less interested in making claims about
the Japanese than in using our view of Japanese performance to test our
intuitions about courage's scarcity. Might it not be reasonably supposed
that courage has to have a moral economy in which it is relatively scarce?

Montaigne thinks the answer is easy: "No matter how great it may be, no recompense is allotted to any virtue which has passed into custom: I doubt we would ever call it great once it was usual."[10] But doesn't an outsider to that culture in which courage is so prevalent hold those people in awe for managing with ease what comes so hard to him and his people? Doesn't the insider take pride in his culture's ability to be known among nations as a culture of warriors who will fight to the death? An individual Japanese soldier may thus not be considered especially courageous as against his fellow Japanese, but he never doubts that he has more than enough to match any enemy he meets, and he knows his enemy will fear him because of his culture's martial reputation. Nonetheless, easy courage seems unfathomable to us as courage, and I think there may be a way to justify our intuition.

Imagine a system of such powerful shaming sanctions that life cannot be lived should one fail to conform to certain group values. Before shooting himself General Saito Yoshitsugu ordered all Japanese on Saipan, including civilians, to make a "general attack." Thus Yamauchi Takeo, whom we met a few pages ago:

> If you were taken alive as a prisoner you could never face your own family. They'd been sent off by their neighbors with cheers of *"Banzai!"* How could they now go home? "General attack" meant suicide. Those unable to move were told to die by hand grenade or by taking cyanide. The women and children had cyanide. Those who didn't jumped off cliffs. Ones like me, who from the beginning were thinking about how to become prisoners, were real exceptions.[11]

Shame bears a close connection with courageous motivation; it might in fact be its chief motivator. But do we want the shame sanction that backs courage to be so powerful that it eliminates choice in some significant way, thus rendering the virtue less virtuous to that extent? It is not at all surprising that such a culture would also be a suicide culture.[12]

Then too we would want to know the rules for the decay rate of cowardice. Is redemption possible in such a culture if on one occasion one fails to measure up? In a culture in which there is no second chance, one in which norms of conformity are so powerfully backed by shame that suicide is the easier alternative to life, we can expect high rates of death before dishonor, with the trigger for dishonor being very sensitive to the touch. One subtle writer on Japanese honor defines their honor system as a defensive one, and contrasts it to the aggressive male honor codes of Homer and the sagas.[13] In a defensive system the main ethical norm is not to stand out, but to conform; in the other the open struggle for precedence is all. Not that precedence isn't struggled for in a defensive system too, but that goal cannot be openly affirmed.

Both Western and Eastern honor systems produce excellent warriors, but it just may be that the defensive one produces more of them by being able to take advantage of the dominating demand for conformity. Each system also seems to have a different starting assumption about courageous potential in the face of death. In the Western aggressive precedence-setting system the assumption is that only the few will not show themselves cowards some of the time. Even Hector must run, Ajax and Diomedes retreat. One can move in two directions in this system, downward out of the honor game into pure contemptibility, or up out of the pack to highly individualized heroism. There is a middle ground in which one plays the game of challenge and riposte, now up, now down, but remaining a player in the honor game. In defensive systems all are expected to measure up, even as it is silently feared that doing so is no easy task, for nothing less will be tolerated. One can only go down. Death before dishonor bears significance in both systems; in one it is a bargaining position or an aspiration, in the other it is honored.

This is an exaggerated picture, needing refinement and qualification. Still, one might seriously entertain the notion that courage of the extraordinary sort the Japanese routinely displayed might be easier for them because of the intensity and uniqueness of their socialization to it. It was, I suspect, harder for McGill to do what he did than for any of the 105 enemy whom he joined in death; he was alone. The pious commitments of cultural relativists sometimes conflict. Those who set such high stakes on the uniqueness of cultures might have to accept that one of the costs of doing so is having to accept that virtues like courage have rather a different quality to them in one culture than in another. Courage just may be easier in some than in others and thus in some sense less praiseworthy if only because less scarce, while in others, as among the Cossacks and other scavenging marauders who greatly preferred slaughtering the unarmed to battling opposed armed forces, courage's substance may have been nine parts pitilessness and cruelty, with no special value placed on exposure to risk; when these opportunistic predators were stoutly opposed their cultural norm was simply to flee.[14] Perhaps the difference in virtue between Western and

Japanese behaviors in World War II can be captured by the difference between doing one's duty and going beyond the call of duty. Japanese culture required the giving of life as a duty demandable by others, whereas McGill in this instance went beyond the call of duty; he volunteered action that could not have been demanded of him. Had he claimed just to be doing his duty he would have sounded falsely modest; a Japanese soldier could, however, without any false modesty, have claimed merely to have done his duty when he charged McGill.[15]

We turn a kinder eye to our own martyrs, but not to all who sought to claim martyrdom for themselves. Here, too, the principle in the West seems to be that martyrdom must be scarce to be held dear. Consider the early Christian martyrs who died testifying to their faith, a faith that holds the promise of eternal bliss. A simple cost-benefit analysis would reveal the good deal being offered: a few minutes, maybe hours, of torment for an eternity of pleasure. In the words of one early father of the church: "And who would not gladly receive tribulation upon tribulation if he is at once to receive also hope upon hope, reckoning with Paul that 'the sufferings of this present time,' by which as it were we buy our salvation, 'are not worthy to be compared with the glory which shall be revealed to us' by God."[16] It seems that no small number of people made precisely that calculation and were volunteering for the bargain martyrdom offered. A rather puzzled and reluctant Roman magistracy was willing to grant their wish if sufficiently provoked, and though some zealous Christian leaders might aggressively counsel martyrdom, cooler voices were concerned about volunteer martyrs.[17]

Something was unseemly about seeking martyrdom because it offered a good deal. It debased its coin, by making for more martyrs than the proper martyr market would bear under ideal conditions. The better martyrdom comes unbidden, and though neither the voluntary nor involuntary martyr had it easy when it came time to die, the volunteer could roughly choose his end when he was ready so that he was not caught unawares and thus not tested in the way the involuntary martyr was. Unseemly too was that the volunteer presumed upon God; he was too greedy for his aureole, as if he suspected God might run out of them before the magistrates got around to throwing him to the beasts, if they bothered to at all.

IT IS HARD, perhaps impossible, to separate the line of argument I have just been following from its politics. It is an ancient tradition to denigrate the grand martial acts of your enemies as something other than the courage that you claim for your own grand actions. If their courage is conceded, then it is a lesser courage or just plain luck. Pericles thus tried to bolster Athenian self-esteem by arguing that Spartan courage was inferior because it did not come naturally as Athenian courage did. Why would the Spartans need to train so hard if it were not to compensate for their natural shortcomings?[18] Besides, he adds, courage is more purely manifested by those, like Athenians, who know the difference between pleasure and pain, who actually have pleasures to tempt them from the hard demands of courage.

Sometimes it is in the interest of one side to admit the bravery of the enemy. It is not just Gallic cynicism that led the nineteenth-century military theorist Ardant du Picq to write of the ancient world: "The conquered always console themselves with their bravery and conquerors never contradict."[19] It seems to be a matter of timing. Once defeated, the war over, the enemy can be allowed their bravery, for their virtue enhances the quality of your victory; but when still embattled it is harder to be so generous to your adversary, and if you concede him too much courage you could scare the living courage right out of your own troops.

One last point on the Japanese that revisits the issue of the scope and specificity of a courageous disposition. Apparently those few Japanese who were taken prisoner were so badly prepared as to how to behave as prisoners that they were very fertile sources of information for interrogators.[20] The Japanese would have an easy answer for this: what should one expect of a man so shameless as to be taken prisoner but that he would also be a rat? How, they might ask, can we train people to die rather than be taken prisoner and also train them to be tough prisoners? Maybe, however, the courage of an entire culture does pay small homage to the laws of thermodynamics. The more a culture musters courage for one task, such as fighting wars, the less it may have for others, such as enduring prison camps or standing up against internal injustice.

Plentiful Courage

The Japanese succeeded in getting extraordinary compliance with the grimmest demands of death before dishonor, but we also claim for ourselves large quantities of courage when the situation warrants thinking of courage as something plentiful rather than scarce. For every quotation one can find about the rarity of courage there is another at hand assuming its abundance, though not its easiness. "Military courage is certainly widespread," says Marc Bloch, but he hastens to add that it nonetheless takes dedicated effort to acquire it.[21] He, one of the greatest historians to have ever lived, had no small amount of it. And if a medieval scholar has it, then who not? We have conflicting beliefs about the scarcity of courage, and we do not seem all that troubled by the conflict. The ambivalence of these beliefs funds the wordplay in Admiral Nimitz's remark about Iwo: "Uncommon valor was a common virtue."[22]

We recognize a courage that is above and beyond the call of duty upon which we confer individualized awards and honor; we sometimes call that heroism, but the distinction between heroism and courage is not consistently maintained, and no great weight should be put on it. Heroic, medal-winning courage must be scarce, or we rightly expect something is awry. Then there is the courage of groups, whole regiments, battalions, or of all the men at the sharp end, who are just following orders, doing their duty, being average soldiers. In some respects it is the courage to be the average soldier that elicits the most respectful incredulity in the average observer.

Have you not wondered how you would have done had you been with Pickett and his men as they undertook that charge into the face of Union fire or with the Union troops assaulting in wave after wave the entrenched Confederate positions on Marye's Heights at Fredericksburg? Would you have held firm in a square at Waterloo? Would you have cracked before going over the top on 1 July 1916 or before the landing craft disgorged you onto an atoll in the Pacific or a Normandy beach? Would you have been able to suppress the knowledge that at least a good portion of your job was to take up some pathetically small amount of an enemy machine-gunner's time and capital so that the chances that some of your comrades would make it to that gun would improve by .01 percent? If you had seen it that way, could you have done it at all? And what if, instead of being the first wave into no-man's land on 1 July, you had been in the second or third, that is, you had known exactly what awaited you? Yet those who were given these orders and duties, with very few exceptions did not refuse them.

The rate of compliance flabbergasts us, because we cannot quite trust that we would not have collapsed sniveling or cowering. It's not just that they did it once, but that they were called to resume the attack later on the same day, or again the next, or maybe a few months down the line. It is one thing to admit we are not up to the grand actions that merit Victoria Crosses and Medals of Honor. As an official matter these are awarded to a person only for deeds the nonperformance of which "would not subject him to any justified criticism."[23] Supposedly there is no shame in not falling on the grenade, even though there must be years of guilt to pay if you owed your life to someone who did. It is quite another thing to be able to do your plain duty when that means storming a well-defended beach. That so many did suggests we would have managed it too. Maybe. And most of us would not care in the least that this courage of doing our duty— for courage is what we would at least partly let ourselves think it was—was prompted by merely following orders, or because we mimicked someone else's courage, or because we could not let our buddies down, or because we were madder than hell, or sick unto death with despair. The point is, we stormed the beach. No, it is not the same as the Japanese style; you could still keep your head down and powder dry and qualify; but it is nothing to sneeze at either. As with Posidonius at Plataea, it was all right to want to come home again alive and even to act on that desire within limits. And should you mistrust that what you had done was courageous and were too confused and fearful or too modest to claim courage for yourself, there were others who would be quick to praise your courage no matter how sheepish or proud that might make you. Your unit leaders would claim the unit's bravery as against others in the larger group.

We expand the fund of courage to its widest extent in those official public honorings of the living and eulogies for the dead. The homage we pay our soldiers who died in battle does not depend on how distinguished they may have been as soldiers; the dead are all understood to have died as heroes, even those who died by friendly fire. The tradition of eulogizing fallen soldiers is old, and though performances in the genre are mostly pre-dictable and dull, there are spectacular ones too: Pericles' funeral oration and Lincoln's address at Gettysburg. It is not just the dead who are coura-geous. We are quite willing on Veterans' Day and Memorial Day to call all those who fought heroes, with "fought" coming to mean "having served" and thus to include even the rear echelon. The passage of time, it seems, brings the rear ever forward and erases differences in virtue.

The good and noble, it is frequently lamented, make up a dispropor-tionate share of casualties. The jaundiced Spartan answer to this was that "spindles (meaning arrows) would be worth a great deal if they could pick out brave men from cowards."[24] Paul Fussell, always suspicious of war sto-ries though he loves to tell them, describes how he was treated as a hero for having been wounded: "In their instinctive generosity, Americans have never understood, God bless them, that the cowardly are wounded as readily as the brave. Shell fragments don't care about the current moral status of the men they penetrate."[25] In a more general lamentation on the same theme a British officer in Normandy in 1944 writes: "That was the trouble with war . . . you might live because you took a risk, or die because you did not or vice versa."[26] The positions are not contradictory. The best probably do die more than their fair share, *and* arrows, bullets, and bombs are not very good at making moral distinctions.

We can better tolerate the relatively sincere belief in high percentages of courage and courageous dispositions after the fact, when courageous action is no longer called for, when no further demands will be made on one's finite fund of courage. An entirely different idea of the proper percentages of courageous people in a given population governs when there is still courageous work to be done. Then we are more modest in our beliefs as to how many can be so disposed. Yes, we exhort them by calling the exhortees courageous before we have much reason to believe they will be, but we are also equally likely to exhort them by provisionally cursing them as wimps and weenies, cowards and chickens, as by calling them heroes.

By our willingness to make the dead paragons of courage we are, I think, endorsing Aristotle's view of courage as the proper manifestation of a specially cultivated courageous disposition. At first sight, it looks instead like quick and easy one-shot redemption conferred for political reasons. Pericles openly says that one-shot redemption is what it is all about; how else to induce people of marginal morals to be willing to die nobly for the city? Those who were not especially worthy before their death, he says, become so by dying for the polis.[27] Jesus, too, appears to support the one-shot view; that's the frustrating message of the parable of the workers in the vineyard: those who work their lives cultivating virtue get no more reward than those who come on board at the last minute. But that would be a superficial reading of what we do by honoring our war dead. We come to understand the dead as properly *disposed* to virtue. They are best likened to the hero in the coming-of-age movie (and so many of war dead are barely more than adolescents) in which the redemption gives the proper sense of an ending precisely because we can now think of the hero as virtuously disposed for now and forevermore. Never mind that he is dead and there is no real forevermore. The reel is at its end, but every year on Memorial Day the polity will rerun it, so that "yet once more, O ye Laurels, and once more," he will perform nobly again as he showed himself disposed to do by dying when and where he did.

6

"I Have a Wife and Pigs"

COURAGE STANDS OUT among virtues not only for the mysteriousness of its psychology and for its capacity to generate good stories, but in other ways too. Consider the relation of courage to pleasure. The argument is made that though a virtue may be difficult and arduous in the acquiring, once achieved it is a source of pleasure to its possessor. The generous person enjoys being generous, as the temperate person enjoys moderation. But it does not make sense to say that courage is enjoyed in the same way without being rather masochistic: there is just too much pain and sorrow and often real extinction in the process. Aristotle noted this long ago and recognized it to be something that distinguished courage from other virtues.[1] Victory is pleasant, but courageous action does not always succeed, nor for that matter is all victory a consequence of courage rather than deceit or luck or being richer; and success too may bring death—which if glorious is part of the payoff but must be "experienced" posthumously in the manner we experience the pleasure of having our family collect on our life insurance—or permanent crippling and disablement—which is more than anyone bargains for: "No soldier desires," writes Abner Small, "not even to save his country, to be torn in pieces by a shell, made a disfigured and hopeless cripple. A man of sense is not built that way."[2] And while we might imagine in the very midst of the fray the pleasant sensation of believing that things are going our way, that sensation may owe a lot more to the courage of our comrades than to any of our own.

No virtue causes quite the confusion that courage does in pinning down just what acts or precise mental states qualify. Seldom can an act of generosity or temperance be mistaken for its opposing vice, or the vice—like tightfistedness, selfishness, or drunkenness—for the virtue. We would never say of a person that he's so selfish that he's generous, or that he sleeps around so much that he's faithful, but we may and sometimes do say (as we are about to see) that he's so cowardly that he's brave. It turns out that some forms of cowardice or shamelessness are able to mimic courage with uncanny particularity.

Courageous Cowardice

Assume for the present that courage, or at least one form of it, is characterized by achieving a state of fearlessness, if only momentarily. Yet some cowards, particularly those who are without shame, also manifest a kind of fearlessness. Aristotle recognized this paradox right at the outset of his discussion of courage:

> The man who is afraid of [disgrace] is upright and decent, and
> the man who is not afraid of it is shameless; but he is sometimes
> called courageous by a transference of meaning, because he has a
> point of similarity to a courageous man; the latter is also a sort of
> fearless person.[3]

Without a prior understanding of the different moral stakes separating honorable from dishonorable goals, the shamelessness of the sociopath, the criminal, and, in Aristotle's world, of the slave and the coward can look remarkably like courage. This shameless person does not fear ridicule or censure; Aristotle goes on to describe him as so degraded that he is undismayed by the prospect of a whipping. In one respect such people are as tough as nails; tough in exactly the way a certain style of action hero is. Why assume, then, that all those we call cowards fear very much, if they fear at all? Imagine the coward who when ordered to go to battle responds not fearfully, but with a Bartlebyan resolve that he prefers not to. And like Bartleby, he will do nothing he is bidden to do unless he feels like it. He fears no reprisal and will stand firm against any attempts to bully him to battle.

Robert Graves tells of Private Probert from Anglesey, who had joined the Special Reserve in peacetime for his health. But 1914 brought more than he bargained for. "In September the entire battalion volunteered for service overseas, except Probert. He refused to go, and could be neither coaxed nor bullied. Finally he came before the Colonel, whom he genuinely puzzled by his obstinacy. Probert explained: 'I'm not afraid, Colonel, Sir. But I don't want to be shot at. I have a wife and pigs at home.' "[4] The colonel tried to shame him. He was ordered to wear the peacetime scarlet tunic, which got dirtier and dirtier from the kitchen work he was then assigned to. His mates called him Cock Robin and made up mocking songs about his red breast. But Probert did not care a whit; he took whatever they dished out. Finally the army gave up; he was discharged as being of underdeveloped intelligence and "went happily home to his wife and pigs."

A British memoir of the Italian campaign in 1944 tells of one Coke, a soldier with a perpetually sour expression, dedicated to "looking after Number One," insensitive to the claims of his comrades situated as miserably as himself.[5] He was not well liked. He had to be bullied into action; he deserted more than once, though when caught the first time he actually looked shamefaced and remorsefully confessed himself a coward to his mates.[6] But that was his last moral moment. Once he admitted his cowardice he became committed to it without shame. We next see him taunting the author for having stuck out an action from which he (Coke) had absented himself. He flaunts his court-martial "as if it were a decoration": "I'll be here when you are pushing up daisies." When the military police come to fetch him, Coke just grins at his old mates. From the back of the truck about to haul him away he turns on them: " 'You silly sods,' he yelled. 'I 'ope you don't get pulled out at Florence!' "[7]

Coke, it seems, is not just interested in number one, but also actively wishes the misfortune of his unit. This shakes the men; they possess an atavistic fear of the power of a pariah's malevolent curse. Not being relieved at Florence is not unlikely, given the malignity of fate and the perverse likelihood of military snafus; so delicate is the balance of fate in their favor, if it is in their favor, that the curse, if not really quite believed in in any serious way, could just tip fate against their hopes. One of them shouts back: " 'And we 'ope you'll be fucking shot!' " To which Coke replies: " 'I'll be alive when you're all fucking dead!' We shook our fists and yelled, but although none of us would ever have admitted it I think we were all a little impressed. Coke had gone down with all guns firing."[8]

Similar accounts abound, of soldiers willing to be whipped from camp to camp and drummed out of the service with nary a twinge; no fear of pain, no fear of censure.[9] Such people unnerve those who observe them. They are not so much loathed as held in a kind of awe, much as the berserk is held in awe; like the berserk they seem almost a species beyond. Nothing touches them. They are a nightmare vision of incorrigibility or clueless-ness, of unrelenting determination to carry out their intentions against a universe whose claims they either do not understand or do not acknowl-edge. They give us the heebie-jeebies in their preternatural imperviousness to social and moral claims and even to threats of physical pain. They are unreachable in a way that even the courageous person who doesn't scare easily is not.

Private Probert has a wife and pigs. Perhaps maddeningly to virtue ethicists, Probert satisfies their vague prescriptions about the virtuous life: he chooses his actions in pursuit of a well-defined life plan, a little narrow to be sure, but otherwise rational, within a well-accepted model of peasant farming; his is an image of human flourishing in the bucolic style, a style seen by many to provide the perfect context for a life of virtue. He is most likely a good husband to his wife and good husbandman to his pigs. Nor should we judge him harshly because he seems to value his wife and pigs about the same. She may well have brought them with her as her marriage portion so that her value is inexpressible independent of the pigs. There is thus some greater seriousness underlying Probert's comedic style than, say, that of the man from Leeds who sought an exemption from service on the grounds that he had to bring his wife tea in bed and had just started a course of hair tonic that would require three months to show results.[10]

Probert is, without a doubt, to be taken at his word: he is not afraid, but given his wife and pigs, both the bliss and the responsibility they represent, he can see no need to get himself shot at. Absent the wife and pigs he has all the makings of a reliable soldier. He might even be a great soldier if he saw soldiering to bear directly upon the defense of his wife and pigs. Nor is Probert completely shameless, for he acknowledges the claims of agonistic manhood. He does not want to be thought a coward: "I am not afraid, Colonel, sir." Not completely shameless by a long shot, but instead, vaguely out of it, not capable of giving reasons that aren't comical, that aren't just the kind, in other words, that will attract the rather Swiftian eye of Mr. Graves; Probert is a man of one dimension and only one dimension, an old-styled humor or vice in a comedy of humors and vices. The man is portrayed as a fool, not a coward, by the most common understanding of cowardice. And that was how the army understood him. He was discharged as mentally deficient, not court-martialed for disobedience or cowardice.

But consider the substance of Probert's foolishness; it surely is not a matter of I.Q. in the strict sense, for he chooses just the right means to gain his desired ends. His mental deficiency is in part a social deficiency. Either he is utterly clueless about how his actions will be judged by others, or if not clueless, and it appears he is not, then he simply doesn't give a damn what anyone thinks of his priorities. But it is more than that; Probert has the luck to be seen as a vulgar clown by Graves and the army, as more comic than criminal. His mental deficiency comes down in the end to his coupling his wife with his pigs. Had he alleged his reason for not going to war to be his wife and kids, even his wife and cows, or his necessity to get in the harvest, or had they understood him to have cooked up the whole thing as a calculated strategy to save his skin, this story would not have been told, for he in all likelihood would not have gained his end.

Coke, on the other hand, is clearly a coward and ultimately shameless about it;[11] he is also fearless in the way that led Aristotle to remark the uncanny convergence of the courageous and shameless character types in their imperviousness to fear. There are two features of Coke's story that deserve special notice. The first is the grudging admiration his total shamelessness elicits from his mates. They can barely disguise their envy of his zealous commitment to a goal they would pursue if they only had the nerve, for none of them wants to be there; each desperately wants to get the hell out alive. In Coke's bizarre inversion of courage and cowardice his behavior exposes a kind of cowardice in themselves captured by the proverb "Many would be cowards if they had courage enough."[12] It is an inversion that becomes a common theme in soldiers' memoirs. Mark VII (World War I) puts it this way: "I understand desertion. A man distraught determines that the last act of his life shall at least be one of his own volition; and who can say that what is commonly regarded as the limit of cowardice is not then heroic?" And this from Robert Crisp, a highly decorated British officer in World War II: "I have always had an uneasy feeling that most conventional cowards are morally braver than heroes. Nothing that happened in the war, around me or within me, inclined me to make any alteration in that assessment."[13] Crisp is not talking about Burdette's good coward who wanted and meant to be brave. The moral bravery of Crisp's conventional cowards is more in accord with O'Brien's view, that courage meant the moral courage to opt out against all the pressures to conform. Theirs is the courage to run away from battle.

Coke has also moved beyond the narrow concern of looking out for number one that characterized his early insensitivity to his comrades. Then they were mere objects of indifference; he has now metamorphosed them into objects of exquisite hatred, a hate he is willing to endanger himself to express. In fact, a group of them were about to arrange Coke's death while on patrol until an officer got wind of the plot and quashed it. Coke taunts his comrades again and again with the imminence of their deaths and the certainty of his survival, for which he can thank his government for having between the wars repealed the capital punishment of cowardice.[14] So gutsy is Coke's last stand that the narrator finds conventional metaphors of martial heroism to be fitting: "Coke had gone down with all guns firing." He ended up being one tough guy. Our anxiety, though, about our guarded admiration for Coke's perversely inverted courage—in pursuit of improper goals (saving his skin) with improper motivation (resentment and hatred)—is reflected by our reluctance actually to use words like courage, bravery, or valor to describe him. Instead we find words of lower register, not quite as ennobling or flattering. Thus nerve, nerviness, and chutzpah, at times even guts and balls, register a small ambivalence for or disapproval of his action, even as we must begrudge some admiring disbelief.

The second point involves the complication of Coke's cowardice by his hatred. J. Glenn Gray, in his book on the moral psychology of soldiering, describes the "constitutional coward" as a person who lacks "a sense of union with his fellows." His comrades "are not able to sustain him emotionally. They are merely part of the external furniture of his life."[15] I am not sure Gray is right. This portrait does not capture that coward, constitutional or not, who is shamed by his cowardice but who lacks the will to overcome his fear; he wishes fervently he were constituted differently, in part because he does feel a sense of union with his fellows; he is deeply envious of those born cooler, less imaginative, less queasy in the gut.

The shameless coward, craven without second thought, comes closer to Gray's description, but the shameless coward, as we have seen, slips by degrees into a near perfect mimicking of courage. Probert recognized no claims of his mates, but he was devoted to his wife and pigs, and in the end not much of a coward either, just unsocialized. When Coke still had some shame for his cowardice at the time of his first desertion he was selfish in the extreme, without fellow feeling for his mates. He fits the description of Gray's constitutional coward. But once he unabashedly gives himself over to his cowardice, his mates become something more than mere furniture. They become enemies whom he cares about with a vengeance; he actively wishes them harm. I see nothing in Gray's formulation of the constitutional coward's detachment from others that wouldn't also describe the lonely heroism of certain kinds of detached souls given to seeking a kind of crystalline principled perfection, the likes of Socrates or Thomas More.

How are we to understand this kind of fearless cowardice of the unshamable? We could declare by definitional fiat that cowardice must be motivated by fear and save Probert from cowardice. But what of Coke? If he is indeed a coward, so one way of arguing would have it, he must be motivated by fear. We must then distinguish between the fear that motivates his avoidance of combat and the fearlessness with which he pursues that goal. We could understand his fearlessness to be particularized to the pursuit of accomplishing a specific goal, a goal erected as the natural end of a more deeply experienced fear. So he both fears and does not fear at the same time. But I am unable to understand the psychology of this view, for though his initial experience of fear of combat set him upon his present course of action, that fear seems no longer to be felt at all. His initial visceral fearfulness played a causal role; it set a goal to pursue—saving his life at all costs; but once the goal got set it detached itself from his original felt experience of fear by virtue of his shamelessness. For he now knows that he isn't going to follow orders to fight, no matter what. The cowardly fear of combat is no longer felt as a passion, but has become objectified as an idea. He is now fearless, a fearless coward.

Or if Coke's fearlessness is granted, the definitional fiat requiring that cowardice be motivated by fear could be satisfied by denying Coke the label of coward. Yet it is one thing to teach a child not to call a whale a fish, and quite another to assume priggish overprecision by insisting that one not call Coke a coward. Coke is a coward and so shameless about it that the initial fear that made him so is now only a fillip, a hypothesis, that set in motion his fearless determination to avoid combat by any means necessary. Contrast Coke's cool determination with the pitiable soldier who so fears that he will crack from fear, so dreads that he will disgrace himself in battle, that he commits suicide the night before going over the top. Is that cowardice? And if so, what of someone who is unwilling to kill himself to avoid combat, who cowers in a fetal position in his foxhole refusing to advance, but who faces his executioners with self-possession? That describes Eddie Slovik (d. 1945), the only American shot for cowardice since 1865.[16] Resolve the tormenting uncertainties of when and how he was to die, and Eddie Slovik achieves a form of resigned dignity.

Cowardly Courage?

In Coke, and perhaps in Probert, the coward's inner state satisfies one description of the courageous person's inner state: fearlessness. But it is also possible to find cowardice and courage converging at the other end of the fear axis, in which the hero shares with the coward an inner state of fear, shame, and confusion. One of the curious facts about some people whom most of us would consider models of courage is that they think themselves cowards, or if not quite cowards they suspect that the courage they are credited with is a sham, that they faked it, hoodwinking others and even themselves. They wonder if they were hypocrites of the sort Jesus described, those whose deeds look virtuous but whose motives are not.

Thus one soldier, John Watney, who performs well, defines himself as a coward simply because he fears, and specifically fears that he will be a coward, even though he does not give in to his fear in a cowardly fashion: "But I was a coward; and the thing I feared more than anything in the world was to break up in battle and give way to that cowardice. I made up my mind that as long as I had the strength, never, under any circumstances, would I allow that to happen."[17] He never did allow it to happen. Robert Crisp again, recipient of both the Distinguished Service Order and Military Cross, denigrates his courage because he was doubly beset with fear, fear itself and the fear of it—the fear, that is, of shame should he succumb to the first fear: "It was some months and only a few more bullets and shells later that I knew my courage for what it was—a reaction to the shame I felt at being afraid, a manifestation of an ingrown complex which survived in a reputation for a sort of recklessness which, somehow or other, I had to sustain and exhibit until some more genuine and significant emotion took its place."[18] Recall the brave Captain Johansen expressing concerns about his own bravery, and note the title of combat-tough Vietnam helicopter pilot Robert Mason's memoir, *Chickenhawk*, a fabulous amalgam of two birds which performs like a hawk but is as fearful as a chicken. If Johansen's tone is wistful and Mason's self-mocking, Crisp and Watney are bitterly self-castigating. One denies himself courage, the other dismisses it as just another form of giving in to fear, as if he were a coward.

How do we understand their psychology? Both men are afraid and then afraid of being afraid. They know that the archetypal coward fears and is dominated by his fear. They know that most cowards, except those of Coke's ilk, also suffer intense shame for their fear and the moral failure they attribute to it. Sometimes they suggest that it is only by the smallest luck that their own fear of shame weighs a little more than their first-order fear of death; they take little solace in that, because, it seems, the balance is almost in equipoise. They suggest also that their fear of shame does not do its work by banishing the prior first-order fear from their consciousness. The fact is that they never cease being scared for their lives, but manage, motivated, they say, by fear of giving way to that fear, to do well in spite of it.

I am not sure I trust them completely; the tone seems too ungenerous to themselves not to be taken without a grain of salt. As was suggested in Doc's case, the psychology of courage may be such a mystery even to those who possess it that in casting about for explanations of their own behavior they fall back on conventional explanations, like fear of shame, call of duty, when their motive was something they could not know in the thick of things because of the noise, the fear, and, above all, the confusion. If they really believed that the fear of shame was motivating them, why all the self-blame? They seem to be suffering from excessive scruples, a disease they caught from that kind of virtue talk that demands that virtuous deeds be done for their own sake, for the love of the virtue, not to avoid punishment or disgrace. That demand may work fine for virtues like generosity and amiability but seems too much to ask of virtues like courage or loyalty. The standard is set too high. The Spartan king Leonidas fails by it; so does Skarphedin Njalsson, the most feared of all saga heroes. Fearing the shame of failure may be the way courage asks to be loved "for its own sake." Or maybe these men endorse a hierarchy of fear-management techniques, some nobler than others, and what they desire is a technique that drives fear, whether fear for their lives or fear of shame, out of their consciousness. They subscribe to a view, it seems, that courage demands, if not quite fearlessness, that fear stay modestly in the background. They are not conceding courage solely to the few psychotics who lack normal fear responses, but they feel that the courageous are those who can push fear out of their heads and bowels and wipe it off their faces when the going gets rough. By that standard they feel they failed, for they were scared.

There is another way to read their anguish. Suppose what they really feel is total passivity, that they are hanging on for dear life as fear calls all the shots, just as it does in the standard case of cowardice. In such a state they cannot distinguish very well the fear of death, maiming, and pain from the fear of shame and being seen as a coward. These fears all coalesce into one big fear that overwhelms their consciousness. But in this hypothetical, fear, plain old fear, comes to their rescue. Fear does not have just one action tendency. Fight is an option no less than flight; if the goal is fear reduction, either action can provide it. By this view the coward is a coward because the socially devalued fear reaction—flight—kicked in instead of the valued one—fight—which by some stroke of luck kicked in for these self-castigating men. Why fear propels one forward, freezes a second in his tracks, and puts a third to flight is inscrutably mysterious to them. And since they cannot trust the virtue of their motive, which they suspect is fear itself, they feel like fakes, frauds, or hypocrites; hence the self-flagellation.[19]

The notion of "critical distance" might be of some relevance. Well-known animal studies show that within a critical distance, that distance within the kill range of the predator, the prey responds to threat by fighting; if still within flight distance it flees if the predator decides to attack.[20] Thus the mouse will run if it can but will bite if it must, its heroism or cowardice resolved by a yardstick. Animals are lucky enough not to have the moral pressure of notions like courage and cowardice muddling the location of the fight/flight tipping point; when in the safe zone the mouse does not fantasize bringing down the cat. When outside the critical zone the prey feels no urge to get even, while the predator prefers not to waste energy chasing on a long shot unless very very hungry. Even the goal of the prey's fighting, once lack of vigilance or bad luck has got it within the critical distance, is not to win, but to reacquire the opportunity to flee, to get back to the flight distance. Not that life is without anxiety once there. I cannot help but wonder about the inner life of those emblems of victimhood in the nature documentary—the wildebeests—grazing with what appears to be casual equanimity within view of the lioness' contemptuous gaze. But could part of the mystery of the human coward and hero, discounting for strength and skill, be a function of their own idiosyncratic internal yardsticks measuring very personalized critical distances?

It thus may be that the mechanism that allows an actor to operate in spite of fear is not self-command or even a greater fear like the fear of shame, but first-order fear itself in its fight mode. Presumably the fight mode also brings with it other passions to mix with the fear that sets it loose: rage, fury, despair, which in some actors succeed in blocking or replacing the experience of fear. Such people might then describe their experience as having *overcome* their fear rather than as acting *in spite* of it, unless it turns out that the experiences are indistinguishable. The type of courage that operates in spite of fear, however, has no choice but to be moved by whatever will move it, difficult as it is to figure out just what that may be. And if it is fear that is moving his courage, then the mind of the courageous person can share significant points of congruence with the mind of the coward. In this view, for what it is worth, the same fear moves each; only the action tendency is different. I will return to this issue later when dealing with anger and its role in fear management.

These men may well buy this view, if only because they do not feel that their self-command performed well enough to take credit. Had their self-command been up to its task it would have better beaten down their fearfulness. The courage of fear-overcoming they aspire to would have had a different feel to it than the one they had, maybe of hot blood, maybe of cold determination, but manifestly not the fear that suffused their being. Thus they feel themselves cowards who faked it, because all they can recall is their fear even though they know their deeds were not a coward's deeds; they don't need an observer to tell them that. But so insistent are the beliefs engendered by a model of fearless warrior courage, a model they even know is not the only model of courage nor the only one they may subscribe to, that the experience of fear makes them, in their own eyes, a chicken, or at best half chicken, half hawk.

Yet maybe these men are just being modest, like Doc, that simpler soul who was not troubled in the least by what he did or did not feel, much to the annoyance of Tim O'Brien. They can indulge the luxury of this self-doubt because they know that whatever they may have felt, they *did* just fine. One suspects they would not have written their memoirs if they had not done reasonably well. It is hard to imagine a craven and cringing coward writing a war memoir, at least a truthful one; the memoirs of those who kept their heads down and muddled through adopt either a self-mocking comic style or, in O'Brien's manner, muse on the horrific psychic and moral demands of war. Vile cowards appear as characters in someone else's memoir.

If modesty is part of the motive of Crisp and the others, it seems to be greatly overborne by genuine anguish, despair, and bitterness. Might it be that these men believe that the simple fact of having survived proves that they compromised too greatly with their fear? Contrast, however, other styles of discrediting one's own manifest courage. In this case the tone is highly ironical, and whatever modesty there is, if not quite false, is not able to hide a certain irrepressible self-delight. The move is not to make courage look like cowardice, in the sense that both are equally motivated by fear, but to make one's own courage look like the most rational way to get to the rear with honor intact. Courage is depicted as utterly unmysterious; it is posed as purely self-interested prudence and nothing more. In this account, courage begins to mimic Coke's fearless and shameless efforts to get himself safely out of action.

Here is Graves explaining why he volunteered frequently to lead night patrols in no-man's land, a task famed for its riskiness and uselessness:

> I went on patrol fairly often, finding that the only thing respected in young officers was personal courage. Besides, I had cannily worked it out like this. My best way of lasting through to the end of the War would be to get wounded. The best time to get wounded would be at night and in the open, with rifle-fire more or less unaimed and my whole body exposed. Best, also, to get wounded when there was no rush on the dressing-station services, and while the back areas were not being heavily shelled. Best to get wounded, therefore, on a night patrol in a quiet sector. One could usually manage to crawl into a shell-hole until help arrived.[21]

It seems bizarre that Graves would think it an advantage to have his entire body exposed, but consider that if he peeps up over the parapet the likely wound was a sniper bullet through the eye or forehead, especially since snipers had their rifles honed in millimeters above the opposing parapet. Much better to put his whole torso out and chance a nice blighty (British slang in the first World War for what the Americans called the million-dollar wound in the second). Graves did get his wound but not as planned; it was by shell not by rifle, by day not by night, and during the third week of the Somme offensive, when the demands on dressing-station services were very intense. Unlike Coke, however, he was willing to get wounded by the enemy.

Confusion

How does one get a fix on one's inner state at crunch time? Civil War veteran Abner Small vented his spleen against Stephen Crane's portrayal, in *The Red Badge of Courage*, of the hero Henry Fleming's inner state. How could Crane represent Henry, a raw recruit, "with a brain fully alive to reason and revealing a cunning course of deception, all in a way apparently realistic . . . but only possible in an imaginative mind before a parlor grate?"[22] Crane, born after the war, never saw combat; Small was there. In his view, battle undid the capacity for reflection and for most thought. In battle all is mystery and confusion. People are brave or craven "in spite of themselves," clueless as to what makes them one or the other or on certain days one and on other days the other. Philip Caputo, a Vietnam vet, notes that battle is so disorienting that one never quite knows how to distinguish fear from confusion.[23] Or as Tietjens puts it in *Parade's End* about the effects of the noise of exploding shells: "If you cannot hear your thoughts, how the hell are you going to tell what your thoughts are doing?"[24] Small affirms: "The shock from a bursting shell will scatter a man's thoughts as the iron fragments will scatter the leaves overhead."[25]

For others confusion is felt as a "helplessness . . . beyond description."[26] Frederic Manning (World War I) describes how battle generates an emotional synesthesia in which individual emotions merge with their opposites so that fear can even become exhilaration or give rise to anger or whatever its emotional opposite may be:

> All the degrees which separate opposed states of feeling vanished, and their extremities were indistinguishable from each other. One could not separate the desire from the dread which restrained it; the strength of one's hope strove to equal the despair which oppressed it; one's determination could only be measured by the terrors and difficulties which it overcame. All the mean, peddling standards of ordinary life vanished in the collision of these warring opposites. Between them one could only attempt to maintain an equilibrium which every instant disturbed and made unstable.[27]

Everyone confirms Stendhal's and Tolstoy's view of battle as a noisy and ironic confusion of forces in which individuals stumble about blindly. Military training assumes that Small, Caputo, and Tietjens are right. Drill, rote learning, repetitive forms, what Keegan calls the "categorical, reductive quality of officer training,"[28] concede the difficulty of thought in conditions of battle; the goal is to wire in habitual and automatic responses and easy-to-administer rules of thumb to help order one's experience in a world run amok. Abner Small grants that deep reflection, cool or anxious, is possible afterwards in tranquillity or before on the edge of the mayhem, but not in its midst. There, it is "the arbitrary military law" that guides action in blind automatism:

> That any man in my regiment, or in the army, analyzed his feelings and marked out any specific line of conduct while under fire, or even thought for five consecutive minutes of the past, present, or future, or measured out or acted upon any theoretical course of conduct irrespective of the arbitrary military law which held him in obedience, is absurd. Afterthoughts are in a sense real, and give a correct résumé of what might have been; but to put an endless and connected train of thought in the brain of a green soldier, so thoroughly scared—by his own admission—that he is not accountable, and set it in systematic motion which shall develop the "Red Badge of Courage," is sheer rot.[29]

Small makes little room for a robust practical wisdom in the midst of courageous action. Maybe before, and in hindsight afterward, but deliberation worth the name seems to be largely suspended as one hangs on for dear life in the midst of mayhem.

Hypocrisy

It might be that courage is immune from a certain type of hypocrisy. If a man is moved to do pious or generous deeds for no purpose other than that of acquiring a reputation for piety or generosity, then in Jesus' view he is a hypocrite;[30] but if a man does courageous deeds because he wants to be known as courageous, or, more precisely, because he cannot bear being known as not courageous, then he is courageous. That is how most honor cultures understand it, and I am inclined to credit them. These cultures were not interested in making courage cheap. They respected it too much for that.

Courage, of course, is susceptible to certain forms of vicious fakery. Take Falstaff, for example. He desires only to seem brave at no risk to himself. Knowing that brave conduct is a most dangerous way to acquire a reputation for courage, he pursues other means. He lies about his deeds, boasting of pasts that never happened, claiming glorious futures that he has no intention of realizing except as material for more fictionalized pasts, and in the present he does nefarious deeds designed to trick others into taking them as evidence of bravery. He thus stoops to stabbing and mutilating corpses so that he can claim them as his victims. If this makes Falstaff a hypocrite regarding courage, he is not Jesus' type of hypocrite, for he does no deeds that are otherwise good except for their improper motive. Jesus' hypocrite still gives real alms to the poor. Falstaff, though, pays his alms with counterfeit coin or, if with real coin, soon defrauds the pauper of them. Falstaff is not alone; stories of unjustly awarded medals, cooked reports, contrived events, invented accounts are common fare in soldiers' memoirs.

THE PURPOSE of this chapter is not to make some easy point about the incoherence of a culture's notions of virtue and vice, about how they ultimately are indistinguishable. For that is not true. Of course there remain areas of irresolvable contention in which one's courage is another's cowardice. Is it courage or cowardice to struggle to survive in a death camp rather than to walk over and touch the electrified fence or get shot for trying to touch it? But it is the psychological indeterminacy of courage and cowardice I most wish to emphasize. No adequate description of either courage or cowardice can reduce them to the presence or absence of a single psychological state. No single psychological state can subsume all courageous action courageously undertaken, and similarly with cowardice. The relation of fear to courage and to cowardice is so rich in possibility that a plausible account could be offered for a fearless cowardice that mimicked courage, just as we could suppose a fear-filled courage that mimicked the inner state of conventional cowardice. Add to these the problem of the "good coward," who, knowing his weakness, still tries again and again, who does not desert before any battles, but crumbles in every one. Confusions like these are pressing enough to lead soldiers to anguished questioning like Burdette's: "But who are the cowards? How are we to distinguish them from the heroes? How does God tell?"[31]

7

Shoot the Stragglers and the Problem of Retreat

THE MILITARY AND its law have struggled to get a fix on the psychology of cowardice too. Consider this provision of the American Uniform Code of Military Justice, which, among other things, criminalizes cowardice:

MISBEHAVIOR BEFORE THE ENEMY

Any member of the armed forces who before or in the presence of the enemy—

1 runs away;
2 shamefully abandons, surrenders, or delivers up any command, unit, place, or military property which it is his duty to defend;
3 through disobedience, neglect, or intentional misconduct endangers the safety of any such command, unit, place, or military property;
4 casts away his arms or ammunition;
5 is guilty of cowardly conduct;
6 quits his place of duty to plunder or pillage;

7 causes false alarms in any command, unit, or place under control of the armed forces;

8 willfully fails to do his utmost to encounter, engage, capture, or destroy any enemy troops, combatants, vessels, aircraft, or any other thing, which it is his duty so to encounter, engage, capture, or destroy;

9 does not afford all practicable relief and assistance to any troops, combatants, vessels or aircraft of the armed forces . . . when engaged in battle;

shall be punished by death or such other punishment as a court-martial may direct.[1]

Making cowardice a capital offense will strike many as a barbaric survival from a rougher age, a time, that is, when few doubted that courage ranked higher than pity or prudence in the scale of virtues. And if many today are reluctant to put even the sadistic murderer to death, what a shock to discover that, as an official matter at least, Congress reserves it for the person who cannot kill at all. Don't worry: although the state has the power and right to execute those who misbehave before the enemy, we are too unsure of ourselves, or maybe even too charitable, to enforce the statute maximally, except once in this century, *pour encourager les autres,* in the bleak Hürtigen Forest in 1945, when Eddie Slovik was shot. Still, we have preserved the option.

Quite independently of its grim sanctions, the statute prompts our attention because of its strangely absurdist quality. Several of the statute's provisions seem merely to restate one another. Wouldn't all cases of running away (1) also qualify as cowardly conduct (5)? Likewise, aren't paragraphs 2 and 8, the one punishing cowardly defenders, the other reluctant attackers, special cases of cowardly conduct too? Surely, the casting away of arms, punished in paragraph 4, is a concomitant of either panicked flight or craven capitulation. Paragraph 7 would execute the soldier so jittery that he overinterprets causes for alarm, while paragraph 3 authorizes shooting the sentry who was not jittery enough to stay awake on duty.

Only paragraph 6—the stricture against looting—marches to a completely different beat. It punishes those whose misbehavior arises from certain kinds of exuberance rather than from fear, panic, or fatigue. Yet, no less than the other provisions, the antilooting provision is devoted to maintaining the delicate balance of forces that keeps armies behaving as armies rather than as crowds.[2] Success can be as disordering as failure. For this reason the Spartans, Thucydides reports (5.73), did not chase an enemy they had put to flight very far, while others feigned flight to prompt their opponents to break ranks in a false flush of success. In this century the initial success of the German offensive on the western front in 1918 was stopped, it has been claimed, as much by the German soldiers stumbling upon stores of wine and cognac as by Allied resistance.[3] But the statute focuses mainly on misbehavior bred by fear, slackness, and failure of nerve, not on the loss of discipline and order bred by greed, cruelty, lust, and other manifestations of exultant riot. Narrow self-interest in the acquisitive style of the looter is not as worrisome to an army as narrow self-interest in the life-preserving style of the coward.

In this chapter and the next I use the statute to explore some aspects of the relationship of cowardice to fear. Here I focus on paragraphs 1, 4, and 5.

Running Away

Isn't running away, punished in paragraph 1, running like hell for the rear, precisely how we visualize the purest cowardice (punished in paragraph 5), just as casting away arms (punished in paragraph 4) so you could run away faster was how Plato and Aristotle envisioned it?[4] In fact the image of running away is so vivid that soldiers have preferred being charged with the vaguer and more abstract "cowardly conduct," considering it less prejudicial and disgraceful than the accusation "he ran away."[5] But statutory provisions that to the normal eye look duplicative will inspire judicial interpreters to invent differentiating glosses, just as language itself never quite allows a perfect synonym. So paragraph 5—cowardly conduct—was read by judges to require a showing of fear as a necessary element of the offense.[6] Cowardice had to be motivated by fear or it was not cowardice, but running away, it was decided, did not need to be so motivated. This strikes nonlawyers as somewhat perverse. Why else would anyone flee battle, run away, if not in panic, terror, or out of simpler fears of death and mayhem? Is this apparently redundant provision there to make sure we can line up the fearless coward before the firing squad, so we can nail Mr. Coke?

The military judges struggled to give running away a meaning that would distinguish it from cowardice. They wanted to avoid defining running away so expansively as to undo the mercy implicit in differently defined and lesser offenses such as "absent without leave,"[7] those acts of desertion that did not take place in the presence of the enemy. One military court became the final word on the subject with this desperate attempt:

> This term [runs away] must connote some form of fleeing from an ensuing or impending battle . . . It appears that to limit the phrase to flight from fear or cowardice is too restricted. It would appear to be more in keeping with the offense, if an intent to avoid combat, with its attending hazards and dangers, is considered as an essential part of running away.[8]

"An intent to avoid combat" is a catchall for whatever motives other than fear might prompt a soldier to run away. What precisely might these motives be? One could, I suppose, run away out of treachery, or out of the most calculating thin-lipped prudence, or out of love of one's wife and pigs as the humane Abner Small supposes for deserters he was asked to round up on leave back home in Maine: "My sympathies, I admit, were often moved for deserters whose love of family was apparently stronger than their love of country. They weren't running away; they were merely going home."[9]

But the narrative suggested by each one of these motives seems incomplete without complementing them with fear of death. The most psychologically plausible motive for running away that dispenses with such fear is fleeing in disgust, sick at being stuck in a situation in which so much is asked of you and so little given you in return; not fear, but the feeling of being ripped off, revolted by unfairness and injustice. But such a person does not run away. The image is wrong; even the notion of fleeing misrepresents the insolence, even the fearlessness, with which he walks, sullenly saunters, but manifestly does not *run* away, while muttering "fuck this." The time Coke *ran* away, he was motivated by fear; later, when he toughened up and knew himself a coward, he didn't run. He held his ground in a one-man mutiny of defiant disobedience.

The judges, however, do not include sullen withdrawal in their picture of running away. Still desperate, they turn to Winthrop's *Military Law and Precedents*, first published at the end of the nineteenth century, in which Winthrop, too, evinces bafflement on this matter, and in good legal form provides authority for his bafflement by citing an older writer who was discussing something not precisely on point:

> RUNNING AWAY. This is merely a form of misbehavior before the enemy, and the words "runs away" might well be omitted

from the Article as surplusage. Barker, an old writer cited by Samuel, says of this offense:—"But here it is to be noted that of fleeing there be two sorts; the one proceeding of a sudden and unlooked for terror, which is least blameable; the other is voluntary, and, as it were, a determinate intention to give place unto the enemy—a fault exceeding foule and not excusable."[10]

The court citing Winthrop citing Samuel (early nineteenth century) citing Barker[11] (late sixteenth century) distinguishes two types of fleeing, the first "proceeding of a sudden and unlooked for terror" and the second of "a determinate intention." Both types, despite Barker's suggestion to the contrary, are voluntary (when I flee in panic, I still intend my flight). But Barker is right to notice that our ordinary ideas about culpability distinguish between the offender who coldly calculates, the picture of self-interested prudence itself, and the one who offends while in the grip of terror or some other strong passion.[12] But our statute does nothing to incorporate Barker's distinction; the statute catches in its lethal sweep the cold calculator and the panicked wreck, whether under paragraph 1 or 5.

Panic, one suspects, is treated more leniently by Barker because it is impractical to do otherwise, not just as a concession to ideas of culpability. Panic usually involves large numbers in headlong flight, and, however harmful its consequences, it hardly makes sense to hand over the entire army to the firing squad. Let them make amends by regrouping and fighting better another day. Barker's distinction between "exceeding foule" flight of "determinate intention" and less blameworthy panicked flight follows immediately upon his discussion of Roman decimation, the practice of killing by lot one in ten of a failed legion. This association suggests that decimation might be suitable in the case of generalized panic-propelled fleeing, but that fully individualized punishment, rated at 1.0 probability rather than at the 0.1 discounted group rate, be meted out to the voluntary calculator of his own immediate best interests, the Mr. Coke shamelessly determined not to stick around.

A prosecution brought under paragraph 5, cowardly conduct, must show, as noted, that the conduct was motivated by fear. This is one of the few areas in the law in which the decision maker is asked to find that the person was motivated by a particular passion, not just to find that the person was in the sway of some generalized powerful passion. How do we prove that fear was the motive? Do certain bodily clues betray him? Was he pale?

Did he tremble, sweat, shed tears, urinate or defecate in his pants? Even if so, such bodily indicators are ambiguous. Heat, too, makes us sweat, while joy, grief, and the cold may make us shed tears. The most lethal saga hero of ancient Iceland grew pale in anger, not in fear. Montaigne observes that both "extreme cowardice and extreme bravery disturb the stomach and are laxative." Even the nickname "The Trembler," he notes, given as an honorific to King Garcia V of Navarre, not as in Aristodemus' case for shame, "serves as a reminder that boldness can make your limbs shake just as much as fear."[13] Dysentery can cause us to befoul ourselves. And the fear of getting caught with one's pants down often leads the soldier, at least in the trenches of World War I, to become desperately constipated.[14] Fear does have a distinctive facial expression, but the expression can be suppressed when one is scared and faked when one isn't.

This is not earth-shattering news. State of mind always ends up being inferred either by legal convention or by the social knowledge necessary to make sense of whatever act or omission whose motivation we are searching for. If one is in a battle and trembles *and* runs away, or cries while curled up in a fetal position and hence cannot advance, then we judge that behavior to be a consequence of fear, and so confident are we of our judgment that we would not believe anyone who behaved in such manner and said he was not fearful.

The law of duress assumes that fear is excusing;[15] but in this statute fear is incriminating. In the civilian world one who succumbs to fear may plead duress to avoid criminal liability; but in battle the soldier may not succumb to fear unless a substantial number of his fellows give in at the same time. In cases of common law duress the defendant is measured against what a hypothetical "reasonable man" would do under like circumstances; but in battle there is no need to have recourse to that hypothetical, for we know whether most held firm or didn't. If most didn't, they are all off the hook, for we do not, in the Roman style, cast lots and decimate the battalion.[16]

Casting Away Arms

The prescription against casting aside one's arms has a long tradition, and it allows us to flesh out further the interplay of shamelessness, fearlessness, fear, and cowardice. In a triumph of the literalism that often characterizes the legal imagination, this prohibition, paragraph 4, is not understood to be implicit in paragraphs 2 (shameful abandonment of a position),

5 (cowardice), and especially 1 (running away). Both running away, except as perversely understood by the military courts, and casting away one's weapons are meant to capture the quintessence of martial cowardice—headlong *sauve-qui-peut* flight. Thus Archilochus, seventh century B.C.E.:

> Some lucky Thracian has my noble shield:
> I had to run; I dropped it in a wood.
> But I got clear away, thank God! So hang
> The shield! I'll get another, just as good.[17]

Tossing away the heavy shield was especially grievous in the phalanx style of fighting that Archilochus appears to have been engaged in, so grievous that the Greeks gave it a special name: *rhipsaspia*. A man, says Plutarch, carried his shield "for the sake of the whole line," because an unbroken shield wall was "virtually impregnable."[18] Thus those accused of *rhipsaspia*, writes Victor Hanson, "were assumed to have been among the first to have abandoned their friends in an effort to save their own lives during a general collapse of the phalanx";[19] these were those rational souls who knew that if flee one must, it was better to be first to do so.

The comic energy of Archilochus' verse is parasitical on the power of the norms he so gleefully confesses to violating. The wit of such self-mockery is possible only because the norm against running away and debarrassing oneself of one's burdensome weapons demands some kind of psychic homage even when not adhered to. To this extent we may read him as not quite given over to utter shamelessness. But we needn't read him so generously; his cheerful cowardice could simply be that inverted courage of shamelessness, what we might vulgarly call the "I-don't-give-a-shit-what-they-think" attitude in matters touching upon reputation, an attitude as unfathomable to most of us as is the berserk courage of the kind that we associate with Alexander the Great. In keeping with his inverted courage Archilochus refuses even to allege fear as the reason for casting away his weapons. It is all a matter of rational choice. His shield, as he observes, is replaceable, something which he is quite pleased to believe is not the case with himself. And although Archilochus knows he will have to fight again (that is one of the risks that running away does not completely resolve unless he is capitally punished for it), it won't be any time soon. He has to get a new shield first. Moreover, there is not the least hint he will do better next time.

With Archilochus compare the keen comedic eye of this Confederate soldier running to beat hell at Sharpsburg:

> Oh, how I ran! Or tried to run through the high corn, for my heavy belt and cartridge box and musket kept me back to *half* my speed. I was afraid of being struck in the *back*, and I frequently turned half around in running, so as to avoid if possible so disgraceful a wound. It never entered my head to throw away gun or cartridge box; but, encumbered as I was, I endeavored to keep pace with my captain, who with his long legs and unencumbered would in a little while have far outstripped me but that he frequently turned towards the enemy, and, running backwards, managed not to come out ahead in this our anything but creditable race.[20]

John Dooley runs his "anything but creditable race" desperately aware of the comedy of trying to maintain the appearance of honor in headlong flight: don't get shot in the back if you can help it and don't throw away your arms, although you realize that they have less than zero value to you now, pure dead weight. He is not unaware of a kind of double competition with his captain, one to see who can get away the fastest and the other to see who can get away the slowest. He envies his captain's benefits of rank: no pack—it is in a wagon somewhere—and no rifle. By this time the weapons of officers are becoming symbolic indicia of rank, like the pistols, whistles, and walking sticks of the British officers who led their men into no-man's land in the Great War. The ambivalence in the account and in the action itself gives the comedy multiple layers.

The heroic ideal of standing your ground at all costs turns out to give way before fear and not an altogether irrational fear, though as with Archilochus the fear is not mentioned directly but supplied by the comic action, giving it its motivating force. Both John Dooley and his captain are still giving respect to the norms they are not quite living up to by adhering to some of their forms: John will not throw away his gun or ammunition— although by denying that the thought ever entered his head he is merely saying that he resisted a temptation that had indeed entered his head—and both he and his captain engage in the farce of trying to prevent the ignominy of being shot in the back by running backward every now and then.

So natural is Dooley's comic talent that he even finds holding firm when desiring to flee an occasion for the triumph of irony at heroism's expense. Three days before his flight at Sharpsburg, Dooley was tempted to run at South Mountain but succumbed to the psychological and social demands of having his bravery presumed upon him:

> I was just making up my mind to make a double quick *change of direction* . . . when a Capt. Mitchell of the 11th Va., who was doing all he could to rally the Brigade, clapped me on the back, saying, "Hurrah for you! You are one of the 1st Va. I know you'll stand by us to the last!" What could I do under such circumstances? Was I to run and prove myself a coward? No Sir! So I just laid down with the others who were making a last *stand*, lying.[21]

In Dooley's "What could I do under such circumstances?" lies an acknowledgment of the magical power on our behavior of others' expectations, especially when those expectations flatter us.

Yet the comic voice with its self-delighting self-mockery indicates that his flight at Sharpsburg may not be culpable cowardice. Dooley can afford to be comic, clearly, because he is not alone in flight. One suspects also that Archilochus can so casually own up to his flight because he was well accompanied. These look like cases of running away so as to live to fight another day—as long, that is, as they do not throw their weapons away. Dooley's attempts to maintain the forms of honor indicate quite well that he means to be back. Even Archilochus intends to return once he gets a new shield, though he will find he faces a foe whose costs of facing him have been subsidized by his contribution to their armament.

When whole units run, cowardice has to be treated differently from when just one person runs. The problem is restoring the spirits of a whole regiment of routed soldiers so that they can believe, as Tim O'Brien came to believe, that courage in the long duration of war requires averaging behavior. Panic is catching; once the contagion gets going, those who catch it have some kind of excuse to solace themselves with; it happens to the best units and they recover. But what of the person who set it all in motion? The first one to flee, the panic generator, may be especially culpable. *The Battle of Maldon*, an Anglo-Saxon poem composed at the end of the tenth century, thus takes care to preserve the infamy of the first to flee by naming him, not because fleeing was itself worthy of remembrance—

scores of nameless souls did the same—but because Godric exited on his lord's horse, leading many others to think in that age of no eyeglasses that it was the lord himself who was fleeing.[22]

Retreating like a Lion

How in heroic culture does one retreat before the enemy so as to live to fight another day?[23] How does one back down without looking like a coward? How does one preserve one's credibility as a person to be reckoned with when defeat is by one part of the dominant ideology precisely what makes you an object of contempt? There must be a politics of prudence, a way of convincing others (and yourself too) that retreat and delay are the wise pursuits of honorable ends rather than mere attempts to pass off contemptible fear as the virtue of reason or even, once Christianity provided the option, as the virtues of forgiveness, patience, and peaceableness. Honorable men on occasion can retreat, run, and maintain their reputations in spite of it. But not without anxiety and labor. What kinds of strategies are available to rescue the situation? Archilochus and John Dooley adopted broad self-mockery, but warriors of limited intelligence like Ajax don't have that sort of comic resourcefulness. Homer, however, comes to the rescue. Blame the gods and provide these honorable warriors with face-saving similes that let them off gently when they must give ground. Ajax thus retreats because Zeus fills him with fear. Even then he does so in the manner of a lion, reluctantly and with many a backward look, like Socrates at Delium.[24] There is no irony here, no mockery of lions or humans, and no self-mockery in the manner of John Dooley.

When Menelaus is in a dilemma about whether to give up Patroclus' body in shame or to fight single-handed, hopelessly outnumbered against Hector and his men, he has recourse to a ready stock of acceptable excuses: "Whenever a man is prepared to go against divine will and fight a man who is honored by a god, then disaster rolls fast on him. So no Danaan will think the worse of me if he sees me backing away from Hektor, as Hektor is fighting with a god's support."[25] And when he retreats, he retreats accompanied by a simile similar to the one that let Ajax withdraw with all decorum: he retreats like a "great bearded lion driven from a farmstead by dogs and herdsmen with spears and shouting: his bold heart within him is chilled with fury, forced against his will to leave the cattleyard. So it was that fair-haired Menelaos moved back from Patroklos." The gods give just enough veil of excuse to let prudence have a chance, for even those totemic animals that emblematize nobility and courage have sense enough to know when to retreat.[26] A lion is still acting lionlike when he gives way, because when he withdraws he does so with appropriate reluctance. If lions and the gods themselves fear enough to withdraw in hopeless contests, then so can Ajax and Menelaus. They suffer no permanent shame, though they must still bear the mini-shame and discomfiture of admitting temporary defeat.[27]

In the much more down-to-earth world of the Icelandic sagas, the heavens are mostly empty or the gods dwelling there do not care much to intervene in human affairs, nor do the authors cover for their characters with choice animal similes. The entire corpus of the family sagas has only 128 similes. For those old Vikings a rose was a rose, an ax an ax, but a man a woman if he let his guard drop for an instant. Saga people had to provide their own excuses to give prudence breathing space amidst the constant pressure to posture aggressively and fearlessly. The saga heroic norm, for example, did not allow a person to deviate from his intended route of travel if he had announced it ahead of time, even though he suspected an ambush. Should there turn out to be no ambush he would be a laughing-stock, and if there was one he still might look cowardly if the ambush offered a battle at something less than ridiculously unfavorable odds. Saga characters actually plot face-saving covers so that they can deviate from an announced route once they learn there is an ambush. When, for instance, a member of Thorstein Egilsson's household intercepts Thorstein along his route to warn him of an ambush, Thorstein makes sure to receive the message out of hearing of his companions so that he can announce (falsely) that it contains an urgent invitation to visit someone whose farm lies along another route.[28]

No hero, however, had to defy death every second; in the sagas it was not always death before dishonor even in those settings in which a most punctilious honor would choose death. Some excuses were admitted. One example merits telling. Hrafnkel, a great warrior given to overreaching in his dealings with his neighbors, is against all odds outlawed by his neighbor Sam for killing Sam's cousin. Sam has the right, indeed the duty, to kill Hrafnkel in order to execute the outlawry judgment he obtained. Sam sneaks up on Hrafnkel, hamstrings him and his men, and then, moved by the fact that Hrafnkel has a large number of dependents, offers him two choices:[29] either to be killed immediately in accordance with the law or to forfeit all his property except a pittance and be banished from the valley with his dependents.

It is Hrafnkel's answer that is of special interest: "Many would consider a quick death preferable to such humiliation, but I shall do as many others have and choose life if I have the chance. I am choosing in this fashion mostly for the sake of my sons, for they will have little opportunity if I die."[30] He admits the pull of the heroic norm, but the pull of life is even stronger. Some of those choosing life may have preferred to die, but were weak of will. Preferring is not doing. But others, like Hrafnkel, know that with life there is hope, and in his world hope means hope of revenge. So though choosing life brings some dishonor it also buys time to redeem honor.

Hrafnkel's second excuse strikes us moderns as touchingly appropriate: his concern for his sons. But, rhetorically, he cannot convincingly claim this reason as his sole reason because it looks so patently pretextual, so obviously an attempt to gloss cowardly motive with a competing virtue of selfless concern for his children. Thus his *"mostly for the sake of my sons"* better to sell the reason's plausibility. The conclusion? Did people think Hrafnkel a coward? Not at all. They counted him as having got his come-uppance, one he richly deserved. They delighted in his discomfiture. But they also knew that he would be back; no one ever doubted his mettle. And the way he came back is why he has a saga named after him; he waited seven years before taking a perfect and thorough revenge.[31] Such is the practical world of the heroic in the sagas. There are ebbs and flows in the life of a hero within which prudence and practicality find a place just as they do in the ebbs and flows of battles.[32]

We need not have recourse to heroic literature to illustrate the strategy of excuse for saving face; we can move from the sublime to the ridiculous. In the absence of gods and honorific animal similes to bail us out, the excuses we come up with to avoid hostile confrontation while pretending to maintain all readiness and willingness to risk it could no doubt be supplied from our own experience. As little kids we somehow heard our moms calling us, or we had to get home for chores or supper, or we couldn't get the clothes we had on dirty without getting spanked; a girl could even allege being a girl. As adults we allege being adults. But the grim demands of the aggressive honor culture of male adolescence was less generous in allowing excuses, especially those by *deus ex machina*.

Coda: Socrates' Retreat at Delium and the Prudence of Flight

When Alcibiades described Socrates' fearless demeanor during retreat he added the thought that it made good sense to look as threatening as Socrates did: "For you're generally pretty safe, if that's the way you look when you're in action; it's the man whose one idea it is to get away that the other fellow goes for."[33] There are many minor paradoxes involving courage, and here is one of them: the way to save your life is to look as if you don't care a pin for it. Some will withhold their fire out of sheer admiration. Thus a rebel skirmisher who stayed to fire after his comrades had fled and then sullenly withdrew with a curse and an obscene gesture so impressed his Yankee opponents that they withheld their fire—"it would be a pity to kill so brave a man."[34] They cheered him instead.

Others hold their fire out of fear. This is Alcibiades' point. When an army is on the run, those who present only a back to the enemy are easy pickings; why take on those still willing to fight? If Alcibiades knows this, we may guess that Socrates did too. He knows that his courageous behavior is individually rational during a retreat; most of the costs it has will be borne by those comrades whose bearing does nothing to strike fear into the hearts of the pursuers. This does not mean, however, that Socrates was motivated by such prudential and meanly interested motives. He was moved to maintain his honor and dignity in the trying circumstances of defeated flight. Too bad if your fellow citizens must bear some of the cost of your virtue by being such easy targets. If they wished to avoid the added risk that Socrates' laudable conduct imposed on them, then they had only to turn and resist; they had no cause to blame Socrates for increasing their odds of being stabbed in the back.

Leaders of fighting men and theorists of combat have frequently stressed to the troops that it is imprudent to turn and run, that those first moments of showing your back to the enemy are the most risky, so that self-interest, prudence itself, counsels staying and fighting or, if withdrawal is necessary, then accomplishing it in an orderly fashion while making sure that the enemy is being faced, though presumably in a slightly less comical vein than Dooley and his captain did it. But that is not the whole story. Suppressed in this account is the temptation to be the *first* to flee, to be the one who first shows his back when the rest of his comrades are still covering it, like Godric at Maldon. It is only generalized flight that makes you easy prey, but even then you gain the advantage of having the odds of your own particular bad ending diluted by the presence of so many of your comrades also ripe for the taking, playing the same strategy as wildebeests in a herd, or fish in a school.

Nonetheless, for the bulk of the men the courageous thing to do may also be the safest. So indelibly marked with courage and rash bravado is the notion of charging and advancing that even when it is the best policy from a purely prudent point of view it does not for that reason lose the luster of bravery.[35] Similarly, in the early years of the Civil War, officers on horseback who ostentatiously exposed themselves to enemy fire were often spared that fire in deference to the courage they were showing. Rash display turned out to buy a safe ticket. Toward the end of the war this deference to gallantry had exhausted itself, and officers became less willing to strike such poses. But few could have thought that when they struck such poses they were merely being prudent, for in fact they were not. They were still exposing themselves to considerable danger. And though it may not have been crazily irrational to be bold, boldness is still no easy feat, and that was why such men gained the admiration that motivated their enemy's forbearance.[36]

8

Offense, Defense, and Rescue

THERE IS A DRAMA within the concept of courage that can be seen as having unfolded historically but also as being reenacted in every generation. The drama pits two conceptualizations of courage against each other, each fighting for the honor of representing the pure form. Roughly it is this: is courage more perfectly exemplified by marching into the teeth of danger, by the charge, by single heroic combat in the Homeric style, or is it best exemplified by endurance, by taking it, by never quitting one's post, by patient suffering over time? The tension can be re-mapped roughly onto other contrasting oppositions: offense versus defense, aggressive honor versus stoic and Christian fortitude, challenge and aggression versus sufferance and patience, physical courage versus moral courage, fear versus disgust, masculine versus feminine. The contrasts are not only substantive but also stylistic. Those on the left of the "versus" tend to be noisier than those on the right, to favor intense expenditures of energy in short bursts with long lazy intervals in between—the masculine; those on the right have a slower rhythm, but are insistent and unrelenting and endure—the feminine. Each set of oppositions also gives rise to its own special stylistic and substantive cowardices, as I shall demonstrate more fully in this chapter, postponing however the masculine/feminine, fear/ disgust, and physical/moral oppositions to later chapters.

Roughly speaking, the courage of offense creates the need for the courage of defense; the courage of aggression creates the miserable conditions demanding another's courage of endurance. One conceptually precedes the other. But on the level of ideology the courage of endurance and patience fights back, claiming precedence for itself. Says a Quaker, bristling at being called a coward by his interlocutor in Walter Scott's *Redgauntlet*, "thou knowest there may be as much courage in enduring as in acting; and I will be judged . . . by any one . . . whether there is not more cowardice . . . in the armed oppressor, who doth injury, than in the defenceless and patient sufferer, who endureth it with constancy."[1] Nietzsche, however, saw the ideology of patient courage as a concerted attack by the weak on the moral values of the strong.[2] Patient courage, in his view, was conceived from the start as an antimodel, a resentfully mean-spirited transformation of the courage of the strong, the exultant victorious, into noncomplaining sufferance, the courage of impotent losers. Before Nietzsche others discerned that the courage of patience and sufferance was serviceable as a cover for naked self-interest. As the fisherman who insulted the Quaker in *Redgauntlet* put it: "all villainous cant and cowardice assumed merely as a cloak to hypocritical avarice."[3]

No new conceptualization of courage, however, succeeds in driving its predecessors from the field. The battle goes on. The old forms of aggressive courage endure, no matter how badly discredited by opposing values of sufferance, forgiveness, and patience or, more concretely, by transformations in weaponry: rifles fired from entrenched positions in the Civil War, or machine guns and artillery shells in World War I. As recently as the Vietnam War Tim O'Brien had to admit that the charge was still *the* test of courage: "It's the charge . . . that is the first thing to think about when thinking about courage."[4] Fighting generals like Grant and Sherman were always suspicious of defensive styles; digging in was seen as cowardly, and many a British soldier in the Boer War and Marine in Vietnam paid with their lives for the built-in bias of their commanders for glorious offense rather than dour defense.[5] Defensive geniuses like Confederate general Joseph E. Johnston were rewarded by being relieved of command.

The preference for conventional aggressive offense is hardly irrational. Going on the offensive from time to time may be the best defense. Thus one Vietnam War platoon leader justifies his sending out patrols day and night because his training told him "that a completely defensive unit is a prime target for an overwhelming attack." The hoped-for conclusion of being on the defensive is breaking the enemy's assault so that you can assume the offensive: "The enemy cannot be beaten," writes the same soldier, "if you remain completely on the defensive; pursuit remains the finishing touch of battle."[6]

Let a war last long enough, however, and the ideal of aggressive courage gets tarnished considerably before the next generation, forgetful, polishes it up again. In the last year of the Civil War soldiers began to dig in on their own initiative. Courage then shifted its style to the capacity to endure, to take it.[7] By 1917 the French army on the western front was in a state of a precisely drawn semimutiny: they would continue to defend, but they would refuse orders to attack. The picture is more complicated once we get outside the context of battle, and even within that context the picture is too much a cartoon. Heroic conceptions of courage more than allowed for a particular kind of glorious defense, usually involving the desperate barring of a narrow pass by few against an overwhelming force. Thus Leonidas at Thermopylae, Horatio at the bridge, Roland at Roncevalles, and numerous heroes of Germanic epic,[8] besides Bowie and Crockett at the Alamo. The defense of a narrow pass was also the epitome of female virtue and honor. Not just female honor: when an Icelandic warrior wanted to mock the martial virtue of his male opponent, he could suggest that his opponent should defend the "narrow pass" of his backside a little better than he had heretofore.[9]

Moreover, outside the confines of war no one wanted to be living around aggressive honor types who saw fit to go around picking fights all the time, exercising their courage by testing that of others. The Old Norse sagas called such people "uneven men," men of no measure; and men of more measured conceptions of aggression would band together to put such troublemakers in their place—underground or abroad.[10] The ideal courage would thus shift its shape depending on whether it was the kind of courage needed to make life miserable for outsiders or to make life bearable for people within the boundaries of a single community. Even within that community, where immoderate aggressiveness was frowned upon, honor and security lay in cultivating a rather threatening defensive style, the look of "Don't tread on me." I will not attack first, but should I be attacked, expect me to make you wish that you had not done so. In this culture of threat, defenders had to be no less threatening than offenders. You showed that your threats to respond to aggression were credible by posturing aggressively, by assuming the offensive from time to time. Nonetheless, the broad distinction between offensive and defensive styles is one that people operating within these varying moral economies were aware of and held to be of moral consequence.

In the U.S. statute prescribing capital punishment for misbehavior before the enemy, paragraphs 2 and 8 define special cases of cowardly conduct, one involving failures on defense, the other involving failures on offense. Paragraph 2 punishes the person who "shamefully abandons" any place "which it is his duty to defend"; paragraph 8 punishes the person who "willfully fails to do his utmost to encounter" the enemy. The "shamefully" explicitly makes defense a moral duty as well as a legal one. Battle itself is a moral contest of sorts, for its goal, as John Keegan and others have noted, is to bring about the *moral* collapse of your opponent, specifically to murder his courage.[11] Keegan's moral contest assumes different moral and psychological claims on the defender from those on the attacker. "It is probably the case," he writes, "that human attackers concede to human defenders a certain claim—which one would call moral but for the ambiguity implied—to their territory."[12] The statute confirms such a distinction. Paragraphs 2 and 8 hold people to different expectations depending on whether they are asked to defend or to "offend." Although violations of each provision involve failures of courage, these failures do not carry the same moral weight.

Courage on defense demands a different mix of virtues and talents from courage on offense, and it seems that cowardice also varies with the different styles of courage demanded. We can, I think, imagine someone who is perfectly courageous when attacked, someone who will not flee, who will even die before abandoning the fight, who at the same time does not have the ability to initiate violence, who, if not quite a mass of quivering jelly, may tend to find too many reasons, with all the trappings of an admirable prudence, as to why it would not be in his or anyone else's best interests to go forward. Such a person may simply have an inertia problem, whether it be from friction caused by a basically peace-loving nature or a hatred of killing unless absolutely unavoidable. But in the context of war that inertia makes him behave as a slacker in settings in which initiative, not inertia, is demanded.

A person so constituted would not strike us as a psychological impossibility. In fact U. S. Grant complained that such was exactly the problem with one of his generals, G. K. Warren. Warren was able to see "every danger at a glance," too many dangers apparently, for he delayed moving until he had made exacting preparations for each of them, with the result that he never got to his appointed place in time to coordinate with others. Still, writes Grant, "there was no officer more capable, nor one more prompt in acting, than Warren *when the enemy forced him to it*" (emphasis added).[13] But we may also see Warren's reluctance on offense as no smirch on his courage at all. Warren is a general. That means his offensive designs do not expose him to any greater bodily risk than defense does. His reluctance on offense may be about risking his men, not about risking himself. He is cautious on offense because he doesn't want to see his men die; he is quick and prompt on defense because he doesn't want to see his men die. Warren lacks hardness, perhaps; and hardness is frequently confused with or deemed a particular incarnation of courage. Grant's gift as a general, and gifted he was, was not to have Warren's scruples about losing men.

The obverse—someone brave in the attack, but cowardly in defense—is hardly unimaginable. Some would cite boxer Mike Tyson as an example, who, when his ominous aggressiveness fails to cow the opponent, either folds sullenly or folds violently, but in such a way that announces he has no intention to stay the course. The courage that depends for its motivation on fury may be better suited for offense than for defense; should the fury exhaust itself before achieving victory, the person is without psychological means to hold on for the duration. Such a person may also feel that his moral standing in a competitive world will be better preserved by claiming "You didn't beat me; I quit."

Offensive Failure: Weak Legs

Offense makes particular demands on courage. Abner Small, recalling the Union debacle at Fredericksburg, describes an incident that occurred during a charge:

> I wondered then, and I wonder now equally, at the mystery of bravery. It seemed to me, as I saw men facing death at Fredericksburg, that they were heroes or cowards in spite of themselves. In the charge I saw one soldier falter repeatedly, bowing as if before a hurricane. He would gather himself together, gain his place in the ranks, and again drop behind. Once or twice he

fell to his knees, and at last he sank to the ground, still gripping his musket and bowing his head. I lifted him to his feet and said, "Coward!" It was cruel, it was wicked; but I failed to notice his almost agonized effort to command himself. I repeated the bitter word, "Coward!" His pale, distorted face flamed. He flung at me, "You lie!" Yet he didn't move; he couldn't; his legs would not obey him. I left him there in the mud. Soon after the battle he came to me with tears in his eyes and said, "Adjutant, pardon me, I couldn't go on; but I'm not a coward." Pardon him! I asked his forgiveness.[14]

This passage is remarkable not just for the literary talent it reveals, but also for the penitent self-understanding of its author, an officer, who has the moral courage to beg forgiveness of one of his men who cannot bear the disgrace of one interpretation of his failure to advance. This is also an account of weak legs, one of many that could be culled from war memoirs and courts-martial, with all the particular moral ambiguity that such cases reveal. The soldier's spirit, it seems, was willing, but his poor flesh was weak. His body just would not respond to the dedication of his will to do the right thing, to go forward. That is one view of the matter: the soldier's view it seems. There are other ways of looking at it.

Weak legs are a near unfathomable mystery. It is the mind-body problem in spades, not as an intellectual exercise, but sadly offering this soldier his most dignity-preserving defense. Without a convincing account of mind and body, emotion and body, conscious and unconscious, we do not know how to apportion blame as between body and will. Though this soldier's fear may be generated unconsciously by brain processes that are old enough evolutionarily to be available to reptiles,[15] he also has self-consciousness, and we cannot read his weak legs without paying heed to his own view of what happened to himself. His own bewilderment, anguish, and frustration at his will's inability to effect his conscious good desire to acquit himself well is not quite the same as the classic case of weakness of will, in which the will is without means to overcome conscious bad desires. All his conscious desires are proper.

Here the will is undone by we know not what. Unconscious desires to flee? Or something more primitive than desire, pure automatic freeze reflex? Or does he will his weak legs but deceive himself into thinking he has willed otherwise? Are weak legs a peculiarly male form of hysteria? Surely some instances resemble classic cases of hysteria, as when the legs give way when ordered to attack, but remain hysterically paralyzed as part of more generalized shell shock, combat stress, or just plain cracking up.[16] Might he know that he is afraid but intends rather to indicate that he does not ratify his fear, that he means to move on in spite of it and is desperately ashamed that an undesired desire for safety is causing his body to defeat his desired desire to move forward? To his mind he is not a coward, even though he couldn't go on. Unlike the good coward, whose legs remained very serviceable for running away, this man's legs do not let him flee either; he just can't go forward: "I'm not a coward," he says with vehement conviction.

Whom or what to blame, whom or what to understand, pardon, or convict? Mr. Small's theory varies with the exigencies of the setting. In the heat of battle Small was not generously disposed toward the shaken soldier. In battle Small's interests were such that he must hold the soldier strictly liable for the poor performance of his legs, whatever the source of their weakness. He had just grounds for suspicion, for weak legs are so easy to fake. The man proves the sincerity of his excuse, however, but only once the battle is over and Small has time and quiet to ponder the mysteries of courage and cowardice is he willing to accept the excuse. The soldier not only now sheds tears of frustration, contrition, and shame, but he had earlier rebuffed his officer's accusation as a man of honor would: he gave Small the lie, the traditional manly challenge to a duel upon an accusation of cowardice. The poor man means well in the aftermath, and Small's lack of certainty as to the psychological and physiological components of weak legs makes him incline toward lenience and thus believe the soldier meant well on the field of battle too. The statute punishing "willful failure to engage" the enemy follows Small in giving some credence to a weak-legs defense, for true weak legs are not understood to occur willfully. If there was a mutiny it was of the legs, not of the will.

Weak legs figure in soldiers' accounts as an insistent motif, seeming to serve as the emblem for the many kinds of fracturing that battle works on the unity of sense and sensibility, but mostly the split between mind and body. The body just goes its own way and the soldier looks on in dismay. This is the body that befouls the soldier's pants during shelling or in the midst of a charge; this is the body that sheds tears, sweats, faints, and even instinctively feints. This also may be the same perverse body that thwarts male desire, as well as male will, as when a man "can't get it up," a case of a weak leg if ever there was one. The same body figures in diverse and often ambivalent ways in how we talk about courage and cowardice: courage is heart, cowardice losing heart; courage is nerve, cowardice nerves; it takes guts to go forward, but the same guts cramp in agony or explode in diarrhea. And when courage is playing on disgust's home turf rather than on fear's it takes "stomach," not guts, to overcome the horror.

Like guts, legs play both sides of the fence; they are as likely to do their duty against a desire to fold as they are to fold against a desire to stay the course. Thus men march asleep, stand at their posts though asleep on their feet; a soldier would prefer to fall out of line, but his legs keep going with a will of their own. One of Tim O'Brien's characters in *Going After Cacciato* can consciously resolve to fall down, yet have his legs refuse to obey—"the decision did not reach his legs."[17] O'Brien inverts the meaning of weak legs to accord with his view that fighting was proof of his moral cowardice. His legs won't let him be the coward that he thinks it is courageous to be.

Then there are the cases, often medal-winning cases, of those who fight on despite failed and very weak legs, who manage to continue when their legs have been mangled by mines or even severed by shells. Philip Caputo writes movingly of his friend Levy who was killed trying to rescue a dead corpsman, even though his legs had been badly wounded.[18] Winner of a posthumous Medal of Honor, Private Herbert Christian, in action in Italy in 1944, had his right leg severed above the knee by cannon fire but continued to "advance on his left knee and the bloody stump of his right thigh, firing his sub-machinegun," killing three enemy and thereby rescuing twelve of his comrades. He continued forward for another twenty yards to within ten yards of the enemy position, where he killed "a machine pistol man" before he finally succumbed.[19]

Irony is present in all manifestations of weak legs; the body makes a joke of our disembodied aspirations, and those aspirations repay the favor by making the body into a bit of joke itself. From the conventional case in which legs give out against the will of their owner, to the unconventional case in which they don't give out even when they are no longer there, Irony smirks from above or from wherever Irony has its mythic home. Weak legs are the governing explanatory force in incidents in which they have been metamorphosed almost beyond recognition. Graves's dark eye gives us this account:

> So [Captain] Samson charged with "C" and the remainder of
> "B" Company . . . When his platoon had gone about twenty

yards, he signalled them to lie down and open covering fire. The din was tremendous. He saw the platoon on his left flopping down too, so he whistled the advance again. Nobody seemed to hear. He jumped up from his shell-hole, waved and signalled "Forward!"

Nobody stirred.

He shouted: "You bloody cowards, are you leaving me to go on alone?"

His platoon-sergeant, groaning with a broken shoulder gasped: "Not cowards, Sir. Willing enough. But they're all fucking dead." The Pope's Nose machine-gun, traversing, had caught them as they rose to the whistle.[20]

This case is almost perfectly congruent with Small's confrontation with his weak-legged soldier. The commanding officer finds his men unable to go forward; they, through a spokesman this time for obvious reasons, testify that they are not cowards; indeed they are as willing as can be ("Not cowards, Sir. Willing enough."), but, being dead, their legs are simply unable to carry out their noble posthumous wishes. Weak legs, by hook or crook, come to explain the failure of almost all failed charges. Death, in this bitterly comic tale, is merely a special and conclusive case of weak legs.

Legs come to be imbued with wills and personalities of their own, whether weak in the attack or strong in reverse. R. H. Tawney, having to break off his career, just begun, as an economic historian, fears at the Somme that his "legs should take fright and refuse to move."[21] An impenitent Hiram Sturdy (World War I), matching the amiable effrontery of Archilochus, was quite willing to subordinate his will to that of his legs, which wanted nothing better than to get out of the trenches: "I bolted, yes, bolted, thought of nothing only jump all those stairs at once ... Was that running away cowardice, if it was it wasn't me it was my legs, they bolted and I had to go with them."[22]

Even airmen participate in the grim irony of weak legs. Helicopter pilot Bruce Crandall (Vietnam) collapses once he gets out of his ship after seventeen straight hours of dropping off troops and picking up wounded in a very hot landing zone.[23] Crandall's deferred weak legs testify to the strength of his will, to the extraordinary burdens the day imposed on his capacity for self-command. Weak legs in bomber pilots in World War II meant not being able to maintain their place in formation, the plane drifting back despite all intentions to do it right.[24]

Not just legs suffer from weakness; fingers get infected too. According to a well-known and very influential claim made by military historian General S. L. A. Marshall in 1946, only 15 percent, and in any event no more than 25 percent, of American World War II infantrymen ever fired their guns in battle, even once.[25] Marshall's numbers may not be plausible, and they have been strongly and convincingly disputed,[26] but for our purposes it is sufficient simply to note the phenomenon as a form of weak legs, however extensive it may have been. These same men did not run, but they could not or would not fire, even, he claimed, when they were being overrun in banzai charges. They were "not malingerers . . . They were there to be killed if the enemy fire searched and found them."[27]

Marshall offers two main explanations. One is a fairly standard case of weak legs, a freeze reflex: "The failure of the average soldier to fire . . . is the result of a paralysis which comes of varying fears." The other qualifies as weak legs too, but a very unstandard case. In this explanation the idea is that people actually fear killing more than being killed. Your legs give out because you fear dying; your finger gives out because you fear killing. What do you expect, asks Marshall, after socializing our citizens in nonaggressiveness and in the value of human life: "[His upbringing] stays his trigger finger even though he is hardly conscious that it is a restraint upon him . . . At the vital point, he becomes a conscientious objector, unknowing."[28] A colleague of mine who fought as a second lieutenant at T-Bone Hill in Korea (he said he could not imagine going forward more slowly than he did, yet when he looked around he was ten yards ahead of everyone else) offers another explanation, which Marshall dismisses: the soldier who doesn't fire at the enemy holds the magical belief that his kindness will be reciprocated.[29]

This same colleague raised another matter relevant to our theme. Weak legs may be the only way of raising the white flag on offense. When I asked him about his fears going up the hill he answered impatiently: "What the hell was I supposed to do? Raise a white flag on an assault? A cook or some rear-echelon guy can raise a white flag. But how do you raise a white flag in a charge?" Weak legs move in to fill the void raised by the dark comedy of surrendering as you go forward in an attack.

There are also weak legs at sea. The statute took its present form in 1950, when it was cobbled together from the Articles of War and the Articles for the Governance of the Navy into a Uniform Code of Military Justice. The weak-legs provision, paragraph 8, it turns out, has its origin in the

Navy articles.[30] The Army always got the weak-legged advancer under various general orders;[31] but the Navy was concerned less with the legs of its sailors, at least until they might have to board an enemy ship, than with the will of a captain to make his *ship* advance. The sailors could be standing on the deck with legs quivering and still be advancing, because the sailor was being borne by a higher will. Weak legs in the Navy, then, were about the metaphysical legs of a ship, whose strength or weakness was solely a function of the captain's will.

The statute punishes only willful failure to do the utmost to encounter the enemy, thus excusing some, perhaps most weak-legged attackers, depending on how "willful" is construed. The question will come down in most instances to whether the weakness is faked or real, happily indulged or desperately opposed. Small's soldier falls on the safe side and should and will be spared the firing squad. Nonetheless cases of unwilled weak legs might still be shameful, as indeed the soldier desperately feared. Shame, unlike guilt, is felt not only for our voluntary failures but also for what we happen to be or couldn't help doing.

Shameful Defenders

Cowardice on defense seems more craven than cowardice on offense. Our image here is of begging not to be killed, turning tail and running, or simply despairing and not just not fighting, as on offense, but not fighting *back*. Failure under paragraph 2 or 8 of the statute is cowardly, and hence shameful, but only for the miscreant defender is shamefulness a formal element of the offense. Mere good intentions are not as likely to save him as they did the weak-legged attacker. Why the difference? There are several possible reasons. One involves the different stakes between losing as a defender and not measuring up as an aggressor. In the paradigm case we understand that the failure to defend means losing all. Weakness on offense means you go home with your tail between your legs, but there is a home to return to. Consider the almost ridiculous obviousness of this statement: the moral demand to defend to the utmost is greater than the moral demand to assault to the utmost. Even within aggressive honor-based cultures that is true. So suspect is the warrant by which people make the first aggressive move that unabashed predators often feel they have to package their aggressive designs as defensive reactions to the aggressive designs of others, as the second move, as paybacks, rather than as actions of an instigator or a prime mover.[32] Even God pretends to play by these rules, alleging the first human disobedience as the excuse to rain mayhem upon mankind for an eternity. However fearful you are, you must defend; but no one expects everyone to volunteer for the forlorn hope, to be first through the breach in the wall. The greater moral value accorded to defense seems embedded deeply in human psychology too: people have been shown, on average, to find the loss of what is theirs much more grievous than the disappointment that attends losing an opportunity to gain what is not theirs.[33]

The defender doesn't have the same kinds of choices or as many as the aggressor, for the latter is the moving party. It is aggressors who get to choose the timing and, crucially, locate the war on the defender's turf. The defender has some choices about how and precisely where to resist: sometimes he must fight pitched battles, but other options are available. The Russians, for instance, let the vastness of their land defeat invaders until it was safe to assume an offensive posture; others have worn their attackers down with pesky gnatlike resistance, as Fabius did to Hannibal. But we should also note that Fabius had to muster reserves of moral courage to persevere in the face of being thought cowardly by his countrymen, who unflatteringly nicknamed him Cunctator (Delayer).[34] Gnatlike resistance, though effective in the end, may in certain warrior cultures not look manly enough to preempt accusations of poltroonery. The prudent warrior must often endure suspect glances and innuendoes about his fearfulness and lack of nerve, as noted above in the case of the southern general Joseph E. Johnston. To be sure, the defensive courage of endurance was always a recognized part of siege and campaign, but in battle it had a tarnished reputation.

The statute may capture some of that mistrust of the justifications for retreat and surrender, holding the defender of hearth and home to a higher standard than the weak-legged attacker. The paradigm we see embedded in the statute—of attacker versus defender of the homeland—grants the attacker the option to plead weak legs from time to time, but the defender's legs must stand firm, at least until the defense is hopeless, in which case surrender, in most cultures, becomes morally acceptable. We seem to feel too that we have more right to ask legs to stand still than to move forward, by which ruse we simply restate the differing moral stakes of not defending as opposed to not offending.

Endurance and Patience

Defense tends to style its courage differently than offense and requires different moral talents. Put aside, for the sake of the broad themes at stake, the fact that good defense often requires offensive tactics and vice versa. Let us stick to the paradigm cases. The paradigm of offense is the mad rush of the charge, that of defense digging in one's heels, metaphorically, and digging in, literally. Offense's courage seems ineffably martial, confrontational; it means working oneself up, by boasts, rebel yells, or rum rations; the disposition for it may be of some use in civil life, but civil life would soon become very uncivil should courage of this style find too many excuses to express itself. Defense's courage is different. It expands readily beyond its narrow martial confines to find ways to exercise itself usefully in wider settings in which it merges with virtues like perseverance, patience, forbearance, and constancy.

The virtues of endurance and constancy that collectively are designated fortitude become the paradigm of courage itself when the source of terror is not a conventional foe to be met in battle but the very authority under which you live and have served. The image of defense as fighting back gives way to horrific images of enduring imprisonment, torture, persecution, death camp, and gulag as with Socrates, Seneca, Thomas More, and the innumerable victims of the evil regimes of the twentieth century. In simpler polities it is about suffering the anguish of exile and outlawry such as those endured by the narrators of the hauntingly moving Anglo-Saxon poems "The Wanderer" and "The Seafarer," or by the heroes of the sagas of Grettir and Gisli.

The expansion of defensive courage beyond battle and siege opens the way for women to participate in a virtue that was once the ideological preserve of male warriors. They jump at the opportunity, the most incredibly tough martyrs of the early church being women: Perpetua, for example, and the slave woman Blandina, who matches Rasputin for indestructibility.[35] Courage as endurance and silent suffering expands even further to encompass distributive injustices, suffered by both women and men, so that—and no wonder the ideology of patient courage comes to justify in part Nietzsche's hatred of it—the poor who did not question the divine order in which clerics grew fat at their expense were counted among the blessed, while those who squawked were revealing their immersion in the sins of despair, envy, and wrath. Cowardice too is thus transformed from running away in battle to giving in to despair, to becoming demoralized, to whining and whimpering, and, depending on the cultural rules regarding suicide, either to using it to cop out or to not having the courage to seek it out.

The contest of moral merit, then, between the courage of taking it and the courage of dishing it out has been there right from the start, embedded in the structure of war. That recognition allows us to revise somewhat Nietzsche's idea of the transformation and degradation of offensive courage into the slave morality of endurance and patience. More accurately the transformation is a story of anciently pedigreed (recall Laches' wise endurance) martial defensive courage's *expansion* into nonmilitary domains. This explains why the transformation Nietzsche saw was never completed: offensive courage never was transformed; it remained to compete with its defensive partner. I don't want to overstate the case. Some transformations did occur, but they were effected by shifts and relocations, by obliquity as much as by overt inversion. And which of the two competing versions was to be crowned as the purer exemplar of courage was contested again and again from the Stoics on.

Aquinas joins the fray and poses directly the question whether "endurance is the chief act of fortitude." He answers yes, but his most compelling reasons are still drawn from battle, though he quickly expands the sense of battle beyond the martial to include the spectacle of martyrdom.[36] The warrior is displaced by the martyr as the purest exemplar of courage, a courage that now means suffering with acceptance. But thus transformed the courage of patient suffering continued to pay homage to aggressive courage, indirectly conceding its primacy by appropriating all its imagery. On the allegorical plane, a martyr like Perpetua sees herself and is seen by her community as arrayed as a soldier or an athlete as she is spitted, grilled, and burned, triumphing gloriously over her foe, attacking the devil and his minions, triumphing over death itself ("O death, where is thy sting?").[37] Rather than just taking it, she is seen as taking it *to* the enemy in the best aggressive style. The diction of martial glory works its magic as it refuses to accept imprisonment, torture, death, and defeat for what they are. The old, aggressive style must retain all its attractiveness and moral force to bless the new, passive style as it does.[38]

Amidst the horrors of the Great War with its own special martyrdom we see a similar appropriation of images of offense to reconstrue the miseries of endurance as being appropriately glorious in the old romantic and heroic way. Thus, like "the Knights of old, who went out to fight loathly dragons which breathed fire and mephitic vapors," Tommy in his gas mask must also fight dragons, but by suffering the fire-breathers to come to him: "How more splendid than that of any beplumed, caparisoned soldier of old, in his courage as he rides, or squats in mud or dust, swathed in his chemical bandages so that all human likeness is lost, awaiting not only shot and shell and steel, but flammenwerfer, asphyxiating gas, lachrymatory gas, stink gas, and other instruments of German warfare."[39] The recasting of armor as chemical bandages, of riding out as squatting in a trench, of dragons as gas and flame-throwers, of splendor as dehumanizing filth, makes Tommy's endurance surpass the active questing of the medieval knight.

The wages of both offense and defense were death, but endurance over the long haul often took a greater toll of a different sort for which there was no compensation in the form of martyrlike glory. For endurance inevitably meant the seepage of courage over time, the drawing down of finite funds, and this drawing down was hellishly bound up, almost necessarily, with the seepage of sanity. The defender got none of the psychic respite that the fury and exhilaration of attack afforded. He just got pummeled, soaked, concussed, and drained of physical, moral, and psychic reserves. He often went mad, not in a burst of fury that added to his reputation for glory, but in an insistent and enduring form that sent him home to be institutionalized, to become, in Wilfred Owen's image, a "purgatorial shadow." Eric Dean, summarizing studies of military psychiatry, thus observes what we might have guessed: "rapidly advancing troops experience low psychiatric casualty rates as opposed to troops in a defensive or stationary posture, who experience feelings of helplessness."[40]

Rescue

Let us return to the statute punishing misbehavior before the enemy. When it comes to rescue—the central theme, it seems, of most contemporary stories of heroism and courage—the statute is relatively mild in the obligation it imposes. In contrast to the heroic demands of the provisions not to run away, not to fail willfully to advance, not to abandon shamefully a position, we move to the diction of practicality: to "afford all practicable relief." Of course, it doesn't make sense to throw good bodies after bad unless it is rational to do so. Presumably one must balance the likelihood of saving the endangered person against the risk incurred to save him plus some value assigned to the overall morale of fighting men who will fight harder for a polity that cares to rescue them. Still, it was hardly irrational for the men charged with saving Private Ryan to question why eight of them should be risked to save someone whose only special claim to rescue was that he was the last survivor of four brothers.[41] Yet even practicable and rational rescue hardly dispenses with the need for courage on the part of the rescuers.

It is precisely in the domain of rescue that twentieth-century battle has made its peculiar addition to the styles of the heroic. Our war stories often become rescue stories even when they start out as efforts in the old genre, sometimes, it seems, in spite of themselves. The film *Saving Private Ryan* thus ineptly shifts from a powerful representation of a very particular Normandy invasion to a general story of a rescue mission that could have been situated anywhere. It is in World War I that stretcher-bearers get Victoria Crosses and in Vietnam that medics get their Medals of Honor.[42] General Birdwell, for instance, Anzac commander in the Great War, said that if he had thousands of Victoria Crosses to hand out he would give them all to stretcher-bearers.[43] Nearly one-third of Vietnam Medal of Honor citations allege some kind of rescue purpose, either centrally as in the case of medics and helicopter pilots, or as a motive adding further luster to grand charges and defenses in the conventional style. Admittedly, in the Vietnam War, because of the peculiarities of American strategy, rescue figured more prominently as a standard part of operations than it did in the pitched territorial battles of the World Wars and Korean campaigns, but Vietnam simply continues a trend already well established earlier in the century. The virtue of those assigned the task of rescue—medics and stretcher-bearers—rises, it seems, as war becomes more nearly total, so that informal truces to gather in the wounded get harder to establish.

In the Civil War the Medal of Honor was more likely to be awarded for rescuing the regiment's colors; and one who stopped in the midst of a charge to aid a fallen companion was liable to be accused of cowardice or, if serving under Stonewall Jackson, to be executed;[44] the helper was seen to be trolling for a morally worthy excuse to justify not going forward. Abner Small tells of another soldier of suspect courage at Fredericksburg, this one, however, blessed with very strong legs:

> In company F was a soldier named Oliver Crediford, a large
> man, of great physical strength. A fellow soldier named Levi

Barker fell wounded, and Crediford picked up Barker and started for the rear.

"Crediford!" the captain shouted. "Come back into the ranks! Leave that man where he is!"

"Cap'n," he shouted back, "you must think I'm a damn fool to let Barker die here on the field."

He kept on going and was seen no more in the battle. If he kept his head to save his skin, I suspect he was the only man that did.[45]

But within fifty years not stopping to rescue begins to require some justification. When R. H. Tawney abandons a wounded man at the Somme he suspects his own motivation for moving *forward*: "I hate touching wounded men—moral cowardice, I suppose. One hurts them so much and there's so little to be done . . . So I left him. He grunted again angrily, and looked at me with hatred as well as pain in his eyes. It was horrible."[46] Cowardice either way, but with a clear sense that the failure to rescue requires some excuse beyond merely alleging the duty to continue moving forward. Frederic Manning captures nicely the resentment the men start to feel when an order not to stop to aid a stricken comrade is issued the night before going over the top. The troops find it evidence of the callousness of the rear echelon to their plight. Says one character: "The bloody fool that wrote that letter [ordering them not to stop to help the wounded] doesn't seem to know what any ordinary man would do in the circumstances. We all know that there must be losses, you can't expect to take a trench without some casualties; but they seem to go on from saying that losses are unavoidable, to thinking that they're necessary, and from that, to thinking that they don't matter."[47] Still, the motives of someone not specifically assigned the duty of rescue remained suspect when he halted his advance to aid a stricken comrade. There was a difference between coming in from danger to escort a wounded man to safety and going out to pull him in. Thus the wry voice of an officer on the Marne: "A few slightly wounded men approached, each attended by two or three solicitous friends . . . These willing helpers were gently pushed back into the fray."[48]

By casting our heroic stories as narratives of rescue are we arguing for a kinder heroic ethic, life-saving rather than life-destroying? Are we witnessing the democratizing of courage and the heroic on the battlefield as we saw courage earlier expanding to include the constant, patient, and persevering? Medics need have no special physical attributes or martial skills. Indeed they are every man or could be every woman, and as such they hold for all of us the possibility of grand action, even if we do not have the body of Ajax or the ability to kill other human beings when it is in our best interests to do so.

Who, after all, got assigned to these rescue details but the worst shots, the meek, the gentle, the miserably unmartial, the musicians, those, that is, whose bodies and style did not predict the usual kind of courageous soul?[49] Take for example this portrait of Corporal Side:

> Side is a remarkable soldier. He looks less like a soldier than any man I have seen in France, and that is saying a good deal. He is short, cross-eyed, bandy-legged, and has a preference for boots and clothes sizes too big for him. In civil life I believe he is a rag-picker, and the character of his profession adheres, as it will, to the man. He joined the battalion two years ago as a stretcher-bearer, and on the 1st of July carried stretchers *under fire continuously* for twenty-four hours. Anyone who knows the weight of a loaded stretcher and remembers the heat, the condition of the ground, and what the firing was like upon that day, will agree with me that the Victoria Cross would have expressed rather less than Side's deserts. However, he for his bravery was promoted to full corporal in the fighting-ranks.[50]

These jobs required more exposure to fire than even the fighting men faced. The medic, as more than one Medal of Honor citation reveals, must hold up the plasma bag in the free-fire zone.[51] Stretcher-bearers must suppress all urges to hit the deck amidst exploding shells, lest they kill their cargo. And each time they come out, they must muster the will to go back into the inferno for another load.[52]

Part of the explanation for the rise of the heroics of rescue is more homely, I think. Rescue comes to dominate as the style of mechanized warfare allows for less opportunity for individual heroic acts in the old style. The distances separating combatants increase; opportunities for glorious charges and single combat become rarer, and, in the case of Vietnam there were very few conventional battles to generate conventional heroics. The only humans seeking immediate attention, who can look you in the eye, are comrades to aid, not enemies to kill, for these have become invisible. In the conditions of mass dehumanizing warfare, the rescuer and indeed the rescued are rehumanized, reindividualized. Rescue also becomes more rational, in spite of the irrational obsession with it, when medical care rises to a level at which the wounded are likely to survive if saved, although that hardly explains the rescue of corpses, as ancient a motive for grand action as there might be.

Rescue involves special rules; it is almost as if it touched on something as deeply instinctual as self-preservation; thus, Robert Graves says a soldier would run a 1.0 risk of death to save a life, even 1 in 20, in certain circumstances, to pull in a wounded enemy.[53] Rescue has a magical power to motivate action. John Keegan notes how difficult it is to get armies to overcome the inertia that self-protection imposes without recourse to some higher object than holding ground or getting new ground to hold: "That higher object is the rescue of comrades in danger."[54] Some have suggested that there is a basic human need to help as much as there is a basic need for help.[55]

The special nobility of rescue seems to immunize it from certain contingencies of success or failure. The glory of the medic who rushes out to save a man who is beyond saving is not tarnished by the ultimate futility of the deed.[56] Whether the practical goal is accomplished or not bears no relation to the worthiness of the risk undertaken. Not so the courage of attack and, to a somewhat lesser extent, defense. There the merit of the deed is tied up in some quite complex way with the success or failure of the enterprise, with its practical purpose. More medals are thus awarded for deeds that lead to victory than for equally grand action that has the misfortune to take place in the context of a general defeat.[57] Glorious defeat is a rather narrow category; most defeats are clouded in suspicions that the general level of courage was not sufficient to the demands of the situation. Going down grandly in defeat is delicately contingent on several key variables that mark the thinnest difference separating glorious failure from dark comedy.

To risk life to give life or comfort seems to have a special motivating power for soldiers, who must welcome the opportunity to have their courage manifest itself in something other than the destruction of life. The ascendance of the rescue narrative can be seen as the continuing expansion of courage into kinder areas even if such kindness takes place in an inferno of shellfire. But so to shift courage's terrain may also transform, if not utterly then at least subtly, courage's substance and inner life. Philip Caputo in a eulogy to his friend Levy who died trying to rescue a man who was "beyond saving" makes Levy all that is courage and sacrifice: "Yours was the greater love. You died for the man you tried to save." Caputo, bitterly and in a way that recalls Christ doubting whether his father had forsaken him, has Levy die *pro patria*. "It was not altogether sweet and fitting, your death, but I'm sure you died believing it was *pro patria*. You were faithful. Your country is not."[58] Rescue makes battle become the place for courage as an imitation of Christ, dying to save others, in which courage becomes love, but without Christ's knowledge that he held the winning hand,[59] more than an imitation then, a true surpassing.

Part of the unfathomability of this soldierly greater love is that his self-sacrifice is not for a friend, but for a comrade. There's a difference. Friendship, according to one soldier, "implies rather more stable conditions" than comradeship, which seems to be characterized by "a spontaneous and irreflective action . . . At one moment a particular man may be nothing at all to you, and the next minute you will go through hell for him. No, it is not friendship."[60] Another wonders at the mystery of the soldier who "will rescue a wounded man under heavy fire to whom an hour before he would have refused to lend sixpence."[61] Comradeship arises in a field of pain and misery and is largely bounded by it; friendship occupies softer and more pleasant terrain. Friendships can exist for a lifetime without ever having the issue of such ultimate sacrifice be any more than a dimly and romantically imagined hypothetical. Soldierly comradeship, in contrast, exists primarily against a backdrop of shared misery or danger. Like courage, comradeship is mysterious, or just baffling, in a way that friendship is not.

There is also the genre of the self-rescue tale, those incredible tales of escape or survival against impossible odds in appalling circumstances. There is no Greater Love here in the usual sense, for there is no friend or comrade to die for; the motive is to refuse death, no matter what. Living is not the easy way out when it would be so much easier just to give up and die. There is also something uncanny about these stories; not only are they tales of Promethean will, but they seem to be stories in which the will may play second fiddle to some eerie power of DNA, raw life's refusal to sink back into the dull clay from which it took so many eons to arise. The chilling power of those true soldiers' tales of escape and evasion that makes them something more than just a chase-scene narrative (which they in fact resemble) is that the heroes' bodies are already broken, often beyond repair, legs shot out, skulls cracked or laid open with gaping bullet holes, massive blood loss, with no water or food, and surrounded by enemy. These tales of self-rescue are tales of the loneliest courage, of suspenseful near miss and close call.[62]

The rescue genre also allows for a demilitarization of courage not unlike the demilitarization that the expansion of the courage of defense brought about as it colonized nonmilitary domains requiring endurance, sufferance, and patience. The courage of rescue and self-rescue, the latter metamorphosing into stories of survival in nonmartial settings, is just the kind of courage that the twentieth century put on center stage in the nightmares imposed by the genocidal totalitarian regimes that give the century its peculiarly pornographic style. The courage of rescue and self-rescue becomes the virtue most needed not in a soldier, but in a next-door neighbor.

9

Man the Chicken

WE ARE HEIRS to two competing conceptions of human nature. The first starts with raw, unaccommodated man as vicious, lustful, violent, selfish, brutish. In this view virtues are necessary correctives, something we impose on our vicious nature in order to survive. The second conception turns the tables: natural man is noble, grand, heroic, generous, only to have his nature suborned by luxury, corruption, and the temptations of vice originating in human civilization. Both views are old and predate by more than a millennium the thinkers we most readily identify them with: Hobbes and Rousseau. In the first view, the brute, as aggressive as he is, can be so without counting courage part of his character. He can kill by stealth in the middle of the night. In the second view, courage would be part of the noble savage's moral paraphernalia, but if everyone were as pure and innocent as he there would be little opportunity to exercise it, unless conditions of scarcity or love of the same object were to set these noble savages to grasp for each other's throats nonetheless.[1]

In the end it doesn't matter much which version you prefer. In both we are stuck with knavish, foolish, vicious humanity; the only disagreement is whether or not we have always been that way. Both accounts agree that whatever our origins, we are pretty wretched. Nor is either view all that concerned with biological and anthropological truth as much as with setting up a rhetorical base from which justifications for various interested political theories can be launched. How could it be otherwise? Except for the few feral children who wander blinking out of the forest once a century offering a most unnatural glimpse of unaccommodated human nature, we have never had occasion to observe humans independent of language and culture.[2] Leave it at this: it would be just as silly to deny humankind's risk-seeking impulses as to deny our risk aversion, to deny human delight in destruction as to deny human delight in construction, to deny human lust for violence as to deny human yearning for peace and security.

Yet it is quite clear that an underlying assumption of the Western heroic tradition is that man is not by nature *Homo lupus*, man the wolf; he is *Homo pullens*, man the chicken, fearful, cowering, craven, easily seduced by ease and luxury in both its gluttonous and lustful forms; his most fearsome biting is more likely to be backbiting than going for the throat. Indeed, when the first list of seven deadly sins appeared sometime in the fourth century, gluttony headed it.[3] Man was portrayed as more tempted by the vices of ease—gluttony, lust, and some forms of what came to be known as sloth—than by the sins of glory—pride and wrath.

The Western heroic tradition assumes that only the few can avoid cowardice. Initial eligibility for the heroic is severely restricted by definition to men of a small class within a limited age range; and even among those who qualify most succumbed at some point to the ready temptation to run to safety, to sacrifice honor in the interests of life when the going got really tough. Hence the elaborate rhetoric of boast, taunt, and egging on and the insistent cultural machinery devoted to ridicule and mockery of anyone who showed fear. Epic and saga can be seen as aspirational manuals: "Time out of mind, strength and courage have been the theme of bards and romances," writes Thackeray, "I wonder if it is because men are cowards in heart that they admire bravery so much and place military valor so far beyond every other quality for reward and worship."[4] If our natures so readily disposed us to risk life and limb there would be little need for the aggressive disciplining of the coward that honor cultures uniformly indulged, no great urge to devote the greatest artistic achievements to telling tales of courage. The heroic style could dispense with the obsessive concern with shame as simply unnecessary; the heroic style itself would be either boring or unintelligible. One anthropologist studying a very violent tribe in New Guinea offered the view that it may take more social labor to inculcate and sustain norms of honor, aggression, and hardness than to raise people up to norms of a less contentious and risk-avoiding style of life, that it is easier and cheaper to train and maintain a society of accountants than a society of warriors.[5]

What though of those people claimed to be utterly fearless? For one thing, they are very rare. It is striking how many of those uses of the word "fearless" do not pretend to describe the inner state of the actor. They are meant rather to register the awe of the observer. "He did not know what fear was" or "he acted fearlessly" means only that "he acted *as if* he did not know what fear was" or "he acted *as if* he were fearless."[6] Some dispute whether there are any naturally fearless people except in fiction and fantasy.[7] True, some people are born without functioning pain receptors. They do not fear pain and are reported to be "eternally giggly and pleased" though they are inevitably scarred and scraped and often suffer ("suffer" takes on a special sense in their case) from badly damaged joints, being unaware when their knees and elbows are being bent in the wrong direction unless they are looking.[8] Even if their joints would allow it, they seem too jovial to make good warriors.

The 2 percent in the studies from World War II mentioned earlier who were not reduced to ineffectiveness after continued exposure to battle seem to be of a special sort, often psychotics or social misfits, as the researchers indicated. This figure may set the maximum number of people who are "naturally" fearless in the face of death, though not necessarily in the face of asking someone out on a date. Even God settled on a number within that range. Of the 32,000 men Gideon mustered to meet the Midianites, 22,000 fled to Mt. Gilead trembling, leaving 10,000. Of those remaining, God takes only the 300 who drink as a dog lappeth; the rest of the 10,000, though not cowards, were clearly not of that elect berserk elite either.[9] Of those who act *as if* they were fearless, some may actually work themselves up into genuinely fearless states, having succeeded in banishing fear by some means, by rage or rum ration, whereas others might be praised as acting fearlessly when in fact they are fighting and struggling at every turn to master their fear lest it send them fleeing.

Fear was a tormenting omnipresence in the heroic world; fear was what you wished to overcome or ignore in yourself and what you wished to instill in your adversary. No one doubted that the average soldier or bloodfeuder was afraid, or couldn't be reduced to fearfulness given the proper circumstances. One paid homage to fear. Agamemnon had images of Terror and

Panic painted on his shield.[10] Before the battle of Gaugamala Alexander sacrificed to Fear; the Spartans built shrines to it.[11] Sure, you recognized that some peoples were more warlike than others, but you also knew that even Spartans could flee in terror, as when they panicked at the battle of Leuktra (371 B.C.E.). Homer insists that the strong-hearted feel the grip of fear; no hero in the *Iliad* does not feel fear at one time or another.[12] Hector runs from Achilles; Achilles experiences fear while fighting Aeneas.[13] Alexander, who feared no one in the host arrayed opposite him, nor the whole host for that matter, was, as already noted, rather paranoid about suspected plots against his life from within his own ranks. (In Alexander's defense, friends impose demands on our courage no less than enemies. Friends are positioned to betray trust and thus to catch us unawares more easily than a known enemy can.) In fact a good many battles, if we may call them that, never got fought because one side ran before there was any engagement.[14]

Though fear is ubiquitous in battle or other violent encounters there have been different views through time as to whether it was acceptable for men of honor to admit openly that they were afraid. (Conversely, it seemed women were heard to voice fear even when not giving voice to it.) It is not until the nineteenth century that we first find soldiers admitting in letters home or in memoirs that they were afraid, but they still took all due precaution about voicing their fears to comrades by adopting, for example, the jocular style that so annoyed Tim O'Brien or the self-berating we observed in Chapter 6. By the time of the Great War, though an officer still had to hide his fear before his men, he at least could own up to a fellow officer that it was a struggle to do so. When C. M. Bowra, new to the front, asked a veteran officer "what one did about being frightened," the officer answered "wisely": "You'll find that you are usually able to hide it." Hidden by habitual English reserve in that "usually" is a world of misery.[15] Before the nineteenth century there was a near universal taboo, at least among those who wrote, against admitting to fear, unless they had already succeeded in spite of it.[16]

Commanders have always assumed the fearfulness of their soldiers. "Fear!" writes the military theorist Ardant du Picq, "there are officers and soldiers who do not know it, but they are people of rare grit. The mass shudders." Du Picq's warriors are reluctant warriors: "Man does not enter battle to fight, but for victory. He does everything he can to avoid the first and obtain the second . . . Absolute bravery, which does not refuse battle even on unequal terms . . . is not natural in man; it is the result of moral culture . . . How many armies have sworn to conquer or perish? How many have kept their oaths? An oath of sheep to stand up against wolves."[17] (A Prussian shell claimed du Picq in 1870; the regimental history recounting his death counts him among the rare brave).[18] The subtlest observer of all, Thucydides, who also served as a general, noticed the tendency of battle lines of the hoplite phalanx to extend by degrees to the right so that each army slowly flanked its opponent's left as it too moved to its right: "This is because fear makes every man want to do his best to find protection for his unarmed side in the shield of the man next to him on the right, thinking that the more closely shields are locked together, the safer he will be" (5.71).

Against this we can pose the observation that few societies have ever had much problem in finding enough young men willing to risk their lives in battle for little or no reason; at least at the outset of campaigns, young males seem eager to test whether they are among those of "rare grit." But once wars gracelessly linger on, these same young men must be held to their posts by ruder force, shame or the prospect of loot having long since shown themselves inadequate to the task. Commanders knew this and urgently sought to counter the seepage of desertion.

One military theoretician, Raimondo Montecuccoli, a general in the Thirty Years' War (1618–1648), an era in which battle combined the press of pikemen with musket fire at close ranges, spends as much time in his treatise detailing stratagems to obviate his own men's cowardice as to activate that of the enemy. Success in battle depended on finding ways to delay the natural cowardice of one's own troops just long enough to give time for the natural cowardice of the troops on the other side to assert itself. He lists devices useful for counteracting cowardice, some rather astonishing: for instance, let the enemy cut off lines of retreat, forbid the inhabitants of nearby friendly cities from admitting any of the troops, dig trenches behind your troops, burn your ships and the bridges you have crossed, delegate certain men to shoot retreating soldiers. When arraying the troops and forming their lines, Montecuccoli advises embedding the cowards in the middle ranks, behind the valorous ones, whom they can follow at less risk to themselves, and hemmed in by other valorous men in the rearmost ranks so that their escape routes are clogged.[19] Cavalry is less useful for combating the enemy than for keeping one's own infantry from fleeing. Besides, horses turned cowardly in battle no less than men; even the Carthaginian elephants that so terrorized the Romans when they first confronted them suffered moral collapse every once in a while.[20]

One can also combat fear by instilling confidence, Montecuccoli notes. Nor does it matter that that confidence is ultimately indistinguishable from crude self-deception and wishful thinking that bootstrap us into performing better than we have any right to expect.[21] "One may conceal or change the name of the enemy general if he happens to have a great reputation." Confidence can also be acquired by the indirection of stimulating

> contempt for the enemy by presenting naked prisoners to the soldier. Once they have viewed the captives' fragile, flabby, filthy, diseased, and infirm legs, as well as their hardly valiant arms, then men will have no reason to be afraid, for they will have had the chance to see the kind of people with whom they must fight— namely, pusillanimous, humble, and tearful individuals.

While you and I might find in this display additional reason to desert rather than fight to the death so as to avoid being taken prisoner Montecuccoli thinks otherwise: "Once they have perceived the wretched fate of such afflicted, shackled, castigated, and emaciated persons . . . they may conclude that it will be better to fall in battle rather than, dragging on their lives unhappily, necessarily experience such contumely and calamity."[22]

Exhortation

If courage were natural or easy, exhortations either as insults and curses— you sniveling bunch of cowards, you chickens—or as challenges—I double dare you—or as rousing speeches would not be needed except to the extent they help coordinate action. Some wise commanders are aware that anything more than a perfunctory "let's-go-do-our-duty-boys-at-the-count-of-three" speech may cause the troops to draw pessimistic conclusions about the commander's own assessment of their present predicament: why else would they need so much rallying to the cause? Those confident in their superiority can do without exhortation speeches as did the Spartans before the battle of Mantinea. Reports Thucydides: "The Spartans . . . spoke words of encouragement to each other man to man . . . realizing that the long discipline of action is a more effective safeguard than hurried speeches, however well they may be delivered" (5.69). Some commanders, in fact, turn their exhortation speeches into anti-exhortation speeches as Nicias did before the Athenian victory at Syracuse: "There is no need for me to make a long speech of encouragement since we are all going into the same battle together. And in my opinion this army of ours itself gives better grounds for confidence than a good speech backed up by a weak force" (6.68).

But Nicias is not finished; he does exhort after a fashion, not by rousing rah-rah, but by cold reason's grimmest assessments of the present situation. He reminds his men that they had better fight well, for they are far from home; they have no place to run; no need to hope for help but from their own hands: "Unless we win, we shall not find it easy to get away." There is nothing cynical or contradictory in Nicias' employing techniques of fear suppression simultaneously with techniques of fear elicitation; fear, recall, can prompt fight as well as flight, especially when there is no place to flee to. For pure cynicism, though, nothing quite beats what the FNGs (fuckin' new guys) were treated to when they first got to Vietnam to punch the clock beginning their year under fire. No sooner were they off the plane than they too were exhorted, not to battle, but to enlist for three years rather than serve out the two required by conscription. The carrot? Reenlist and you get a cushy job in the rear. Here is Tim O'Brien again giving us the speech of the battalion Re-Up NCO:

> Sure as I'm standing here, one or two of you men are gonna get your legs blown off. Or killed. One or two of you, it's gotta happen . . . I'm not trying to scare shit out of you. But you better sure as hell be scared, it's gotta happen. One or two of you men, your ass is grass. So—what can you do about it? Well, like Sarge says, you can be careful, you can watch for the mines and all that, and, who knows, you might come out looking like a rose. But careful guys get killed too. So what can you do about it then? Nothing. Except you can re-up.[23]

Armies, we see, play it by ear. When courage is required, there are techniques for engendering it; but cowardice is the expected baseline, the backdrop against which virtue must struggle to assert itself, so why not make use of it to fill certain staffing needs? The modern bureaucratized army can use cowards as well as heroes and indeed treats the former rather well.

One would love to assign some more honorable reason to the rhetoric of re-upping: is it not prudent to weed out those men who would by their cowardice endanger their buddies in the field? Or, given cowardice's contagious

power, should it not be quarantined to the rear? But I doubt these charitable justifications. Why assume that those who self-identify as cowards
after having been scared by the NCO's speech will in fact give way to their
fears in battle? Most untested soldiers would have considerable anxiety
about whether they will prove cowardly and might think their anxiety
proves their own cowardly nature; but once in battle most manage to do
their job. The strategy of recruiting by appeals to cowardice could well
weed out as many good combat soldiers as bad. The cynical explanation
looks like the right one: prey on, even nurture, fears and vices for the benefit of meeting recruitment quotas; let private vices produce public benefits
in the best Mandevillian style.[24]

Self-Exhortation: Boasts and Vows

La Rochefoucauld remarks in several places how much easier it is to trick
ourselves than to trick others, and that though we can't bear being fooled
by our enemies or betrayed by our friends, we are quite pleased to fool
ourselves.[25] It is easier, however, to fool ourselves in some respects than in
others. We are likely to think ourselves smarter, prettier, handsomer, wit-
tier, more entertaining, and fairer minded than we in fact are. But we are
not as readily given to thinking we are more courageous than we are, at
least with anywhere near the facility with which we deceive ourselves
regarding other virtues and advantages. Not that we don't have techniques
for tricking ourselves into courage, but we are also more likely to know that
that is exactly what we are doing; with courage the tricks we play on ourselves are not quite as inadvertent, as indirect, or as out of consciousness as
most self-deceptions are; the soldier tossing down his rum ration knows he
is imbibing a chemical remedy for strengthening courage or blunting
cowardice.

If we doubt our courage, if our inner life is one of anxiety and fear, we
don't usually fold our tents immediately and admit failure. Our sense of
shame prompts us to make attempts to get by one way or another. People
are not just left to their own devices to invent these stratagems; culture
provides many models for bucking ourselves up. Not even tough guys like
Beowulf could do without them. He and his early Germanic companions
made liberal use of boasts and tough talk before combat as ways of raising
the stakes of moral and martial failure. Boasts are not just boisterous public
claims to precedence and glory; they also assume the psychic priority of the

fear that tempts flight or withdrawal from the honorable game of glorious risk-seeking. True, Beowulf might still have great confidence in his courage and boast because it is a conventional line in the script of any would-be hero. But unless the hero pushed himself to perform tests that he himself recognized as uncertain of their outcome, that he understood truly to be tests *for him*, he would have to accept that he was just faking it, performing a charade, even if his level of playing it safe exceeded everyone else's level of derring-do.

There is very little distinction between the boast and the vow. One imperceptibly slides into the other. They are strategies of precommitment, of raising the moral and social stakes of failure by undertaking to suffer special ignominy for having foolishly presumed more glory for yourself than you were worthy of. The boaster not moved to suit his actions to his words makes himself a fool as well as a coward, a classic buffoon of Western comedy: the big-talking soldier, the *miles gloriosus*, who times his entries, like Falstaff, at "the latter end of fray and the beginning of a feast."

A reasonably functional facsimile of courage can be had in bottles; drugs and drink supplemented the exhortation speech or put one in a frame of mind to be roused rather than sickened by it. In the early Germanic world one also needed drink to get in the mood to boast and vow. When Godric, the coward I mentioned earlier, fled on his lord's horse at Maldon in 991, his disgrace was even more foul because in the mead-hall before battle he had been talking big about not fleeing. That one needed ale to prime the pump of boasts is a powerful testimony to the seriousness of their consequences. You had to impair your reason before strapping the burden of the boast to your soul.

Drinking in the heroic world, as still vaguely in our own, was a competitive affair. People cared who could drink the most, and, once drunk, they also competed as to who could make the most poetically powerful and most daring boast. The next morning could bring serious regret, more than the usual regret of hangover. *The Saga of the Jómsvíkings* tells of a group of Vikings sickened by what they have vowed to do the night before, knowing the chances of coming out alive are just about nil. One of them tries to beg off by claiming that drunkenness voids the vow, but he doesn't press the point very insistently. So off they go to their doom. There were other risks in priming the boasting pump with drink: it is said in Beowulf's praise that he was a paragon among men because "drunk, he slew none of his retainers."[26]

Proper boasting can be an emblem of magnanimity, and the apt boast can approach the sublime when the truly great reveal thereby their knowledge of their own greatness. Such boasts achieve their sublimity by dispensing with the form "I did or will do such and such"; they take the form "I am X, and what more need be said?" The most priggish adherent to norms of modesty and self-effacement would concede the grandness of Alexander's exchange with Parmenio: " 'Were I Alexander,' said Parmenio, 'I would accept of these offers made by Darius.' 'So would I too,' replied Alexander, 'were I Parmenio.' "[27] Parmenio, a commander of considerable virtue, was no slouch, but woe to him who would presume to position himself as Alexander.

American culture is split on the propriety of the boast, largely along racial lines. Hyperverbal rhapsodic trash talk, rapping, exuberantly delighting in its own rhetorical fecundity, is colored black even though Beowulf and dozens of Homeric characters show that it also has a place in one well-attested strand of the classic Western tradition.[28] Contrasted to it is the antiboast of those who find boasting immodestly vulgar; call it the U. S. Grant–Clint Eastwood tight-lipped style. The less said, the more threatening it is understood to be; and the more wittily said, the greater the glory: "Go ahead; make my day" achieves its modest sublimity by using the form of a threat to cover the immodesty of its implicit boast. In a similar vein, Marc Bloch records the "heroic reply" of a man in his unit, "so much finer because of its obvious innocence of any literary pretension." When one panicky soldier cried, "the Germans are only thirty meters away from us" this man replied, "Well, we are only thirty meters away from the Germans."[29]

Threats and Faking It: The Eyes Have It

Boasting is not designed just to help overcome one's own fears; it is also meant to instill fear in others. The boast is assimilated to the larger genre of threats. Both boasts and threats suggest the strategy of faking it, bluffing, and other forms of posturing designed to trick yourself into courage and to fool others into thinking you have it.

According to one astute view, a successful threat is one that never has to be carried out, for if you have to carry it out it did not work as a threat.[30] The trick is in selling the threat, in making it credible so you will not be called on to enforce it; this is largely a matter of appearances, of reputation, and just looking like the type who is ready, able, and likely to back up his demands. This theory of threat makes all threats converge on bluffs; even in those cases in which the threatener can more than back up his threat, he would, remember, prefer not to have to carry it out. That way he gets what he wants on the cheap, and experiences the delicious satisfaction of seeing his mere desires deferred to.

Those reputed to be courageous, for instance, as well as those known to be a little crazy, have a much easier time selling their threats than those known as cowards or as purely rational. (Rational people are predictable; they will always attempt to operate in their best interests; crazy people cannot be trusted to do so.) The advantage in appearing courageous (or crazy) is getting to avoid testing your courage on every occasion on which it might be demanded. But there's the rub: even making a threat, even risking a bluff, makes certain demands on something approaching courage. There is the grave risk the threat won't work and you will have to deliver. To be sure, there are excuses of varying plausibility you can make to save face if you back away from your ultimatum. You can try to appear forgiving or forbearing or just too contemptuous of the other to care one way or another. But if you failed to sell the threat in the first place there is no reason to believe you will be any more successful selling your excuses for not delivering. Nonetheless, so great are the cost advantages of being able to fake it well that it is to the advantage of those who fear they are cowards to develop techniques to appear brave.

BEING LOOKED AT is threatening. The threat lies in focused attention, as of a predator eyeing its prey (or an emboldened prey warning off a predator). It's not just humans who can be stared down. The negative meaning of staring seems already fixed in a primitive portion of the brain. There are toads, various fish, and insects that gained a selective advantage by developing pairs of large spots located on their bodies that counterfeit the staring eyes of an individual of a larger species.[31] Even reptiles, birds, and fish, it turns out, don't like being stared at by something that looks as if it might be able to make a meal out of them. Of course not all staring eyes are threatening. A mouse does not make the cat ill at ease by staring back. But in that range in which the hierarchy is unstable there is an implicit threat in meeting another's eyes that must be removed either by averting them or by cultivating looks of deference, submission, or insipidness so as to disarm the gaze. Even that doesn't totally solve the problem, for gestures of submissiveness are easily faked and can also mock (or challenge) their object if the deference displayed isn't precisely calibrated.

Let me expound more fully by presenting an allegory of eyes, faking, and courage. Suppose a poor guy—poor because the underdog and thus having a claim on our pity—is accosted by a big guy who wants to fight him, mostly because he just wants to beat up poor guy, but who alleges as a reason that poor guy was looking at big guy's girl friend in study hall. What is poor guy to do? Focus the question more narrowly: what is poor guy to do with his eyes? Poor guy does not want to cave in immediately, so he intends to meet big guy's eye. But he is not sure he is up to doing that.

To fix his eye is not only not to back down; it is something more, because the pecking order has long been established. Everyone knows that big guy is dominant in the fighting, if not in the social and academic, hierarchy. So poor guy understands that not to assume the submissive is to challenge big guy even though big guy challenged him. But "challenge" is the wrong word to describe what big guy did by calling poor guy out. Challenges work up the pecking order; what big guy is doing is engaging in a kind of ritualized reassertion of his dominance; no challenge there. Such is the catch-22 of dominance hierarchies. The dominator can pick the fight and then accuse the lower person of rebellion or revolt if the lower does not immediately make gestures of submission.

All poor guy's resolve is focused on keeping his gaze focused. He is trying to take things one step at a time, the immediate goal being not to relinquish his dignity until he absolutely must. Still, he is not sure he can keep his eyes fixed on big guy with a look that says, "Don't tread on me." It will have to be the look that says that, since poor guy is not about to verbalize a threat to big guy. The audience already congregating would break out in derisive laughter if he did. But he has already held his gaze too long to back off now and not get beaten up; he is embarked for better or worse. He fears he may have made a big mistake, but he can't deny that he experiences some small self-congratulation for being daring enough to risk faking it as he is. Faking, he is finding out, takes its own kind of courage. The complete coward would have groveled or run or said he was sorry for looking at the girl right from the start.

Just as one man's panic can turn into the panic of a whole company and one man's courage can help embolden those about him, could it be that if one part of your body plays the courageous part, in this case the eyes, other body parts will take up the role too? Well, say the spine and shoulders (but manifestly not the gut, which is still churning), if the eyes can stand up to big guy like that, maybe we can too. Aren't our bodies something less than a unity and more a loose confederation, a collection of parts each with a small will of its own? The cases of weak legs suggest there may be some poetic and psychological, if not quite physiological, truth to that.

Let's leave poor guy frozen in his *tableau vivant* and cast a cold eye on some of the implicit assumptions informing the allegory. Poor guy's story resembles that of an adolescent-coming-of-age movie: the poor guy backs down the bully merely by standing up to him; or if the bully doesn't crumble so easily, poor guy learns martial arts and then beats the bully into submission. But what if the story doesn't end that way? What if the bully doesn't crumble and is just too tough to be beaten? Here's the question. Does one incur less risk of being thought cowardly by trying to stand up and failing than by not trying at all? Can you opt out of the game to greater advantage than if you stay in and flop? The answer depends on a host of variables. It depends on how you fail; it depends on how long it takes you to fail; it depends on how creditable your reasons look for not playing. If you are Achilles and refuse to compete in a chariot race, as he does, you can arrogantly claim that "I would certainly take first place and carry the prize away to my hut" and not have people snicker although they could hardly love you for it.[32] Achilles is doing more than not playing though; he is not playing but still claiming a counterfactual victory in the race to be run— that is, he is playing by not playing. But this option is a respectable strategy only for the select few whose skills are well established; they can pretend to be, maybe they actually are, above the game because they have already acquired sufficient honor or reputation that their nonplaying will not be seen as purely faking it, a coward's desperate attempt to cover.

Cowards, too, might be better served by not playing than by playing and losing. Few would argue that you are better off for going to war and collapsing in fear before the first battle, cowering, whimpering, unable to carry out your assignment, than for finding a way to stay out in the first place. It is the difference between being suspected a coward and, in the most tragic outcome, being sentenced and shot as one. Recall Robert Burdette: "There were scores of ways of keeping out of battle without actually suffering the charge of cowardice."[33] Yet it is standard wisdom in the schoolyard, if not in war, that you are better off standing your ground and fighting than cowering in disgusting cravenness. This wisdom, however, needs reevaluation.

Standing your ground, so the argument goes, elicits the respect of the person about to make you his punching bag and, if not his respect, then that of others who might also try to abuse you once it is revealed what easy pickings you are. Cowering, running away, cringing is supposed to intercept any pity that might extenuate the beating you will get once he catches you. And catch you he will, for, as with Achilles, the strong are no less likely to be fleet of foot than the weak, rather more likely in fact, since human weaklings are seldom blessed like gazelles; besides, if he can't run you down now, he will corner you later.

The counsel to stand your ground seems merely to restate a certain ideology of courage as if it were fact; it looks suspiciously like an exhortation tailored to an audience of suspected cowards by alleging the pure prudence of courage. But the advice might serve the bully's lot much better. Standing up to the bully who likes beating up weaklings often only gets him madder; the weakling playing at bravery lacks fighting skill and practice; he may also find that he is unable to compensate for his low threshold of pain or for a thirty-pound weight difference. The folk myth that the bully crumbles when the going gets rough owes its tenacity to a large dose of wishful thinking; bullies are often pretty good fighters, no less so than lions who also prefer to cull the infirm or newborn wildebeests from the herd or go after three-day-old Thomson gazelles.

Bullies include in their number not just those who pick on the weak because they cannot pick on the strong, but those who pick on the weak yet also do quite well against the strong. What they like is aggression, low risk or high, and they have, as a usual matter, an extraordinarily high pity threshold. Whatever respect you might gain by sticking it out against them depends not just on making a pretense of sticking it out but on how well you actually do. You are only slightly less a laughingstock for being knocked down in ten seconds, knocked out in twenty, than for running away, especially if you can run away with the comic bravura of Archilochus or John Dooley. Running or sticking it out—either way you lose, unless you acquit yourself fairly well in the fight and cause some verifiable damage or put up a good show before you succumb by remaining defiant to the bitter end. The conventional argument has yet one more step: so you fought and were not even close, but by showing your willingness to fight, even if you are without skill, you will buy future reprieve. Maybe, maybe not. It is not even clear that you buy yourself any self-respect. The miserable fantasies of revenge of the person who got badly beaten are no less frustrating than those of the guy who ran away.

Poor guy sadly suspected this darker account might be true, but he was gambling that his eyes would do the trick, that they would work as a threat, that they would unnerve big guy just enough so that big guy would decide to shift into some face-saving tactic that allowed him to back off. Suppose that big guy laughs contemptuously at poor guy, says he's not worth the time of decking him, and turns away. How does poor guy then assess his own performance? He cannot feel triumphant, for though he suspects he has beaten big guy in this encounter, he did not beat him up. In the contentious world of teen encounters he and everyone else knows that big guy is still dominant. What poor guy mostly feels is relief for having extricated himself from this encounter without getting beaten up. He has no confidence that his dignity has been preserved; he suspects that if his showing got him any respect at all it was of those people he never feared to begin with.

Soon after his extrication cowardly thoughts start to intrude. He begins to fear that big guy will come looking for him again. He suspects that the next encounter of this type with big guy or anyone else won't be much easier, that it still will take all his effort to muster the courage to glare back, to stare down, for he knows that he has little martial force to back up the lack of submissiveness he intended his eyes to declare. Moreover, he begins almost immediately to torment himself with vehement hopes for evil to befall big guy from any source.

Poor guy, we may think, is being harder on himself than he should be. He showed courage, the more so because he had nothing to back up the threat implicit in meeting big guy's eyes. Call it foolhardiness, but can poor guy be faulted for having been born smaller and weaker than big guy? Can he be faulted for having been raised in a social class that devalued fighting, or for not having older brothers to toughen him up? Is it unfair that big guy got his training on a regular basis, getting beaten by and beating his brothers and neighbors? What's the virtue in growing up like that? Yet it turns out there is a virtue in growing up like that; that is exactly what encounters like this one reveal. Poor guy suspects he is blamable in part for not working to counter the hand dealt him by nature by toughening up. And although poor guy may have some very deep contempt for those guys who go out to fight every Saturday night and seem to take pleasure in it whether they win or lose, he is also deeply envious of their talent, if that is the right word for their competence in such matters.

THE HARRIS SPARROW lives in groups, and the males have a dominance hierarchy. Relative rank in the hierarchy is signaled by a patch of dark plumage on the breast and head; the darker and more extensive the plumage, the higher the bird in the pecking order. The issue that intrigued experimenters was why lower-status birds didn't cheat and develop dark plumage.[34] Why, that is, didn't they fake it like poor guy? So the experimenters painted the feathers of low-status birds black. These fakers got nowhere. Other birds did not defer to them, and they stayed right at the bottom of the hierarchy. Then experimenters injected low-status unpainted birds with testosterone. These birds got aggressive, asserted themselves, but they stayed low in status because no matter how tough they got they didn't have the dark plumage to keep the others from treating them like low-status birds. They got no respect for their toughness. To gain respect they had to *look* tough, not just be it; that is, they had to have the capacity to make their threats believable. These tough birds with untough looks thus had to fight every time they wanted to assert themselves, which by definition means they had not risen in the hierarchy, for the top dog rarely has to fight; he just threatens with his black patch. Toughness without black feathers didn't make it, and black feathers without toughness didn't make it. But when experimenters painted the birds that they had injected with testosterone, these birds at last got respect, which means their mere threats worked. Now report the authors: "this time the cheating worked." But they are wrong. By "this time" the birds were not cheating at all; they were really tough and had a badge to prove it.

Poor guy reads the tale of the Harris sparrow and despairs. You need real toughness to back up the show or you are stuck at the bottom. Yet poor guy takes solace: Harris sparrows have only one badge of dominance, and so faking it can take only one form: paint your chest and head black. Humans, though, are more resourceful at cheating; there are more codes to manipulate and more complex rituals to fiddle with to gain local advantage. Humans are given to faking, whether they are good at it or not; so much of civility depends upon it. Those who find their way into the top half of the various pecking orders to which they belong often suspect that they got where they are because of no small amount of buffaloing others both above and below them. Fakes, clearly, are less likely to be exposed as fakes if they possess the advantages conferred by certain natural endowments. It helps to look the part, though as those sparrows show it is not sufficient. We can paint our own feathers black by cultivating a look of toughness, but it will take a lot more than paint to disguise a miserably unmartial body.

For those locked in the middle or lower ranks of physical toughness there are times you might wish to look threatening as a way of avoiding having to be tested; there are equally other times when you wish to look nonthreatening in the extreme in hopes that that will buy you the sufferance, even the benevolence, of people who threaten you.[35] Tobias Wolff offers an example of the face he put on to charm unseen but suspected snipers as he plodded along jungle paths in Vietnam: "What I tried to do was look well-meaning and slightly apologetic, like a very nice person who has been swept up by forces beyond his control and set down in a place where he knows he doesn't belong and that he intends to vacate the first chance he gets."[36]

When we hold our heads erect and whistle a happy tune we only half hope that no one will suspect we are afraid; it is more that the performance is so obviously indicative of fear that we will charm the hostile other into thinking we are too pathetic, cute, or submissive to harm. Who has not found himself laughing too heartily at some big guy's vulgar humor or agreeing to all kinds of preposterous views on who is the best quarterback in the league just because we walked into the wrong bar? We seem to have endless inventiveness in coming up with shameless gestures of bonhomie. Do we really believe that our amiability is not read for just what it is? After such encounters do we congratulate ourselves on our ability to negotiate so well the pitfalls of cross-class, cross-ethnic, cross-racial, cross-age interaction? Or do we feel contemptibly craven as we retreat into fantasies of wishing we were that big, tough, powerful, and effortlessly threatening? Not so we could go about threatening others; no, we wouldn't admit to ourselves such small-minded resentments, but so we could relax, just relax, and not feel so shamefully threatened.

I have been describing threatening encounters in which faking and bluffing is directed mostly toward an opponent who can see you. This is the classic paradigm of epic and the heroic; it is about gauging your courage, toughness, skill, and strength in the presence of the opponent, where both can look each other in the eye. War once had much of that heroic possibility built into it until technology succeeded in enlarging the battlefield so that the enemy became invisible, though you feared you were visible to him.[37] You lost the most sovereign remedy for overcoming your fear: *seeing that your enemy's fear was as great as your own*. All the gestures your premodern counterpart employed to scare his opponent now look like empty charades, meant only to buck yourself up. Looking tough or acting crazy doesn't mean a thing to a shell lobbed your way. But there remains one constant between face-to-face antagonisms and those played out over long distance: you are observed by your comrades and friends. They may be the hardest judges of all, for they are also often your competitors for honor within the group; and it is largely their views that mold the way you will judge yourself.

The Rear Echelon, Doing Just Enough, and Malingering

One of the most frequent strategies of making do is doing just the minimal amount that will satisfy the demands of honor. This method requires some genuine exposure to risk, but even that level of exposure can be manipulated by the skillful operator. La Rochefoucauld, always alert to the myriad forms of hypocrisy and mean self-interest, notes that in war few men care to risk the continual exposure to danger necessary actually to win; most look just to cover their own reputation for honor.[38] The Roman general Scipio purchased a lifetime of honorable safety toward the rear by one recklessly daring act in his youth. He was too important to his country alive, says Polybius, to risk himself for the sake of conventionally daring displays.[39]

Scipio's strategy may work for generals but for very few of lesser rank. Even generals feel the need occasionally to polish their reputation for courage by visiting the front in the midst of battle as Patton sometimes orchestrated in a not very risky way. From the home front's perspective a general who sends his men to fight looks like a hero though he is safe in a command post to the rear. But the men at the sharp end exempt very few of the rear echelon from their contempt: in their eyes the rear is made up of shirkers, imposters, and hypocrites who can readily give orders that expose others to death and danger while staying well clear of harm's way themselves. "Rear echelon," as William Manchester notes, is "the most relative of phrases":

> Your definition of it depended on your own role in the war. To
> the intelligence man out on patrol near the Jap wire, the platoon

CP [command post] was rear echelon; to the platoon it was the
company CP; to the company it was the battalion CP; to the
battalion it was the regimental CP . . . until you reached the PX
men who landed at D-plus-60 and scorned the "rear echelon"
back in the States.[40]

The condemnatory bitterness contained in the concept of rear echelon is
inextricably bound up with a sense of outrage that the rear echelon win
medals, more than can ever be justified to the fighting men, and go home
to tell war stories. Each person closer to danger sees the danger those further rearward think they are enduring to be a joke; those near deny the possibility for true courage to those more remote because the latter's risk level
does not rise to a point where those at the sharp end would concede that
courage is even possible. Merely to be stationed farther back, moreover, is
understood to prove one's lack of nerve. In memoirs from the Great War
the very uniform of the staff officer transforms its wearer into a Vice of
False-Seeming in a late medieval morality play.

But I stray. There is a friendlier gloss to put on the behavior of doing
just enough to save your honor than La Rochefoucauld, not known for the
generosity of his sentiments, is willing to grant; moreover, this interpretation is readily available to those of lesser rank, to those who actually have
to do the fighting: it is the notion of doing one's fair share. It is all fine to
hope that the war is concluded during the time you are doing your share,
but at some point one rightly feels he has discharged his duty though the
war drags on.[41] Frontline soldiers begin to feel there is a limit to what the
polity can ask of them when so many others are not sharing the risk.

If the higher authorities were not willing to relieve the men who had
done their fair share, the men made accommodations with their counter-
parts on the other side. Much has been made of these kinds of arrangements, from the pickets in the Civil War who would exchange rounds of
songs, even food and tobacco, to the various understandings achieved
across the moonscape of no-man's land on the western front.[42] Though the
men were still honorably willing to give their all in battle, they bought
themselves some relief from certain kinds of daily risk, earning a little less
anxiety about being sniped at as they shaved, washed, or defecated. One
British soldier describes the mutual restraint of German and British patrols
as they crawled around in the night in no-man's land amidst the shell holes
and corpses each pretending "that they are Levites and the other is a good

Samaritan, [passing] by on the other side, no word spoken. For each side to bomb the other would be a useless violation of the unwritten laws that govern the relations of combatants permanently within a hundred yards of distance of each other, who have found out that to provide discomfort for the other is but a roundabout way of providing it for themselves."[43]

There is fair share as it concerns the risk of exposure to death and maiming; then there is the fair share of all those thankless tasks that are part of soldiering: burying, lugging, cleaning, digging. Some hope that doing more than their fair share of those miserable tasks will help make up for deficits that they worry exist in their accounts on the high-risk ledger. "The only compensation about doing more than my share is that it lulls the fear of failure. At least I am pulling my oar," says one officer on the western front who felt the need to justify why he helped the men with the grunt work.[44] Burdette's good coward always took the "smaller portion for himself . . . in scant-ration times."[45] There is thus a complex moral economy in which people trade in a specie of misery; if one can't fight well he can at least lessen the burden on those who do by undertaking to do some of the fighter's share of the drudge work. One must take care not to seem overeager to compensate in this manner or risk looking almost officiously craven, but the noncomplaining pitching in above one's share would, it seems, compensate partly for other shortcomings.

The one who does just enough to maintain his honor might shade by degrees into the malingerer and shirker. There are those who fake courage but thereby end up doing brave deeds, and there are those who just fake and fink out. The creativity, ingenuity, and brazenness needed to fake courage pale beside that devoted to generating credible face-saving excuses for disappearing from the front or for not getting sent there in the first place.[46] I need not rehearse them; our own lives hold so many instances, though enacted in nonmartial settings. Malingerers and shirkers do not pretend to courage, but some are good enough at faking that they may actually escape having their courage questioned; that is, they escape being considered cowards.

It is the very shameless aplomb, the cool, of a certain class of malingerer that leads Tim O'Brien to reject Hemingway's formulation of courage—grace under pressure:

> But somehow grace under pressure is insufficient. It's too easy to
> affect grace, and it's too hard to see through it. I remembered the

taut-faced GI's who gracefully buckled, copping out so smoothly, with such poise, that no one ever knew. The malingerers were adept: "I know we're in a tight spot, sir. I wouldn't go back to the rear, you know me. But—" then a straight-faced, solid, eye-to-eye lie. Grace under pressure means you can confront things gracefully or squeeze out of them gracefully.[47]

Too bad that the coolheadedness it takes to lie convincingly to avoid danger is not transferable to aid the same person to operate courageously in the face of it. Nor are these adept malingerers as perversely admirable as Mr. Coke, that fearless coward, for he made no excuses at all.

The next two chapters take us directly to the matters of courage's semblances, those states that for one reason or another people feel share the look of courage but lack a special something that makes them fall short of the pure virtue.

10

Praised Be Rashness

SOMEWHERE IN OUR educations most of us have heard vaguely tell that Aristotle viewed virtue as a mean. To the extent that we paid any heed, we mistook the adage as bland counsel for moderation and included Aristotle in a class with parents, teachers, clergymen, doctors, and other sorts whose advice prompted a roll of the eyes. Not that moderation isn't a good thing on occasion, but Aristotle had something else in mind. The theory of the mean is more a theory of propriety, of getting things right given all the vagaries of setting, timing, passions, and persons, which will not always be satisfied by middlingness. Some occasions appropriately demand either all or nothing. I will provide just enough of a sketch of Aristotle's theory of virtue to launch us into a discussion of rashness and its mottled reputation.

For Aristotle, virtue is the joining of right action and right feeling or emotion. For the emotion to play its proper role it must occupy a mean between two extremes, one in which the emotion is excessive, the other in which it is deficient.[1] A virtue is itself a mean condition, having, in his model, not one but two opposing vices, one caused by a deficiency of proper feeling, the other by an excess. The doctrine of the mean works quite well for virtues that involve the modulation of a single desire; temperance, for instance, means finding just the right amount of desire for food and flesh, somewhere between asceticism and luxuriation. But the theory runs into trouble with courage, for courage is not a simple matter of getting a single appetite right.[2] The failures of the theory of the mean to explain courage have been noted by several commentators. Here is the gist of two of the theory's problems.

Courage, says Aristotle, is a virtuous mean situated in a field of two emotions: fear and confidence. The one who has excessive "confidence is called Rash, and the one who shows an excess of fear and deficiency of confidence is called Cowardly."[3] Courage is thus equally opposed by the vice of cowardice and the vice of rashness. Aristotle seems to recognize one problem for the theory of the mean right away. Courage, he notes, seems a lot closer to rashness than to cowardice. This is why, he says, people talk loosely of courage as cowardice's opposite when rashness, more properly in his view, is cowardice's true opposite. But this concession obscures the strength of the sense we have that courage is of an ilk with rashness, rather than opposed to it; and cowardice, we sometimes feel, is opposed to rashness no less than to courage, no doubt because rashness seems to mimic courage so well.

Another problem, one Aristotle does not appear to recognize, arises from his requiring that courage get two emotions right: not only fear, but also confidence. Confidence bears some connection to fear management, but it is more complex than mere lack of fear. To squeeze fear and confidence onto a single emotional axis so that we can find its mean requires considerable massaging of the definitions of fear and confidence and still leaves us with an implausible psychology of the virtue. I leave to a footnote further discussion of this particular problem;[4] here let us consider how Aristotle understands rashness and the rash man.

Aristotle's Rashness

Aristotle defines rashness in relation to confidence, not in relation to fear. He distinguishes the rash person who has excessive confidence from the person "who carries fearlessness too far," who is fearless when he shouldn't be. This latter person, he says, has no special name. Aristotle calls him insensate and a maniac, a type he believes to be readily found, as we saw earlier, among the Celts, who fear neither earthquake nor flood. The Celts, insufficiently human to be possessed of human vices, are more akin to dumb, apparently really dumb, beasts.[5]

And if we think him unfair to Celts, he is not much fairer to the rash man. His portrait rings false. In contrast to the Celt, who takes fearlessness too far, the rash man is "a boaster and a pretender to courage; at any rate he wishes to *seem* as the courageous man really *is* . . . and therefore imitates him where he can. Hence such people are usually cowardly as well as rash, because while they make a show of confidence when circumstances permit, they cannot face anything fearful."[6] This portrait does not oppose rashness to the vice of cowardice at all; rashness, implausibly, predicts cowardice, Aristotle's rash man being no more than Falstaff, a fearful coward trying to fake it and not being very convincing in his performance. This is hardly a convincing portrait of excessive confidence and is manifestly unfair to any rash people I have known. If I needed people more likely than average to face danger when it mattered as well as for cheap thrills, I am sure I would score better than random by selecting people known to be rash.

William Tecumseh Sherman, in a love-hate admiration for certain southern "young bloods" that the northerners couldn't match, "sons of planters, lawyers about towns, good billiard-players and sportsmen, men who never did work and never will," hardly thought that their rashness was anything but a natural outgrowth of a most exuberant courage; it seems courage was equally a predictor for rashness as rashness for courage. This from a characteristically straight-talking letter to General Halleck:

> War suits them, and the rascals are brave, fine riders, bold to rashness, and dangerous subjects in every sense. They care not a sou for niggers, land, or any thing. They hate Yankees *per se* and don't bother their brains about the past, present, or future . . . They are splendid riders, first-rate shots, and utterly reckless; Stewart, John Morgan, Forrest and Jackson, are the types and leaders of this class. These men must all be killed or employed by us before we can hope for peace.[7]

Other people, some quite recently, follow Aristotle in defining rashness absurdly as a kind of cowardice in order, it seems, not just to render homage to the Aristotelian theory of virtue, but jealously to keep the honor of courage from such types as the rascals Sherman wanted to kill.[8] More politics of courage? Let us give rashness its due: at worst it is a semblance of courage, sometimes a pathetic one, but still not a contrary or a vice opposite to courage, and sometimes it is a very good semblance indeed; in fact rashness by degrees insensibly merges with courage.

Semblances of Virtue

Semblances of virtue are something less than the pure virtue, usually because motivated in some less than perfect way. The action looks good; the deed produces the desired results, but something is lacking in the inner state of the actor. We could even rank the semblances according to the worthiness of their motivation, gridding them between near perfect virtue at the top and a pure fake at the bottom.[9] Much of the politics of courage is taken up with determining what will win praise as the real thing, or what must make do with being denominated a mere semblance or, worse, what ends up excoriated as a vice.

Aristotle lists five semblances of courage.[10] They are actions motivated or informed by: (1) the fear of shame or the desire for honor; he calls this civic courage, which, in his estimation, though very close to the real thing, is not motivated by desiring virtue for virtue's sake; (2) experience and skill in facing the specific danger; (3) spirit, fury, rage; (4) optimism about one's chances; and (5) ignorance of danger. At least four of these semblances—all but number 2—can easily lead to actions that are rash in a generally acceptable view of rashness, not in the contrived caricature of it as a Falstaffian cowardly boaster. I depart from the Aristotelian model to the extent that I want to reestablish rashness as a very good semblance of courage, not the vice Aristotle would have it be. In the next chapter we will deal specifically with the Aristotelian semblances.

Rashness and Risk

I want to distinguish two kinds of rashness, one involving what we sometimes call thrill-seeking, in which incredible behavior is mobilized on behalf of ends perceived to be of little social or moral value; the other is the more usual sense of rashness in which the question is primarily one of reckless means. The triviality of the ends is signaled by their justifications: "because it is there," as in mountain climbing or eating from any forbidden tree, or "because it feels neat, it gives me a high," as in bungee-jumping or skydiving. This is the rashness that we associate with daring for daring's sake; it is about the love of risk, danger, and thrill. Thrill-seekers may purchase the best equipment, have medical rescue units at hand, they may, that is, go about their dangerous activity in a prudent way and still not be absolved of the charge of a certain kind of rashness. The triviality of the end coupled with the level of risk relegates it to the domain of rashness.

Some might prefer to call such risk-seeking action daring or just plain stupid, and reserve rashness for a certain style of hastiness and thoughtlessness in the means of pursuing goals, worthy or not. But the thrill-seeker is not best characterized as stupid even if the thrills are cheap. Stupidity is a vast category that has considerable overlap with rashness, but then stupidity has been thought to have areas that are congruent with courage too. Not all rash action qualifies as stupid, nor all stupid action as rash. There is a notable distinction between those too dim to recognize risk or to discern the inadequacy of their plans to deal with it, and those who, keenly sensitive to risk, hunt it down or welcome it when it comes by chance.[11] And how do we understand the stubborn desire to retain risk as part of the system when it could feasibly be lowered, as in the case of the British divisional commander who refused to permit the use of steel helmets when they became generally available in 1916 because he thought they would make the men go soft?[12]

No small amount of the impetus toward rashness of the thrill-seeking variety comes from the prospect of being thought daring and reckless by the risk averse. Their "tsk tsk"s are as much sought after as their "ooh"s and "ah"s. The impulse to seek danger may owe only a little more to the pull of thrill than it does to the push of the desire not to be counted among those who not only welcomed bicycle helmets but who also saw fit to attach rear-view mirrors to them.

If risk-seeking for unworthy goals is rash, then not undertaking risk to achieve valued goals is by one description overly cautious, by another cowardice itself. Robert Graves, with some ironic indulgence in which rationality, reason, and calculation become their own joke, discusses how he, "like everyone else" on the western front, had a "worked out formula for taking risks":

> In principle, we would all take any risk, even the certainty of death, to save life or to maintain an important position. To take life we would run, say, a one-in-five risk, particularly if there was some wider object than merely reducing the enemy's manpower; for instance, picking off a well-known sniper, or getting fire ascendancy in trenches where the lines came dangerously close.

When it came to saving the enemy wounded there were competing views. Some groups, like the Canadians, who felt they had a score to settle, took no prisoners and shot wounded enemy; others, like Graves's regiment, as we saw, would undertake a one-in-twenty risk to get them in.

> An important factor in calculating risks was our own physical condition. When exhausted and wanting to get quickly from one point in the trenches to another without collapse, we would sometimes take a short cut over the top, if the enemy were not nearer than four or five hundred yards. In a hurry, we would take a one-in-two-hundred risk; when dead-tired a one-in-fifty. In some battalions where morale was low, one-in-fifty risks were often taken in laziness or despair.[13]

The general point is quite clear: the more valued and worthy the goal, the greater the willingness to incur risk to bring it about. That, after all, is how we show we really value the goal; otherwise we are merely paying lip service. Another point is that the precise rationality of how to achieve valued goals may be undercut from time to time by exhaustion and despair. By articulating these themes probabilistically, as Graves does, some interesting points emerge. Once, say, a value of running a 1-in-100 risk is assigned to a goal, it becomes by definition rash to undertake greater risk to achieve it. If you judge something to be worth incurring a 1-in-2,000 risk, then to take a 1-in-1,500 risk of death is rash if done with awareness of the increased risk, stupid if done with no awareness, even though the total risk being run is hardly suicidal. Rashness can thus describe actions that are not all that objectively dangerous if you undertake them incurring a higher, but still manageable, risk than you have already decided that goal merits.

Once, however, the probability of harm drops low enough, neither courage nor rashness is part of the picture. If I am running a 1-in-100,000 risk to bear a message to Garcia, then doing so is not making much of a demand on my courage, and not to do so for fear of the risk would be timorous beyond acceptability. Still, if I could do it at 1-in-100,000, then to incur a 1-in-80,000 risk to do it would not seem to be rash either. The risk is just too remote in either case. And presumably if climbing Everest subjected the climber to only a 1-in-100,000 risk of death, he would lose all interest in climbing it, since it would already have become a family-vacation site.[14]

What level of risk must there be for courage, rashness, or thrill to be a possibility? How do we know where to draw the line? If we can't quite trust our own emotions, we take our cue from the cultural sortings of these things. When most people would fear or most would thrill we are roughly in the zone. We do know that locating that line is not reducible to a formal calculation; it is consciously part of Graves's desire to debunk the heroic that he purports to reduce it to numbers in the first place, as if courage and cowardice were a matter for the actuary. But then he does not reduce it to *mere* numbers. The numbers are given in reference to goals and assign them their moral rank—saving a life, taking an enemy position, hauling in the enemy wounded—for which courage is demanded in the face of the risks assigned the goal, but in ever-diminishing amount as the risk declines. Yet even at the level of debunking, the level of pure dry and wry numbers, he reminds us that at some level of risk the possibility of both courage and thrill is born.

And below that level? One drops into the world of insurance reps, or, even worse, one bottoms out in my university town, where a group of parents at a local grade school armed with snow shovels scattered the child-delighting snowbanks that the plows had tossed up, lest the children incur the risk of tumbling in the snow. (The grade school had already banned footballs from the playground because the ends are pointed.) Although risk aversion this excessive may kill any chance of greatness in any domain whatsoever, is such mind-boggling caution cowardice? We can imagine such people so aggressively insistent on lowering remote risks and opportunities for fun for their kids that they would fight and kill to achieve it; they might even be granted a very small amount of moral courage for risking being seen as so nerdy if it weren't that they were impervious to such shame. Cowardice and timidity, though often generating similar revulsion in those who must observe instances of both, are not quite the same thing in all instances. But though all timidity is not also cowardly, we rightly suspect that timidity may often indicate a cowardly heart.

Rashness with regard to means has a stylistic component. Not just any imprudent course of action qualifies as rash. If I am risk averse and take too long to move into action for fear of not having accounted for all the dangers and having developed plans to meet each of them, I may in fact be increasing the risk of failure by seeking to prepare for all the risks. Though such behavior might be called silly, fussy, hyperrational, timid, it would not be called rash even though it has unwisely lowered the chances of success.

Stoical passivity, too, does not qualify as rash, even though by some measure it seems perversely to prefer self-indulgent defeat to any active strategy standing a reasonable chance of success. Then there is stubbornness, which might be thought of as the rashness of irrational persistence, such as that of the commander who unwisely will not retreat because it looks cowardly. Rashness more properly describes the irrational embarkation on a new course of action.

Rashness usually requires a certain sense of hastiness, of not taking one's time to think things through, of not being able to postpone when postponement makes the most sense. It is more than that though. Rashness is not just inadvertently achieved by haste or thoughtless passion. Some have a conscious preference for the riskier way, choosing it with their eyes wide open. This preference is often incorporated into a certain style of aggressive honor. Honor, in one of its most historically prevalent forms, demands both rashness and courage, not really seeing all that much difference between the two, for to be honorable one must be seen as willing to incur risk in the pursuit of honor, to risk purely for risk's sake, not for the thrill, but for the reputation that comes with having tested oneself in fearful conditions.

By one way of thinking, rashness, if not exactly thoughtless, simply refuses to make thought bear on action in a way generally judged to be rational, for it always seems to prefer the very short-term to the mid- or long-term goal; that is why it is rash. "Rash" is thus the way we describe actions prompted by having one's reason overborne by those passions that we think of as "passionate," that is, emotions that rile us up, like anger and indignation, grief, love, and jealousy; yet rashness is also about being motivated by passions that sap us of caring, like despair. Rashness can be prompted both by excessive confidence and by the utter lack of it. So too not all rashness need have the look of fury; we can even imagine a purposive kind that is motivated by quiet love or grim hate, or rashness with a stiff upper lip in the style of English phlegm. Yet, when we send to central casting for the rash man, if he isn't hotheaded, vengeful, overzealous, madder than hell, a stickler for honor, we will send back for another.

Rashness and Deliberative Courage

Moralists of a certain stripe despair over rashness. They want virtue to travel cozily with reason; they also seem embarrassed by the unseemliness of loud, boisterous, rebel-yelling, thrill-seeking, honor-loving rashness, so that rather than let courage subsume such behavior in its wide embrace they propose a courage that starts to look like a special case of prudence. No doubt courage depends on some recognition of danger and risk; otherwise the lucky stupid person is courageous.[15] Nor do I think that this reflective deliberative courage is not wondrous and courageous; it is just not the whole story, nor is it without its own niggling associated vices, such as coldness, hardness, and cruelty.

Philosophers can discuss courage in terms like this: "Some aspect of practical wisdom's ability to deliberate, decide, and then inform action is absent in each of these five semblances [of courage]. Truly courageous actions rest on practical wisdom's astute judgments about situations, personal capacities, and justifiable goals."[16] Doesn't this view of deliberative courage feel wrong, too abstract, too intellectual and much too bloodless, more concerned to defend against rashness than against fear? Is it not confusing strategy sessions and planning with what it takes to carry through on the plans? Rarely does a common soldier talk like this about battle; this way of talking seems dedicated to denying courage to the private soldier and claiming it as the preserve of the rear echelon, the politician, or the philosopher.

Am I being unfair? I conceded deliberateness to Aristodemus in choosing to rush headlong into the Persian ranks; I also conceded him some amount of tactical deliberation once embarked on his one-man charge, that kind of quick thinking that improved his chances of killing a large number of Persians before he got killed himself, wisdom as a kind of seat-of-the-pants application of know-how one step up from raw instinct. But this kind of philosophic discourse clearly wants something more than knowing whether to feint right or feint left or how to apply one's sword to a neck. It demands, it seems, the intelligent assessment of risk in relation to goals. It means figuring out what's worthy and the most worthy way of going about achieving it.

So anxious is this discourse about the vice of rashness that it wishes us to play outside consultant to ourselves so that we can compare theories of moral accounting to come up with just the right evaluation of ends, just the right means to carry them out. Surely something of this sort will be needed to fulfill the stringent calls made for fine-tuned assessments of risk, for "nuanced rational judgments about what is pertinent and valuable,"[17] for the correct evaluation of the worthiness of ends so that one can determine when safety must take second place to the advancement of those goals, for recognizing the locations of the fine line that keeps prudence from veneering cowardice and desires for honor from prompting foolhardiness. But intelligence and deliberation, as we shall see in the next chapter, are just as likely to lead to despair or cowardice. Whatever capacity it is that accomplishes all these nuanced judgments, it cannot be the ability to keep your head in a crisis, for that is what many believe courage is.[18] We can't explain courage by saying you need courage to have courage.

In Chapter 4 I already registered doubts about this way of talking about courage, but I do not mean to overstate my case. Reason and deliberation have their role in courage, but so do unreason and rashness. First I will praise rashness and after that clip its wings a bit. The deliberative model of courage denies by fiat courage's intimate relation with rashness. But rashness often gets the job done. No amount of deliberation would lead to actions quite as successful, and "praised be rashness for it," as Hamlet says. To be fair, rashness can also be put to the service of rationality. Game theorists have detailed the ways in which it may be rational to cultivate a reputation for irrationality, and to do so credibly, as we noted briefly in the context of threats, it may be necessary to be really rash on occasion.[19] The commander who burns his ships or the bridges behind him is leaving himself no option to retreat. Such strategies suppose that it might be better for his prospects and detrimental to those of the enemy to let them have the opportunity to deliberate between advancing and retreat, best to bestow upon them the opportunity to choose among competing options, while denying himself the opportunity for choice by precommitting to the path from which he now cannot deviate. That too, though rash and very risky, is a kind of courage. And it involves the reasoned decision to be rash, reason and rashness converging seamlessly.

I wonder if the modern philosophic discourse hasn't shifted courage from the grit of battle to primarily noncontentious settings, the dangers that threaten threaten abstractly or hypothetically; they aren't felt. Neither the dangers nor the fears they engender are sufficiently particularized. And they seldom involve facing off against another human being rather than against the weather; and though facing a hostile Mother Nature surely requires courage, it does not do so in quite the same way as with fighting a human. Nature doesn't need courage to pose a threat to you; a human enemy, however, will be drawing on reserves of the same virtue you are drawing on, and one of the things that is being contested is who has the most of it. Being rash might be as helpful against a storm as against a human, but against only one of these adversaries will your rashness or prior reputation for it have an effect. A storm doesn't care one bit about your virtue. A human, though, will sit up and take notice when you burn your bridges, when you forgo, riskily, the ability to deliberate further. Whatever the opposition between deliberation and rashness, they make quite better companions than this kind of virtue talk is willing to allow.

Hamlet's point, though, when he praises rashness, is not strategic; he is talking about the benefits of complete inadvertence with no reason sneaked in the back door. Unless we are motivated rashly from time to time, he says, we will achieve less optimal ends than if we deliberated, plotted, weighed, and evaluated. True, our impulses get us in trouble; but they also get us out of some situations, not just serviceably, but with panache. Moreover, it is hardly our reason that keeps us from rashness so much as our fear. Most rash and raging actors open up one eye, at least to squint. Haven't you noticed that your own propensity for rashness, to the extent you have one, picks its moments in which to indulge itself? Imagine a constitutionally hot-tempered soul who is of slight build and not a very good fighter. Is he not likelier to let his fury take control when the person who is assaulting his friend is one his "practical wisdom" knows he can beat? Is it even possible to describe the perception by which he recognizes that the guy opposing him is six feet six inches and 250 pounds a matter of deliberation? The knowledge that he cannot win does not take much reasoning or deliberation; it is felt instantly at some subcortical layer of the brain as fear, rather than deduced in the most evolutionarily recent portions of it. If you know you can win, it doesn't take much courage to do so; if the outcome is uncertain, then your courage is gauged and, ever more so, the longer the odds against your success, until those odds begin to bump into the certainty of your not having a chance in hell. Then it is surely rash to try, but courage is still part of the mix even then. How can rashness not become an ever stronger ingredient in the constitution of courage itself as the odds of success grow grimmer?

There are indeed settings in which courage can be the endpoint of some kind of deliberation, as when one has time to concoct a strategy that will need courage to be implemented. But in so many instances there is not much time to deliberate; courage is often demanded in emergencies. The haste that informs rashness must also inform courage. One just dives in; he who deliberates is lost. Courage's job in this case looks exactly the same as rashness', for it is courage or rashness that gets us over the hump, over our fear, hesitancy, self-doubt, and our reasoned evaluations of risk. How can we ask that this be completely a rational or deliberative process? Once in the water or the burning house, we deliberate, I have supposed, as to how best to bring the person in or out and to get ourselves home safely in the process. But this is not a very interesting deliberation requirement, for only the person intent on suicide does not deliberate to this extent.

Rashness is part of the politics of courage. Calling someone rash is a way of dismissing often awe-inspiring action as being of less virtue than deliberate courage. Many of those called rash are people who simply don't scare easily or who seem to thrill to fear or who just get mad as hell or who just don't give a damn. These sorts do not fare well among most philosophers of virtue, who seem desperate to give them bad grades. I suspect an unavowable class issue is lurking here. Courage is always threatening to be vulgar; unless it is tied up with reason and wisdom it would be too readily available to those shameless slaves who do not fear beatings, to thick-necked soccer hooligans and Saturday-night fighters, to disgraced canceled beings like Aristodemus, and to women, who are always accused of being more susceptible to passion than to reason in their motives. No sooner is one of these easily-angered rash types (Achilles) or thrill-seekers (Odysseus, Beowulf) or plain old brawlers (Ajax) of the right social station and gender than he is made into an epic hero. So when Nicias in *Laches* denies courage to the rash because their actions are not based on the knowledge of the proper grounds of fear and hope, he does not just intend to deprive animals of courage, but "many men, many women, and many children" whose actions otherwise look pretty impressive (197b).

I am not arguing for calling the insane man who believes himself bullet-proof virtuous, or for honoring those whose fearlessness is bought at the price of insensibility and dimness, Aristotle's Celts. Courage clearly requires some sense of risk and danger, even if that is not always accompanied by fear or always exactly conscious. Pure insensibility and pure stupidity do not qualify. We need not deny the virtue of rashness in order to admire deliberate courage also. Rashness comes in all degrees and a wide variety of styles, most of which allow for and indeed assume that the rash person is aware, at some level, of the risks he runs. In some styles he loves the risk; in others, the risk is recognized but is not heeded; in yet others he prefers taking his chances as to the level of risk. If we fear that the rash are at times stupid, that stupidity is not of the kind that cannot see danger, but rather of the kind that doesn't let the perception of it lead to prudent action.

The proponents of deliberate courage are rather uncharitable to those more passionately motivated and also to those more dispassionately reck-less out of a conscious delight in risk-seeking, the thrill-seekers. The rest of us cannot deny the awe and rightful respect we have for certain kinds of reckless action. Even those modern philosophers distrustful of the moral status of reckless courage concede that "there is often something almost flattering in our ascriptions of recklessness. It is as if we prize courage so highly that even its thoughtless extremities may not altogether extinguish our admiration."[20] Samuel Johnson notes that rashness "is never men-tioned without some kind of veneration," and he offers an eloquent defense of our veneration:

> It may be laid down as an axiom, that it is more easy to take away superfluities than to supply defects; and, therefore, he that is cul-pable, because he has passed the middle point of virtue, is always accounted a fairer object of hope, than he who fails by falling short. The one has all that perfection requires, and more, but the excess may be easily retrenched; the other wants the qualities requisite to excellence, and who can tell how he shall obtain them? We are certain that the horse may be taught to keep pace with his fellows, whose fault is that he leaves them behind. We know that a few strokes of the axe will lop a cedar; but what arts of cultivation can elevate a shrub?[21]

There is something rather compelling about Johnson's metaphors.

If we find the daring that is involved in trivial thrill-seeking blame-worthy in some respects, it is not because the substance of that daring is all that different from the substance of courage except for the worthiness of the ends sought. Nor is it that the ends are bad, as in the case of Mr. Coke's shameless cowardice, only that they are trivial. Might it be that we find the courage expended in thrill-seeking blamable because we really do believe that courage is a depletable resource to be jealously guarded and expended only when it matters, when the goal reaches a certain level of seriousness? The vice of thrill-seeking rashness then is that it is a kind of masturbation, matching two of the reasons we find masturbation troublesome: it is feel-good self-indulgence that at its best is only a deformed second best and because, by some atavistic attachment to medical theories of humors that have not been current for nearly three centuries, it is understood as a wasting of a scarce substance, a spilling of a valuable seed on unfertile ground.

In order to give such masturbation a positive spin, we might rename it and call it training or practicing courage. I wonder if rashness and thrill-seeking aren't, more accurately, what it means to exercise courage in dull times. In a time when demands on our physical courage are rare, we must contrive occasions for courage. (Think how much better it is that courage be exercised in sport and skydiving than in activities like barroom brawling, freebooting, and mercenary soldiering.) It is a common belief that excellence in contact sports is a pretty good predictor for physical if not moral courage. The remark attributed to Wellington that Waterloo was won on the playing fields of Eton is probably as good a social and cultural explanation of the virtue of the English officer corps as any. When Robert Graves, while recovering from wounds, was assigned to training replacement officers, he sorted the men by how they played games, "principally Rugger and soccer. Those who played rough but not dirty, and had quick reactions, were the sort needed."[22] So thorough is the prejudice that we are ever so mildly shocked to discover that a certain Herman Sallee, who lettered in football in college, was court-martialed for cowardice: before leading his first patrol in Korea he collapsed in tears and terror—"I just can't do it." More telling is that Lieutenant Sallee introduced the details about his athletic record in his defense. It was designed to show that he was not dispositionally a coward, but that he was genuinely physically ill at the time of his failure. The court was unmoved.[23]

Consider too how readily we can construct a rather dubious portrait of a courageous person of the deliberate type, who keeps his goals in mind, figures out the best way to advance them, and does not let fear deter him from achieving the valued goal. He appears fairly often in movies and literature as a dispassionate and able leader, good at his job, and frequently in the uniform of the enemy, for with coolness often comes a kind of hardness, an unpitying sensibility that can easily slip into methodical cruelty. Tim O'Brien, testing the philosophers again, writes of a lieutenant the men called Mad Mark. Mark was not rash in the least; he was coolly deliberate in everything. O'Brien, somewhat unfairly and inaccurately, describes Mark as practicing "more or less an Aristotelian ethic." He was purely professional; he hunted men with no more anxiety than if they were deer and very effectively. "Like Aristotle, Mad Mark believed in and practiced the virtue of moderation; he did what was necessary in war." "He carried a shotgun . . . and the shotgun itself was a measure of his professionalism, for to use it effectively requires an exact blend of courage and skill and self-confidence." Because of its limited range, you have to "see the enemy's eyes," and that "requires courage and confidence."[24]

What got Mad Mark his name was his calmness; he never showed fear: "He was insanely calm." It is his calmness, his ability to keep cool under the most trying conditions, that led the average grunt, extremely astute on these particular matters of moral psychology, to realize that Mark was crazy. A sane person with perfect poise might want to show fluster in some settings, might, indeed, have to show fluster in some settings to be perfectly poised. Mark never flustered, and that showed that something was wrong with him. Evidently, we have come to resist accepting that humans ought to possess this deliberative kind of courage, for we suspect it is a form of insanity. Mark may well have been insane, but even so his insanity took the form of mimicking a model that moral philosophy holds dear.

Reexamine the significance of the shotgun, which O'Brien reads as an extension and emblem of Mark's courage and confidence. Even Mark is not above playing the rashness game; what else is the shotgun about, a weapon that must usually be used rashly (because you have to get so close) or cruelly (because of the particularly messy way it has of disorganizing a human body)? A shotgun can hardly be better at killing the enemy than a rifle; it seems more designed to send a message to his own men. In a rather inventive way Mark's shotgun continues the tradition that saw officers' weapons become mere indicia of rank. His shotgun is the equivalent of the World War I officer's whistle, walking stick, or saber: it is virtually useless, but important symbolically. Yet unlike those fastidious continental officers, for whom it was déclassé to kill, Mark bears his shotgun to reveal his special election as a killer, a person who prefers to kill absolutely and messily when he kills, to lead by showing exquisite poise in the face of the horror he creates.

Clipping Rashness' Wings: Wisdom, Cunning, and Prudence

For all my praise of rashness, the heroes of saga and epic I so admire knew they had to make some accommodations with prudence. Life expectancies were short enough without adding indiscriminate death-seeking behavior to the hellish mix of disease and famine. After all, only the most psychotic of berserks didn't wear a helmet; and no one eschewed a shield, at least at the start of a fight. Tough men of honor were prudent in the extreme about the quality of their weapons and protective armor. They made other com-promises too. The real trick, as we touched on in Chapter 7 when dis-cussing retreat, was to find ways to maintain honor even as one backed off, backed down, or simply took to the sidelines to catch one's breath. No one won every encounter, but a man of honor made people believe he was still to be reckoned with nonetheless, that there would be a next round.

But here is the problem. For these men born into cultures of honor, pru-dence was psychologically trying, and the psychological costs were rather different from those we bear when, say, we prudently try to resist pleasure's siren call.[25] For they rightly feared being thought fearful and justly worried that all those envious others with whom they were competing for honor would gladly assign the worst possible motivation to inaction or to retiring action. Retreats and various forms of forbearance brought taunts of cow-ardice from opponents; nor was it certain that your comrades, envious of your standing, would deny themselves some pleasure at your anguish. Complains Shakespeare's Ulysses:

> They tax our policy, and call it cowardice,
> Count wisdom as no member of the war,
> Forestall prescience, and esteem no act
> But that of hand.[26]

The system had a built-in bias toward rashness to avoid insinuations of fearfulness and cowardice; indeed courage itself is biased heavily toward rashness. And though a reputation for rashness, as we saw, could pay divi-dends, more often than not, your rashness, if predictable, would make you easy pickings for a coolly smart opponent.

The Vikings had a proverb right on point: "Only the slave avenges himself immediately, but the coward never does."[27] The proverb posits two poles of temptation, Aristotelian ones at that: the temptation of anger-impelled rash action of the thoughtless slave versus the temptation of fear-impelled nonaction of what was understood as effeminate cowardice. The moral order of revenge thus lay figurally bracketed by animals at one end and women at the other. The proverb's view of practical wisdom comes down to finding the proper timing, somewhere between right now and never. Prudence was not always about turning the other cheek; it was not about not hitting back, but rather about hitting back in the most effective fashion, which meant getting the timing right. To be sure, wisdom was at times about knowing whether to hit back at all; but it was just as much about knowing when to hit back and whom to hit and having the self-command and courage to act accordingly. In feud, for example, with its my-turn/your-turn style of conflict, it is sheer stupidity to hit back immediately. Delay itself is a weapon; one toys with the opponent, forces him to excessive vigilance, interrupts his sleep with anxiety, and makes him and his kin live with fear. Delay is the power to terrorize; only a fool would waste one of the most maliciously delicious aspects of having the ball in his court. How different prudence looks in that world, before it became a commodity peddled by insurance companies and actuaries.[28]

Only the rashest of hotheads didn't understand that not all wrongs could be righted immediately; one might have to suffer contumely for a time as did Achilles (sulkily) and Odysseus (with outward calm but with great inner turmoil); intelligence was an honorable asset and could even be combined with physical acumen within a single person.[29] If not, alliances could be formed between those with brains and those with brawn. Even the brawny, those who managed to do well over a reasonable length of time, knew enough to take counsel from the wise; and of course, one of the chief ways the wise displayed wisdom was by recruiting brawn to their cause.

Wisdom was understood to inhere not only in strategy, but also in having the skills or being able to muster the means needed to effect the strategy. In Old English, for example, one warrior at Maldon is called "wise" (fród) for spearing in the neck a Viking who had just wounded him.[30] In the violent world of honor, wisdom was not quite separable from knowing how to kill well, which meant not just sending your victim on the road to Valhalla, but also finding a way to avoid joining him for the ride.

Honor cultures recognized wisdom as a virtue, as long as wisdom was put to the service of gaining or preserving esteem, to the extent, that is, that wisdom furthered courage's cause. In these cultures it is hard to separate wisdom from cunning, even from cruelty at times. Some rough agreement began to emerge that certain classes of deceit were dishonorable—undertaking a truce so as to betray the other party—while others were gray enough to allow already honorable men to put them to use—like taking advantage of an opponent's foolishness, instances, that is, in which your courage was less called into question than the other's stupidity: "For it is not said," writes Montaigne, "that we may not, at the right time and place, take advantage of the stupidity of our enemies just as we do of their cowardice."[31] Cunning, then, had its proper role, and, according to the ancient Chinese military theorist Sun Tzu (fifth century B.C.E.), it should play the dominant role: "All warfare is based on deception. Therefore, when capable, feign incapacity; when active, inactivity. When near, make it appear that you are far way; when far away, that you are near. Offer the enemy a bait to lure him."[32] In the Western tradition, the wise man was not just smart, he outsmarted: thus the image of tricksters like Odysseus, Njal and Sturla of the sagas, Jacob, Joseph, and David of the Bible. They are winners, though given to unsavory tactics at times; and although you may be too scrupulous to want them on your side, you definitely do not want them in the ranks of your enemy.[33]

The problem is that even acceptable cunning and deceit suggested the tactics of a coward too fearful to meet his opponent face to face. Would a man of courage kill like a thief in the night? Would he poison? What about the moral status of feigning flight in battle? Is an improperly cunning tactic one that does damage without openly presenting oneself for reprisal, so that feigned flight in battle is acceptable because you are still exposed, but guerrilla warfare and surely terrorism are trying to get away with something for nothing? Thus the low status of archers: Paris gets blamed for standing well rearward and picking off Greeks with his bow, good at it though he was and considerably more effective at killing Greeks than those undertaking more risk where the hacking and hewing was going on. We find some people developing a lawyerlike ability to obey the letter but not the spirit of norms against taking unfair advantage. One Icelander prods awake the men he has sneaked up on, so as not to commit such a shameless act as to kill sleeping men, and instantly dispatches them before they know what is upon them.[34]

It is often the case that what the loser considers trickery, the winner considers wise tactic. Those victimized by cunning have an interest in claiming their cunning enemies to be cowards, too afraid to fight fair and square. And cunning persons also must not be quite sure that they are properly motivated. But then does cowardice lie in stabbing your enemy in the back unawares, or in not having the cold hardness to treat him so if the opportunity arises? Hamlet wasn't quite sure. Mores attributed to Machiavelli undertook to recast courage as hardness and cunning as the willingness to indulge cruelty if need be; courage was the determination to do whatever it took to achieve one's ends. Not to take advantage of opportunities was a sign of softness, the mere "craven scruple" that marked indecision.[35]

Anxieties and uncertainty on this score abound. Why is Odysseus a man of honor though a trickster? Might it be that he is respected for his wisdom because he is also as strong as an ox and a good wrestler? Thus David in the Bible and Egil in the Icelandic world can be admired for outsmarting others because they were also reckoned warriors of impeccable mettle. Even the unhairy Jacob was a good wrestler, though cravenly fearful before his amiable brother, and very good at lifting heavy stones.[36] Then how does one account for the estimability of beardless Njal, the wisest and most subtle of strategists and tricksters, who makes not the faintest pretense of being a warrior? His force is uniformly applied by others' muscles. It seems that wisdom is accepted on its own terms, that is, independently of the physical prowess of its possessor, more readily if the wise man is old; if young, he must show consistent ruthlessness and cunning in counsel. Most wise men, the Nestor types whose role it is to offer prudent counsel, are old. Yet they seem to think that their counsel has a better chance of being heeded if it is larded with tedious retellings of their own youthful martial glory. The young find them mostly boring. By being associated with old age, wisdom comes to mean boredom before it gets suspected of being cowardly.

Tactical and strategic cunning, unlike courage, is a virtue that cannot always speak its name. A culture can honor one or two cunning men of its own race, like Odysseus, as manifesting virtue by their wits, but when a whole gender is considered cunning, as with women, or a whole people, as with Jews (Greeks were viewed this way by Romans),[37] cunning is assigned a distinctly negative value. Victories obtained by guile, notes Montaigne, are somewhat tainted; those overcome by deceit rather than by valor, he says, do not admit their inferiority to the victor.[38] That doesn't prevent the cunning victor from coming to have genuine contempt for the stupidity or gullibility of the loser. And what does it mean to recognize that you have been overcome by the valor of the enemy? One man's valor is often another's bullying. Suppose you are Judea losing to Rome, Grenada to the United States, Poland to Germany, Hungary to the Soviet Union; did you lose to their valor? Did the presence or absence of their valor (or yours) have anything to do with it? In the end the victors often come to accord their consciences with expedience. They see in their victory the proof of their valor and, as was mentioned earlier, they sometimes come to recognize the need to confer valor on the defeated so that they can claim the necessity of their own to overcome it.

SO, YES, THERE is a place for practical wisdom in the hostile world in which courage and cowardice are chief among virtues and vices, but not quite in the genteel way moderns are wont to talk about wisdom, prudence, and reason. In settings demanding courage—which are also settings crawling with relentless temptations of cowardice—wisdom, prudence, and reason mean steeliness, ruthlessness, and deception.

Stupidity, Skill, and Shame

ONE STRAIN OF PHILOSOPHY, as we have seen, desperately wants to define courage so that it not only is consistent with intelligence but also requires some manifestations of it in reasoned deliberation. But the very capacity of discernment that so often characterizes intelligence is just what folk theory believes is more likely to prompt fearfulness than bravery; it is partly, though only partly, the problem of that "craven scruple of thinking too precisely on th'event" that so prompted Hamlet's fit of self-loathing.

The Problem of Brains

One of the most salient features of intelligence, it is rather insistently believed, is its ability to find good reasons for worry, whereas those without that ability sleep well and march blithely on. And since no defensive faculty would be sensitive enough to do its work if it did not generate some false positives, this capacity must also generate certain not-so-good reasons for worry as the price of being able to do its job well.[1] Intelligence, by this view, best displays itself as intelligence by discerning risk, by identifying cause for concern.

We even come to suspect that those who discover difficulties and perils are somehow smarter than those who figure out ways to get out of them, since these saviors do not need raw intelligence so much as know-how and virtues like tenacity, cool, confidence, and courage to implement their know-how. Indeed, the person of limited intelligence and imagination, who sees but one way out and sticks to it, may have a higher rate of success than one who discerns a number of options and must choose among them or overcome desires to abandon one course for others. Joseph Conrad makes great comedy out of Captain McWhirr, whose mental dullness is the exact virtue needed to get him out of a typhoon, preserving his human cargo against all odds; never mind that it was his dimness that got him into the fix in the first place.[2] But to have avoided the peril would cast intelligence again in its role as the prompter of safety first, affirming its kinship with prudence but also with unsavory cousins like timorousness and cowardice. Intelligence seems to be more the provenance of the pessimist than of the optimist, of the fearful than of the brave, of the self-critical than of the person with high self-esteem.[3]

Surely there is some truth in that ancient wisdom. Thucydides, again, has a perfect speech for the occasion. Here is the setting. Demosthenes, heading a small Athenian force of sixty hoplites and some archers, is about to try to prevent a vastly superior Spartan naval force from landing at Pylos (425 B.C.E.). He marches his men down to the sea and exhorts his desperate band as follows:

> Soldiers, all of us together are in this, and I do not want any of you in our present awkward position to try to show off his intelligence by making a precise calculation of the dangers which surround us; instead we must simply make straight at the enemy, and not pause to discuss the matter, confident in our heart that these dangers, too, can be surmounted. For when we are forced into a position like this one, calculations are beside the point: what we have to do is to stake everything on a quick decision. (4.10)

No doubt Demosthenes has a different view of the use he will make of his own intelligence, but his mordant observations assume that his men will demonstrate theirs by engaging in a competition of wits whose end will be to come up with the most pessimistic description of their present bad circumstances.

Intelligence shows off by seeing difficulty and by exposing the vanity of any ameliorative gesture as so much delusion and wishful thinking. The view is roughly that hope is irrationally seductive and the provenance of idiots (the Greeks had a distinctly less generous view of hope than Christians did).[4] Demosthenes concedes that their straits are so dire that there is no point in trying to prove them worse than any fool can already see they are. So spare me, he says, your wit. When the situation is this bad, "calculations are beside the point." Refined tactics require time for deliberation, and they have no time; given the circumstances, sound policy, wisdom, and rashness converge. Don't think; just charge. Thinking will only prompt despair.

Demosthenes, however, doesn't stop there; he still has to convince his men to fight, for they are not without the tempting options cowardice offers: either to run or to lay down their arms and beg quarter hoping it will be granted (not a sure bet by any means).[5] He has some work ahead of him. He proceeds by trying to suggest that their plight may not be as bad as it looks, noting for instance that the enemy has a difficult place to land. He tells them to ignore the difference in numbers since only a small portion of the enemy can be brought up against them given the narrowness of the landing place. He knows, however, that accentuating the positive of their position is not the best rhetorical strategy to employ, since the bleakness of their situation has already been conceded. Instead he asks them to shift their point of view, to see things from the Spartan side. They are operating from ships and "on the sea quite a number of circumstances have to combine favorably if action is to be effective. So I consider that the enemy's difficulties make up for our lack of numbers." Above all, he says, you, as Athenians, "know from experience all about landing from ships on foreign shores and how impossible it is to force a landing if the defenders stand firm and do not give way through fear of the surf or the frightening appearance of the ships as they sail in."

Demosthenes himself plays the very role he would deny his men—showing off intelligence by discerning every possible point of danger—but from the Spartan vantage point. He demonstrates how a smart Spartan, one who by definition has the capacity to discern risk and cause for worry even in good times, would exercise his intelligence. Put yourself in Spartan shoes; see how scared you men of intelligence would be if you were they. By itself, though, that move wouldn't work; it requires recourse to a powerful bit of knowledge not quite avowable except in circumstances this bad. The Athenians know the Spartans must be scared stiff because, says Demosthenes, we have been in the exact situation the Spartans are in now and were scared stiff ourselves. In fact, the Athenian troops know the Spartans have even greater cause for concern than Athenians would in the same circumstances, for the Athenians are used to fighting from ships whereas Spartans are not.

The speech is rhetorically and psychologically masterful. Demosthenes' wits did not undo *his* courage, but he did not need them to embolden himself. Rather his courage kept his wits functioning so that he could use them to aid the cause of his men's faltering courage, undone in part by their wits. The men are now moved to behave courageously though it was hardly their reason that got them there, but rather Demosthenes' rhetorical skills which marshaled the appearance of reason to the cause of passion, inspiring confidence when all reason would undermine it. Demosthenes rallied his men by conjuring up their past fears, which they then could attribute by sympathetic imagining to their Spartan enemies. Intelligence plays two roles here, one in the men and another in the leader: the men's intelligence undermines their resolve until their leader uses his intelligence to suppress theirs so as to get them to accept a more sanguine view of their situation.

It is not just analytic smarts that keeps company with cowardice. Cowardice is likewise believed to correlate positively with imagination, although the imagination that undoes courage is not the kind that makes for good poets, but a very specific imagination: one that exercises itself almost exclusively in picturing disaster, and not just any disaster, but ones that befall *me*, the imaginer. What exactly would it be like to have a bullet pierce my brain; would I know it when it happened; would the experience of it be an eternity collapsed into a second and then what if . . . ? "Happy are those who lose imagination," writes Wilfred Owen. "My imagination, that cursed imagination of mine," laments soldier Philip Caputo.[6] Mostly, imagination merely provides the illustrations for a text of disasters that intelligence has already written. Those, however, whose imaginations are so structured as to imagine disaster only for their enemies are the beneficiaries of one of those limits of mind, such as optimism and overconfidence, that allow people to do courageous things simply because they think the odds are all in their favor.

Optimists, the Furious, and the Insane

Aristotle believes that optimists manifest a semblance of courage, a semblance ranked somewhat lower than the semblance based on fury or rage. Fury and spirit, Aristotle recognizes, often serve as "an accessory" to true courage, though they lack the perfection of reason.[7] But the optimistic are confident in danger, he says, only because they have never experienced defeat. They don't think they can lose, "but when the result does not turn out as expected, they run away."[8] Aristotle makes his optimistic person's confidence a function of past success, and surely this is a reasonable basis upon which to construct justifiable optimism. Consider, however, an optimism that arises solely from a capacity for self-deception, independent of any basis in past victory. In the extreme case, the confidence of such an optimist is completely unassailable. Failure can always be explained away: the other side got lucky; they cheated; it wasn't really a defeat anyway. This optimist does not run when the going gets rough; he may well stick it out, charmed by the belief that no bullet has his name on it. But why do I adopt such an ungenerous tone? There is ample proof that positive thinking, self-deceptive though it may be, gets results.[9]

We may want to distinguish between those who are high on themselves as a matter of disposition, a given aspect of their character not needing external confirmation—those sometimes annoying souls of undentable self-esteem—from those who try to trick themselves for the occasion, optimists for the nonce. There is the courage of congenital optimism, and then there is that which comes from the rum ration, the boast, the vow, the exhortation speech, or even, at times, from the application of reason. In analogous manner, we should distinguish between those people who use techniques that trick themselves into fury and rage and those people who are by nature furious, cursed or blessed, as the case may be, with a short fuse. The techniques used to elicit fury look remarkably like those designed to increase confidence, with the rum ration and exhortation figuring prominently. Why aren't these ploys, some of which we just saw Demosthenes make use of, designed to raise confidence in desperate situations, appropriate aids to virtue? A soldier moved to give his utmost by the effects of a rum ration or an exhortation speech does not lose his chance at courage. If the rum or the speech fails to do its job, he is still blamed as a coward, so we should praise him when they work. Commanders are willing to take semblances of courage wherever they can get them, and not just commanders, but the doers of the deeds themselves, who welcome any trick they can play on their minds that will let them behave in a way that is not shameful. Imagine the high command saying, "Sorry, men, no awards for valor in the last show: too much yelling, too much boasting, too much rum; do without the rum next time, boys, and you will have it just right."

Isn't there a reasonable case for being more charitable to the ironically or artificially deluded than to the constitutionally self-deluded? The first has to do some work to trick himself; the other can't seem to avoid not tricking himself. The person who struggles to let one part of his consciousness wink at another part to buy some assistance for his beleaguered disposition for courage deserves some credit. Such suspension of disbelief is itself a sign of one's commitment to courage; it might well be part of what it means to have a disposition for courage. How different is this from cultivating courage by boxing, fox-hunting, wrestling, or rugby? Why do I want that irony, that twinge of awareness of the self-trickery as trickery? No doubt it is my own politics of courage that desperately hopes to keep it separated from insanity, fanaticism, and the annoying optimism of the self-esteem crowd.

One Civil War soldier argues that courage is getting to whatever state it takes to "nonrealize" danger: "Courage is merely a nonrealization of the danger one is in owing to excitement, responsibility, or something of the sort."[10] Yet it is hardly clear that this soldier includes the self-deception of the constitutional optimist or the insensibility of the Celt as acceptable ways of achieving the nonrealization of danger. Since "responsibility" follows on "excitement," he seems to be raising the ante so that his "something of the sort" is not meant to include just any kind of distraction, but only those of a certain dignity. He does not go so far as to say that courage is the forgetting of fear by any means. Still, his view is more generous than that of the philosophers who follow Aristotle (though Aristotle himself is fairly generous) and also of some bitter moderns, such as Vietnam war correspondent Michael Herr, who are deeply suspicious of the moral value of actions that pass for courageous: "A lot of what people called courage was only undifferentiated energy cut loose by the intensity of the moment, mind loss that sent the actor on an incredible run; if he survived it he had the chance later to decide whether he'd really been brave or just overcome with life, even ecstasy."[11]

IMAGINE A PARANOID schizophrenic who musters all his might to face up to the phantoms that hound him. What some might wish to call the paranoid's courage can rather be seen as a phantasm analogous in quality to the phantasm that gives rise to it. Call it quasi-courage, dress-rehearsal courage, not quite a semblance. When Ajax awoke from his fit of insanity to find that he had slaughtered only sheep and not the armed men he thought he was killing, he was not about to excuse his disgrace by arguing that it took just as much courage to kill sheep he thought were warriors as to kill real warriors. The sympathetic observer is much more likely to be charitable to him—in fact the observer might be inclined to think the incident worthy of tragedy—than the sufferer is likely to be to himself should he ever recover his wits. The willingness to grant the deluded person courage is something of a sop, well intentioned as it may be.

Compare Ajax's case with the case in which the danger thought to be present is very likely but for some reason fails to materialize. A soldier storms a pillbox only to find it abandoned. He would win no medal for the guts it took to face the danger he thought was there; but most of us would speak of the courage it took to make the charge, more of us than would grant Ajax courage in killing sheep, while the soldier and his buddies might share a grim laugh, or experience the hysterical laughter of relief at the bad joke that, thank God, just occurred. We do not pity the soldier; we think him lucky; whereas we sympathize with the struggle of the sick man to face his terrifying phantoms, as much from an understanding that, like Ajax, the poor person would be mortified to be seen as his pitiers who wish to confer courage on him see him.[12]

Ignorance

Aristotle distinguishes between the optimist and the person whose courageous deeds are accomplished in ignorance of the danger. He considers these ignorant souls inferior in virtue to the optimists because they have no self-confidence. The optimists flee only when their self-confidence collapses, while the person unaware of danger flees as soon as he discovers the danger. In reality it can be hard sometimes to divide the proportion of stupidity between these two types, for just as we imagined that the optimist might be constitutionally so optimistic as never to doubt his bases for confidence, so the ignorant person might be so dim, or spacy, as never to be able to perceive the amount of risk he incurs. Presumably Aristotle means to distinguish between the insensate Celt, who is by nature incapable of fear, and the ignorant person, who fears quite well once he realizes he is in danger.

What, however, of the person who prefers not to know what he is about to face, the better to manage his fear and maintain his resolve? He is not ignorant in Aristotle's sense; he is all too aware of the proximity of danger. He just doesn't want to know any more than he does; he wants no particulars, and wishes that he could get the whole looming knowledge out of his head. His will not to know more than he does (and his wish to know even less) is a way of readying himself to face what he must. There are also those who feign ignorance of risk as a way of behaving coolly, sometimes sublimely, in the face of danger. The image is of a certain kind of English phlegm or Israeli contemptuousness. Though they feign ignorance of risk, they are not feigning their cool. They are not like the Celt, because they understand the risk. In this box belong types like Grant, Rabin, Wellington, and those numerous intrepid Englishwomen who penned their travel memoirs during the nineteenth and early twentieth centuries.

Skill and Experience

Here I want to flesh out the two remaining Aristotelian semblances touched upon in previous chapters: the semblance of skill and experience and the semblance of what Aristotle calls political or civic courage, which though "very like courage proper" is deemed inferior because it is motivated primarily by negative sanctions, fear of shame, disgrace, or punishment, rather than by the virtue itself.[13] Experience, according to Aristotle, gives one the ability to recognize false alarms and so to remain cool in situations in which others panic or fidget. The training and skill of these men (Aristotle has professional soldiers in mind) increases their odds of success in battle. But when they see that things are not going their way, when the usual advantage their skill provides disappears, then these "professional soldiers turn coward." Their experience allows them not only to discount false alarms more accurately than the inexperienced can, but also to recognize cause for real alarm earlier. Not surprisingly, then, they are "the first to flee, while the citizen troops die at their posts."[14]

This semblance has some of the substance of the courage of the mythical bully, who fights well when he is rightly confident of victory, who is good at recognizing the weak and beating them up. That is not quite a fair picture. These professionals are also the people who make a living doing dangerous work, and they should not be deemed less virtuous for being good at their job, itself a virtue of sorts. We don't admire the bomb-disposal expert less because he is an expert. Moreover, the experienced soldier who sticks it out when he knows the situation is hopeless will be manifesting more courage than the person whose inexperience still lets him hope, lets him believe that the odds are not insurmountable, when in fact defeat is certain.

Recall though the nearly universal intuition noted in *Laches:* the more skilled a person is at dealing with a specific danger, the less we credit courage rather than skill for the success; and as a corollary we believe the person who has to face these dangers without skill and training is displaying more courage precisely for sticking it out when the odds are stacked against him. There are qualifications of course; the unskilled person cannot be holding firm because he is one of those fools of self-esteem who believes himself skilled when he isn't; he cannot just be plain stupid; his virtue requires that he have the tragic knowledge of the unfavorable odds.

Few of us, however, would prefer to give up our expertise for the sake of being thought more courageous for not having it. There is no denying our admiration for the expert even when he is up against a less skilled person who has only his courage to recommend him. We admire the experience of the expert, his professional cool, his success, his hardness and dedication; we defer to him because he is a winner more than because he is courageous, although no doubt he is that too. His coolness and expertise, though, occupy a slightly different ground than does courage, for just the reason that we know the present challenge is easier for him than it is for the less skilled. We don't want our courage too easy, except on Memorial Day. But we credit those who have acquired the skills of a dangerous and risky expertise with their past courage in gaining that expertise, in their perseverance; they have proved their courage in the past, and they confirm a disposition for courage by engaging in such high-risk work. Don't they have to war against their own fears that their time is running out?

Others, however, have argued that training and skill, far from detracting from courage, often make sure that it is possible. Training offers the means to intercept confusion and panic so that one's virtue can get a footing and get oriented. Thus Robert Gajdusek in his memoir of World War II: "But thank God for discipline and training, for experience which gives knowledge to create space in which bravery can exist."[15] Gajdusek's claim is less that training gives confidence than that it buys time in which one can try to do one's duty; by allowing a person to fall back on drilled responses, training dispenses with deliberation and relieves some of the pressure on self-command. It is not to be pooh-poohed.

Aristotle collapses the semblance of skill into the semblance of optimism by having both types turn tail the moment their perceived advantage disappears. This is too hard on the professional soldier (in Aristotle's world a mercenary), just as we saw that it is also an inadequate account of the self-deceiving optimist. Make that mercenary a citizen and he will behave as a citizen, but when hired to fight as a mercenary he will bring a certain self-interested prudence to his battles. He will fight well enough to preserve his reputation as a mercenary worthy of his hire. He may run when a citizen soldier wouldn't, but he cannot run before his fellow mercenaries deem it is justifiable to do so, and presumably his skills will reduce the number of instances in which he will be tempted to run. He may not evince the special courage of the citizen, but then except to the extent that both citizen and mercenary are risking life, the stakes are not as high for him as for the citizen protecting hearth and home as well as his own heart. The philosophic account of deliberative courage must concede the virtue in the mercenary abandoning the fight before the citizen. Given the lower stakes the hired soldier has in any particular outcome, it would be foolhardy for him to treat his commitment as if it were the same as the citizen's. When he is running he may not be running as a coward (do cowards go into that line of work to begin with?); he is running as a virtuously prudent man.

But there are times when courage and courage alone is being tested, and in these settings skill can be understood to compromise courage to the point where a person might ostentatiously waive any advantage conferred by his training or special expertise. Montaigne describes the effect this view of skill's dubious relation to courage had on French dueling practices:

> The honor of combat consists in rivalry of heart and not of expertise; that is why I have seen some of my friends who are past masters in [fencing] choosing for their duels weapons which deprived them of the means of exploiting their advantage and which depend entirely on fortune and steadfastness, so that nobody could attribute their victory to their fencing rather than to their valor.[16]

Again we find rashness praiseworthy, not for the beneficial outcomes it may yield as when Hamlet praised it, but because rashness is the only way one can be certain that one's courage is what is being tested rather than other cultivated excellences. Not just cultivated excellence either; elsewhere Montaigne mocks natural advantages of strength and size: "To have stronger arms and legs is the property of a porter, not of Valor; agility is a dead and physical quality . . . A man's worth and reputation lie in the mind and in the will: his true honor is found there. Bravery does not consist in firm arms and legs but in firm minds and souls."[17] What is a big strong guy to do? Forever be deemed of untested courage, it seems, unless he submits to the Handicapper General.[18]

This fetishization of courage was not merely confined to highly formalized duels but even allowed ideas of fair play to spill into battle itself, where it was not advantages acquired by skill that were abjured but other kinds of beneficial happenstances that prevented the contest from being a true test of courage. In the early years of the Civil War there are cases of commanders declining the advantage of surprise and firing over the heads of an unwary enemy to allow them a fair chance.[19] Likewise it has been argued that the British in 1916 failed to take full advantage of the surprise their newly invented tanks gave them because of a belief that surprises were unsporting.[20] The idea of fair play received as great an assist from the ideology of honor and courage as from softer sentiments like pity.

Fear of Shame or Desire for Glory

According to Aristotle, to be courageous because one fears the shame of cowardice, or because one will be punished, or because one aspires to the glory and honor that come with a reputation for courage, though still praiseworthy, is less worthy than to be courageous because it is a fine thing to be so.[21] Aristotle was quite willing to make generous accommodation to glory-seeking and honor, but the modern ethicists that follow him are more hostile to shame-driven courage. They argue that the person motivated by honor, fear of shame, or punishment is not sacrificing his safety for some higher good, but calculating the best way to get more safety as he defines it. No matter that his understanding of safety may lead him to choose death rather than a life of shame; he has simply made the calculation and found it less painful to attack and die than to run and live.

In contrast, the truly courageous person, so the argument goes, reaches a point where his safety, no matter how conceived, will cease to matter to him as much as the external goal; it is for the good of that goal that he sacrifices the good of his safety. He is not, by this argument, seeking more safety in pursuing that goal. His commitment to the goal puts a limit on the value of his own safety; a point is reached where safety is not part of the calculation. Such is the man who is motivated courageously, not weighing two evils that threaten his safety to see which, in his view, is safer, but choosing between two goods that cannot be weighed on a single scale of safety.[22] Plato, recall, makes a similar point when he compares the bravery of soldiers unfavorably to that of philosophers. Warriors "face death . . . through fear of something worse."[23]

As good as that sounds, I just can't buy it. Any theory that reduces the heroes of epic and saga to something less than courageous has to be flawed fatally. Imagine telling Hector, Alexander, or Beowulf that he was manifesting only second- or third-rate courage. Let's give some credit to those "men of old" in Sparta who, as noted in Chapter 2, regarded courage as "fear of censure and terror of disgrace."[24] Unless people are lucky enough to be genetically courageous, how are they to be trained up to courage without recourse to competition and shame, the fear of disgrace? No culture I am aware of has seen fit to dispense with shame in the cultivation of courage.[25] We may not want to make the virtue so cheap that everyone has it, but we also do not want to make it so impossibly difficult that only a few can ever possess it. Shame avoidance, in the context of Western honor systems, might give us just the right amount of courage. In the Japanese context I suggested it might give us too much, where shame becomes so coercive as to be almost indistinguishable from being whipped (literally) to battle.

Remember that for honor-based cultures there was no higher goal than honor and glory and its corollary of shame avoidance. Honor culture erases any meaningful distinction between service to some noble principle and the avoidance of shame or the acquisition of honor. The entire moral order is subsumed under the larger goal of honor; there is no higher principle. This is why Aristotle, much more conversant with honor culture and its assumptions than we are, pretty much collapses civic courage into courage proper, by making true courage a matter of facing noble and glorious death fighting the polis' battles. But since one's own honor is so intimately connected with the honor of the polis, the pursuit of personal glory puts one at the service of the polis in any event.[26] Shame-driven courage looks just fine to me, and it is hard to see how the citizen soldier devoted to the welfare of the polis could avoid being caught up in it.

But let me make the case, if I can, for some possible ways of conceptualizing a non-shame-driven courage that is available to more than just saints and an occasional hero. Shame, by conventional understanding, is the miserable experience of being *seen* in disgrace. So try framing the question this way: Would the person do the courageous deed if he were all alone, if he could back out unseen? This question gets at some of the suspicions about the quality of the courage motivated by shame avoidance. If the courageous shame-avoider would take the coward's way out were he able to do so unobserved, then we would rightly want to discount somewhat the moral value of his courage.

No one doubts that it is harder to be courageous alone than in groups, even for that ideal person whose courage is not driven by the fear of disgrace. The presence of others stimulates one's courage not only because of the fearful prospect of shaming oneself in their eyes or because they will praise and honor one's successes, but because they also offer assistance just by being there; their presence is a solace. The pull of their companionship (and their need), just as much as the push of their monitoring eyes, greatly aids one's embattled resolve.[27] Thus soldiers desiring to fall behind, to drop out, will keep up with their advancing comrades because being alone behind is more frightening than being together under fire.[28] And then there is the moving image recorded again and again of soldiers huddling together under fire, leaning against one another as children do with their mothers, bunching against all orders, because the closeness of other living bodies helps sustain them in their tribulation. Yet even with the support of comrades, soldiers testify to feeling ultimately very alone: Gajdusek notes that "the forces of the moment force [the soldier] back upon himself, alone and unaided finally, no matter how backed up and surrounded by his buddies and support groups."[29] All the comradeship in the world, according to Frederic Manning, cannot overcome the loneliness of it all: "Every private soldier is a man in arms against a world, a man fighting desperately for himself, and conscious that, in the last resort, he stood alone; for such self-reliance lies at the very heart of comradeship."[30] But this existential loneliness, for all its misery, does not offer the option and temptation of evading the demands of courage that being physically alone does.

The awareness of the special achievement of lonely courage led people in the Great War to respect the valor of those occupying low-status non-shooting jobs—ration carriers, message runners—who often had to go it alone and who thus had the option to take refuge unseen in a shell hole and compose an excusing story. So appalling were the conditions, so deep the mud, so intense the shell fire, that such stories hardly needed concocting.[31] The special aloneness that night imposes—special because we suspect we are not alone at all, but rather in the presence of hostile others whom we cannot see—adds to the psychological burden: "Under danger, in the dark," says a French soldier in the Great War, "one feels a kind of particular horror at finding oneself alone. Courage requires to be seen . . . To be alone, to have nothing to think about except oneself . . . The soul abdicates quickly and the flesh abandons itself to shudders."[32] No wonder Napoleon held no courage equal to two-o'clock-in-the-morning courage, the kind he felt he possessed. Harold Macmillan (World War I) speaks of the panic he experienced at night, wounded, separated from his companions. It causes him, like those other courageous men we observed, to downgrade his displays of courage to mere sham:

> I suppose that courage is mainly, not wholly, the result of vanity
> or pride. When one is in action—especially when one is respon-
> sible for men under one's command—proper behavior, even acts
> of gallantry are part of the show. One moves and behaves almost
> automatically, as a member of a team or an actor on the stage.
> But now it was all over; I was alone and nobody to see me. There
> was no need to keep up appearances and I was frightened.[33]

Courage is generally easier to muster when observed,[34] easier in the day than at night, but still not easy for all that; it is harder when alone, but classic views of shame aside, one does not have to be actually seen to experience shame; we only have to see ourselves as others see us. To the extent that you value courage, any failure of it, observed or not, will bring about the unpleasantness of shame. You hold in your mind's eye the judging eye of your moral community, if, that is, you are not shameless. There is no reason to think your own inner eye will go easier on you than will the eyes of others; rather the contrary, even though there is good reason to distrust the self-indulgence that underscores the claim that self-loathing is harder to bear than being loathed by others. In any event, the person who is courageous alone does not prove that he was still not motivated by the standard concerns of the honor/shame moral economy.

Solitariness increases the chances that this is a person who may indeed break free of the honor/shame system in his virtuous motivation, achieving thereby the philosopher's Perfect Virtue. This is a person who could have concealed cowardice with credible excuses, but chose to do the right thing when he had safe ways out that he could have kept to himself. It just might be that this person's virtue is motivated independently of the approbation or disapprobation of real or imagined viewers. At least the odds are greater that he does the right thing because it is the right thing and for no other reason. Yet his inability to see himself play the coward might mean only that his sense of shame long ago did its work in molding his character.

We have not yet quite escaped shame, even with solitary courage. Consider this: there are deeds that take courage to do, the nondoing of which is not cowardly. These are the deeds beyond the call of duty, deeds of supererogation.[35] Yet even here honor, glory, and shame play a role. Although one can refuse to volunteer for a forlorn hope without being thought cowardly, those who come forward may do so in part because they are jealous of their reputations for courage. And those jealous of their reputations would run the risk of shame if their prior reputations marked them as the kind others would expect to volunteer.[36] The world of supererogation is not without its own competitions for glory. Saints competed for the honor of most holy, no less than epic heroes, whose heirs the saints were, competed to be proclaimed best in battle.[37] Even those courageous souls not given to seeking glory may hold themselves to personal standards higher than the culture generally demands. Like the practicer of lonely courage, they would feel shame for not being true to their own standards. Their internal eye would visit shame upon them should they fail.

Less grandly but more interestingly, it may be that people are moved to volunteer for a forlorn hope or some other suicidal task less to avoid shame, since no shame inheres in not volunteering, than to avoid embarrassment. Imagine that a commanding officer, before the men, asks for those willing to storm the wall. Painfully awkward silence. Seconds seem like minutes, and to avoid the generally embarrassing scene some poor sensitive soul says he will volunteer, just because he cannot bear the embarrassing silence. In less dire circumstances, teachers are saved by a similar impulse in some poor student who volunteers an answer to the teacher's question solely to dispel the awkwardness of the classroom's deafening silence.

Supererogation doesn't quite free us from shame's tentacles either. I will make one last attempt to paint a courage that avoids the taint of honor and shame: Courage may be one of those virtues which is best realized not when pursued for its own sake but when it arises as a by-product of some other virtue's natural expression. Take the case of Lorenzo, an Italian mason, who lives outside the camp at Auschwitz-Birkenau in which Primo Levi suffers. He smuggles food to Levi every day without recompense, "because he was good and simple."[38] He incurs considerable risk to help his countryman, a risk he seems less concerned about than Levi does on Lorenzo's behalf. He speaks little, is not stupid, perhaps a bit strange, but indubitably decent to the core. He could be deemed rash regarding his own safety but not rash in the way of a thrill-seeker or hothead; there is no style of rashness at all; he sees a fellow Italian suffering, and he shares his food with him, no more, no less. His actions are but the expressions of his goodness and simplicity. He seems so simply good that courage is not the issue. He cannot imagine doing other than what he is doing. It may not be exactly that his goodness intercepts all perception of risk; rather his goodness makes him somewhat impervious to it, almost pushing the perception out of active consciousness. Of course he knows that if the Nazis catch him the consequences will be severe, but that knowledge does not bear on his decision to help Levi. To the extent that he lets risk affect his actions, it is to make sure that he performs them with sufficient precaution and guile so as not to get caught, because getting caught would prevent him from sustaining Levi. There are thus days when he is late delivering extra food because it would have been too dangerous to do so at the usual time.

Is Lorenzo's courage any different from Doc's in running out to save his wounded platoon mates because that is what medics do? The cases are very much alike, but Doc is a soldier in combat whose duties are necessarily dangerous. That setting does not allow courage to play a supporting role to some other virtue; courage dominates the moral terrain. One is always aware that one's capacity for it is being tested and drawn upon. The deeds that make up Lorenzo's goodness are more banal. They are individual small gestures, accumulated over weeks, a massing of homely, simple, relatively insignificant actions. He finds some extra food; he gives it to a starving man; he says an encouraging word or two. No single action of his is grand in the way Doc's actions are. But Lorenzo is courting real danger. It is not as if he is being fired at, but danger is ominously present; he is, after all, operating in a regime of terror. Is it, then, as a psychological and moral matter, his disposition for kindness that allows him to do what can also be described as acts of courage, or is it courage that comes to the rescue of his disposition for kindness? In Lorenzo's case it seems to be the former, or at least that is how Levi presents it. Lorenzo does not see himself as courageous; he does not even feel himself all that tested by the risks. He is just being Lorenzo, not unaware of the risk but not obsessed with it either. It is there as so much background against which his decency exercises itself.[39]

The same issue of indirect courage is raised by Jesus' description of that unsurpassable love of laying down one's life for one's friend. Courage in this formulation is subsumed into love, love as total self-sacrifice. Mightn't we see the motivation of those soldiers who throw themselves on grenades almost instinctively as being more centrally manifesting that Greater Love than courage, whereas the equally self-sacrificial behavior of charging an enemy machine gun is more about perfect courage than perfect love? Excepting those who in an instant fall on a grenade, courage in the conventional shame-avoidance settings of contests of honor or battle can never be a mere means to an end. It always is in some respects desired in its own right and sought after, since that is where honor lies. This is no bad thing despite the impossibly rigorous demands that certain moralists would want to impose. But in the regime of greater love, it seems honor and shame are on the back burner. It is the perfection of love that is sought, a love so great that it needn't even know or like the person who is rescued by it. Courage is how this love must reveal itself, for it has no other way. Does deliberation fit in this picture? It can, but it need not. Like Doc, you hear someone yell "Medic!" and respond to the call.

I do not want to push these musings too far; I am struggling to find one way in which it makes sense to think of a perfect, though subordinated, courage realizable outside the constraints of shame (and honor). Unlike Captain Johansen, who was concerned about the quality of his courage, people like Lorenzo and the men who fall on grenades may not have contemplated the quality of their courage or courage at all. The man who falls on a grenade has only an instant to react. But those people, like Lorenzo, who extended courageous kindness over weeks and months could not bear to think they did not have the courage to stand up to injustices they saw.[40] It is perhaps this kind of distinction making that has forever made clerks—intellectuals and academics—the object of laity's scorn that they should trouble themselves as to whether Lorenzo and others like him are best seen as kind and decent with courage aiding those virtues or as courageous in a good cause. We are blessed either way by such as they.

I 2

The Shape and Style of Courage

IN CHAPTER EIGHT we met Oliver Crediford, "a
large man, of great physical strength," and Corporal Side, "short, cross-
eyed, bandy-legged," with "a preference for boots and clothes sizes too big
for him." One was a coward, the other courageous, but against type. That is
why the authors took special care to provide these characters with a physical description. Tim O'Brien, recall, was concerned to make his beloved
Captain Johansen blond. We want to believe at some level that courage
has nothing to do with body types, that it is about will and spirit and greatness of soul, and yet that belief struggles against a deeply held contrary
belief that there is a very distinct and predictable relation between courageous or cowardly disposition and body type.

We attribute virtue to healthy and beautiful bodies and vice to ugly and
sickly ones. Even virtues that only indirectly touch on embodied existence—benevolence, graciousness, and intellectual virtues—still have to
overcome the reluctance in others to cede merit willingly to those whose
physicality displeases. We may feel guilty that we feel that way, we probably
should feel guilty that we feel that way, but in spite of two millennia of
Christian discourse to the contrary, we still understand too well the disgust
Odysseus had for thick and ugly Thersites and the mockery Hephaestus

had to endure from his divine kin for being crippled.[1] If even abstract intellectual and moral virtues seem to fit certain body types better than others, then what of those virtues and vices that implicate the body directly? Courage, cowardice, and the virtues and vices that govern sex and sexuality put the body, its urges and behaviors, front and center. Even moral courage is not disembodied; it makes little sense to us independent of metaphors and the very fact of standing tall, standing up, standing firm, of not taking it lying down.

Fat and Thin, Short and Tall

Courage and cowardice star in moral narratives, in epic, romance, tragedy, and comedy. We thus have traditions of various duration that dictate the conventional casting of them, dressing them up just right so we know them when we see them. And since there is a favored image of what the courageous person and the coward look like, ironies and comedies abound when the body is cast against moral type. We expect, and not without some reason, that the well-built, big, strong man has a body that predicts courage; the skinny, spindly guy, one that predicts timidity and probable cowardice. The short, if stocky, are also thought to be tough as nails; and not all fat means cowardice: think of the fat that graces the guts of the guys on Harleys. We distinguish, it seems, between soft fat and hard fat, the former gained by eating big through weakness of will, the latter by drinking big with a will to violence. One got chosen last in games; the other was the guy no one could bring down, the guy for whom the receipt of pain was largely hypothetical, an idea that came to him indirectly via the pleasure he took in dealing it out to others.

Fatness is considered such a vice that though we may know fat people to be tough on occasion, we are reluctant to cede them any virtue for it (few virtues are allowed the fat: joviality and perhaps generosity).[2] And it is not surprising that a medic who forfeited the love of his unit would also be fat, his other deficiencies seeming to be wholly predicted by his bodily failings: "Unfortunately Doc looked like the individual he acted. He had pimples and was overweight . . . and would not carry his load."[3] The very thickness of fat, we suspect, makes fat people insentient; they are Aristotle's Celts, too brutish to feel fear, the flesh so overwhelming the spirit that any inner life is as obstructed as we imagine the arteries of such bodies to be. So wedded are we to the moral limits of fat people that we will engage in all kinds of self-deceptions to prevent any dissonance from disrupting our commitment to what certain types of deeply moral, deeply thoughtful characters must not look like. Thus when Gertrude declares Hamlet "fat and scant of breath" during his duel with Laertes, modern editors have come to the rescue with glosses to show that "fat" meant sweaty and out of shape, but manifestly not fat.[4] Hamlet fat? No way.

There is a rather complex moral history to fatness; it was always associated with gluttony, and gluttony was never held to predict courage. And though it did not predict cowardice either, it was hardly an accident that our leading literary glutton is also our leading literary coward: Falstaff, that "obscene greasy tallow catch," "a roasted Manningtree ox with the pudding in his belly," so fat that he "lards the lean earth as he walks along," is also a "coward on instinct," a "sanguine coward," a "true bred coward."[5] Courage, remember, was the prerogative of the noble, who enjoyed their feasts, the mere fact of being able to afford to eat well being a privilege of their condition. But, as we saw with Beowulf, feasts were cast in the form of competitions in drinking and boasting, so that gluttony was enlisted to the cause of courage; the warrior feasted on his loot, the hero delighted in his drinking bouts, but they were not gluttons in the sense that a good meal ranked first among desires. Eating and drinking were foreplay to fighting (and fornicating). Courage was not denied to the hefty or even to the portly, but there were limits. A horse could bear only so much weight before it foundered.

The glutton, however, he who made his belly his God, cared not for courage or anything else that got in the way of his pursuit of culinary pleasure, tickling the palate and filling the maw. In one sense the glutton is reckless in the face of death; but his heedlessness toward his health is very different from the rashness that sends a person up Everest or diving out of airplanes. Not all kinds of risking death carry the same meaning or bear the same predictive value for courage and cowardice. On occasion, though, we might imagine the glutton mimicking courage or reckless abandon in the courageous style. Should the cook ruin his sauce, he might risk physical violence; should his table grow spare, he might undertake the risks of law-breaking to obtain the means to eat. Falstaff took to highway robbery, but in the end was too cowardly to see it through properly.

Much of the history of beauty and fashion can be summed up simply as doing what it takes not to look like the poor;[6] just having clothes that were not rags mostly did the trick up until the Industrial Revolution, but even naked bodies carried the indicia of rank. Beauty is mostly what the poor are not, to this very day. Thinness, when the lot of the poor, was hardly the virtue it has come to be among us. When the poor were skinny and emaciated, the rich were rounded and portly; when the bodies of the lower orders grew fat amidst the plenitude of cheap calories the agricultural revolution put on the table, the rich eventually responded by imposing the burdens of thinness on themselves. But this meant that portliness couldn't have been antithetical to courage, since the rich and powerful by ideology combined both, even though the hyperobesity of Falstaff already marked the gluttonous coward.

The transition that divorced fat from courage does not occur overnight. Falstaffian sorts, like Joseph Sedley in *Vanity Fair*, continue to play the role of the obese coward, but it was still possible in World War I for an upper-class officer to be both portly and brave. Such is the case of Tietjens in *Parade's End*; his portliness occasions no jokes at his expense. But by World War II the fat officer is denied moral authority. If he does well it is by way of redemption. William Manchester introduces Tubby, a fat lieutenant painted as a comic pretender to courage, only to have him instantly wasted leading a charge which no one would follow. So strong is the assumption that his fatness would lead to mirth at his death that Manchester felt obliged to record that "there was no malice in the section; they mourned him as they would any casualty."[7] Paul Fussell, however, does penance for the treatment the short and fat Second Lieutenant Abe Goldman got at his and everyone else's hands ("his arrival brought joy to every anti-Semite in the battalion"). Goldman redeems himself by showing great courage under fire and great dignity when wounded. Goldman played according to type until it mattered, and in his case Jewishness was added to the burden that shortness and fatness had already imposed on his virtue.[8]

Shift the setting to Stalin's purges, in which an interrogator with all the power in his hands failed for his fatness to frighten Eugenia Ginzburg, though admittedly she was hard to scare under any circumstances: "Bikchentayev was again ranting and thumping his desk, but I was not afraid of him. Comic roly-polies should not be appointed to these flesh-creeping jobs; they don't carry conviction."[9] But some roly-polies are not very comical, rather sinister in fact. We don't find it fit to call them roly-polies when they are. So ungenerous are our moral assessments of the fat that we are quite willing to see them as having a special talent for cruelty and perverse pleasure: not a few Roman emperors come to mind, Henry VIII, and the assorted villainous fat clerics of legend.

This is all about male bodies. We have no secure cultural rules of thumb about the shape and size of female courage. I want to reserve this discussion for later, but for now suffice it to say that it is a grim reminder just how excluded by ideology women were from the core of courage that there is no clearly favored body type that is both female and courageous that isn't substantially masculinized. Nor is courage about old bodies, male or female, which become degendered by age in any event. The old are largely nonparticipants in the courage game except at one grand moment: when called on at last to die without importuning the young with complaints.

It is not just the fat who suffer, but the short, and the thin, unless sinewy; the thin may even suffer more than the short if they are tall and hence step into the category of geekiness. Tallness, however, usually is a savior, mostly for the fat (and by definition for the short). For if a fat person is also tall, he is metamorphosed into "big," which reopens all kinds of moral possibility. If the fat are also politically powerful they command deference for their power if not for their fat, as the case of Winston Churchill might attest. Power transforms fat into what the Germans call *stattlich*, which English only partly captures by a combination of "portly" and "imposing." Those whose bodies lower expectations regarding the courageous possibility of the soul they house—the skinny, the fat, the short, the physically inept, the old, the feminine, the effeminate—should also be the beneficiaries of those low expectations by being excused from the demands of courage altogether, yet it is not clear that such is the case.

Jean Améry, an unprepossessing physical specimen, tortured by the Gestapo, admits he would have revealed anything to get the pain to stop; alas, he had no secrets to reveal. Can physically weak types like himself, he wonders, get to excuse their moral failure because of their physical weakness? "If we agree to a reduction to the purely physiological," he says, "then we run the risk of finally pardoning every kind of whiny reaction and physical cowardice." We cannot excuse the cowardice of the physically unendowed, at least not completely, and we don't, for even if we excuse them somewhat we still hold them and their failures in contempt. "But," continues Améry, "if we exclusively stress the so-called moral resistance, then we would have to measure a weakly seventeen-year-old gymnasium pupil who fails to withstand torture by the same standards as an athletically built thirty-year-old laborer who is accustomed to manual work and hardships." Can that be fair? He throws up his hands in despair. Having been tortured himself, torture suggests to him only bitter images of impotence, mental and physical: "We had better let the question rest, just as at that time I myself did not further analyze my power to resist, when, battered and with my hands still shackled, I lay in the cell and ruminated."[10]

But when wretched physical specimens do great things it is a matter of special note. Corporal Side was not the only mismatched marvel in the unit of Mark VII. Mark's memoir can be read as a hagiography of a certain Jackson, "that little wisp of a man," his best NCO. Jackson is remarkable for enduring, for keeping cheerful under the most appalling conditions, and for never thinking of himself:

> I bid him good night . . . thinking of heroism and wherein it con-
> sists. This is the unostentatious kind. Here's a wisp of a man with
> a permanently troublesome knee. He has just come from
> trenches, said to be worse than Ypres in 1914, where he has done
> two men's work, besides helping crocks out of the mud, support-
> ing them and carrying their rifles. Under the foulest conditions
> his spirits have never flagged . . . Now, when by all the laws of
> Nature he ought to have dropped half-dead, he has appointed
> himself to the role of Florence Nightingale, and has not even left
> himself room to lie down. I cannot sleep for thinking of him.[11]

Jackson's courage is feminized in Mark's mind, not just because he cares for the men, nurses them and endures, but because he is but "a wisp of a man." Yet Jackson does not suffer moral diminution for being thus feminized. Quite the contrary.

But woe to the person whose body marks him for grand things who then turns tail, for he must suffer more than the disgrace that awaits the average coward; he must suffer the joy his failure gives to those who have always felt themselves diminished in his presence, envious of his physical-ity. Abner Small cannot disguise a certain mean delight at the failure of a towering "Apollo-like" creature to make it through the training period, with "his step, his confidence; and a new-born scowl and close mouth denot[ing] firmness and courage . . . bristl[ing] all over with fight."[12] The middling and scrawny love it when the big and brawny collapse in terror.

And rather than own up to the meanness that informs this delight, they justify it as Goliath getting his comeuppance. Rifleman Bowlby, hardly a hero himself, is not quite displeased that Meredith, the biggest brawler in the company, is so scared of getting killed that he won't join the attack. William Manchester follows suit in delighting in the collapse of the unit tough guy under artillery fire, and even though he had nothing but contempt for his fat lieutenant, as we saw, he insisted that those "good athletes" with their perfect bodies fought no better than "ectomorphs and endomorphs." Manchester takes care to note too that though he was nicknamed Slim for his slight build, he was known in his unit for the enviable size of his virile member.[13] Some body parts, it is believed, can compensate for the shortcomings of others.

We are meant to conclude that the playing fields of Eton, which were believed to have made those undeniably good English officers what they were, were not about training bodies, but about getting the right frame of mind into whatever body one brought to the game. But might we also not understand the special terror Japanese and Vietnamese soldiers prompted in their Western opponents as gaining a boost from their smaller bodies, which were perceived as perversely related to the amount of courage and martial energy they brought to bear? Yet, however justifiable, so tenacious are the beliefs about the relation of body type to courage that they have unabashedly survived the equalizing power of force multipliers like guns. The trigger finger of a ninety-eight-pound weakling should be as effective as a body builder's. But the skinny guy with a gun remains ineffably what he is, overcompensating for his lack of natural endowment, trying too hard, playing the fool. Only the gun is deferred to, until he reveals himself truly to be a man of courage burdened by having been miscast as to body type, a David with a sling. The big guy with a gun may also be seen as overdoing it, but not as overcompensating for overdoing it. Something else seems to be driving this reluctance to let guns democratize courage across all body types; I suspect that we hold some deeply primitive belief that the paradigmatic test of courage is in hand-to-hand fighting, a pitting of the unmediated strength of one human against another, not a testing of nerve carried out at long range. Our intuitions war with each other on this: we think of courage as embodied in strong bodies but then discount the courage of those with strong bodies because it comes easier to them for being strong.

Class, Profession, and Toughness

Few would doubt that the miner and longshoreman are tougher and more likely to be courageous than the accountant and adman. We also cherish the belief that courage and cowardice map themselves on to professions and even on to specialties within professions, thus holding the issue of class constant. Within the rarified physical world of the academy, who would not expect anthropologists and archaeologists to stand a better chance of courage than literature professors or computer scientists? Indiana Jones is thus cast as an archaeologist, not only because that provides the excuse to send him to exotic places, but because his physical prowess would be unimaginable if his professional life preferred libraries to the outdoors, airy ideas to material artifacts. The success among academics of Robert Parker's tough detective Spenser owes much to the delightful fantasies generated by a bibliophile who can kick the living daylights out of the uneducated. And further down the ladder, do we not expect the truck driver or butcher to be more the warrior than the baker or the confectioner?

Mark VII, again marveling at the disjuncture of body type and courage, describes the company sergeant major, a "tall, thin, dark man . . . with a long hooked nose and a slight stoop." But "he wears the DCM [Distinguished Conduct Medal]." And his captain informs Mark that "he is the bravest man in the regiment." He brought in fourteen prisoners single-handed on 1 July. He is a confectioner with a young wife and child.[14] This CSM looks anything but a hero, no doubt because he suggests a Jew, and he is a confectioner to boot.[15] The Medal of Honor citation of Eric Gibson, which is sufficiently remarkable for its aggressive grandness of action, leaps out from among 3,000 others because Gibson was the company cook.[16] And no one was braver, even to the point of crazed rashness, than Siegfried Sassoon, poet. Graves records that Sassoon was especially motivated to keep up "the good reputation of the poets as men of courage."[17] The idea of poets as men of courage might sound laughable to us, yet there was once a time, which romantic poets like Byron tried to recapture, that recognized that the inspiration that prompted poetry would also prompt battle glory (just as battle prompted some of the greatest poetry). King David and the Viking Egil Skallagrímsson, among others, were not only their people's greatest warriors but also their most renowned poets.[18]

The comedy of the inappropriate incarnations of courage and cowardice has an overtly political dimension. Body types (and obviously professions and jobs) are not randomly distributed across class and ethnic boundaries. Just as we know today that the fat are not likely to be as educated, as wealthy, or as from California as the thin, so in Britain the wispiness of a Jackson or the bandy-leggedness of a Side predicted their class fairly well. The diminutive stature of the English lower orders, the miserable fruit of industrialization, is frequently observed in memoirs of the Great War, as indeed is their sorry contrast with the tall Germans; height requirements were lowered more than once during the war so as to be able to replace the slaughtered legions. In March 1915 a Bantam Division of men between five feet and five feet three inches had been organized (the previous minimum had been five feet three inches, which had shortly before been reduced from five feet five inches, which in turn had been reduced from five feet eight inches).[19]

The incarnation of courageous and cowardly possibility reproduces the antagonisms embedded in the social hierarchy. Bigness did not predict courage when, depending on the precise period, it came in the guise of an Irishman or an American country bumpkin, to say nothing of blacks. Soldiers from the towns make sure to note every big country bumpkin that collapses in tears; good farmers find the city toughs first to run in battle. James McPherson discovers a "remarkable unanimity" in the letters home of Civil War soldiers of middle-class background discussing the cowardice of street bullies: "It isn't the brawling, fighting man at home that stands the bullet's whistle the best"; "Roughs that are always ready for street fighting are cowards on the open battle field."[20]

One can assume that much of this is very selective vision. The range of performance in battle within any class or profession varied from heroic to craven with enough instances at either pole to confirm or disconfirm any prejudice. We have examples of the delightful mayhem wrought on ideological complacency by unavoidably grand performances by people who were not supposed to give them. Lord Moran laments the day universal conscription brought such "plainly worthless fellows," "the worst product of the towns," into settings where their "bad stock" revealed itself plainly. Good soldiers "are not bred from bad stock." But what to do when the bravery of the "cockney soldier" becomes a legend, that is, when city toughs turned out to make very good soldiers?[21]

Never doubt the resilience of upper-class complacency. If the cockney's stock goes up, upper-class stock does not go into decline. The upper class just goes ahead and takes the credit. Thus, for instance, the unspoken import of Wellington's famous remark that his men were "the scum of the earth, mere scum of the earth" was that he could turn such scum into the world-beating soldiers that they were.[22] Much of the increase in value of the cockney soldier in Moran's case comes at the expense of middle-class stock, especially those segments of the middle class who see themselves as models of probity and prudence but are seen in turn by their social superiors, in Yeats's hostile image for them, as contemptible adders of the half pence to the pence. The qualities that led to their peacetime success, their risk aversion and selfishness, are exactly what lower the value of their stock in war. The lordly classes in Britain, when Moran was writing in the 1940s, were not yet willing to accept the self-serving claims of heroism more consistent with American capitalist ideology, which considers the "entrepreneurial risk" of investing in some Silicon Valley startup rather than in government bonds to be a sovereign predictor of the kind of recklessness and toughness needed to make it in battle.

There is so much at stake in these beliefs that the truth will never be forthcoming. We still cling to a belief, shared by the objects of it, that the lower orders are tougher than the higher. Isn't this the view God takes when he has Gideon assemble his shock force from those who lap up water at the brook with their tongues? He is not just looking for bestial berserks, but for those who flunk the test of good manners, the vulgar, knowing full well that the odds are that these are men whose vulgar toughness you can trust in battle.

By using the word "tough," we withhold some of the virtue that goes with courage. Like Pericles' view that Spartan misery makes for Spartan toughness and that their bravery was not as praiseworthy as that "natural" Athenian courage that was not undone by the good life, the better-off want to think that the worse-off come by their courage not as a demonstration of their virtuous character, but by Pavlovian conditioning. Toughness, a mere semblance of courage, has been thrust upon them by inurement, and since when does the hand get praised for getting callused, though surely that callus is more praiseworthy than the soft hands of one who quits when he gets his first blister. Lacking Pericles' reasons for denigrating Spartan virtue, we are now more willing to see Spartan toughness as the meritorious end of a chosen regime of self-denial, dedication, and commitment. When, however, the toughness is that of our own lower orders, we see them as anything but Spartan-like: they made no choices; they were put into mean streets and learned the way of them. Yet the norms of democracy make it harder for us to deny so complacently the courage of the low, to exclude them from courage by definition, as the medieval lords did their peasants, and the Homeric heroes did Thersites and their slaves. Is it some form of democratic compromise that recognizes the virtue of toughness, readily concedes it to the lower orders, honestly envies them for it even while suspecting that it limits the possibility for a richly imaginative inner life or is the result of having none?

For the most part we collapse toughness into courage and have no need to distinguish the two, except when, acting like competitive Greeks, we want to determine whose courage is most praiseworthy—the intrepid enlisted man's or his equally brave officer's, the street-fighter's or the corporate whistle-blower's. Self-serving as it is, there is something about the Periclean position that does not go away so easily. When a different kind of conditioning, the playing fields of Eton and all that, produced the extraordinary stiff-upper-lipped bravery of the young subalterns who endured the trenches of the Great War, we do not hesitate to call them brave, as evidencing the truest virtue; not just tough, for often they were not tough, just brave. Is it the most blatant class bias to do honor to the playing fields but to begrudge the mean streets the virtues they give the lower orders, seeing one as revealing the benefits of cultivation, the other as yielding mere inurement to suffering? The unequal distribution of medals among officers and men would suggest no small amount of bias. But less sinister may be that the bias is also supported by a belief that the better-off have overcome more to produce actions as grand as those of their men. We grant them extra credit for having to overcome refinement and a soft life to do courage's dirty work.

The fact remains, however, that the people most likely to be at the sharp end are not the well educated and comfortable. A platoon leader in Vietnam puts it this way:

> In vain I looked for the archetypal platoon of romantic fiction. The kid from Brooklyn wasn't there . . . The incipient poet never made it. The rich mama's boy out to prove his manhood stayed home . . . The selection process continued for the unfortunates drafted so that those with some education or particular skills would be diverted from combat service. Even among those who made it to Vietnam, the vast majority never saw combat. Only those without skill, without schooling, and without friends, or

those who were obstinate in the face of ceaseless proselytizing against their obligation to serve, made it to the field.[23]

In Britain, it is the men of Ulster, the Clyde, the highlands;[24] while in America, and depending on the war, they are the blacks, Hispanics, poor southern whites, Irish, Slavic, and Italian city toughs, all versions of Wellington's scum of the earth who for all their failings made great soldiers and fighters.

The American white middle class generally believes that race and ethnicity predict toughness, if not quite courage; blacks are assumed to be tougher than whites, and among whites anyone is believed to be tougher than Jews unless they are Israelis, who within a generation inverted the stereotype of Jewish diasporan effeminacy and passivity into that of the Sabra soldier, efficient, cool, and not to be messed with. That transformation was also understood to effect a change in body types. The cultivated lack of physicality and pallor of the yeshiva *bocher* gave way to the cultivated dark physicality of the Sabra, and martial virtue followed as the night the day.[25] We are more than willing to grant that bodily size and shape are not perfect predictors of courage, yet we refuse to think that they have no predictive value. Strong bodies provide the basis for confidence, and confidence, from Aristotle onward, has been considered part of courage's anatomy; healthy, strong bodies make their possessors optimistic and thereby help undo some bases for fear. And we believe they are more likely to come through despite Montaigne's belief that such natural endowments have nothing to do with true courage.

Courage and Complaint

Courage can be quiet or vocal. We have already touched on the differences between tight-lipped, terse styles—the sagas and Clint Eastwood—and the more verbose and rhapsodic styles of Beowulf, the Homeric heroes, or the trash-talk of the dozens and rap. But can courage whine? Can it even complain? Here, as in so much else, context is crucial, but there are some plausible cases to be made for absolutes nonetheless. No complaint, no matter how justified, can be stated in a whining tone without undoing the virtue of the speaker's position. Could Achilles, sulking in his tent because he was wronged by Agamemnon's high-handedness, possibly have presented his claim in a whining and wheedling tone? Would the Greeks have suffered that, even from him? Wouldn't he have had to make his complaint pass as a complaint and not a whine? Yet Homer describes him as crying, and when Odysseus and others try to placate him he pouts and rehearses several times his grievances while refusing Agamemnon's splendid reparations.[26] It is partly our suspicions that he was whining that make Hector so much more attractive for modern readers. Those heroes, however, had very selective filters on their ears, so that the complaints of lowly Thersites are heard as a whine, while Achilles' whining is heard as a complaint.

So anxious, however, are some styles of courage to avoid anything approaching the unseemliness of whining that they eschew all complaint. In fact one prevalent view of courage is that it is nothing more than not complaining. Modern war forced this style upon the soldier. In Eisenhower's formulation, courage, "real heroism," is "the uncomplaining acceptance of unendurable conditions."[27] And though the style of noncomplaint maps on to the courage of endurance, perseverance, and patience, it is not unique to it. Noncomplaint can also be a feature of aggressive courage. In the saga world, for instance, the assertion of a claim does not take the form of complaint so much as of threat or of ominous prediction as to what will happen should the rightful order not be reestablished.

Complaint can be consistent with courage, can even be courage itself when it is made to a hostile authority or to a powerful enemy who is the source of the misery complained about and from whom the risk of retaliation for the complaint is real. But to complain to those who have no causal connection to one's misery starts to be heard as a whine no matter how deeply and elegantly intoned. And to repeat complaints, no matter how justified, also transforms complaint into wheedling and whining. We try to exempt those incessant complaints we make to God by larding them with praise and gratitude and calling them prayers, but one suspects that enduring incessant complaint is the burden God must suffer for wanting worshipful humans.

In the unfathomable degradation and misery of death camp and gulag, what moral basis could there be for complaints that would only be heard by others whose misery was as great as the complainer's? Those who did not complain were praised for it. Milena, in a German camp, "never wasted a single word on her own suffering."[28] Those who did were blamed: Mina, in the misery of a cattle car in its month-long journey across Siberia, "complained a good deal about her ailments, and this was not popular in the car, where the unwritten law was 'Suffer in silence.' We all of us in fact had plenty to complain of."[29] Do not blame their lack of pity: "Before we can feel much for others, we must in some measure be at ease ourselves," writes the subtlest theorist of sympathy, Adam Smith.[30] A death camp survivor concurs: "One unhappy man doesn't pity another."[31] In gulag and lager there is no distinguishing noncomplaining toughness from courage; they become congruent. Just as there is a recklessness that is inseparable from the courage of aggression, so the courage of noncomplaint has its own form of recklessness. Vera Brittain, working as a nurse's aid during the Great War, laments the death of a young soldier whose preventable death was due "to an over-conscientious determination to endure; he had refused to complain until too late."[32]

The reputations of various ethnic groups concerning their propensity for complaint are well known. A norm for noncomplaint can exist equally in cultures characterized by individualism—the English with their stiff upper lips, for instance—and by suppression of the individual into the group. Again the Japanese set a standard, incomprehensible to those, like myself, raised in a culture and class in which pain is mostly avoidable and voluntary, and complaint rewarded. From Hersey's *Hiroshima*:

> To Father Kleinsorge, an Occidental, the silence in the grove by the river, where hundreds of gruesomely wounded suffered together, was one of the most dreadful and awesome phenomena of his whole experience. The hurt ones were quiet; no one wept, much less screamed in pain; no one complained; none of the many who died did so noisily; not even the children cried; very few people even spoke. And when Father Kleinsorge gave water to some whose faces had been almost blotted out by flash burns, they took their share and then raised themselves a little and bowed to him, in thanks.[33]

Can't we imagine a person who in important matters is the model of courage itself, who can suffer intense pain and face serious danger without giving way to fear, who nonetheless is a hypochondriac on a daily basis, fretful, complaining about lack of sleep and niggling pains?[34] Contrast that person with the person who when ill remains cheerful, who complains not at all, who pretends to feeling well without expecting to be congratulated for it, who actually succeeds in masking just how lousy he feels, but who is extremely risk averse and when exposed to danger tends to be easily frightened. Neither type argues well for that idealized courageous disposition that never fails either in substance or in style, and neither is an implausible character type, not even rare. Just more problems for a unified theory of virtue. We prefer our heroes not to fuss about a hangnail, not to whine, yet we must acknowledge that courage often plays against type; courageous people can't all be blond and reticent like Johansen.

Suppose, however, that focusing on small and immediate annoyances serves as a coping mechanism that staves off despair and insensibility. Whining and niggling help shore up the soul against grand despair. Hence the chronic grumbling and griping of soldiery from the beginning of time. Grumbling about cold, heat, forced marches, and fatigue had none of the stigma of openly owning up to fear.[35] Grumbling, however, is not whining. Grumbling bound the men together and helped preserve their spirit; whining does no such thing. Tone of voice is all-important in determining how charitable we are willing to be to such ways of coping. As for those non-complaining types who never trouble others about their own chronic pains and discomforts, they build up so much goodwill that we cut them all kinds of slack should they show some unseemly risk aversion.

Style matters a lot, especially when courage becomes more a matter of defense than of offense, more about taking it than about dishing it out. Patience and endurance are nine-tenths a matter of style; it is, after all, mostly about suffering *in silence*. The hypochondriac, the complainer, the whiner do not qualify as good stoics or Christians, but the courage of aggression should still be available to them, as it was for that chronic complainer Achilles (and Egil in the saga world). Hypochondria, complaining, whining are not cowardice; they do not augur running away; they are their own distinct vices, ones, in fact, that exasperate us so much that we are rather uncharitable to those who have them—so uncharitable that we may even call them cowards, unless, like Stonewall Jackson, a noted hypochondriac, their fearlessness in battle is so great as to give them inexhaustible credit to purchase indulgence for their hypochondria. Still, whining is to the ear, it seems, as fat is to the eye; those vices that annoy or disgust are often more stiffly punished, though informally, than those vices that we know to be of greater moral and practical moment, like faithlessness and cowardice. To the extent that cowardice is failure under *big* pressure, we are more willing to understand how easy it is to succumb, especially when natural aversions to pain and death are the forces to be overcome. But we expect everyone to face up to little things when the pain and discomfort are merely annoying and life is not seriously threatened. Cowardice may be more excusable than being a pain in the ass.

Finally, what about the person who, after acquitting himself acceptably, the danger now passed, collapses in tears or hysterical laughter, trembling, even vomiting or befouling himself? Has he revealed himself as less courageous by not maintaining his self-control until all the inner turmoil the danger prompted has subsided, or does all demand on his self-command cease with the passing of the danger? The answer will depend to some extent on our understanding of the psychology of the postdanger collapse, on our view of the moral psychology of courage, and on our narrative theory of courage. If acts of courage are stories with beginnings, middles, and ends, when does the end occur? When the danger has been faced and dealt with? Or does the story require that the camera stay on the person to see if he behaves with proper dignity afterward, by showing suitable regard to modesty rules or to the norms of bodily control? Those who want a colder, wiser, more prudent courage will prefer a more controlled ending, but I bet most of us would find a final scene of collapse touching, a sign of just how much this person is still one of us. The legs of the helicopter pilot, mentioned earlier, giving out as they did, reveal to us, but even more clearly to him, the physical and psychic costs of what he had done. If he did not know until then, it was only because he needed his legs to tell him.

I 3

The Emotional Terrain: Fear, Hope, Despair

FEAR—OF DEATH, of pain, of disgrace—is the main ground of courage. Fear is obviously just as crucial to the psychology of cowardice, though not exclusively, as we saw with those fearlessly shameless cowards. But other emotions also have a place in the domain of courage: anger, vengefulness, shame, embarrassment, relief, hope, confidence, despair, indifference, disgust, pity, sorrow, grief, caring, love, boredom, and the absence of all affect—insensibility. Some of these emotions are an aid to courage in its dealings with fear; some, like disgust, are as likely to defeat courage as fear is. Many of these emotions can play both sides of the fence. Fear can impel fight as well as flight. "Love can make cowards of the brave and heroes of the timid."[1] Despair can lead to complete torpor and lassitude or, by stimulating other emotions, impel a berserk charge. Grief and sorrow can motivate surrender or revenge.

My account of courage so far has already had much to do with fear, directly and by implication. How could it not? But I need to say more here about fear and fear management; in the next chapter I will take up some other sentiments that aid, threaten, or otherwise impinge upon courage: disgust, anger, and relief.

Fear in Heaven

It is next to impossible to imagine what human consciousness would look like without fear playing a fairly large role. What would life be like with no fear of the unknown, of death, of nonbeing? Fear helps animate the world, making us feel the world's fascination and thrill as well as its power and danger.[2] Our very sense of aliveness seems inseparable from our fears. Some low-intensity fears may even be prerequisites to reasoned decision making. It has been demonstrated, for instance, that the ability to act on perceptions of risk requires some intuition that "something's up," a vague kind of apprehensive hunch, a mild foreboding.[3] It has also been supposed that alertness and fear are just points on a continuum of arousal that is part of what it means to be sentient and clued in.[4] This reaffirms Demosthenes' view, articulated to his ragtag band awaiting the Spartan seaborne assault, that fearfulness may be connected to intelligence in some nonrandom way. Nietzsche saw a different kind of virtue in humankind's fearfulness: it fuels our fearsomeness: "And has the world not lost some of its charm for us because we have grown less fearful? With this diminution of our fearfulness has our own dignity and solemnity, our own *fearsomeness*, not also diminished?"[5] Nietzsche's fear is that with no fear come bland complacency and torpor. Most others fear the opposite, that without fear there would be nothing but violence, disorder, and unlimited aggressive self-assertion. "Nothing civilizes a Man equally as his Fear," writes Bernard Mandeville in the early eighteenth century.[6]

Fear seems so much a part of what it means to be human that to see Jesus as fully human we have to believe him capable of fear; we may even have to see him afraid. Three of the gospels oblige us. He fears in Gethsemane: "O my Father, if it be possible, let this cup pass from me."[7] The cup is his martyrdom. This passage threw Origen, in the third century, into a tizzy. "Someone," he says, "who did not examine the meaning of Scripture closely might think that . . . even the Savior was afraid in the hour of the passion. But if he was afraid, one might say, who ever was courageous?"[8] Christ a coward? For Origen, courage is not about overcoming fear; courage means being fearless. Origen must make considerable use of his substantial exegetical talents to absolve Christ of what to his mind is cowardice. But others continued to make impious intimations about Jesus' courage. It was reported that when the humanist Lucilio Vanini was being led to the stake in 1619 to be burned as a heretic for his atheistical views, he uttered, in

Mandeville's estimation, a "Sentence too execrable to be mention'd." It was this: "Christ sweated in cowardly [*imbellis*] fear at his end, I die without fear."[9] Vanini's tongue was cut out before he was burned. Most of us would not share Origen's anxiety or think to blaspheme as Vanini did, for we would grant that most courage, the kind available to common nonheroic humanity, means doing battle with fear.

If the human experience is unfathomable without fear, must it also be the case that to experience heavenly bliss we need to carry the capacity for fear, if not fear itself, to heaven? The question occurred to Thomas Aquinas, who asked "whether fear remains in heaven."[10] The psychology of heavenly bliss is not easy to fathom. Whence comes the pleasure in heaven if there is no ache of desire? What of the "joys" of relief that depend upon the recent cessation of pain, threat, or the avoidance of disaster? Does one experience relief the first moment in heaven knowing one is not in hell, but never again? Must there then be traces of pain in heaven too? One long-lived tradition supposes that some portion of the joys of the blessed in heaven lies in contemplating the pains of the damned in hell.[11] Pleasure, the view was, requires some contrastive state in order to be understood and felt as pleasure. That's why orgasm can't last; if it did it would simply become a new benchmark that would soon either bore or cloy. The pleasure of watching the damned, though, amuses only if there is some memory or some capacity for imagining and indeed sympathizing with their agony. How can the blessed understand the pains of the damned enough to delight in their suffering or to be relieved that it is not their own lot if they cannot, at least imaginatively, experience their torment, anguish, despair, and horror? In this kind of heaven, the idea of fear (and relief) is alive and well: "The everlasting punishments of the wicked will not be altogether useless," says Aquinas, "because the elect rejoice . . . that they have escaped [such torments]."[12]

Even the decorous Aquinas can't quite disguise that the elect's rejoicing in their own good fortune is part *Schadenfreude*, a perfect German word to name the pleasure we take in another's misfortune. But that does not mean the elect need fear except in a hypothetical way. Aquinas concedes that there is an attenuated fear in heaven, a perfected "filial fear," which is the fear of giving offense to paternal authority. It is distinguished from "servile fear," which is fear of punishment. Servile fear is banished from heaven, "since such a fear is excluded by the security which is essential to everlasting happiness." Filial fear, though not banished, is present only in shadowy form since the evil that is feared filially, the "non-subjection to God," though possible in nature, is "impossible in the state of bliss."[13]

Can servile fear really be completely banished, as Aquinas claims? How can filial fear not suggest the possibility of servile fear, the fear of God punishing failures in proper displays of deference and obedience, failures, that is, in showing the proper respect of filial fear? Is there no collective memory in heaven of Satan's disobedience and of what happened to him? Are the blessed, unlike the fallen angels, utterly untemptable?[14] Aquinas argues for "the security of everlasting happiness," but is there nothing the blissful souls can do to forfeit that security? Wouldn't the memory of Satan's sad tale give them some anxiety that they might have forbidden thoughts? With that anxiety fear has its foothold in heaven. Aquinas does not agree with the gist of these rhetorical questions. The case can be made that heavenly bliss is such that it is secure against any worry of giving offense to God. The fear would be more the fear of letting someone down whom you desperately loved. But if that's the case, then guilt and regret make their way into heaven too, which is also something to be feared. If heaven is to house identifiably human souls, some form of fear must be there even if only of an attenuated filial kind.

With fear thus transformed by the state of bliss, what happens to courage? By one view, it disappears with the rough-and-tumble occasions that call it forth in this life. Courage is a virtue that depends on scarcity, danger, death, and pain. More than any other virtue, courage is unintelligible without embodied existence. And for many, even for some who may have been courageous, the precise attraction of eternal bliss is that it eliminates the need for courage. One suspects, however, that Satan's disobedience was in fact a *sin* of courage. It is not just that heaven lacks the conditions and opportunities necessary for courage; it is that courage there is not a virtue at all, but absolutely a vice. In heaven courage can manifest itself only in disobedience.[15] Yet even if all possibility for true courage has been removed from the heavenly scene, do not the souls understand what courage is? Are they tempted by remembrances of its glorious presence on earth? If the souls understand and enjoy watching the sufferings of the damned, might they not also possess enough imagination to fantasize courageous possibility in heaven? But that way rebellion lies, and the souls, evidently, are unable to entertain that thought, nonsubjection to God being impossible in the state of bliss. By expelling Satan, God confirmed that courage had no place in heaven except as a memory.

Fear of This and That

We are rather promiscuous in our use of the word "fear," and this is true for more than English speakers. The same problems arise in Latin, for instance. We say, "I'm afraid that it might rain tomorrow," simply to voice a preference; no fear is felt.[16] The construction "I'm afraid that" or "I fear that" has fear operating as a modal verb on the order of "prefer," "wish," "would." This is, needless to say, not the terrain of courage. True visceral fear can also be understood to embody a preference—the desire to escape or obliterate the source of fear—but it is something more than a mere indication of a preference, for it grabs us and threatens to take over. Yet even visceral fear encompasses a domain larger than the domain of courage and cowardice. Courage is about big fears only and then only about those of a certain dignity. Aristotle, remember, limited it to fears of death in battle. We are willing to expand it beyond battle, but at some point we understand the expansion to have moved us into a world of metaphor, a world of virtual courage, even farce, as when images of battle and attack, courage and cowardice, are wedded perfectly to courtship and seduction, scary though they may be.[17]

Fear is a genus that includes many species.[18] Many of these species we have words for, like dread, fright, trepidation, angst, anxiety, horror, terror, panic, awe, respect, consternation, dismay, alarm, the sense of foreboding, ominousness, the heebie-jeebies. Some of these fears are positioned on a scale of varying intensity; some reveal fear's strange connection with worshipfulness, respect, and hierarchy, as in the sense of being God-fearing. Anxiety is usually thought to indicate a generalized unfocused fear whose object is unknown. By degrees it comes to subsume the fear of the other shoe dropping, of being set up for a fall when absolutely nothing seems to be threatening at all. Fear seems to have different feels depending on its precise basis. I experience, for instance, the fear I have of someone who can beat me up physically differently from the fear I have of someone who can beat me up mentally; the respectfulness in each case is felt differently. There are also all those fears with no ready nonscientific name that we distinguish by their various objects, sometimes as phobias: fears of cats, rats, bats, dogs, bogs, mice, lice, heights, flights, water, worms, sex, speed, space, race, constraint, cocktail parties, office hours, old friends, Friday the 13th, and fat.

Take fear of the dark: it is more than just terror, apprehension, and dread; it has so many nooks and crannies, it is its own entity. Nor do we escape it by falling asleep. Our dreams make sure of that. Fear in its various forms, along with frustration, is one of the more dominant affects of our dream life.[19] No matter how safe the streets or how remote the possibility of war, we face grim and gruesome tests once we fall asleep. In dreams we enact situations that demand courage. We are accosted, we are in war, in the camps. And we fail; when we turn tail and run, our dream feet leaden, stuck in dream mud, laboring in slow motion, we fear the dream is something more than a dream, that it is predicting fairly astutely what we suspect our behaviors would be were we ever asked to fight a real war or stand up against waking injustice. It's when the dream is a happy one in which we rout the enemy, save our children and parents, stand up to the concentration camp guard, and win the damsel that we know, right as it is happening, that we are in a dream. The knowledge that our courage is but a fantasy makes our good dreams sources of embarrassment.

Like fear of the dark, fear of death is a large house with many rooms. And it is probably evolutionarily adaptive that this is the case. First fear death as death, then worry about discriminating precisely about whether you most fear death by drowning, starvation, asphyxiation, piercing, beating, stomping, falling, freezing, burning, artillery shell, or rifle bullet.[20] As encompassing as the fear of death is, however, it does not wholly include other focused object fears. These have their own structures that involve more than the fear of death. Fear of strangers is not only about fear of death; it involves the more complex set of dangers that an undomesticated human poses. Fear of pain will even send some to seek death to avoid it. Torturers, the true experts on these matters, thus take great care to deny their victims any easy means of killing themselves.

Our fear systems do not always discriminate that carefully between dangerousness and frighteningness. True, frighteningness has to be a pretty good indicator of dangerousness or our fear systems would be without selective advantage. But it is far from perfect. Degrees of danger often require analysis, close attention, refined judgments, and careful application of reason; frighteningness is an irrational but hasty judgment that makes up in speed what it lacks in refinement.[21] One World War II study found that soldiers did not always fear weaponry to the degree it posed a risk of death. Only 38 percent of the men rated as most frightening the same weapon that they rated most dangerous.[22] Stuka dive-bombers were one of the most feared but one of the least lethal in number of deaths caused. The shriek of their engines spooked the men. Once a weapon gets a merited reputation for lethality, however, it becomes feared even if it doesn't shriek, as with the notoriously effective German 88mm gun.

Most often frighteningness works quite well as a surrogate for dangerousness. The most dangerous weapons also figured very highly on everyone's most fearful list. Still, the sad fact that the experience of wolves and Jews attests to is that the costs of the mismatch in perceptions between dangerousness and frighteningness are borne less often by the misperceiving frightened person than by the unfortunate object of his fright.

Contagious Fear

Fear, as noted in Chapter 7, is contagious.[23] If the contagion is especially virulent and spreads rapidly, we speak of panic. Someone else's fear can put us into a state of alarm, unless we are certain that whatever is frightening him poses no risk to us. And the state of alarm is its own kind of fear. Once we are alarmed or given over to fear we are very susceptible to interpreting events in line with our worst expectations. Thus it is that in battle, any unexplained rapid movement to the rear can set off a panic. S. L. A. Marshall tells of a general flight triggered by a sergeant who hastened back to the aid station to get attention for a wound he had just received. Any "precipitate motion in the wrong direction is an open invitation to disaster."[24]

The effects of fear's contagion, though reasonably adaptive to small hominid groups a million years ago, had to be prevented in battle; otherwise armies threatened to disintegrate into panicked crowds. Images of contagion thus prompt images and strategies of inoculation. These shots in the arm stung. Philip Caputo witnessed a tough sergeant curse and kick the living daylights out of a marine veteran who collapsed in tears sobbing that he couldn't take any more combat:

> Sergeant Horne bulled up to the marine, kicked him in the ribs, and pulled him to his feet . . . Horne's face was scarlet and fierce beneath its flaring moustache. He shook the marine violently. "You're a fucking coward, but you're going and you'll take it. You'll take it as long as I do." Holding the man by the front of the shirt, he shook him like a rag doll. "YOU HEAR THAT, YOU FUCKING COWARD? YOU'LL TAKE IT AS LONG AS I DO." And none of us did a thing to stop Horne because we felt the same terror. And we knew that that kind of fear was a

contagion and the marine a carrier. So, shake the hell out of him, Sergeant Horne. Beat him, kick him, beat that virus out of him before it spreads.

The medicine worked. The marine recovered, his fear of battle overcome by a greater fear of the big, bull-chested Horne.[25]

Caputo presents one kind of bitter medicine against fear's contagiousness. Fear can prove to be its own sovereign remedy, the more immediate fear canceling the more remote. "The fear of today," says a character in Raymond Chandler's *The Little Sister*, "always overrides the fear of tomorrow."[26] Primo Levi speaks of how the most immediate misery blocks perception of the remoter one, which continues to run in the background. "Human nature is such that grief and pain—even simultaneously suffered—do not add up as a whole in our consciousness, but hide, the lesser behind the greater, according to a definite law of perspective . . . And if the most immediate cause of stress comes to an end, you are grievously amazed to see that another one lies behind."[27]

New fears can replace earlier fears or merely block them for a time. Sometimes, too, the sight of fright in others can work to alleviate the misery of fearing simply by justifying one's fear. When Eugene Sledge, scared out of his wits, saw the hollow terror in the eyes "of those fine Guadalcanal and Cape Gloucester veterans . . . I no longer felt ashamed of my trembling hands and almost laughed at myself with relief."[28] His is not a rare response to fear-stricken looks in others; his fear likes knowing it is shared by select others, for though he still fears, he no longer feels foolish for fearing.

Aristotle addressed directly the issue of whose frightened looks should relax you and whose should cause you alarm. It depends on relative social rank. You should not feel fear, he says, when those to whom you think yourself superior do not feel it.[29] And by necessary implication a look of fear on the face of your superiors will have an irresistibly contagious power. Does a child forget the face of her terrified parent? War correspondent A. J. Liebling found two kinds of person consoling in a dangerous time: "those who are completely courageous, and those who are more frightened than you are."[30] In contrast, Michael Herr was not very consoled by those who showed no fear as they were about to hit a hot landing zone in Vietnam and was even more frightened by those who showed as much fear as he felt himself: "All you could do was look around at the other people on board and see if they were as scared and numbed out as you were. If it looked like they weren't you thought they were insane, if it looked like they were it made you feel a lot worse."[31]

Contagious Courage?

Liebling, in the passage just cited, reminds us that though fear is contagious, courage seems to be so too. Other observers make the claim explicitly. "No matter how lowly his rank, any man who controls himself automatically contributes to the control of others," says Marshall. "Fear is contagious but courage is not less so. To the man who is in terror and verging on panic, no influence can be more steadying than that he see some other man near him who is retaining self-control and doing his duty."[32] Yet one wonders if courage is as virulent in its contagion as fear. Does courage even spread by contagion at all? When I grow alarmed by your fear, my newly acquired fear now has a life of its own and will persist until new evidence arises to show that no danger threatens. But the courage I catch from you is likely to continue to need your presence to sustain itself; it is too delicate a thing to go it alone. Whatever courage I catch from you owes less to any newfound confidence in my own powers than to my belief in your confidence in yours.

Fear jumps from one person to another despite the will of the recipient. To catch courage, it seems, I also have to *want* to catch it. Fear only has to overcome my sense of well-being to win control of my inner spaces; and my sense of well-being is very fragile. It doesn't take much to undo it. Courage, in contrast, has to overcome much more robust defenses before it can infect me. Courage must battle my fear and roil, and the battle is not an easy one to win, for courage is called for only in situations in which it is natural to fear, in which the setting is indeed dangerous; my fear, in other words, has every reason to stick around.

Courage, when it spreads, then, is not so much caught as mimicked.[33] It can also be ordered. The order is no less salutary in its effect than rum, exhortation, and boasts. Confused and fearful troops often need only a command to focus their wills and discharge their dangerous duties. Commanders have witnessed with wonderment their orders magically reestablish order amidst confusion. Grant's order to demoralized men at Fort Donelson "acted like a charm. The men only wanted some one to give them a command."[34] In Humphrey Cobb's *Paths of Glory*, Colonel Dax finds that giving an order helps him overcome the incipient panic he feels:

"The mere issuing of a command always inspires confidence. It doesn't matter whether it is a necessary command, or even a correct one . . . It inspires self-confidence even in the man who issues it."[35]

The magical mechanism of the order that elicits obedience to authority works in a subtler way than threats and violence in the manner of Sergeant Horne. The command simplifies the world; it confirms that authority is acting authoritatively; it reenacts the proper roles of order-giver and order-follower; it makes complying take less resolve than disobeying; and it embarrasses the order-recipient to refuse. That Bartleby the Scrivener finds it so unembarrassing to refuse politely every order given him is what proves his bizarreness and so unnerves the readers of his story.[36]

Courage effected by orders, however, is not courage by contagion. The magic of the order inheres in its being in the imperative mode, in its providing a task and distraction. It owes little if anything to whether the commander is spreading his courage about as if he had sneezed it on to his men. But there surely is something infectious about the bootstrapping of confidence that occurs simply as a result of being among many arrayed in rank, marching in step, or holding a line together.[37] Take away a soldier's feeling of support and he panics. But his confidence grows on seeing the might and number of his friends, the grand array of his army's weaponry. Sledge, before he boards a landing craft to invade Okinawa, finds that the sheer "immensity of the fleet gave [him] courage."[38] This spread of confidence is a kind of contagion, and though some of the confidence may owe a little bit to the "schooling effect"—that your odds of getting eaten are lessened by the presence of so many succulent buddies to tempt the hostile forces before they turn their attention to you—it is still nothing to sneeze at.

In the end, however, one knows that fear is much more catching than courage or confidence. One dram of evil packs more punch than an equivalent dram of good.[39] Take the case of the calming effect of another's calm. Calmness is contagious but it is not virulent like fear. Your calm works better to *keep* me calm than to *make* me calm; whereas your fear works just as well or even better to make me fear than to keep me fearing. If I feel we are in a touchy situation, your calm is only slightly more likely to calm me than to fill me with doubts about how alert you are, or, as in Michael Herr's case, it might only lead me to believe you are insane. Worse yet, your calm, rather than assuaging me, might make me add self-loathing and shame to the fear I so palpably feel but cannot get rid of, a fear that is mocked by your calm, not soothed by it. The best thing to be said for your calm is that it keeps you from being a source of contagious fear. Even that has its alarming aspects: for when you, a calm person, finally do show alarm, you will be very alarming indeed.

But not all fearful persons are equally capable of generating alarm, as Aristotle pointed out. There are times when your fear will only make me have contempt for you for having it, especially if you are one of those with a reputation for being too easily alarmed. Yet even if you are a Cassandra prophesying doom by your mere terrorized look, the very fact that we have such a ready stock image to describe unwisely unheeded alarmists suggests that I will show enough concern, if not quite fear, to scan the horizon for myself when she prophesies. There are no such readily available images that counsel me to catch your calm. For we seem to possess a powerful inkling that bad omens are more likely to be true than good ones, and that these latter are really malign tricks of fate to make us unwisely unwary.

Fear's Tense: Hope and Despair

Fearful conditions, the omnipresent lethal danger of battle, raise havoc with the simplest of temporal references by suffusing them with unintended irony. A conventional "See ya later" loses its routine innocuousness, prompting instead an intense pang of fear, as if the complacent assumption of futurity contained within the phrase were a jinx. Mark VII enduring on the Somme puts it this way:

> The cloud of uncertainty that hung above us every moment while we were under fire, putting its minatory query before the least anticipation, is lifted, and we are free to say "In an hour's time," without challenging Fate with the phrase. When freedom to anticipate is being persistently challenged, one understands as never before how much man lives by hope. To be deprived of reasonable expectation—even of the next moment—is the real strain . . . It is the perpetual uncertainty that makes life in the trenches endurance all the time . . . We have to forget "I shall." It is this constriction of hope that depresses men in the trenches. "If" stands before every prospect, and it is no small "if" in this war.[40]

Mark's world may be short on hope but it is not short on hoping. The presence of all that threat and danger sets him to hoping, indeed rather more than he would wish. That is as it must be when one is in misery, at least until misery gets so bad that it leads to utter despair. His hoping is one of the ways by which he reveals the consciousness and presence of his misery. For most of us in less threatening circumstances, hope exercises itself over longer future spans. I can say I will do this or that in five minutes without hope entering into it; Mark can't, and that is the sign of the dire straits he is in. The "constriction of hope" does not mean less hoping but that hope must operate in vastly more foreshortened time spans than it is used to operating in.

When things are going well we hope too, but not in the gut-grabbing way we do when we want to get out of danger. Amidst moderate pleasure we hope for greater pleasure; most bones we have to pick with the present are processed as hope, a gray sentiment if ever there was one despite Christianity's insistence that it is pleasurable and a virtue. Hope is the recognition of incompleteness that sets us yearning. But that is small potatoes compared to the hope that torments Mark, the hope to be alive in the next hour.

Hope and fear have been linked from early times as bearing some important relation to each other. Both are said to be future directed, one involving expectation of good, the other expectation of evil. That is Aristotle's definition in the *Ethics*, and it is followed by and expanded upon by Aquinas.[41] Fear and hope are also claimed to be linked psychologically as well as formally. If you cannot hope, say Aristotle and Aquinas, you cannot fear.[42] This view also makes its way into popular understanding: Vera Brittain can thus declare that "having now no hope, and therefore no fear," she did not pick up the paper to read the casualty lists.[43] Fear does indeed seem to have an eye to the future even when calamity is already upon us: will it hurt more than it already does, will it never end? But despair, having no hope, does not necessarily undo fear. I can know I am to be hanged, even be resigned to its certainty, and still fear that death. Though when and how I will die is certain, just what the experience of such a death will be can still be a source of fear.

There are always uncertainties to be resolved even in the midst of larger despair. Moreover, some forms of fear generate an accompanying despair, that panicky fear that you are trapped, that there is no way out. Says one soldier: "Apart from fear, my other most pronounced feeling was despair. We were obviously the playthings of fate."[44] In the view of another soldier who had "stood in one damn fox hole for forty-seven days," despair and fear could coexist, though it is tiredness rather than fear that he blames for causing the despair:

> Sometimes they pushed a fellow so long, they are too tired before they even start fighting. They don't give a damn whether they get killed or not. They lose courage. They don't aim, can't hit the ground fast. They're scared all right but they don't care. When they're running they run about fifteen yards and then start walking—don't give a damn.[45]

To be scared and not care? Isn't being scared one form of caring? According to this soldier, caring consists in getting the body to move in certain sensible ways, like running rather than walking, or diving for cover amidst a hail of bullets and shellfire. These men take more risks not because they feel no fear but because they are too tired, sick, and despairing to act in accordance with their fear.[46]

Despair is not not fearing; rather it is not giving a damn even though you fear. It means fear gets detached from its functions and action tendencies; it gets stuck in the morass fatigue imposes on the world. We met this phenomenon earlier but discussed it more abstractly as a matter of probability: "In a hurry," Graves observed, "we would take a one-in-two-hundred risk; when dead-tired a one-in-fifty. In some battalions where morale was low, one-in-fifty risks were often taken in laziness or despair."[47] There is no need to think that fear cannot accompany hopelessness or lassitude. Despair coexists quite well with many sentiments. Only hope is excluded by definition, and even that cannot hold. What of the despair-induced rage that makes despair such a good motivator of berserk fury? That very fact led Aquinas to annex a certain hope to despair. The assumption is that despair means torpor, but add a dash of hope and you get violent and often courageous action. And what is the nature of that hope? What else but the hope of revenge: "For they who despair of flight, strive less to fly, but hope to avenge their death."[48] One of life's most ecstatic pleasures, revenge, can attach itself to despair.

The passage from Graves raises another issue concerning fear and futurity as well as hope, confidence, and despair. We can position each of these sentiments with regard to their relation to beliefs in the face of various odds. Confidence, we might say, is the belief that the odds are with you. Hope is the desire for good things in the face of fairly long odds; otherwise hope would give way to confidence, or to expectation or awaiting.[49]

Despair is a belief that the odds against you are impossible. The pessimist is distinguishable; he still hopes but believes that his hope will be of little avail since his luck is to draw the unlucky number whatever the odds. The pessimist need not be all that fearful; he is readily distinguishable from the timid and the cowardly, who seem disposed to believe the odds are worse than even they, at some level, know they are.

Fear Management and Magic

Boasting, faking, exhortation, rum rations, giving or taking orders, small-group cohesion, various self-deceptions regarding confidence, cultivating rashness and seeking thrills are only a sampling of means of managing or otherwise dealing with fear. There are still other ways that deserve a word or two, and there will be others we will leave undeveloped. Some fear-management techniques have an eye toward prompting courage; some, those that deal with styles of flight and freeze, truck with cowardice. Some of these means require training to overcome natural reflexes; others are themselves natural reflexes, part of our biological makeup, and come unbidden. One of the stranger examples of the latter is that symptom of battle shock in which men fall asleep in the midst of furious battle as they curl up to avoid shellfire. This is not the sleep of Alexander the Great, indulged to show the steeliness of his nerves,[50] but a fear response that humans seem to share with ostriches. No nightmare that might threaten such sleep could be worse than the reality that wakefulness poses. This reaction, however, is rare enough to give the men who succumb to it credit for cool under fire.[51] It can be seen as a special case of weak legs, paralyzing the entire body and consciousness itself, but significantly less mortifying to its sufferer.

Sleep is not the only way of burying our heads in the sand. The thinnest of covering, clothing itself, makes us feel so much less vulnerable than nakedness. Soldiers find some measure of comfort behind the flimsiest of cover if it makes them feel less exposed even though in fact it provides no protection whatsoever. Tietjens in *Parade's End* takes solace in the cover provided by a paper bag: "If you are lying down under fire—flat under pretty smart fire—and you have only a paper bag in front of your head for cover you feel immeasurably safer than you do without it."[52] Marc Bloch put a scarf over his face in "hope that it would diminish the force of any hit."[53]

The proximity of other bodies provides comfort too. The bunching phenomenon mentioned earlier seems hardwired within us.[54] Huddling, hugging, cuddling assuage fear. The Roman legion and the infantry square gained their effectiveness in part not just because the strength of numbers prompted confidence, but also because close bodies provided a much more primitive comfort. Men could literally lean on each other. Bunching made good sense until exploding shells, grenades, and land mines made it foolish, and it is a consistent feature of twentieth-century war memoirs that platoon leaders find it next to impossible to maintain proper separation of their men on patrol, who feel blindly drawn to one another. One subaltern on the western front describes the phenomenon in a letter to his mother:

> The book of rules says spread out, don't get hit all at once. In practice this happens. The men turn to their officers for protection as though their saviours endowed with power from above. Mutual and moral support is gained by close proximity. The men bunch and hunch . . . We are dazed and bewildered and dazzled by the noise and near misses. Try as I will to get my fifty spaced out, they must creep back for the comforting assurance weaned from close companionship.[55]

No small amount of magical thinking informs our desperate tactics against fear; what else could let one be comforted by the cover a paper bag affords against shrapnel? Prayer, complex as it is, is also meant to work magic. Although as a strictly theological matter despair is evidenced by the inability to pray, in the foxhole prayer is a sign of despair, of a sense of utter helplessness in the face of dizzying noise and exploding shells. Though it is not true that there were no atheists in the foxholes,[56] those who had never before been especially warm to the idea of God but who found themselves praying couldn't help but recognize the grim comedy of their action. They had to work hard to fashion prayers that they could live with and that would also work just the right amount of magic to capture the heart of the malignant Being who had got them in all this trouble in the first place. One person promises God to believe in Him if he gets out alive. Another starts to bargain with God but breaks off in midprayer: "This is the time to make a deal. Then I thought: I've never been very religious. He isn't likely to want to deal. So I got up and starting looking for somebody, anybody."[57] When prompted by fear and anger, prayer—precation—drifts toward imprecation. Curses, after all, are themselves prayers. Consider the form of that most common of curse/prayers: goddamn it.[58] Many believers, however, just lose their faith. One religious soldier, when he saw what a shell could do to human flesh and bone, gave up on the possibility of the resurrection of the body, and with that prop gone his God came tumbling after.[59]

God found he also had competitors. He had to share part of his authority with the pagan deities Luck and Fate. Luck and Fate figure in the simplest soldier's tales much the same as the gods figure in the *Iliad*. How could Luck and Fate not intrude given the lethal randomness that tormented the spirits of those at risk? Soldiers mused obsessively on why him and not me. Where amidst the carnage did reason and will fit in? James McDonough, who lived through Vietnam, puts it this way:

> Rational decision making or technical and physical skills may save you once or twice. But a man in combat is exposed a thousand times. A gust of wind blows at the right moment to take the mortar round ten yards farther to explode harmlessly behind you. A tree grows for fifty years only to absorb the grenade fragment that would otherwise have entered your heart. A blade of grass, a bent branch, or an article of equipment deflects a speeding bullet enough to send it harmlessly through your flopping shirt or boneless flesh—or savagely through your brain or liver. And as you move mindlessly through the replacement system, the whim of an unseen clerk sends you to a unit in a quiet sector—or to a unit that will take its men like lambs to the slaughter.[60]

The eerie magic of close calls, the black-humored bad luck of friendly fire, to say nothing of the vast conspiracy of earth, air, fire, and water that the "short-timer" believes is seeking to do him in just as his tour of duty is about to end, make a soldier, in Herr's words, "a luck freak, an evil-omen collector, a diviner of every bad sign."[61]

Luck exists in a strange moral economy with courage. Feeling lucky, no different from any spurious source of confidence, can fuel courage. Yet the obsession with luck is its own kind of cowardice, making you suspect that what courage you have is working at cross-purposes with your desperate desire to get home in one piece. Like courage, good luck is also depletable, and one must take care not to waste it. Vietnam vet Tobias Wolff astutely saw the fear that tormented him as economizing on his luck: "Fear won't always save you, but it will take some of the pressure off your luck."[62] Fear is the way you show that you are not taking your luck for granted, not presuming upon it. Luck demands more than prudent husbandry; it demands worshipful respect. Fear thus pays homage to the sardonic Powers That Be, Fate and Luck; it means you are not assuming their benevolence. Those minutes of respite from fear purchased by simple unwariness, a precious moment of miraculous fearlessness, tax your luck and must be compensated for. So grim were the accounts that Luck kept that one North Vietnamese soldier reports that many of his comrades felt as if good things, "small acts of love," were "a bad omen, as though happiness must necessarily call down its own form of retribution in war."[63] Equanimity, optimism, and moments of pleasure are charged off to your luck account. Once you are committed to a cosmic order in which Luck and Fate are the controlling deities, by "taking the pressure off your luck" fear can compensate for some of the miseries it causes.

Fear, then, is not without its charms, not so charming, though, that you don't wish it would go away or at least behave as a politer guest during its stay. We struggle to cabin it and we have recourse to more magic to assist us in the desperate task. There is the talismanic magic of small gesture. The body itself mobilizes against fear magically in ways less overwhelming than falling asleep under fire or losing the ability to move one's legs. Eugene Sledge describes how before an attack the "men had squared away their gear and had done their last-minute duties: adjusting cartridge belts, pack straps, leggings, and leather rifle slings—all those forlorn little gestures of no value that released tension in the face of impending terror."[64] The magic of these forlorn gestures is of limited potency; doing them doesn't bring good, so much as not doing them would spell certain doom. They represent refusals to be contributorily negligent in one's own bad end.

These semiautomatic nervous gestures are also desperate attempts to claim one's humanity and dignity, to make sure that, amidst the engulfing disordering terror, your shoes are tied, your clothing hangs right, and you are properly arrayed, especially since you are about to die. Fear has a way of making you feel as if you are falling apart or soon about to. These gestures are meant to hold you together by mooring you to details. That is why they involve tying, buttoning, buckling, straightening, folding, ordering, wiping away dirt and sweat. Gestures of this sort may be the most touchingly human, the saddest actions undertaken to deal with fear that there are.[65] They assert in the gentlest way that one cares to give it a good try, that if one is going to turn coward, it will be as a "good coward." Burdette's good coward, remember, took care to order his equipment just right. Sledge finds these gestures pathetically touching too; because they are such sadly puny defenses to mount against the monumental danger at hand. But these small activities are of value; if the readiness is all, this is the stuff of readying.

There is the magic of cover, of bunching, of hiding one's head in the sand. The restriction these freezing actions impose on physical movement may help manage fear in some settings, but limiting freedom of movement is just as likely to cause panic in others. Movement has its own magic, independent of how rational it may be, that matches the magic of freezing. Certain movements make people feel as if they are assisting fate in their own interests, even movements that are purest reflex. Ducking and flinching when hearing a rifle report may be irrational, but the mere ability to move, to dodge, makes people feel they are less likely to be hit by flak or shrapnel or traversing machine-gun fire. Never mind that the bullet you duck is already behind you. The space needed to make these sorts of movements seems to be a part of the reason World War II bomber pilots favored the B-17 to the B-24.[66] Quarters were more cramped in the B-24; the poor leg room over the long haul was uncomfortable, but a higher psychic price was paid because the lack of space restricted the ability to flinch at flak bursts; pilots felt more like sitting ducks than they already were.

Leg room aside, bomber pilots also felt the choking constraints of holding position in formation. Whatever equanimity was gained from the improvement in the odds of survival by flying in formation or by standing shoulder to shoulder in phalanx, legion, or square was partly undone by the restrictions these formations imposed on freedom of movement. Oh to be a fighter pilot or a skirmisher who can zig and zag. The fighter pilot managed to turn evasive action into a mark of flying mastery so that, instead of being discredited for cowardly impulses, he got credited with rashness, dash, and panache. Zigzagging was the way helicopter pilot Robert Mason would take off and land in hot landing zones. The guys teased him about it, telling him he was as likely to zig into a round as away from one. "Look, Mason, if it's your turn to die, that's it. You can't control the odds. It just wasn't your day to get zapped." But Mason feels that he dodged the bullets that missed rather than that they just missed all on their own, even though he concedes that his friend "was right of course."[67] The belief in the magic of his own agency brings a certain small measure of equanimity. As with those forlorn gestures of steadying and readying it is less that zigzagging prompts a powerful sense of control, than that not doing so would be unbearable in its requirements of holding still (an admission that the courage of endurance may be harder to achieve than the courage of action). His buddy, however, is hardly the voice of pure reason. Magic controls his thinking too. In his world it is either your day to get zapped or not; the Norns, the Fates, not the rationality of your actions, determine whether your thread is to be cut now or on a later day.

The fearful person is not just left to his biologically determined reflexes or to his own pathetic devices. Soldiers are trained, and what is training if not directly or indirectly a set of fear-management techniques? Training, too, is not without its magic, the magic of automatism, the alchemy of turning men into machines, or of grafting a new set of reflexes onto the more cowardly ones of flight and freeze that nature equipped us with from the start. Is it not magic when a dead man will complete the drill steps he embarked upon while still alive?[68] Officers are given ready rules of thumb to apply under horrific circumstances; the men are drilled so that their bodies will automatically carry out tasks in spite of fear, or, if the poor soldier is lucky enough, his automatism will displace his fear altogether. Automatism is its own kind of courage. Don't we who only stand and wait look on in admiring disbelief at people able to do their job under such circumstances? Let us catch our courage where we can.

There is, however, a colder way of looking at it. Military theorists, it has been noted, assume the fearfulness of men rather than their courage; drill and discipline are as much concessions to individual weakness as measures to ensure the coordination of large groups. An individual in isolated combat needs courage to do well, but a coordinated troop of a thousand can get by on considerably less personal virtue as long as discipline supplements individual shortcoming. Raimondo Montecuccoli in the seventeenth century and Ardant du Picq in the nineteenth understood that. That's why, to draw on an example du Picq takes from Napoleon, 3 French soldiers will be defeated by 2 Mamelukes, but 1,500 Mamelukes will be beaten by 1,000 Frenchmen.[69] The parts don't add up to the whole in either case: the whole of the French troop is greater than the sum of its parts, the whole of the Mamelukes less. The former need drill to supplement shortfalls in individual courage; the latter need drill to coordinate their too plentiful and disrupting courage. But pure discipline beats pure courage when the numbers get large enough. That too is a kind of alchemy.

The Emotional Terrain: Disgust, Anger, Relief

THE COURAGE OF ATTACK is about fear pure and simple. The courage of endurance is more complexly motivated. Fear is a big part of the picture, but it must share with disgust the lead role as the passion that must be subdued or otherwise managed. Fear and disgust converge in horror, a genre and a sentiment that is the signature of the twentieth century—gulag, death camp, trench warfare and battles lasting months; heaps and fields of rotting corpses, mangled bodies, excrement, offal, mud and muck spontaneously generating plagues of flies, maggots, and rats that eat the human beings they displace. Pigs, fed up with being food for humans, join the macabre feast: "pigs eating roast people" is the arresting image with which Philip Caputo opens his memoir, epitomizing to his mind the "horrors so grotesque" that characterized the upside-down world of Vietnam.[1] An enveloping vileness beyond description means that the courage of industrialized war in the past 150 years is not just about facing fear but about facing down the oppressively vile smells, sickening sights, and loathsome touchings of corpses and rats that corrupt the spirit before they kill.[2] Dirt first, then death, or rather dirt as death: "The whole zone was a corpse," writes Edmund Blunden of his sector on the western front, "and the mud itself was mortified."[3]

Disgust

St. Helier Evans is sent out to dig "a hastily pegged out site" in no-man's land. A flare goes up, and he goes down on his hands only to find "them touching jellylike swollen faces." He slips and loses his balance on "wobbling, bloated bellies." The stench, he says, was indescribable.[4] Stuart Cloete stumbles and finds to his horror that his hand has gone through the abdomen of a French corpse, roughly "of the consistency of Camembert cheese." "It was days before I got the smell out of my nails." That is precisely the problem with disgust; the disgusting doesn't wash away easily. Fear tends to decay rapidly once the source of danger is removed; disgust has a very slow decay rate; it lingers like foul odors in the air. The disgusting is sticky, slimy; it pollutes, contaminates, and binds with and suffuses that which it touches; it corrupts. That is the horror of it; there is no cleansing oneself without painful and demanding rituals of purification. Even then there is no guarantee that one has washed it all away or passed it all through. No wonder Cloete feels that the Frenchman under his fingernails would poison him: "I remember wondering if I could get blood poisoning and thinking it would be ironic to have survived so much and then be killed by a long-dead Frenchman."[5]

The rotting corpse as neighbor, already a motif in some Civil War writing, becomes an oppressive theme of Great War memoirs that continues, though less insistently, through World War II, diminishing at last in Vietnam, where bodies are magically helicoptered away from the scene as soon as practically possible. But when the helicopters can't get in, as during the intense fighting in the jungle heat at Ia Drang, the stench of rotting corpses makes Vietnam smell just like the Somme in July or Okinawa in May.[6] Not just corpses decay and emit appalling stenches, but you do too. Trench foot rotted the flesh. Yet, as bad as soldiers had it, their disgust was mostly a regrettable by-product of an enterprise that was part of an honorable tradition; contrast the Nazi practice of purposely drowning people's spirit in excrement and vomit as they journeyed for days packed in railroad freight cars to the camps.[7]

Disgust imposes all kinds of Hobson's choices. Primo Levi, interned in Auschwitz, describes the disgusting warmth of the urine that spills on his bare feet from the slop bucket that it is his turn to empty; however repugnant it is, he says, better that it happen to him than to the bunkmate who sleeps foot to head with him.[8] That is disgust versus disgust. Sometimes it is disgust versus fear. It is November 1916, on the Somme. Mark VII sets the scene:

> Whoever it is we are relieving, they have gone already. The trench is empty. In the watery moonlight it appears a very ghostly place. Corpses lie along the parados, rotting in the wet: every now and then a booted foot appears jutting over the trench. The mud makes it all but impassable, and now, sunk in up to the knees, I have the momentary terror of never being able to pull myself out. Such horror gives frenzied energy, and I tear my legs free and go on.

Mud and rotting corpses, extrication is near impossible. Either you get sucked in by the horrific or you suck it in when you inhale the stench; either way you lose. Those who know the *Alien* movies will understand the horror genre's obsession with ingesting slimy things and in turn being ingested by them. Here the mud works as mucus, and the corpses, soon to be mud but never quite reduced to it, too cheesy for that, offer the real thing.

Mark is now confronted with a dilemma:

> Turning sharply around a bend I come upon a fearsome sight. Deep water lies in a descending right-angle of the trench, and at arm's length from me a body has fallen face downward in the water, barring the way. Shall I push the body aside and wade, chancing the depth of the water, or shall I get out on top and double across the corner? . . . Ten to one a German sniper is hiding on the forward slope below. If I try the water it may prove too deep; even if it isn't, I shall be wet to the thighs, and there are four days to go; besides that body . . . If I go over the top and the sniper hits, what a kindness he might do me! I am up now, running and dodging. Twice the sniper fires, but I am more troubled to dodge the bodies than the sniper's aim. Now over, and slap into the trench.[9]

The choice is a clear one: wade through muck safe from sniper fire but at the cost of pushing aside a sodden corpse blocking the way, or leave the contaminating dead and the thigh-deep ooze and face the bullets. In this hellish calculus plain old fear of fire loses out to disgust for the watery, slimy, clammy, and smelly. Better a clean death by fire than such polluted death-in-life, a pure cost-benefit analysis, very deliberate, in which courage does not seem to figure at all. Such is the horror of this hell that choosing to face fire to avoid corpse-filled water means facing corpse-carpeted land. But the corpses up there are dodgeable, and Mark takes greater care to avoid them than the bullets aimed at him.

Eugene Sledge structures his memoir on the opposition of fear and disgust. The first half, his experience at Peleliu, is about fear; the second half, Okinawa, is about disgust. Sledge suggests that it takes more of whatever it is—courage, endurance, just holding yourself together without going insane—to suffer the assaults of the disgusting than to suffer those of the fearsome. Neither, however, is to be wished upon anyone but an enemy. The terrain of Peleliu is brittle coral under a stifling sun. The images are all of heat and dryness. Disgust is present but secondary: he is disgusted by his own filth and by the corpses lying about, but fear dominates the account. Not so once he gets to Okinawa. No memoir of the Great War matches the disgust-evoking power of Sledge's Okinawa. Dryness gives way to mud and maggots, which had the grace to appear as flies on Peleliu. On Okinawa death literally shares your foxhole. Sledge digs one hole right through a rotting Japanese corpse before he gets permission to angle the hole a bit to the side of the rotting remains.[10]

> If a Marine slipped and slid down the back slope of the muddy ridge, he was apt to reach the bottom vomiting. I saw more than one man lose his footing and slip and slide all the way to the bottom only to stand up horror-stricken as he watched in disbelief while fat maggots tumbled out of muddy dungaree pockets . . . We didn't talk about such things. They were too horrible and obscene even for hardened veterans. The conditions taxed the toughest I knew almost to the point of screaming.[11]

Sledge begins to rot himself—body and mind. He pulls off strips of dead flesh that slough from the soles of his feet;[12] and the horror, the stench, the gobs of rotting human flesh teeming with maggots come close to driving him insane. It is only by the most concerted effort that he can keep from going over the edge. We needn't join Sledge amidst the corpses to visit the disgusting: the mud was more than enough for some. Siegfried Sassoon stared irritably at his mud-encumbered boots: "I was always trying to keep squalor at bay, and the discomfort of feeling dirty and tickly all over was almost as bad as a bombardment."[13] The tickliness presumably means lice, but lice are not maggots. Soldiers are horrified by their own uncleanness: "We were all lousy and we couldn't stop shitting because we had caught dysentery. We wept, not because we were frightened but because we were so dirty."[14]

How much easier in some respects the lot of the soldier who did his campaigning before the sixteenth century, before, that is, the civilizing process would have given him a sense of refinement regarding bodily functions. A soldier in the fifteenth century was no more likely to be lice-infested than a nonsoldier. Neither soldier nor nonsoldier would have been too chary of finding private spaces for defecating, and the standards for wiping up afterward would have been abysmally low in either case. The noncombatant would have found the cold, wet, and filth of the soldier's camp not much more trying than the cold, wet, and filth of his peasant hovel or for that matter of his lordly castle. Indeed, leaving home for war had its compensations; at home only the lord could enjoy the benefits of fleecing peasants, while the peasant at war at least enjoyed the possibility of looting another lord's peasants and maybe even rich town dwellers. What a change for the modern middle-class soldier. Sledge thinks himself in "hell's own cesspool"; his medieval and early modern counterpart, admittedly with some exaggeration, felt right at home.[15]

The assault of the disgusting works to move soldierly courage in the direction of the courage of the prisoner, inmate, or nurse: the courage of enduring the revolting and repulsive without throwing up, cracking up, or opting out. Some women keenly perceived that the disgusting was just what gave them the possibility for showing their stuff, since battle, the conventional martial courage of offense, was denied them. Vera Brittain clearly sees the disgusting as just that, the woman's domain of the heroic. She thus wishes to "emulate the endurance" of her fiancé at the front by nursing the badly broken bodies shipped back home: "I seized with avidity upon all the unpleasant tasks of which [the other nurse's aids] were only too glad to be relieved and took a masochistic delight in emptying bed-pans, washing greasy cups and spoons, and disposing of odoriferous dressings."[16] Sledge's experiences on Okinawa are more than matched by those of Japanese student nurses cleaning up the mess on the other side: "Pus would squirt in our faces," but they toughened up and "grew accustomed to the smell of excrement, pus, and the maggots in the cave, but the smell of death there on that road was unbearable."[17]

The courage of enduring the disgusting was different from that of enduring the pain inflicted by the torturer; that latter kind of courage always prompted awe, and the time span of the endurance required was measured in minutes and hours, the intensity of the torment making minutes, even seconds, seem like an eternity. The strength of soul it took to face smells and filth rather than consciousness-destroying pain meant enduring interminable, soul-destroying discomfort, with interminability measured in weeks, months, and sometimes years: cold, damp, and endless revolting assaults on the senses, unrelenting foulness, unavoidable, and draining, very draining. These discomforts were not mere discomforts, not just niggling annoyances, for the stakes were high. These foulnesses were death's minions, not a disembodied allegorical Death. Allegory doesn't smell so insistently of rotting corpses.

Cowardice is usually understood as failing in the face of fear. Does it make sense to speak of cowardice as a failure to do proper battle with disgust? Is squeamishness or fastidiousness cowardice? Might there not be courage displayed in the pursuit of privacy and cleanliness? Kipling paints such a portrait of a soldier he calls "The Refined Man," who insisted to the death on taking care of nature's needs privately:

> I was of delicate mind. I stepped aside for my needs,
> Disdaining the common office. I was seen from afar and killed . . .
> How is this matter for mirth? Let each man be judged by his deeds.
> *I have paid my price to live with myself on the terms that I willed.*[18]

The refined man narrates from the grave, because he could not bear to defecate in the presence of others. He knows there is a vulgar comedy to his death; he was sniped taking a dump. Nevertheless, he defies those who find the way he died a matter for mirth. He has no regrets. Had he to do it again he would run the same risks. His commitment to his fastidiousness is something he willed; it is not, he argues, neurotic anal compulsion, not the result of his unconscious impelling folly when safety could have been gained merely by accepting the "common office." If there is an unavoidable comic indignity in getting shot "doing his duty," that indignity pales, in his mind, beside the indignity of having to do it observed by others. He postures as a Prometheus, a romantic hero willing to brave all to realize the perfection of his own soul. And he is very convincing as long as we repress the image of what he was doing when he died, caught with his pants down.

Courageous? Maybe. He was surely no coward. But is there not associated with certain varieties of fastidiousness, the kinds we might narrow more properly to squeamishness, an effeminacy that has considerable overlap with cowardice? The boy who could not skewer the worm on the fishing hook, or was timid about pulling the fish off the line once caught, who would not pick up toads, who would not camp out because he could not bear lack of toilet paper or the idea of squatting in the woods, was not considered very manly. To the other boys he was a wimp. This is not quite the same as a coward, but the boys would feel fairly confident that such squeamishness would predict cowardice. After all, the settings in which bravery is demanded are not always clean and neat. Danger is often messy, smelly, and dirty. The refined boy would be excused as merely eccentric only if he had already acquitted himself well in the face of fear. If the refined boy was good at fighting or sports, his disgust for worms and toads would subject him to good-natured teasing, but his moral stature would be reasonably secure. His toughness in the face of fear or pain buys him some relief for his weakness in the face of the disgusting.

Both those who crack too quickly because of disgust and those who cave in too readily to fear would make for pretty bad soldiers. A prosecution for cowardice, which, recall, required a showing that the offending conduct be motivated by fear, could be recast to include an aversion driven by disgust, for the disgusting things he fears are the very messy, smelly stuff of interminable battle. Most likely, though, those who are felled by disgust will be treated as medical casualties, dismissed with no small contempt for not being able to toughen up.

Anger

Fury, spirit, rage, anger motivate behavior that, if not honored as the purest courage, is still deemed, in Aristotle's estimation, to be a reasonably valued semblance of it.[19] Fear is pictured by many as having a mutually exclusive relation with anger in settings understood to be dangerous or frightening: the more anger, the less fear.[20] Anger is thus frequently enlisted to do battle against fear.[21] We trust passions to do better battle against fear than reason. When reason works to quell fear it usually does so by activating fear-opposing passions like confidence or other competing fears. Anger and confidence are not the only passions that oppose fear. Mandeville lists an unsavory collection that serves equally well: avarice, vanity, ambition, to which we might add hatred and lust.[22] But anger has a special privilege in that it is more conventionally annexed to courage because anger looks to revenge, a common theme in stories of courage. The prospect of revenge, in Aristotle's opinion, actually makes anger pleasurable.[23] How much more pleasant to have our courage moved by anger and the delights of revenge than by the self-laceration of shame. Anger enlivens us and helps us mobilize the full extent of our physical powers. It purifies the spirit with its fieriness.

Would it were that easy. A lot of cowards are plenty angry too. The way the discussion usually goes is that fear is the given, the starting point, and then anger arrives to oust it. But fear, quite clearly, is just as good at dampening anger as being dampened by it. Anger need not overcome fear, need not displace it; it can coexist quite well with fear despite the traditional view. So often the object of our justifiable anger is just too tough to take on, or our fears make him look too tough to take on whether he is or isn't. Anger need not lead to revenge, but to mere fantasies of it, which, for whatever compensation they might offer, come soon to oppress us with our own sense of weakness precisely because we know that it is all fantasy and that we don't have the guts to follow through. It is one kind of coward who is so dispirited as not to recognize insult or offense or be moved to anger because of them; it is quite another kind who feels those wrongs exquisitely but whose anger never succeeds in displacing his fear or in moving him to action. This is a person many of us know so well, having played the role enough times ourselves to count him close kin. Such a type can even acquire a reputation as a person of great self-control, a model citizen, as long as he keeps his vengeful visions to himself.[24]

I suspect though that the story of how anger and fear work to thwart each other is more complicated than one of ousting or overcoming. Philip Caputo describes the emotional turmoil elicited in a soldier who sits in a cramped helicopter that carries him into a hot landing zone. Unlike the infantryman in a ground attack, he has no freedom of movement. That costs him the illusion, he says, of having some control over his destiny. Trapped and powerless, he begins "to feel a blind fury toward the forces that have made him powerless." Then fury and fear engage in their intricate pas de deux:

> His blind rage then begins to focus on the men who are the
> source of the danger—and of his fear. It concentrates inside him,
> and through some chemistry is transformed into a fierce resolve

to fight until the danger ceases to exist. But this resolve, which is sometimes called courage, cannot be separated from the fear that has aroused it. Its very measure is the measure of that fear.[25]

Caputo's account is one in which fear and anger combine to generate courage. It is not so much that one opposes the other. The chemistry is more complex. The anger that generates the resolve which is sometimes called courage is inseparable from fear. It is as if anger is an avatar of fear, a form of it, a transformation that fear works on itself. The anger is not some pure reagent anger; it is fear with a different face.[26]

Not all anger is fear transformed. Anger arises independently of fear all the time, as when a person lashes back at those who have wronged him, or when we burn with indignation at injustice suffered by others. But the anger that propels courage in the face of fear might just be fear experienced as anger. This might be what fear has to do to produce the fight reflex, rather than freeze or flight reflexes. Yet the anger that impels the fight reflex is never not recognized as also being fear: fear and anger become one, yet distinct. Sounds a bit like attempts to explain separation and unity in the Trinity, and why not? It is fitting that the mystery of courage should, at least in some aspects, mimic that mystery too.

This account adds one variation to a psychology I hypothesized in Chapter 6 to account for the "cowardly" courage in which the actor thinks his courage false because he feels so much fear despite doing brave deeds. Here the actor feels both fear and fury, but because his fear is felt as fury he is able to explain his success without lapsing into self-castigation, whereas without the rage, brave people filled with fear feel like cowards and are confused, even as they carry on with success. Caputo's account is not unlike Frederic Manning's description of the confusion and merging of opposed emotional states into each other—"One could not separate the desire from the dread which restrained it . . . the collision of these warring opposites."[27] But Caputo is not talking about confusion; he is quite clear about the experience and sorts it out fairly well. Fear and anger do not start out opposed and collapse one into the other; the resolve called courage is generated by a fury that is more than just fueled by fear; it is that fear with a different face.

Caputo's rage focuses on those who are the source of the danger, the enemy. How fortunate. For the resolve that his anger engenders would not be courage if it did not find the right object on which to vent itself. There always is a risk that such anger could be redirected mutinously, though being shot at nicely reestablishes the enemy as the immediate object of anger, letting off the hook the superiors who put one in the enemy's line of fire in the first place. This is one reason why mutinies seldom originate among the troops actually engaged against the enemy but rather among those in the rear areas.[28]

Relief

We think of courage and cowardice as keeping company primarily with the emotions that prompt them or stand in their way—fear, anger, disgust, fear of disgrace, sense of duty—and stop there. What, however, of the emotional aftermath? Shame is the consequence of cowardice, but what is the emotional consequence of courage? Is it pride? Perhaps, but only if we are certain that we were courageous or, even if uncertain, manage to be convinced that we were by the sincere reactions of others. Exhilaration? The ecstasy and pleasure of victory? Sure, if your courage was part of a victory; but what of the courage displayed in defeat?

The ecstasy of victory seems in many ways to be a species of relief, relief that it wasn't a defeat. The exultation in the defeat of your foes gets so much of its energy from how easy it would have been for the tables to be reversed. In the vanquished you see what you managed to escape. The thought is perfectly captured by Vietnam vet James McDonough, who describes his feelings after a firefight as he looks at the enemy dead:

> Could it be—repugnant thought that it was—pleasure that one feels at the sight of an opponent's body? How could a civilized man feel such a thing? Perhaps the emotion was born of relief. Ground combat is personal . . . It is a primordial struggle . . . Emotions flow with an intensity unimaginable to the non-participant: fear, hate, passion, desperation. And then—triumph! The enemy falls, lies there lifeless, his gaping corpse a mockery to the valiant fight he made. Your own emotions withdraw, replaced by a flow of relief and exhilaration, because he is dead and not you . . . Do that once, twice, three times, and repeat it again later in the day. Do the routine the next day, then again. Soon the emotions become confused. The sense of relief is identified as pleasure in being alive, and life itself is purchased at

the cost of someone else's death. Kill or be killed: the emotional result is pleasure at the sight of the enemy dead.[29]

Is that shocking? Those pleasures that are owing in part to the cessation of prior pain, prior anxiety and fear, prior desire, involve relief. Our most intense pleasures fit this grim model. The pleasure of sexual orgasm is in big part a relief from aching desire. Even the book we pick up and find ourselves delighting in was often picked up to obtain relief from present fecklessness. There are, of course, pleasures that do not involve relief. They happen unexpectedly or as part of the simple routine of being around people you love. They may generate longings for more, or wistfulness about their evanescence, but they do not receive their initial positive valence from the cessation of prior negative states.

In soldiers' memoirs relief changes its focus over time. First, there is the relief of finally getting into action, the relief that relieves the misery of waiting, of the wretchedness of boredom, suspense, and fearful anticipation, the relief from all that uncertainty and self-doubt about the quality of your courage that will finally get resolved one way or another.[30] If the rhythms of your assignment allow for it, you may have accesses of fury and then little ones of relief accompanied with small surprises and self-congratulation while the testing is in progress (hey, I'm doing okay, I'm actually doing it). And then there is the cathartic relief when the first test is passed. You actually managed not to disgrace yourself, though you are not quite sure how it happened that you didn't.

Once, however, you are relieved to find that you didn't or won't disgrace yourself, the quality of your courage ceases to matter as much. Relief comes to characterize the sensation of disbelief as you emerge alive and in one piece yet again from another brush with death. Even this relief is experienced differently by different people. For some, as described in the passage above, relief informs a glorying pleasure in seeing the enemy dead. For others it is less glory than lassitude, a torpor of shame, almost postcoital, what T. E. Lawrence described as "the physical shame of success, a reaction of victory, when it became clear that nothing was worth doing, and that nothing worthy had been done."[31] Similarly, but without regard to the general success of the mission or one's personal performance in it, others will feel hollowed out by the cessation of such overwhelming fear, barely able to pull the psychic pieces together as they slowly reawaken to a life they had already given up on.[32] Others may laugh hysterically or burst into tears, or show evidence of more embarrassing signs of catharsis. In contrast, the miserable long-drawn-out demands made on the courage of endurance means that moments of relief will be less intense, not so much the "Phew, I didn't disgrace myself" or "Thank God I'm still alive" as the sensation of momentary respite from cold or heat, or the pleasure of finding an unexpected extra bite to eat.

Imagine an attack with a series of intermediate objectives, a hedge and a farmhouse. The hedge is taken after a brisk fight. The men are relieved at the success. Now come two problems. The first is that relief undoes the resolve to continue, for relief is primarily a sentiment of conclusion. It ends stories; it does not begin them or play proper roles in their middles. Relief prevents the men from reassembling their sense of urgency; so the farmhouse is not taken. The second is the problem of rebound.[33] Relief does not work by swinging you back to some prior neutral state. It bounces you back to feeling much better than your real circumstances suggest you have a right to feel. Relief often prompts a false sense of security. And with unwarranted rosy views of the world comes careless complacency. But the external world isn't obliged to ratify your complacent view of it; you are asking for trouble.

We needn't suppose that the first objective was achieved after a brisk fight. The same rebound occurs when an anticipated hard fight doesn't materialize.[34] S. L. A. Marshall reports that one company that did not meet anywhere near as much resistance crossing the beach at Normandy as they had expected started "to act as if they were at a clambake." "Success," says Marshall, is "disarming," precisely because of relief's rebound effects: "When the tension suddenly relaxes through the winning of a first objective, troops are apt to be pervaded by a sense of extreme well-being and there is apt to ensue laxness in all of its forms and with all of its dangers."[35] The costs of relief are at times greater than the costs of fear, because, strangely, relief is more disruptive of rationality. Our reason coexists rather well with fear, which keeps us alert to our environment; it does less well in the face of relief-induced exhilaration. And look how promiscuous we are in our readiness to find relief. Pain is not just something to be relieved from; pain can also bring relief, as when it replaces another pain; it needn't even be a lesser one. Variation is itself a kind of relief. Hope, too, provides a species of relief by transforming a mere wish that things improve to a belief that they will, hope thereby metamorphosing into faith.

15

Courage and Chastity

THERE IS NO getting around the fact that courage, as traditionally conceptualized, and conceptions of manhood are intimately bound up with each other. The connection holds across time and space. There are exceptions, but they are the kind that prove the rule.[1] Courage and a certain manly ideal imposed costs on men and costs on women, though not in quite the same way. Roughly it is this: men bear the burden of living up to a murderous and terrifying ideal; women bear the burden of being excluded from living up to it, which, though saving them from fighting wars, was forever used to justify their subordination. Women, instead, in many cultures, were relegated to the virtue of chastity. In the discussion that follows I sketch out the part the traditional conception of manly courage played in creating a miserably anxious masculinity and in helping maintain a miserably constrained world of opportunity for women. The focus will be on ideologies of courage, and only indirectly on men and women who are burdened with or benefited by them. To report on these ideologies and how they prompt pain and support injustices is not to endorse that ordering of courage's world. As I stated in the Introduction, these particular understandings of courage have traditionally allowed it only to men at the upper end of the social hierarchy. Courage was understood to mirror and justify the inequalities of the social hierarchy. This historical and cultural baggage still imposes its burdens, though mostly, now, on women. Democracy and mass-conscripted armies made it very difficult to continue to deny courageous possibility to the ranks of men previously excluded. Start first with the way we talk.

Diction and Insult

So bound up is courage with manhood that it is nearly impossible to speak of it without invoking male body parts or the word for man itself. Greek *andreia* (courage, literally manliness) is derived from the stem *andr–* (adult male).[2] The Hebrew root G-B(V)-R (man) yields GEV(B)URA (courage). Latin *vir* (man) gives us "virtue"; although in modern English "virtue" has come to indicate general moral excellence, it used to mean, more narrowly, in earlier English as well as in Latin (*virtus*), courage, valor, forcefulness, strength, manliness. The expansion of the sense of "virtue" from courage and manly forcefulness to encompass all virtue is thus not only about extending the scope of courage beyond the martial but also about expanding the notion of manhood. As an adjective or adverb "manly" means courageous, forthright, frank, and is meant not just to mark the positives associated with the conception of manhood, but to build that conception by distancing itself from negative traits associated with or imposed upon children, women, and, yes, old men too.

Courage, manliness, manly virtue, is defined less by what it is than by what it is never supposed to be: womanish or effeminate. The unmanly man becomes a symbolical woman.[3] He is the sissy, the pussy. He manifestly doesn't have balls. Both "balls" and "pussy" are vulgar terms, but because the first is an honorific I do not have to feel the least apologetic for writing it, whereas I honestly feel I must apologize for "pussy," whose vulgarity is not softened by doubling as an honorific. The vice that inheres in references to the female overpowers the virtue inherent in references to the male. Consider, for example, the different effects the Latin prefix *ex* (out, from) has in "emasculate" (*ex* + *masculus*) and "effeminate" (*ex* + *femina*). *Ex* cannot prevent *femina* from retaining its female gender, though in grossly parodic form, but *ex* castrates the underlying male in "emasculate," regendering him female, making him no man at all.

So deep is the misogyny that informs the philology of courage and cowardice that when a female term is used to praise a man it is really a male term in drag. Take this case: "He is one tough mother." "Mother" is one word for woman that all men hold dear, but not so dear as to make calling a man a mother praiseworthy. For the "tough mother" is not a mother at all, but a "motherfucker," who by some small concession to decorum has been euphemized by suppressing the second element of the compound. The honor in being so called is an example of slang's power to make the bad stand for the good, as in "He's a real bad dude," but even this kind of inversion cannot make a female term pay homage to a male ("He's one tough pussy" just doesn't work, even for a woman, whereas "She's got balls" is a compliment). "Bad" can mean good, but "woman" can't mean man. We honor the "tough mother" because the implied second element of the compound—"fucker"—allows a real bad male to be transformed into a real good male, not a good woman into a good man.

The insult of calling a man a woman, a boy a girl, is as old as the hills and travels well. Hector, in what can only be described as trash talking, calls Diomedes, who flees before him, "no better than a woman."[4] Gudrun, the enterprising heroine of *Laxdaela Saga*, goads her brothers to kill her ex-lover by comparing their spirit unfavorably to that of a farmer's daughters.[5] And in the 1960s Tim O'Brien records how he and his friend Erik were addressed by their drill instructor: "A couple of college pussies . . . You're a pussy, huh? You afraid to be in the war, a goddamn pussy."[6] The style of reinforcing aggressive male-gendered courage by contrasting it with some conventional notion of womanly softness is remarkably tenacious.

These insults support an ideology whose central claim is that courage, especially of an aggressive martial variety, is masculine, just as weakness and softness, and by implication cowardice, are feminine. The claim is not, however, that all women are cowards or that all men are courageous; even men, especially men, one could say, know that is not true. The claim is that for men to be men they must be courageous; otherwise they are like women, only lower. Cowardly men are allowed none of the virtues women have for being women, and they are understood to be embarrassments as much to women as they are to men. To call someone a "sissy" or a "pussy" is really to create a new entity, not woman, not man, but a womanly man, an un-man. But the category of the womanly man depends on a prior ungenerous notion of the courageous capacity of women. Women, however, were generally excused being called cowards; being called "woman" was enough. Neither courage nor cowardice was, according to this ideology, available to them.[7]

Staying a Man

In highly competitive male honor systems manhood is always at risk, for a man is unmanned not only by having no courage but simply by having less of it than the person facing him. Failures of courage expel him from his presumptive gender. Most men will spend some part of their moral lives out of their proper gender. In saga Iceland these issues arise in striking clarity. The men there lived in a culture of insult in which their courage, their manliness, was frequently questioned and challenged by other men and by their own women. A wife, a mother, and sisters were keen observers of their men's mettle, and they were unrelenting in derision unless he undertook to measure up. The most frequent insult was to call a man a woman or a would-be woman. The insults focused directly on sex acts; the coward was a man who let his anus be used as a vagina. Remember the man, mentioned in Chapter 8, about whom it was suggested that he wasn't very good at defending "the narrow pass" between his legs. One didn't have to be the passive partner in a homosexual coupling to be thus accused. But that was understood to be the natural endpoint of a man who took it lying down, so to speak. Tim O'Brien's D. I. had the same end in mind for him a thousand years later: "'What the hell we do with puss in the army? We fuck 'em, don't we?'"

Man was a category that biological males had a hard time staying in, despite the initial presumption in their favor.[8] Even Egil, whom no one would have thought to mess with when young and who was so successful that he managed to grow old, was mocked in old age by the serving women to whose space he was relegated to lament his sexual impotence.[9] The Vikings had a proverb that made the point brutally: "The older a man gets, the more a sissy he is."[10] Moreover, it was not just that men constantly risked falling into metaphorical womanhood with any decline in their power, whether martial, sexual, or economic; it was also that some women were credited with more manly virtues than their men. No small number of saga women, sharp of tongue, hard of heart, and cold of counsel, were admired for their toughness and praised with the same words used to praise men. The admiration was unambivalent as long as they were still womanly. That meant no cross-dressing. One woman was thus mocked as mannish because she favored, it seemed, men's clothing, but even so the mockery cannot avoid paying homage to her enterprising vengefulness.[11]

These women were exceptional, and it was harder for them, clearly, to rise above womanhood than for men to fall into it. But they suffered little downside risk; if they didn't emerge from the mass of womankind they remained what they were: women. They suffered no individualized opprobrium. But the men had to struggle to stay where their biological form said they should be or else sink into figural womanhood. As the best writer on this topic says, "if a woman's ascent into the masculine took some doing, the man's descent into the feminine was just one real or imagined act away."[12] No wonder the men were so anxious about their reputation for courage. That reputation was manhood itself, and to be thought cowardly was to be dishonored as *ragr*, an Old Norse word translators usually render as "coward," which doesn't quite capture the gendered message it explicitly bears: a man anally penetrated as a woman. With that in mind the proverb I rendered as "the older a man gets, the more a sissy he is" could be much more vulgarly translated without distorting the sense.

Anxious Boys and Men: The Female Gaze

The ideology of courage may shamelessly stack the deck in favor of male possibility as opposed to female possibility. But courageous possibility, because not certain to be realized, because only a possibility, makes for a very anxious masculinity. It is remarkable how anxious this masculinity looks whether in Homer, an Icelandic saga, or an American high school. Look how sensitive guys as tough as Achilles are about every slight. Not just Achilles. Much of boyhood, even for sybaritic middle-class Americans, is a mandatory series of testings of daring and physical toughness the goal of which seems to be as much to develop anxieties and sensitivity about the state of one's toughness and how one stacks up as to develop courageous capacity itself. The testing begins well before puberty and subsides when we no longer care, no longer count, or move off into gentle or pacified zones, where contention is often diffused or denied. In modern middle-class life a man's anxiety over the quality of his courage has pretty much been dissipated by his mid-thirties or has been confined to neatly bounded athletic contests. In heroic society, though, men are anxious as long as they are expected to bear arms, well into their fifties in some places.

Boys of my generation were constantly subjected to "sissy tests." Need I supply the various forms? Most involved seeing who could endure great pain without crying uncle—holding a lighted match, jumping off ever higher places, playing various versions of a game of chicken, or just being bad: breaking windows, sassing back to grownups, but during a time when such behavior meant certain beatings from an adult who was not afraid to exercise meaningful authority. These tests did little to resolve the deep anxiety; they rather augmented it. It was never understood that by passing them you had proved yourself courageous. You only proved that at that instant you were no coward. You had denied the negative, which in this nonmathematical order was something less than claiming the positive. You were not a sissy, not a girl, at least until the next time. Everyone knew what a sissy was. You were more reticent about claiming courage. Courage's ineffable mysteriousness made it always seem to be just another 10 percent more than you had given when you had given your best or 10 percent more than you had endured when you had endured your most. You never escaped, for all the testing, the anxiety and fear of sinking into unmanhood.

Why this need to organize the moral order of courage and cowardice in such a transparently defensive way? Part of the gendering of courage piggybacks on another gendered opposition: action versus passivity. According to the dominant ideology, with a compliant reality often confirming it, man's world was outdoors and active; woman's, whatever amnesia this involved about who actually did the work, was to be protected, private, inside, behind doors. But the main metaphoric force behind the active/passive distinction was the sex act itself.[13] Men had to get erect and penetrate; from their perspective they were the ones who had to do something; women only needed to lie there, even though such lying could be a pretty unpleasant experience. For men the risk of physical failure was the risk of moral failure, and failures could not be hidden or faked, at least not from their female partners, who just might decide to make it known. As one male law student put it: "We have to play chicken every time we go to bed." Might the ideology of courage owe something to male resentment at being so exposed? This is no small part of the reason that the language of courage, campaigning, and combat maps on to courtship, seduction, and copulation. But this rhetoric seems to be less about conquest and the breach of a defended position than about overcoming fear, fear of shameful failure, fear of inadequacy, fear before such an overpowering object of desire, fear of what in the world to do afterward. Both doing what it takes to make life and doing what it takes to take it are scary. That's why rum rations are needed for both, and many an old soldier found it easier to charge the enemy than to face up to courtship and coitus.[14]

The male ideology had it that a legitimate sex act only posed risks for a woman well down the road; that's when she had to deliver. Her risks, once she proved to be fertile, were of a different order, mostly physical, not shame, but unspeakable pain and sometimes death.[15] Childbirth gave men cause for anxiety too. Parturition confirmed maternity and womanhood, sealed it with indubitable proof. It did no such thing for manhood, at least not before the era of blood and DNA testing. Paternity was always maintained as a fiction, a legal presumption, and required a lot of wishful thinking by husbands, while, on the other side, male lovers loved paternity's deniability. There is also the vague male suspicion, when considering the prospect of childbirth, that men weren't quite up to taking what it took to be a woman. When literal push came to shove men were not sure they could bear a pain the intensity of which they could not fathom. Such pain could be explicable only as punishment for some unspeakable crime on the order of disobedience to God.[16] Battle seemed preferable. In addition to such bad-faith justifications as the biblical account for women's pain, men's sense of inadequacy, perhaps their small guilt, generated compensatory behaviors ranging from the sweetness of couvade, in which they undertook to share and mimic the woman's pain, to its much paler avatar in the scripted behavior of the American man of the 1950s who paced up and down shielded from distressing sound and sight. Even the Lamaze style is concerned to bolster male feelings of insignificance: now the man is "coach," charged with the awesome responsibility of counting and reminding the woman to breathe on cue. We have come so far that my dear father admired my courage for being present at the birth of my kids.

One more source of male resentment, though attenuated in our time, figured greatly in earlier cultures of honor. If passivity was thrust upon women, with it came the power to watch and talk about what they saw; or if they were prevented from watching they still could talk about what they heard. Watching and hearing meant judging, and women became the scorekeepers, the arbiters of male competence in combat and competition, not just in bed. Back then it was the female gaze through which so much of male honor and reputations for courage and cowardice were filtered. It was not only Viking women who kept track of and so cuttingly impugned their men's manhood, or simply declared themselves divorced in disgust. In Mediterranean cultures the women composed songs that preserved male feats of honor and disgrace.[17]

Women were the rememberers in these simpler cultures. That's what scorekeeping means in honor cultures: remembering every wrong so that it can be properly paid back by the men. Women gossiped. They denied sex to their failed men, but mostly they just humiliated them if they showed the least bit of fearfulness or cowardly propensity. These tough mothers did not want cowards for sons. And they found very charged ways of letting them know that. It was women, after all, who raised their sons up to the demands of aggressive honor and held their sons, husbands, lovers, and brothers to its highest standards. One Gothic matron lifted her skirts to expose her private parts to her fleeing son and scornfully asked him if he wanted to climb back in;[18] a Confederate woman sent her petticoat to a man who refused to fight;[19] during the Great War young English women accosted fighting-age men in civilian dress on the streets and handed them the white feather of cowardice, often, it seems, not distinguishing all that carefully between civilians and wounded soldiers in mufti on home leave.[20]

Much has been made of the so-called male gaze's being privileged in so many cultural forms, giving us our world mediated through the eye of male desire. But put in the long perspective, it is not quite clear whose gaze was more anxiety-provoking to whom. No wonder Medusa's looks killed. She was that judging female eye that forced men into battles they might have preferred to talk their way out of. If Freud wanted to see her as a projection of men's fears of castration, her decapitated head to his mind suggesting the easy severability of certain body parts, I prefer to see her threat as more public and less hidden in the darkness of psychosexual fear. Her eyes may indeed unman men, but by judging them cowards.[21]

Women judged what they saw, and they lashed those who fell short with their tongues. If watching and judging meant being relegated to the sidelines, tongue-lashing was considered to be a form of active involvement and precisely the type of action those not allowed or unable to bear arms should be taking. Leave it again to the saga Icelanders to put it in words. Says one woman: "It is manly for someone who can't do the rough stuff to be unsparing with the tongue, to say what might be of use."[22] Her advice is intended to include old men and all women, and what she means is that those not able to fight should goad those who can, unrelentingly. A woman's tongue could mock the enemy too, but her chief role was to keep her men going forward by deriding them. Those women who were specially energetic at goading their men were feared and respected. But they knew too that this was a second best, making a virtue of a severely restrictive necessity, a paltry form of courage in which their courage worked to endanger others more than themselves and which justified men in thinking them ruthless and scheming.

Yet if goading was to work, men had to care about what their women thought. These women were not so contemptible that men did not care to be thought well of by them. And though women may have been partly playing a role that men expected them to play, the scripted nature of goading made women no less terrifying to the men who were the objects of their taunts, laughter, and sneers. A rough rule of thumb in these aggressive cultures might be this: a man was more scared of other men than of his own group's men, but more scared of his own women than of other women.

The Restricted Domain of Women's Courage

It was not just male mean spirit or psychosexual anxiety that argued for exclusion of women from martial glory and the domain of courage in earlier times. There were practical reasons to do so. When weapons technology imposed range limits measured by a stone's throw or an arrow's or a spear's flight, when death-dealing meant punching, stomping, hacking, hewing, and stabbing, the difference on average between male and female muscular power made excluding women sensible. There is also the fact that as a purely biological matter women's reproductive capacity is dear; men's comes cheap, though this seems to have not prevented numerous cultures from engaging in preferential exposure of baby girls, making women's reproductive capacity even scarcer. No wonder these cultures might have to raid others for their women. Much primitive war is thus about capturing women, not territory. Give me Helen and I go home. And the number of men who died to re-abduct her mimics the number of male sperm cells that must perish in their effort to fertilize one egg.

Women were manifestly not excluded from pre-industrial combat for fear they might get raped if taken prisoner. That was their fate anyway if their men lost. Ideology could be scrapped in the interests of practicality too; sometimes you needed your women to join the fight. Thucydides thus speaks admiringly of the women of the Corcyrean democratic faction who "joined in the fighting [against the oligarchic faction] with great daring, hurling down tiles from the rooftops and standing up to the din of battle with a courage beyond their sex."[23] Likewise Icelandic women who defended their kinsmen with force were praised for their actions.[24] But women were not allowed to march out to fight, even though they could gain honor by defending.

Women's virtue was ideologically tied up with sex, either in bearing children, preferably sons, or in not bearing them unless officially given the right to. Whereas the meaning of virtue eventually expanded to accommodate all excellences a man would wish to claim, for a woman the meaning of virtue contracted into a tight little ball. Her virtue in this ordering depended ultimately on the condition of her sexual availability; it meant meeting the demands of chastity, for without that she was denied all virtue.[25] This restrictive locating of feminine virtue in the vagina is more than confirmed negatively by the term "woman of easy virtue," meaning prostitute. Montaigne, writing in the sixteenth century, describes a system of values that has only recently relaxed its hold but has not yet ceased completely to obtain:

> Our passion, our feverish concern, for the chastity of women results in *une bonne femme* ("a good woman"), and *une femme d'honneur, ou de vertu* ("a woman of honor" or "of virtue") in reality meaning for us a chaste woman—as though, in order to bind them to that duty, we neglected all the rest and gave them free rein for any other fault, striking a bargain to get them to give up that one.[26]

Such a narrow sense of virtue left women little ground to exercise courage except in the defense of chastity. Courage had no independent footing. How many women had the example of Lucretia forced upon them as uninvitedly as any potential male interested in rape? And what of the poor daughter whose father, St. Hilary of Poitiers, asked God to take her from this world rather than that she should marry and lose her virginity? God obliged; and to her father's great joy, she died soon after his prayer.[27] She died to preserve virginity; many others died for failure to preserve theirs. This is not uncommon fare in the Mediterranean basin whether among Muslims or Christians.

But Lucretia's example was not the only kind of heroism a strict chastity regime allowed; womanly heroism could also be achieved, in rare and desperate circumstances, by sacrificing chastity, conferring it as a gift.

In Greece in 1941 a truck loaded with gaily dressed women passes Robert Crisp riding toward the front. "Good God," said one of his mates named Oxo, "a three-tonner full of tarts." Their Greek Army guide needs to be told that tart means prostitute. "No, no!" he says, "Prostitute, no! They are, what you say . . . volunteers." Comments Crisp:

> In any other circumstances it might have sounded funny. Instead, it was strangely moving. All those young women, like a lorry-load of cattle, off to the market-place of the battlefield to satisfy the appetites of the soldiery—yet making of it an act of joyful dedication which was as heroic as any act of valor . . . Not even Oxo could persuade himself to say something ribald.[28]

Given the uncompromising Mediterranean attitudes toward chastity we can understand Oxo's reverence. These women are going to their social death, to satisfy men's appetites, like animals to the slaughter whose flesh will fill human maws. Crisp is honest enough to see that there can be little sexual pleasure in this for the women; theirs is not the pursuit of pleasure, but a gift of that to the men who are also being led like cattle to slaughter. Their heroism is in letting themselves be degraded for the larger cause and in doing so cheerfully, so that the men get greater pleasure than they would from women taking no pleasure in doing a grim and distasteful duty. It is their cheerfulness, analogous to a soldier joking in the face of death, that makes the scene so moving to the British observers. The valor of the girls depends in this case on the chastity norms being solidly and unassailably in place, so that it is a worthy recompense for the valor of the boys. Hence their sacrifice.

Chastity enforcement for women parallels courage enforcement for men. Cowards were lined up and shot or ran gauntlets or were ostracized; similar sanctions awaited women for failing the demands of their defining virtue. Women, however, were involved in a battle without respite during the same part of their life cycle in which the men were exposed only inter- mittently to the rigors of combat; but then in some cultures honorable men would be called on to avenge unwelcome attentions to their women, so that men's courage was tested in feud in defense of their women's chastity. Thus it was that men as well as women died to maintain the chastity regime. There was a strict moral economy linking women's chastity and men's courage. If a group's men were courageous their women would be chaste; cowards' women were unchaste because, almost by definition, a coward wasn't threatening enough to ward off unwelcome advances to his women. Of Albania, Margaret Hasluck notes that "a man slow to kill his enemy . . . risked finding that other men had contemptuously come to sleep with his wife."[29]

Early Christianity, touched on briefly earlier, expanded the opportunities for women to display courage independent of chastity and be credited with it, until obsessions with virginity contracted them again. When it came to the courage of endurance, women martyrs overmatched the men. Pagan persecutors helped too by showing themselves disposed to give both women and men the opportunity to test themselves in the face of death. At Lyons in 177, twenty-three women died, twenty-four men; at Scilli in 180, five women and seven men.[30] But it is the women who stand out in the accounts, for a variety of reasons: because their courage ran against the complacent assumptions of courage's ideology, perhaps too because they added some extra spice to the implicit pornography of these garish violent rites that so characterized the Roman world;[31] but mostly because of their extraordinary capacity to endure torture, as in the case of Blandina at Lyons, or because they were self-consciously concerned to make their deaths legendary, as with Perpetua, who orchestrated her exit in grand style, taking care to keep a prison diary of her last days.

But once the church was secure, occasions for martyrdom were rare; those that there were fell to the lot of apostles, all men, off in distant lands importuning pagans. Women's courage lost the main arena in which it was allowed to compete on an equal basis with male courage. The glory of martyrdom gave way to the inglorious fortitude of patient poverty. Poverty offered no grand orgiastic spectacle on which all eyes focused; there was no conceivable way the diction and imagery of warrior courage could be marshaled to sweep the slow and insistent miseries of a lifetime into its ambit in the way the intense, bounded suffering of martyrdom could. There was no earthly glory in patience and poverty; but there was earthly glory in martyrdom to add to the heavenly payoff. And the earthly glory was so great that the women martyrs bought themselves relief from that insistent niggling about their sexual status. Says Peter Brown, "Only a very trivial man would have asked if Blandina had prepared herself for the presence of the Spirit by practicing sexual abstinence."[32] Perpetua was the very image of attractive fecund femininity. The women martyrs were often not virgins at all. It was courage, not virginity or chastity, that was being tested.

Escaping Chastity

Officially excluded from public life and politics, with their virtue made a function of sex, there was not much conceptual room for women's courage. Relocating women's courage to childbearing hardly emancipated their courage from their sexual organs. Nor was it clear that bearing children tested courage. Until not long ago, if one was fertile and married there would be children unless the man was a dud; there was no escape and thus no option for cowardly flight. Can courage exist if there is no cowardly option other than entering a nunnery? But the inevitability of an event, its inescapability, doesn't undo courageous possibility. We all have to die; and we make moral distinctions among people by how tastefully they manage their departure; and we are wont to see those who do so in a dignified way as courageous. So too women, I suppose, kept a quiet tally of who did well and who did not when giving birth. Given the options of flight offered by contemporary anesthetics, epidurals and such, there has arisen of late a parturition macho among women. The gentlest of women may feel just an inkling of glorying at the expense of her epidural-succumbing sisters when she refuses to cry uncle and does it the old-fashioned way.

Yet it is in the context of chastity that a particular style of womanly courage begins to emerge. In many nineteenth-century novels women brave social disapproval to assert themselves for love, or for freedom from the largely sexual shackles that confine them. Stendhal portrays these women as unambivalently courageous; they intimidate the men about them, not by their supreme desirability but by their strength of character. So too, but to a lesser extent, Maggie Tulliver, Hester Prynne, and some of Wharton's heroines. Forced into a regime of virtue as chastity, a woman's courage comes to be seen as having the force and strength to pursue love and desire, to self-realize, to risk social opprobrium and still manage to do this in such a way that, though whispered a whore, though ostracized and gossiped about, she can satisfy herself and no small number of her tormenters that she is rather larger than life. Surely the creators of Mme. de Rênal, la Sanseverina, Mathilde de la Môle, Hester, Maggie, Tess, and Ellen Olenska did not expect their readers to hate them or prissily reject them as immoral and fallen. Though some, like Lily Bart, Tess, and Hester, were to be pitied, the others were quite frankly posed as objects of admiration for their fearlessness, and even objects of envy for their courage, their greatness of spirit, their recklessness if you will.[33]

Some of these women clearly resent not having conventional courage available to them. Maggie desperately longs for the grandness of action denied to women;[34] and Mathilde de la Môle in *Le rouge et le noir* (*Scarlet and Black*) goes so far as to devise an explicit theory of courage that will admit not only the peasant man she loves but herself too. For Mathilde, courage is more than meeting cannon and charging in battle; it means risking ridicule. She accepts that the men from her own social class who bore her are conventionally brave when it comes to combat or a duel, but that is "mere" bravery to her. Courage in her view is breaking the bonds of convention and scripted expectation. She wants action whose grandness comes from a specific kind of recklessness—not being a slave to one's fear of shame. One must risk looking foolish to achieve greatness.[35] The merely brave fear showing bad form; they are brave because it is too embarrassing not to be; but her Julien, she thinks, has no such fear. Mathilde's courage is the courage to be thought shameless. That is the risk she feels she must take so that she, a woman, can gain the ground to show fearlessness, bravura, in short, courage.

By grounding her theory of courage on the willingness to risk ridicule and shame, Mathilde makes courage available to women for breaking the constraints that chastity imposes on them. The same theory may also, she hopes, allow a mere peasant boy with brains access to the highest society ladies if he is brazen enough.[36] One could trivialize her theory by reducing it all to a matter of a quest for orgasm. In fact, Stendhal trivializes it too by showing that the theory is just as likely to lead to grand bedroom farce as to heroism.[37] Does it make sense to compare the courage of Tommy in the trenches, who has to crawl through corpse-laden mud, wire, and fire on a fruitless patrol, with the quest for erotic pleasure? Even if the price of pleasure was death? We should, though, be more charitable and see her theory, in spite of the cultivated flippancy with which she presents it, as a serious attempt to stake out something that we call moral courage, which has come to be understood as precisely the kind of courage it takes to risk opprobrium, shame, and derision in the pursuit of higher goals. And moral courage, though never completely separable from physical courage, as will be shown in the next chapter, was not hedged in with all the old aristocratic male baggage.

But does Mathilde bring us woman's courage at the price of making her indistinguishable from Probert and Coke in Chapter 7? The problem is similar to the one that so concerned the church at various points in its history: what to do with people following their own inner lights, who claim to be the sole arbiters of their consciences. Without some outside control how do we know if we are not just plain shameless and too self-serving to have a clue that we are? The problem is finding a way to limit the range of self-realization so that it is clearly something more than self-indulgence. It's not as if there is no virtue in chastity (at least to the extent it is a necessary component of fidelity), and we should be just a little suspicious of someone who finds it too easy to toss it to the winds. Surely then it would not be courage we were dealing with. There have to be ways of judging the worthiness of the desire that transgresses the disputed social norm and the intolerableness of the injustice that the social norm works before we will bless the transgression of that norm by thinking it courageous rather than reckless or just immoral.

Clearly, not everything goes. Short of finessing the issue by declaring sexual pleasure to be *the* essential component of human flourishing not to be restricted in any way, the narratives developed some rough rules that legitimated the desire, saving it from charges of being nothing more than a libidinous quest to scratch an itch. If the desire qualifies as true love, all kinds of sympathy are mobilized on its behalf. We have been trained by a multitude of narratives to root for the star-crossed lovers against ungenerous public opinion, parents, and querulous, unattractive spouses. But true love, though necessary, is not sufficient. Mathilde knew that; she understood that to transgress norms of chastity is courageous only if you pay a price, no matter how justifiable your cause. You have to be more than just willing to pay; you actually have to pay it. You have to give something up; in her case it was social standing, wealth, and public esteem; the price was even steeper for Maggie, Hester, and Mme. de Rênal. The man who charges a machine-gun nest and lives is no less courageous for living. But when pleasure is part of the goal rather than the extirpation of an enemy position, we want the anticipated costs to be borne to make sure we aren't merely justifying self-indulgence, debasing courage's coin by declaring orgasm courageous.

But Mathilde and her sisters, constrained to fight their battles for self-realization by resort to erotic transgression or flouting social norms, are out for more than pleasure. Although orgasmic ecstasy complicates the courage issue, it doesn't undo it. Mathilde can claim that she too has as her ultimate goal the extirpation of an enemy position, the enemy being the double standard that limits her ground for courageous action so narrowly to the sexual domain. I suspect that she would concede the puniness of that option; it is the very smallness of the field on which her courage is forced to exercise itself that is the object of her revolt. We can thus excuse her for the pleasure she obtains along the way toward realizing the larger goals.

But gains are made. No sooner do upper- and middle-class women win to themselves moral courage in the erotic domain than, starting in the mid-nineteenth century, they start to carve out a domain of generally recognized feminized physical courage by doing battle, as suggested earlier, against disgust and horror in conditions of considerable danger in war. In the well-known case of Edith Cavell (d. 1915), a nurse could even be formally executed by the enemy for carrying out activities that she felt flowed naturally from her commitment to saving lives.[38] The nurse, though eroticized by the men she assisted, was courageous independent of her relations to the norms of chastity. One even guesses these norms had to have been relaxed just a bit to let nurses go off to the front. The wartime nurse then claims a part of traditional martial courage for women that is visible to men and conceded by them as courageous in a way that so much of the manifest courage displayed by pioneer and immigrant women was not. The courage of the pioneer women was too readily subsumed into the old style of patient poverty, and thus rendered invisible, and, moreover, they were not of the "right" social class.[39]

The Great War, as we have seen, did more to contract the domain of male courage than to expand the possibility of female courage. Remember that courage was now seen to be a finite resource readily exhaustible by the continual moral seepage occasioned by the relentless horror of the trenches. Not only did the amount of courage available to an individual diminish, but its style began to shift also, for the charge, that purest emblem of aggressive courage, had been rendered mostly uselessly suicidal and stupid. Male courage began to become more a courage of endurance, to assimilate itself to a courage equally available to women. In the First World War the tests of endurance were borne almost exclusively by the men who fought; not so in World War II, which was as much a war against non-combatants as against soldiers. Women as well as men got to test their mettle in death camps, bombing raids, and gulag, settings in which tired metaphors took on a new, horrific life. "On the march back," writes

Eugenia Ginzburg, "numbers of [the men] had died like—I was going to say 'like flies,' but at Kolyma it was truer to say that flies died like people."[40] The flies join those pigs Caputo saw eating roast people, and with the simplest metaphors turned upside-down and inside-out, why shouldn't courage, too, have a sex-change operation?

When it came to enduring the unendurable, the camps gave further confirmation to what men privately suspected but would never officially admit: women were tougher over the long haul, both psychologically and physically.[41] Ginzburg looks through the barbed wire at the men's compound:

> Although one might have thought the men were stronger than we were, they seemed somehow more defenseless and we all felt a maternal pity for them. They stood up to pain so badly—this was every woman's opinion—and they would not know how to mend anything or be able to wash their clothes on the sly as we would with our light things. Above all, they were our husbands and brothers, deprived of our care in this terrible place.[42]

If the women were in fact doing better it was not because they were getting demonstrably better treatment. In a Western version of the same nightmarish world, a French prison in 1917, e. e. cummings, hardly a sentimental softy, makes no bones about how much worse the women had it than the men: "Not only were they placed in dungeon vile with a frequency which amounted to continuity; their sentences were far more severe than those handed out to the men. Up to the time of my little visit to La Ferté [the prison] I had innocently supposed that in referring to women as the 'weaker sex' a man was strictly within his rights. La Ferté, if it did nothing else for my intelligence, rid it of this overpowering error."[43]

Women, having been trained for centuries in abjection, in making do with leftovers, in both the material and moral worlds, tended to be realistically practical, toughened by their lot. Then too, although it is suspiciously canting to say so, they may have been better at helping and caring for one another over the long haul of captivity. Men did well with the glorious sacrifice, the greater love of the falling-on-the-grenade variety, but withdrew between times. Such grand gestures were signatured male—a one-shot burst ending in death or exhaustion.[44] The women may have come in better equipped to endure these hellish conditions. Even more favorable to their courageous possibility than to the men's is that the women did not have to suffer psychic emasculation if they didn't rush the guards, if they didn't fight back physically. The women could survive without being subject to charges of cowardice for making the accommodations necessary to survive, for if that aggressive courage was not allowed them, neither was the cowardice for failing to uphold a model deemed inappropriate to them. Not that women survivors wouldn't feel survivor's guilt; that is a different issue. But they could survive and be credited with courage of the first order, a fully realized courage, utterly appropriate and admirable.

Such courage is not quite as appropriate to the men. They still must pay homage to a heroic model that shames them for enduring the not-to-be-endured. They were supposed to take arms, real ones, against their sea of troubles. Never mind that conditions made that next to impossible. That doesn't erase the effect of millennia of a male model of courage that the men are failing to measure up to. Yet it is not quite right to say that the courage of endurance is gendered feminine, except in the special sense that women were not excluded by ideology from it. That courage has always been available to men as well as women, to Socrates in his cell and to Perpetua in the arena. But it is feminizing in some small respects to men, because the ancient grand model is there to mock it as cowardly, as taking it lying down, and we still subscribe enough to that model to fear that it has a point.

Primo Levi, ever the best writer on this regime of abjection, describes the death of a man who is to be hanged for having played some part in blowing up a crematorium. The inmates are called out to watch him die. "Perhaps," says Levi, "the Germans do not understand that this solitary death, this man's death which has been reserved for him, will bring him glory, not infamy." The Germans read out his sentence and ask the assembled if they understand.

> Who answered "Jawohl"? Everybody and nobody: it was as if our cursed resignation took body by itself, as if it turned into a collective voice above our heads. But everybody heard the cry of the doomed man, it pierced through the old thick barriers of inertia and submissiveness, it struck the living core of man in each of us: "Kamaraden, ich bin der Letz!" (Comrades, I am the last one!).

Levi says he wished he could say that a voice rose from the midst of this "abject flock" to answer the condemned man's call, to give him "a sign of assent." But all were silent. The man quivers in death. Levi bursts into a lament of self-loathing at the destruction of their souls: "There are no longer any strong men among us, the last one is now hanging above our heads." He walks away unable to meet the eye of his best friend Alberto, both "oppressed by shame."[45]

The last one is the last *man*. That is one of the possible meanings of his deeply ambiguous last words. "I am the last" is directed to the Germans to indicate that they have gotten all who participated in the revolt. Don't blame any others. He also could be understood to be exhorting those skeletal men assembled to watch him die to make sure he is the last victim, as in "Comrades, I am the last man these bastards are going to kill." But his words are also a reproach to the living captives, that he at least is a man, the last of his sad people to behave as one. That's how Levi comes to understand him. He concurs with the most pessimistic reading. Yet Levi still possesses his "living core of man," his capacity for shame; he is not so unmanned as to be shameless. He still measures his moral quality against the highest and grandest image of masculine courage. Even in the camps among the abject, the active image of grand heroism, going down with guns blazing, sets a standard that reminds those who have given over their whole being to the day-to-day struggle to survive, with its constant machinating for extra calories, how paltry a triumph mere survival is.

Levi puts us in an impossible situation. It is not for us who have not suffered to agree with him in his self-reproach. Only he has the right to blame and shame himself. Yet we cannot suppress a kind of proto-reproach for all those who stood there and watched; we are disgusted by their docility. Where is the courage in that kind of endurance? Do we need anything more than this vignette to explain the Israeli commitment to a most aggressive kind of warrior ethic in the old heroic style? Notice too how gendered the reproach is. The men who fail to act as "the last one" did are not men. Set the scene in a women's camp, and the women, if equally abject in their unwillingness to encourage the condemned person, are still women. They are not expected to rush the guards. Those who do will be admired, but those who don't will not be the objects of the same kind of contempt.

Yet there are arguments to be made for the virtues of struggling to stay alive.[46] If the enemy's goal is to exterminate your kind, then managing to live defeats his aim. And there is something remarkable about the sheer refusal of DNA to stop doing what DNA does: endure so as to make more of itself. We find ourselves crediting life itself with the virtue of courage simply for surviving extreme conditions. That's why we bestow a quasi-heroic status on those who survive exposure to the cold or mine collapses or being cast adrift at sea. But if we are to honor life itself for not giving up, then that is an honor that seems more appropriately bestowed on life embodied as a female. Women have to live, they must; it is their bodies that bring forth life. Besides, as noted earlier, biologically speaking, male life is cheaper, more readily expendable.

Women's Macho

The feminist movement has in the last thirty years rejected abjection of any sort. The courage of endurance, patience, sufferance, though in some settings admirable and worthy of awe, was too serviceable as a sop to justify keeping women in subjection, by honoring them for being so good at dealing with abjection. Western women sought and obtained the right to strive for old-style offensive courage, in athletics and in war, not as nurses, not as goaders of their men, but as primary actors. Muscles were in; so too were martial arts and contact sports. Since it was precisely the old gendered theory of courage that lay at the ideological core of women's subjection, why not claim that aggressive courage for themselves? They suspected that unless all styles of courage were open to them they would always be treated as second class, weak, incapable of real courage even though everyone knew they could take their lumps. The goal (admittedly the feminist movement is not of one voice on this) was to make aggressive courage publicly women's own, to be able to hit and hit back and be honored for it. And it is also possible that it was the nineteenth- and twentieth-century re-invention of woman's courage in its war against chastity that enabled its expansion into the ancient preserve of warrior courage.

When aggressive courage is adopted as their own, does that courage become feminized, or do the women who train for it become masculinized? The courageous avenging heroines of certain popular culture forms—notably the slasher film and other low-budget horror genres—make their combative girls into something more and less than girls.[47] They sport women's bodies, to be sure, very attractive ones in the eyes of the teenage boys who make up the audience; but these tough girls are gendered masculine, because, it seems, that is the way the boys who identify with them want their courage served up. These heroines fight back; they avenge wrongs done them; they can kill, thus surpassing tough saga women; they appropriate the gaze that film theory identifies as male. Mainstream movies like the *Alien* films with Sigourney Weaver as a Rambo figure would simply have been inconceivable as little as thirty years ago, though their progenitrixes would have been already leading exciting lives somewhat earlier in comic books. But in pop culture the old aggressive courage stays masculine even when it is being enacted by female bodies.

The transition from one kind of womanhood to another makes for some awkward occasions. How, for instance, is a woman to shake hands with a woman? Should it be a firm shake? Would that be trying too hard? Should one just start medium and adjust fast? She shouldn't offer a limp, passive hand, but what if one woman gives another a limp hand, which is then awkwardly crushed by the one shaking firmly? This has little to do with courage, but it does have to do with certain trivial consequences in the real world that flow from the adoption of masculinely gendered styles of courage and toughness. When I once asked about woman-to-woman hand-shaking practices in a seminar, one woman said, "I squeeze hard and hold it. I'm not going to be the first to back down. You know, it's like I'm a woman and so are you, so let's see who gives in first." Many were stunned by the easy appropriation of the male honor culture of challenge and riposte, literally itching for a fight in a handshake.

When will we know that women are accepted as official players at aggressive combative courage? It is already granted in sports, woman on woman. Some are better at delivering hits and taking them than others, and they are honored for the virtue. But what about when it is woman versus man, say, as in a war? We will not know that women have made it when they win silver stars or Medals of Honor. It will be whispered that the award is suspect, infected by the politics of courage, bruited about that it was granted because she was a woman, not in spite of it or independently of it. So how will we know? The answer is fairly easy. We will know women have made it when it is fully believed that they can be subject to a court-martial for cowardly conduct. Leave it to one of Stendhal's women—Mathilde de la Môle again—to make an epigram for the occasion: "I can see nothing conferring honor . . . except sentence of death. It's the only thing that can't be bought."[48] Until cowardice can be attributed to a female, without such behavior being dismissed as just coming with the territory or as so much "femming-out" on the order of shrieking at a mouse, the old order will still govern and do its work in restricting options for women, even as it relieves them for the moment from the oppressive and anxious burden of having to live up to the demands of aggressive masculine courage.

In the meantime, either women have not yet been given enough opportunity to be cowards in combat, or the men who still seek to reserve jealously for themselves an exclusive courage intimately tied to their conception of manhood have been loath to drum them out for cowardice when the occasion arises. Not that women aren't drummed out, but, you guessed it, it is for being unchaste. Thus two highly publicized cases in 1997: the first woman B-52 bomber pilot, Kelly Flinn, and Lt. Colonel Karen Tew, both of the U. S. Air Force.

16

Moral Courage and Civility

NOT UNTIL THE nineteenth century does the term "moral courage" appear in English. It is meant to distinguish physical courage, the courage to face death and pain, from a different kind of courage. Henry Sidgwick, in Victorian style, offers this definition of moral courage: people "facing the pains and dangers of social disapproval in the performance of what they believe to be duty."[1] Mathilde de la Môle, in the previous chapter, captured the sense of it more vividly, though she did not yet give it its own name: the willingness to look like a fool, to suffer disgrace in the interests of higher principle or right, which for her meant self-realization in loving whom she would, at the risk of her social standing and reputation for chastity. For us moral courage has come to mean the capacity to overcome the fear of shame and humiliation in order to admit one's mistakes, to confess a wrong, to reject evil conformity, to denounce injustice, and also to defy immoral or imprudent orders.

Is Moral Courage Ever Divorced from Physical Courage?

It is a frequent theme among soldiers, Tim O'Brien's constant theme, that as hard as physical courage is, it is easier than moral courage, easier to be shot at than to be laughed at and scorned, thus too some of the import of the proverb cited earlier: many would be cowards if they had courage enough. Moral courage plays to a different beat than does the general kind of physical courage demanded of soldiers. Moral courage is *lonely* courage. It often requires making a stand, calling attention to yourself, or running the risk of being singled out in an unpleasant and painful way. Modesty, fear, even stage fright pose themselves against it. Physical courage can just happen. You go to war; you're ordered to attack, you do. You are never singled out, you remain part of the group, you follow orders, having been trained to do so without too much questioning, if not grumbling. When, however, physical courage requires egregiousness, isolation, loneliness, we saw that it requires moral reserves on the order of those we are presently supposing moral courage regularly needs. It is the loneliness that makes moral courage so especially commendable, and in its finest instances it is as admirable and nearly as sublime as the most tragically moving examples of physical bravery.

Let us accept as fact that the manifestly physically courageous may not be especially morally courageous.[2] People will face death rather than fol-low the dictates of their conscience when it tells them that they are risking their life for something trivial, wrong, evil, or just a mistake. The harder question is to what extent moral courage can exist independently of physi-cal courage.[3] Does the willingness to face up to dishonor and ridicule buy one admission to courage's privileged ground independently of any judg-ment about how well you would persist in the face of physical fear? In Chapter 12 I noted that moral courage draws to it, almost naturally, images of posture. One stands up, one takes a stand, one stands firm. One can even be said to charge ahead. Moral courage embodies itself metaphorically as a soldier, a fighter. Are these just ways of talking, mere metaphor, or are they something more? To the extent that moral courage takes determination, grit, and passion, the body must come along for the morally courageous ride. But we might want more of the physical than just that. First let's exclude some claimants to moral courage, some for being more aptly cases of physical courage in good causes, the others for not being sufficiently risky to qualify as courage though they may be moral.

Those cases often described as examples of moral courage that most impress us seem to impose substantial risk of death and imprisonment: the people in Nazi-occupied lands who sheltered Jews, for instance. We think of these people as moral heroes, but is their courage moral courage or just plain courage? They do not fear ridicule; studies have shown them to be rather nonconformist types who march to their own drummer.[4] They simply can't imagine acting otherwise. They are like Primo Levi's helper, Lorenzo, and their courage seems to blink at the considerable physical risk their actions pose for their own safety. To compare such as these with those who overcome fear of censure, of being marginalized, even of losing a job seems to involve comparing great things with some lesser, though still very admirable, kind of courage. This is why most nonviolent resistance to oppression is about courage pure and simple. Beatings, imprisonment, pain, even death are part of the risk. Rosa Parks may have had moral courage a-plenty, but to do what she did took plain undifferentiated courage. Not all forms of civil disobedience qualify as courage. It is one thing to demonstrate against nuclear power in the United Kingdom, quite another to sit-in at a lunch counter in Mississippi in 1964 or to publish truth in Argentina in the 1970s.[5]

George Orwell has a field day with the "moral courage" of pacifists in World War II Britain compared with what pacifists had to risk in World War I. His diction reproduces unapologetically the themes of the preceding chapter with men falling into effeminacy and women goading their men by impugning their manliness:

> In 'seventeen to snub the nosing bitch
> Who slipped you a white feather needed cheek,
> But now, when every writer finds his niche
> Within some mutual-admiration clique,
> Who cares what epithets by Blimps are hurled?
> Who'd give a damn if handed a white feather?
> Each little mob of pansies is a world,
> Cosy and warm in any kind of weather;
> In such a world it's easy to "object,"
> Since that's what both your friends and foes expect.
>
> At times it's almost a more dangerous deed
> Not to object; I know, for I've been bitten.
> I wrote in nineteen-forty that at need
> I'd fight to keep the Nazis out of Britain;
> And Christ! How shocked the pinks were! Two years later
> I hadn't lived it down; one had the effrontery

> To write three pages calling me a "traitor,"
> So black a crime it is to love one's country.
> Yet where's the pink that would have thought it odd of me
> To write a shelf of books in praise of sodomy?[6]

Orwell reminds us again of the politics of courage. In pluralistic societies the most craven conforming to the demands of the group you identify with, that "mutual-admiration clique," can still be presented as if it were an act of courageous defiance as long as you believe your group is by some tally outnumbered or "disempowered" in the wider polity. Orwell disallows courage under such conditions; though you may be inconvenienced in the wider polity, the safety net provided by your own group, among whom you are now counted as a person of consequence, means the risk you incur is not sufficient to test your capacity for moral courage. It isn't lonely enough. That is why those excessively risk-averse parents in Ann Arbor who knocked down the snowbanks showed little moral courage for risking being thought nerdy; they were playing to a sufficiently large audience of their own, feeling very secure and self-satisfied that they were doing the rest of us benighted souls a service.[7]

Yet here again there are roughly zones. Pluralistic society does not undo the possibility of all moral courage just because any position one might take will find some supporting constituency. There are cases in which real costs and real pain are borne by the person who takes his stand, and the very support and honor that he wins by taking it are, to his mind, part of the pain and shame of his action, not some unintended benefit. A young upcoming Israeli colonel, Eli Geva (a brigade commander at age thirty-one) ruined a promising military career by refusing to order his troops into Beirut in 1982; he was largely responsible for scuttling the high command's plan to go in: "I don't have the courage to look straight into the eyes of bereaved parents and tell them their son fell in an operation which I believe we can do without."[8] The peace faction that honored him for the stand he took were not his people; they were people for whom he normally had contempt, and I would guess that he would hardly have derived much solace from being welcomed by such as them as a man of moral courage. Note too how Geva, honoring all the requisite modesty norms, describes his morally courageous refusal as a failure of the moral courage needed to face grieving parents. He also immediately volunteered to serve in the ranks to show that he was not afraid of dying in what he believed to be an unwise cause; he did not want his moral courage sullied by suspicions of physical cowardice.

Orwell raises another point. There is also an inertia in the reputation certain actions acquire. If an action is once deemed courageous, it takes time for it to cease being claimed as courageous even though it no longer takes much courage to do it. In Britain, to be a pacifist in World War I took some "cheek," so that pacifists during the next war see themselves as reproducing the courage of their predecessors because the deed of resisting war has, by those earlier actions, become typed as requiring moral courage. But the stakes have changed. It is hard to claim moral courage for acts that raise no more than one-tenth the eyebrows they once did and in which you are well accompanied by a self-sustaining group quite pleased with its own high moralism. Much more courageous is the ten-year-old bedwetter who steels herself to risk attending a slumber party.

The obstacles that oppose moral courage—derision, ostracism, loss of status, demotion, loss of job—are not trivial. But even here physical fear, not just fear of being seen as foolish, contemptible, or disgusting, may be part of what needs to be overcome to manifest moral courage. Have we become so secure in our persons that we don't fear a fist in the face for taking unpopular stands? A person of moral courage cannot be so physically a coward that a mere threatening glance would dissuade him from his noble purpose. Moral courage is largely hypothetical to the physical coward, for the level of safety the physical coward would demand before he would take his moral stand can rarely be met; not all moral courage has the good luck to strut on the stage of a faculty meeting. Let us then settle on this: moral courage may not require physical courage, but it may be undone by physical cowardice, the kind of risk aversion that plagues people whose imaginations make physical dangers seem horrifically and palpably present though they have no greater likelihood than one over Avogadro's number.

Reconsider the women of the last chapter whose moral courage was mobilized to oppose chastity norms and the larger social order that so limited their opportunities for flourishing. They displayed a fearlessness and resolve that we could safely predict would have stood them just as well in battle. Maggie Tulliver, unflinching before the gossip of St. Oggs, is also fearless and cool headed in the flood that kills her. Stendhal's women cede nothing to their men when it comes to courage of any sort. These women would not make psychological sense, they would surely not elicit our sympathies to the extent they do, if they quailed at much of anything that hindered their struggle. I do not want to collapse moral and physical courage. The distinction is worth maintaining at some points, especially, as I will soon show, when it is soldiers who make the distinction: it does matter that the fear to be overcome is of ridicule rather than of death; it does make a difference that moral courage depends much more on satisfying a requirement of loneliness than does physical courage which need not satisfy it at all. But, though distinguishable at some points, they overlap at others and often fade into each other. The metaphors of physicality that describe moral courage as standing up are thus more than "mere" metaphors. Moral courage needs enough physical backing not to be deterred from its moral agenda with laughable ease.

People speak loosely; we often confer moral courage on those who display good intentions in matters that need physical courage, but who can't follow through. What makes the "good coward" good is this kind of effort. The willingness to expose himself to risk, given his fears, is itself a kind of courage, but it is not properly physical courage, since that is precisely what he lacks. His praiseworthiness, like that of the person of moral courage, is that he is willing to endure derision or disgrace in order to keep trying to make good. There are other cases. Thus Jean Améry, who blames his own lack of physical courage for his "willingness" to tell the Gestapo everything they wanted to know just so they would halt the torture, is credited nonetheless with moral courage by Primo Levi for joining a resistance movement that made him a likelier object of Gestapo torture.[9] Burdette makes much the same move as Levi by coming up with that perfect expression "good coward." We want somehow to indicate the greater moral stature of such people in contrast, say, to those whose aversion to risk, whose fear for anything that might happen to their bodies or careers, keeps them from testing their courage of any type in any domain.[10]

Moral Courage versus Physical Courage

There is one setting in which the contrast between moral and physical courage is vividly drawn, for they are set against each other in true combat. We have met the problem before. How does one retreat or delay battle when it is prudent to do so and maintain honor? Moral courage is the courage of the military leader who is willing to risk his reputation for courage, to suffer shame, in the interests of reason and effective action toward the goal of ultimate victory. This was the courage of Fabius Cuncta-tor, of Joseph E. Johnston, of Tolstoy's Kutusov in *War and Peace*. Moral courage is the courage not to attack grandly when grandness is also foolish; it means enduring nasty insinuations as to the quality of your courage. In this setting moral courage is, perversely, the courage not to face death, or at least to postpone facing it. It is the courage to act in accordance with rea-son against the powerful pull of that martial honor which is always threat-ened by any behavior that is susceptible of being interpreted as motivated by fear or cowardice. The opposition between physical and moral courage couldn't be more sharply drawn, for by this time the punishment of high ranking commanders was limited to disgrace, demotion, or reassignment, and not the Carthaginian treatment of crucifixion.[11]

I find it a nice irony that moral courage—the very concept arising as part of a general trend to demilitarize courage, to suit it better to the demands of civilized society, to democratize it so that it is available to civil-ians, women, the old, and the low—achieves its perfect instantiation right back on the battlefield, where it must fight not against injustice, but against the dominant understanding of courage—against, that is, physical courage itself as it rushes headlong into rashness and stupidity. (Recall that the experience of twentieth-century war reveals another possible distinc-tion between moral and physical courage: physical courage is a depletable resource, giving out after continued demands upon it; moral courage just might grow stronger with exercise.) But because the moral in this moral courage of retreat is having the "boldness" to back away from immediate physical danger, people are going to be suspicious of its true motivation, just as they mistrust the courage of the draft dodger.[12] It thus may be that this kind of moral courage can be risked only by those who have already proved their physical courage. Otherwise no one will quite believe it isn't just a fancy excuse to save your skin.

When Siegfried Sassoon, already decorated for bravery, publishes his vehement protest against the war while recovering from wounds, his friend Robert Graves worries that the army will "read it only as cowardice, or at the best as a lapse from good form." Even worse is that Sassoon's comrades back in the trenches won't understand it.[13] Not unlike Eli Geva, Sassoon ends up volunteering to go back to the trenches once he finds that the protest is merely going to get him declared pathetically crazed with shell shock rather than court-martialed in grand style. So much the warrior is Sassoon that he cannot abide not getting properly "wounded" for his moral courage; he wants punishment, not pity. Punishment will dignify his protest precisely because it helps assuage doubts as to the protest's proper motivation. As I argued for women like Mathilde, who violate chastity norms, it is not sufficient that he merely risk punishment; he must actually incur it. Just as the integrity of their courage is compromised by the pleasure being sought, so is his by the particular danger being avoided.

U. S. Grant makes his own relation to moral courage a minor theme in his *Memoirs*. In the Mexican War he finds himself in a forward position when "an order to charge was given, and lacking the moral courage to return to camp—where I had been ordered to stay—I charged with the regiment." Commanding a regiment before his first combat in the Civil War, he approaches the brow of a hill expecting to meet the enemy on the other side. He finds his heart "getting higher and higher until it felt to me as though it was in my throat. I would have given anything then to have been back in Illinois, but I had not the moral courage to halt and consider what to do; I kept right on."[14] Grant can't help sending small sneers in the direction of moral courage, knowing full well that it is capable of being falsely claimed by suspected cowards.[15] He invokes moral courage as a shill so that his drolly announced failures of it become suitably modest ways of claiming physical courage, or, more accurately, of denying cowardice.

Grant is indeed genuinely modest about his substantial courage, both physical and moral.[16] Modesty, however, does not prevent him from claiming, though obliquely, moral courage in one setting:

> I do not believe I ever would have the courage to fight a duel. If any man should wrong me to the extent of my being willing to kill him, I would not be willing to give him the choice of weapons with which it should be done, and of the time, place and distance separating us, when I executed him. If I should do another such a wrong as to justify him in killing me, I would make any reasonable atonement within my power, if convinced of the wrong done. I place my opposition to duelling on higher grounds than any here stated. No doubt a majority of the duels fought have been for want of moral courage on the part of those engaged to decline.[17]

This is a rhetorically complex passage. Are the higher grounds of his opposition to duels his belief in the moral cowardice that is displayed by fighting them, or some other ground not made explicit? With typical Grant-like grimness he also lets us know he doesn't like improving the odds of those who have wronged him before he executes them. Grant doesn't go for posturing in the style of impractical gallantry. The contrast with Lee on that point is a cliché of what used to be taught in grade school as American history. The physical courage he denies himself at the beginning of the passage is the denial only of a certain foolish wasting of courage, nothing more. He does not even disclaim that he may not be forced to duel when he has wronged another if his attempts at atonement should fail to settle the dispute.

Grant, of course, cannot decorously claim moral courage for himself. Even more than in the case of physical courage, the question of whether you are displaying moral courage, especially in those settings in which the act of moral courage is also one that extricates you from immediate physical danger, is not your call to make. So Grant's rhetorical hands are tied and there is thus more than a hint that he means to let anyone know who cares to think he does not have the nerve to kill, that he will kill. There is no escaping, either, that this is U. S. Grant talking. The name has an extraordinary threat value; and if anyone can feel secure enough to disclaim his courage to fight duels it is he.

Grant's moral courage is not of the stand-up-and-oppose-injustice variety. It is about swallowing pride, about not responding to insult, no matter how meanly motivated it may be. Grant had this kind of moral courage, the moral courage of endurance in abundance. Notice, then, that moral courage, no less than physical courage, comes in an aggressive style and in a passive style. Grant complemented his offensive style of generalship and commitment to aggressive physical courage with a most powerful moral courage of the opposite stamp: he suffered attacks on his character in silence, endured calumny with uncomplaining dignity.

A nonsuspect moral courage might also be more easily achievable by a general, since as an older man, justifiably stationed rearward, his personal physical courage is less an issue than his willingness to order young men to test theirs. Hardness, rather than conventional physical courage, is his virtue. If a general's moral courage is tested when he retreats or postpones engagement, the subaltern or lower-ranking officers at the sharp end are tested when they defy orders to attack given by commanders to the rear. Think of the moral dilemma; the officer risks court-martial for insubordination, but, depending on the situation, not to defy the orders means not only death or capture for himself and his men but also the possibility that the men may not even obey the order if he gives it to them. What to do, then? The moral courage it takes to refuse the order is doubly compromised. Not only does the officer have to live down the intimation of his physical cowardice and lack of toughness, but he may also be tempted to refuse the order to avoid the embarrassment of having his own authority defied by his men. Easier it may be to stage a one-man mutiny himself than to be one man opposing the mutiny of his own company.

Safer Times, Times of Plenty

Why did it take until the nineteenth century for English speakers to name a distinction between physical and moral courage? The answer though complex in the particulars is fairly easy to summarize in a rough way. There is little need to carve out a notion of moral courage in an age in which it was so clearly understood that courage of whatever sort meant that your body was ultimately at risk. The solitary woman who opposed those denouncing a witch stood a good chance of being burned as one herself. It is only when people can rely on not being killed or beaten for voicing unpopular opinions that physical fears can be separated from fears of rejection, ridicule, and disgrace. No need to call Socrates physically courageous during the retreat at Delium and morally courageous while in prison resisting temptations to connive with what he considered to be ignoble and unjust opportunities to escape. Plain courage would do in both cases, for in both instances he exposed himself to physical extinction. But by the nineteenth century in western Europe the upper and middle classes had become secure enough in their persons that people could undertake to support unpopular causes, to stand up against injustice, and not die or be imprisoned. The price they paid was loss of social standing, being despised by "decent" people. This often entailed serious economic costs—loss of job, relocation—and the psychological costs of knowing oneself so despised; but they were spared the scourge, which at times may have seemed preferable.

Moral courage owes its distinguishability from the larger domain of courage to several converging influences. The civilizing process, commercial culture, and more effective government and law all combined to pacify the public order.[18] Civility and public order are good things. But some worried that courage would get rarer when noncontention, tolerance, and polite accommodation replaced a most punctiliously sensitive and aggressive honor. In the older cultures of honor, courage was always testing itself. The ethic of revenge meant one had to posture fearlessly even if actual lethal encounters were often nipped in the bud by friends or by other intervenors who negotiated peace. To be too ready to accommodate and forgive was cowardly; people were not so willing to praise your sweetness of spirit if they suspected it was a mask for pusillanimity. In the commercial world, however, people had better things to do than avenging past slights. Men's interest became strongly biased toward future opportunity rather than toward past offense, and not just the short-term future either, but a future long enough for thirty-year bonds to mature. Peaceful public order did not prevent men from importing the diction of battle into finance or from trying to convince themselves that it took courage to make money, but such gestures were obviously and embarrassingly compensatory efforts, fantasies of manliness to make up for the unmanning that people feared luxury and peace had effected.

The ancient view of stoic bent was that wealth, luxury, and soft peace made a society and its men effeminate; virtue risked suffocation in fleshpots and ever more contrived sensual indulgence. Nations and institutions that got fat, it was believed, fell. Even those brilliant theorists of the new prosperous order of the eighteenth century who reject this ancient wisdom and find virtue in wealth and refinement—Mandeville, Smith, and Hume—worry about courage's well-being amidst so much amenity.[19] Smith sees the loss of martial virtue as a real cost of commercial society, though he admits that, as a practical matter, courage is not as practically necessary as it is in barbaric societies. Given the costs of weaponry, a commercial society will be able to annihilate its poor courageous barbaric neighbors by virtue of its superior weapons technology. Its wealth can readily make up for shortfalls in individual courage. But courage is too important for general moral character to let it languish: "Even though the martial spirit of the people were of no use towards the defence of the society, yet to prevent that sort of mental mutilation, deformity and wretchedness, which cowardice necessarily involves in it, from spreading themselves through the great body of the people, would still deserve the most serious attention of government."[20] Smith, we see, cannot imagine a distinction between moral and physical courage; failure of the latter is a moral disease that mutilates and deforms all moral possibility. It behooves society to train its people up to courage even if the occasions to exercise it will be infrequent, indeed, even if it "were of no use towards the defence of the society." As a fiscal matter it is not cheap to maintain ancient manly virtue, but Smith thinks it well worth the cost.

Hume is more optimistic about the effects of wealth and refinement on courage:

> The arts have no such effect in enervating either the mind or body. On the contrary, industry, their inseparable attendant, adds new force to both. And if anger, which is said to be the whetstone of courage, loses somewhat of its asperity, by polite- ness and refinement; a sense of honour, which is a stronger, more constant, and more governable principle, acquires fresh vigour by that elevation of genius which arises from knowledge and a good education.

This sounds like wishful thinking. Why think that this new, "more con- stant, more governable" honor will be tough enough when it comes to doing courage's rough work? Hume answers by playing a variant of the same trump card Smith did and one we saw advanced by du Picq in Chap- ter 14. One wild barbarian may be able to lick two civilized soldiers, but 1,500 barbarians will lose to 1,000 disciplined soldiers. Warfare had changed its style; it is no longer a series of aggregated individual combats: "Courage can neither have any duration, nor be of any use, when not accompanied with discipline and martial skill which are seldom found among a barbarous people."[21] Refinement, the discipline of work and edu- cation, the curbing of rough passions, makes men stay in line, shoot straight, and obey orders.

The Risk of Social Ineptitude

One problem with moral courage is that it must recognize its occasions very precisely. Physical courage is given more room to play in; it is at home in games as well as in war, in defense of a bauble or of one's life. When excessive, as in rashness, we still can't help but admire it. Moral courage is not given as much leeway. Its excess is often priggishness and officiousness which have none of the charm of rashness. If your moral courage takes the form of owning up to mistakes or confessing wrongs, you must take care not to turn such confessions into occasions for self-indulgence and self- aggrandizement in the style that has come to dominate American public dis- course. If your moral courage is of the kind that demands opposing dominant norms, beliefs, and opinions, then the risk is that it will degenerate into mere nonconformism and end in egoistic assertiveness. It is this so-called moral courage that Dostoyevsky's insufferable Underground Man wished he had more of so he could make more scenes and generate even greater embarrassment among those who had the misfortune of dealing with him.[22] Moral courage needs to ground itself seriously as when it stands up against racism, anti-Semitism, sexism, or complacent injustices, and even then there is that nervous line where priggishness may start to compromise morality.

Once manners and refinement had advanced sufficiently in the higher levels of society so that violence was unlikely to take place at convivial gatherings, but the norms of a general aggressive honor were still very much in play, say from the sixteenth to early nineteenth centuries, it could be argued that good manners and refinement needed implicit physical threat to make sure people repressed their ruder urges. In short, some continued to see virtue in a regime that insisted on keeping moral courage indistinguishable from physical courage. You want to give offense and annoy by violating community norms? Be prepared to back it up with your body.

Concern about nervy intrusiveness led Mandeville, early in the eighteenth century, to argue the public benefits in having people fear for their lives in polite conversation. Dueling, he says, is a good idea. It keeps "ill-bred Fellows" from befouling good conversation with their self-assertive vulgarity. Fear makes for civility, and those who advocate abolishing dueling should understand fully the cost of doing so:

> The dread of being called to an Account keeps abundance in awe, and there are thousands of mannerly and well-accomplish'd Gentlemen in Europe, who would have been insolent and insupportable Coxcombs without it . . . It is strange that a Nation should grudge to see perhaps half a dozen Men sacrific'd in a Twelvemonth to obtain so valuable a Blessing, as the Politeness of Manners, the Pleasure of Conversation, and the Happiness of Company in general, that is often so willing to expose and sometimes loses as many thousands in a few Hours, without knowing whether it will do any good or not.[23]

Though Mandeville knows he is being somewhat outrageous, he is only half joking. No moral courage in his world, it's still all physical, for refinement and soft manners are themselves bought only at the point of a gun or an épee. Make things too secure and in his view the whole genteel edifice will come toppling down in a plague of coxcombery. Yet so powerful is the mere threat of violence that very few duels actually have to be fought to secure the public benefit of good manners. Six people a year sacrificed to the cause of decent society, a bargain at the price. In our more exasperated moments we will sometimes half jokingly join in Mandeville's whimsy, for such self-assertive boors and prigs are parasites on our civility. They can indulge in the complete complacency of knowing that they will not be punched, challenged to a duel, or subjected to blood vengeance for giving so much offense. Mandeville, though, already assumes that courage has been so undone by advances in refinement that he can count on the coxcomb being physically fearful; what, however, if he is an Ajax or an Achilles who turns all conversation to complaint about not being properly deferred to and can lick anyone whom he offends?

Would that it were that the only cost of our good manners was having to endure nerviness and self-interested assertiveness in ill-mannered others; we also suffer because we feel tainted by our own good manners. One of the hidden costs of the civilizing process and the suppression of old-style honor is that rather than feeling proud of our graciousness and restraint, we feel instead as if we were chicken. To be sure, others are relieved, even grateful, when we do not make a scene by attacking those who offend us. So grateful, in fact, that they think us well-mannered, poised, tactful, rather than craven or cowardly. But we do not completely concur. Hours later we find ourselves inventing witty ripostes we should have made to the offender. The French have a perfect term for this: *esprit d'escalier*, the wit of the staircase, those perfect cutting remarks you think of after you have left the scene and are heading out and down the stairs. We even may tell counterfactual versions of the incident to others in which we cast ourselves as actually having said what we would have said, had we had the quickness to come up with it at the time and the nerve to say it. Such stories, we fear, are the revenges of cowards.

We accept that it is a good thing to be polite and poised, even at the cost of feeling somewhat cowardly when we are, knowing that we confer thereby a gift on well-socialized bystanders who repay us by playing the coward in the interests of social uneventfulness when it is their turn to suffer the assaults of nerve and chutzpah. By so doing, however, we construct precisely that moral community that is capable of preferring great injustice to great embarrassment, even at times to minor embarrassment.[24] The very real risk we run is that of selling out matters of moral moment (including the rightful claims of people showing moral courage) to our desperate desire not to be embarrassed. Sometimes you may just have to work up the nerve to make a scene and tell the boor to shut his mouth.

In the end we need constant guidance from larger moral principles, and from practical wisdom, to help distinguish moral courage from mere bad manners, or to tell when bad form is saved by moral courage because the goal is worthy. Practical wisdom (for which we have finally found a place in courage's world) must tell us whether, when, and how to make a stand. Not every offensive joke is worth challenging. Not laughing at it is often all that is required. It also makes a difference who the teller is, whether the person is basically decent or truly defective morally, whether weak or powerful. So strong, however, are the norms against scene-making that even reprimanding the weak is no easy task, even harder than not laughing at the boss's miserable attempts at humor. Our vision is often clouded; we need the verdict of detached observers or our own consciences at some later date to know what we should have done. But that puts us right back to the frustrations of *esprit d'escalier*.

Café Coronaries: The Martyr for Manners

The usual literature assumes that men are often willing to die to avoid shame, but the sadder truth is that they may be even more willing to die to avoid embarrassment. Shame is about big moral issues, embarrassment about minor screw-ups for the most part, but frequently no less painful in the short haul. Embarrassment is about present quandary; it puts us to the burden of doing something *now*, and with our poise paralyzed to boot. Shame provides no present option; it is too late to do anything now, except to disappear. The process of rehabilitation, if allowed, is a long one beyond any present quick fix, except in suicide cultures. Occasions for embarrassment are also more frequent than occasions for shame. Earlier, I hypothesized men volunteering for a forlorn hope just to break the excruciatingly awkward silence when the request for volunteers goes unanswered. There is no shame in not volunteering, only embarrassment for the silence. The first awkwardness of not knowing what to do or say, or seeing that others are embarrassed because they do not know what to do or say, is a most powerful motivator of desperate action. Embarrassment brings me back to the interplay of courage, cowardice, and good manners. There is another mystery here to describe, if not to solve.

You are at a fancy restaurant; you have a searing pain in your chest that radiates down your arm; you feel faint and begin to sweat. You fear you are dying of a heart attack. You are no hero; you have run from every fight you could have been in. Yet, rather than make a scene, rather than call unseemly attention to yourself in this moment, rather than look pathetic and pitiable, rather than embarrass those present by having such bad manners as to choose so badly your time of departure, you sit and suffer in silence. You do not wish to die, yet it appears you are willing to; you cannot get up the nerve to scream or even to let a groan escape; you cannot even find it in you to suggest ever so discreetly that you think you are not feeling well, that you need help. You vaguely hope your companions notice that you are out of sorts and will ask whether anything is wrong; but you are not sure that you won't so understate the truth out of embarrassment that they would be easily able to interpret the seriousness of your needs in line with their desires to continue the convivial occasion. Maybe the pain will just subside; how disgraceful it would be to have called attention to yourself if the whole thing were no big deal or, for that matter, if you were going to die anyway.

And what humiliation if it turns out to be gas, an attack of reflux. You remember with horror the one occasion you did mention in a public setting, in as unobtrusive a manner as you could muster, that you had excruciating chest pains and could not catch your breath. That small communication destroyed the conviviality of the event as you were rushed to the emergency room. It was gas. Gas, mind you, not even angina. Gas is a disorder, no matter how painful, that can never rise above ribald comedy and fail to elicit giggles and guffaws. There is shame in being seen as so fearful as to think you are dying when you are not; it proclaims your cowardly disposition. How many times can you claim to be dying and not make your exit? Though there be shame for acting so fearfully if in fact it turns out you are in no danger, that is a problem for the future should you survive the present predicament. The immediate problem is that you are simply too embarrassed to spoil the company by suggesting that you may be dying, too embarrassed for their sake for the burden you impose on them, as well as for what it says about your lack of manners and your apparent excessive fearfulness.

Is this not a form of heroism? Is this not unobtrusiveness raised to epic proportions? Dying in homage to good taste and good manners, like

Kipling's refined man! Is this not the kind of courage that the civilizing process demands of its adherents? If fear of shame pushes soldiers over the top into no-man's land, fear of embarrassing yourself and others by looking foolish or by otherwise making a demand on their capacities for poise and tact has you drift stoically, with all small dignities preserved, into the valley of the shadow of death. Haven't we a case of inverted moral heroism? Dying quietly in order not to rock the boat, not to stand out at all, "not to object," as Orwell says, even when all rational self-interest demands it to save your own skin.

The answers to these questions that are only pretending to be rhetorical questions are not so easy. One thing is clear. This silence is not courage, moral or otherwise, even though it may qualify as a martyrdom for the cause of good manners. Why is this silent sufferer any different from the soldier who charges forward because he is too embarrassed and too fearful of shame not to? There are differences: the soldier's response to fear of shame fits into an age-old narrative of courage. The norms of honor value precisely that motive, though most ethicists are not so generous. There is also a big difference in the kind of mettle it takes to face death when it is being delivered hostilely by another human rather than by natural internal causes. Our poor martyr for manners has no such glorious tradition into which to fit his behavior. He will merely be thought stupid or obstinate for not looking better to his own interests. Should he die in the restaurant he will still have made a scene, though he will be spared most of the awkwardness of it. The norms against not making a scene might be some of those that grip us most powerfully, but that does not mean that we also do not know them to be trivial when measured against life. It is just that they are so hard to violate knowingly. That is why, in fact, we have come to honor the person of moral courage who can rise against them while, unlike the coxcomb and boor, feeling most exquisitely their grip in his gut. But then our dying man is not a coward either, physical or moral. We cannot, it seems, get ourselves to deem anyone cowardly who goes to his death decorously, hiding so well his pain and fear.

Fixing to Die: A Valediction

OUR MARTYR FOR manners felt most acutely the problems of how to make a proper exit. Recall now Aristodemus, the Spartan disgraced at Thermopylae and cheated later of his just prize at the battle of Plataea, whose tale was told in Chapter 2. Aristodemus' story was as grimly comic as it was tragic, and its comedic aspects share something with the gray comedy of the martyr for manners. Aristodemus' tale can be seen as the farcical account of a man who, no matter what his intentions, turns his homecomings into sources of shame to himself and of embarrassment to others. He makes a habit of coming home when propriety demands that he not. On one occasion—Thermopylae—cowardice led him home purposively when he should have died; on the next occasion—Plataea— courage, born of a desperate wish to erase the shame of his first ignoble homecoming, brought him home inadvertently when he meant to die. No matter; his success was again a breach of decorum and good taste. Grand deeds are more properly done by proper men, not by those disgraced as cowards. In his case decorum demanded a less glorious performance in battle unless he were politely to die in the process.

But there is another component, in addition to his being a failed creature, to the awkwardness of his second homecoming. Aristodemus intended to die and failed to realize his intentions. He gave others reason to rely on the immediacy of his death; he was even understood as having obliged himself, in a way, to die in battle. Coming back alive thus transformed his martial success into yet another failure, not of the magnitude of the first breach, but a failure nonetheless, a failure of good manners, for he had taken his formal leave and was not supposed to return. He had, after all, been fixing to die.

Start with a homely example most of us will have experienced. You run into a colleague going about her usual business two days after saying farewell to her at her going-away party. Shouldn't your colleague have had the grace to disappear upon the conclusion of the party, leaving behind only what the leave-taking ritual allows as appropriately left behind: an e-mail address, some memories, and a vacant office that others will jostle for in a smaller reenactment of Odysseus' and Ajax's competition for Achilles' armor? The sense of awkwardness confirms that the formal closure provided by the ritualized farewells of the party has been violated. The ritual inaugurated a new era in which the parting person is no longer to intrude her bodily presence without engaging in other special ritual activities. There are no clear rules for handling the physical presence of that person again so soon. The prior performance of the leave-taking ritual means that such a subsequent encounter can no longer be "business as usual." She is now socially "gone," and she should have gotten her body to accord with her new social status. If she is to be seen again, that reseeing must fit the special contours of something known as a "visit," which has its own peculiar ritualized features with its own specific expectations. Otherwise she is to be seen only in photographs; not heard but only heard about, unless she phones long distance.

Doesn't the awkwardness of this unscripted encounter reproduce the awkwardness of Aristodemus' second homecoming, writ smaller to be sure but in other respects fully analogous? Fixing to die is a final farewell. Here too the person can come back properly only in the status of a visitor, albeit mostly an unwelcome one: as a ghost, an afterwalker, an unsettling memory, or as other similarly unpleasant special statuses we impose on the unliving that register our deep anxieties about death and our equally deep anxieties about visitors. (Notice how often we picture death as a visitor and visitors as bringing death or the plague or as simply plaguing us.) Although their coming back after dying may make for horror, their coming back from the brink without dying, after farewells have been said, makes for awkwardness, which in some bizarre way can be almost as unnerving.

The state of fixing to die need not be accompanied by a unique inner state. All that it requires is behavior that leads others to believe one is in that special zone. It could be implied by illness or explicitly assumed by vows. It could be accompanied by a grim sense of purpose, an ebullient desire for glory or martyrdom, or by dark despair in which the farewell takes on the tone of a "good-bye to all that." The status need not be chosen by the subject as much as it is conferred upon him by the understandings and expectations of others, as when one contracts certain kinds of diseases. But whatever its origin, fixing to die is a special, almost magical, ritual state, and it often finds itself playing a role in courage's drama.

The Kaiten

The Kaiten is a special torpedo that the Japanese brought into service toward the end of the World War II. The warhead carried 3,000 pounds of explosives, powerful enough to sink an aircraft carrier if properly aimed. Everything was in the aiming, and to ensure that this was a smart torpedo, a human pilot was provided with room right behind the warhead. Behind his space was the missile's propulsion system. If the Kaiten hit its target the pilot died one kind of death; if he missed—the Kaiten once discharged was not recoverable—he died another kind of death. The first way was glorious, the second a humiliation the price of which was variously starvation, suffocation, or, more properly, suicide by self-detonation. A submarine could carry five or six Kaiten on its deck with a special complement of five specially chosen humans to pilot them who could enter the missile via special hatches while the sub was submerged.

When the call was made by the commander of Yokota Yutaka's school for men "who burn with a passion to die gloriously for the sake of their country" to man a new weapon, Yokota was desperate to be chosen. He was not in the least deterred by the commander's disclosure that there was no hope of returning alive; that was the attraction. He took training deathly seriously: "If you'd had two lives, it wouldn't have mattered, but you were giving up your only life. Life is so precious . . . That's why we trained like that. We practiced that hard because we valued our lives so highly." Yokota had fantasies of sinking an aircraft carrier or a cruiser, no mere destroyer for him. He "didn't want to trade his life for anything as small as that."[1]

The ceremony of departure is a highly formal affair in which the pilots bid farewell to life and are invested with a ritual short sword. Another Kaiten survivor describes the ceremony as a thrilling show. "It was almost like the departure for battle of a great general and his samurai warriors in the feudal age." For this man, too, the meaning of the Kaiten was not that life was cheap, but that in an age of tank battles and massive assaults by forces numbering in the hundreds of thousands, when even the air war was "no longer the clash of lone warriors," the "Kaiten was still an individual affair." Hence the elaborate ritual and the grand send-off, heroic in the old style.[2]

Yokota describes how he and the five others cultivated a certain bravado, a joking in the face of death. It would have been the meanest disgrace to have shown any signs of fear. One man in their training group did so, and Yokota cuts him out of his group pictures. Yokota is fixing to die; he focuses all his being on dying right, which as he envisages it has two aspects: maintaining composure in the face of death and hitting a worthy target. They crawl into their torpedoes. Yokota is in number four. But only two ships are sighted and only three Kaiten launched. He is ordered to come back in. "That," he says, "was the moment I really wanted to die." Notice the force of that "really." It is not meant to suggest that he did not want to die in his Kaiten taking down a thousand enemy with him; quite the contrary. He wants to die for the pure shame of having failed to do so. That "really" means wanting to disappear leaving no trace of ever having been. It is less a wish to die than a wish never to have been born.

Yokota's story degenerates into a tragicomical farce. On his next encounter with Allied ships his Kaiten couldn't be fired because of a cracked fuel line; the other three fired just fine. Again, all dressed up and no place to go. The crew of this mission had, like Yokota, all been pilots who had not been able to launch on their prior mission, and all had vowed, before they departed, that there would be no accidental returns this time. But Yokota comes back. At the base he meets another pilot who has had the same bad luck; both "wanted to crawl into a corner and die from failure." Their own appropriate horror at their shameful condition does nothing to assuage the disgust they inspire in other Kaiten pilots for having come back alive; they are considered cowards. They get beaten savagely by those who have been passed over in favor of these two losers who cannot die for trying. And then the war ends. Yokota is devastated; he weeps uncontrollably, not, he says, because Japan lost the war, but for not having accompanied the other Kaiten pilots in death.

Yokota, like Aristodemus, does everything he can to die, but the gods are too comically disposed to let him carry it off; a myriad of near misses keeps him alive as if to mock his heroic pretensions. His fellow pilots consider his failure inexcusable, partly because it is comical, even though they do not find it a laughing matter. They show no willingness to let Yokota off the hook by attributing his failure to misfortune rather than to him. What precisely was his fault, what did he *do* that could justify beatings severe enough to cost him his hearing in his left ear?

The easy answer is that he disgraced them by disgracing himself; he should have died as he vowed to do in the way he vowed to do it. His formal farewell forecloses his coming back in the flesh. To his fellow pilots his return generates something more than the mere awkwardness and befuddlement of running into an acquaintance who lacks the good grace not to be seen after her going-away party. The stakes are higher here. This is the world of honor and shame and its defining virtue and vice: courage and cowardice. Yokota's fellow pilots are not imposing standards of judgment on him that he doesn't hold for himself. He is mortified by his own failure; he too would have beaten someone like himself, just as he had cut out the picture of the man who trembled when he boarded his Kaiten. He does not plead on his own behalf the special difficulty of having to get ready to die not just once, but several times, a torment those who succeeded in launching the first time did not have to face.

Yokota contemplated suicide, and this of course is what he should have done. In Japanese warrior culture suicide is a well-scripted ritual in which shame becomes partly redeemable by choosing an honorable exit in which you relieve others of having to bear your presence and relieve yourself of their scorn should you not so relieve them. Recall Pantites (Chapter 2), who hanged himself because of the shame of having survived the slaughter of the Three Hundred. Pantites chose suicide in a culture in which killing oneself was not as positively valued an option for escaping the pains of inadvertent shame. He was left to improvise without great cultural support.[3] Yokota, it turns out, was considerably less willing to blow himself up for shame than to blow himself up for glory, and this is read as cowardice by his peers. Yokota wanted to die, contemplated suicide, got some explosives to do it up right, but by that time the war was over, and by his own admission he "didn't have the guts to blow [him]self to bits." Does his failure of nerve prove, in the end, that the beatings and self-mortification were justified, that he was rightly culpable for his own bad luck? Was there some failing here that could justifiably be seen as cowardice? The bargain he struck with the moral order was that he was not to come back; the bargain was unconditional, rendered so by a rite of passage that marked him as someone fixing to die, to whom all farewells had been given.

How could Yokota be welcomed back when Aristodemus was not? Aristodemus, moreover, had carried the day against the enemy. His success in battle transforms his failure to die from an issue of intense shame to one of mere embarrassment for not having had the *tact* to die, more a social failure than a moral one. The comparison between Yokota and him is not quite apt, because of the different role suicide plays in each culture and because one man cannot die for winning and the other cannot die for losing. It will take some time for both to be full moral members of their communities again, if ever, and if ever, more time for Yokota than for Aristodemus.

Yet we still want to say it was not poor Yokota's fault. Put aside the fact that in spite of the official view that blame should follow blamable intentions, that it should figure only for those actions that could have been willed otherwise, we still insist on blaming the stone that trips us, swearing at the door sill on which we stub our toes, hating the person whose brakes fail and who smashes our car, and grumbling about the obese person who boards the full flight even without regard to whether he sits next to us. Fixing to die raises somewhat different issues for attributing blame for failure. When one aspires to glorious death, the failure to gain it turns the aspiration into pretentiousness. The aspiration itself may be praiseworthy, but failure to gain the aspired end seriously risks making the aspirer something of a fool.[4] Yokota's ambitions, undertaken with proper motivation and dedication, thus become, by virtue of his coming back home, risible pretensions rather than the noble goals they were before the gods jokingly intervened. So what if he is at the mercy of circumstances beyond his control? He took the risk that circumstances would not sort themselves out in his favor, a risk that left him open to derision and shame. In his culture, suicide was an option made to order for such failure, and he couldn't get himself to go through with it.

Raising Lazarus

Sir Thomas Browne (1605–1682), that most subtle and strange of writers, finds himself meditating on some points that he fears might lead some, but not him, to doubt holy writ or the wisdom of its claims. One must be engaged in intense tempting of oneself to be able to come up with the occasions he finds troublesome. Would any but the most skeptical of believers think to raise these?

> I can read the history of the Pigeon that was sent out of the Ark, and returned no more, yet not question how shee found out her mate that was left behind: that Lazarus was raised from the dead, yet not demand where, in the interim, his soule awaited; or raise a Law-case, whether his heire might lawfully detaine his inheritance, bequeathed upon him by his death; and he, though restored to life, have no Plea or title unto his former possessions.[5]

Lazarus, poor soul, was not fixing to die; he had already been dead four days and was smelling rather bad when Jesus resurrected him. Jesus never asked Lazarus whether he wished to come back (that would have required a miracle of a different order—a dead man speaking); he also never asked Lazarus' sisters if they wanted him back. John's account shows that Jesus was not in the least bit interested in their desires. He had his own fish to fry, for it was He who was fixing to die. Jesus may have inferred such a desire from their manifestations of grief. But it is just that inference that Browne shows is not warranted. Mary and Martha's grief did not take the form of wishing Lazarus back; it took the form of wishing he had never died in the first place. The distinction is not a trivial one. And thus they register impatience with Jesus for having failed to attend Lazarus in his final illness, an illness they assume Jesus could readily have cured. This being the week before his last entry into Jerusalem, Jesus wanted a bigger miracle than a simple cure, and he purposely tarried to provide the occasion for a display that would impress even those who already believed in him.

Browne, however, who at some level does not wish to have wicked thoughts but is not altogether displeased by the psychic mischief they cause when they intrude as a consequence of the very wish not to have them, suggests that none of the family members may have been all that pleased with the miracle. Lazarus has made a lame homecoming very much as Aristodemus has done, but even lamer after the manner Browne indicates. If Yokota comes back shamed, Lazarus comes back destitute, at the mercy of his sisters' charity, if they were his heirs, for his death automatically transfers the title of his estate to his heirs. He would surely stand the best hope if Mary and Martha were in fact his heirs, but it is quite certain that they are not; his property undoubtedly passed to some unmentioned male relative to whom Lazarus and his sisters must now beggar themselves. No wonder Martha and Mary are so peevish with Jesus' tardiness, for they too have been rendered destitute by their brother's death. Browne hints at a certain thoughtlessness in the miracle, a certain callousness to what it would mean to force someone into the tactless behavior of coming back once he said his final farewell. More than just awkwardness is at stake; property titles also hang in the balance.

Two Twists and Scalp Cane

Scalp Cane, a Cheyenne, grieved the death of his brother, who had been killed by the Crows.[6] As in so many honor cultures, the grief of warrior-aged men manifested itself properly in revenge.[7] A certain grand revenge might also contemplate joining your dead kinsman in death by dying in battle against his killers. So Scalp Cane "mounted an old man on his horse, and together they rode up and down the Cheyenne village, the old man crying for all to hear, 'Here we have Scalp Cane with us today. Look at him now, ye Cheyenne. Tomorrow he will have left us. Behold him! tomorrow he will be with us no more.'"

Scalp Cane had entered the ritual status of someone fixing to die. It entitled him to special privileges before the battle. He could, without giving offense, take meat from anyone or whip others who were in his way or were slow on the march. In other cases, after the formal announcement of no return, women would sing songs of encouragement, or the person about to die would himself sing death songs. But tomorrow came, and Scalp Cane came home with it. The Crows sent the Cheyenne fleeing, and Scalp Cane fled ignominiously with them. "After that day the standard greeting for Scalp Cane was, 'Hello, you are back? You don't look like a ghost.'"

Likewise, Two Twists, moved by the lament of an old man whose sons the Crows had killed in battle, vowed to die meting out revenge upon them: "My friends, behold me; I shall never return from this raid."[8] Two Twists came back too, but not before he went hurtling into the Crow breastwork, wreaking havoc among them. The other Cheyenne watched him disappear over the breastworks fighting hand-to-hand. Inspired by Two Twists' example, they charged and routed the enemy. Two Twists came home to a rather different welcome from Scalp Cane's. But there was still awkwardness. There remained the matter of the vow. A consensus was reached that Two Twists was to be excused from it because he had honored it in spirit if not in the letter. Nor would they agree to let him go out fixing to die again; they released him completely from his vow. The jurisprude Karl Llewellyn extols what he considers the Roman-like legal genius the Cheyenne exhibited in the case. The people saw that promises had purposes that should not be thwarted by formalism and literalism: "All the men saw that the essence of the promise had lain not in its wording, but in uninterrupted glorious exposure, which he had performed."[9]

The difference between the cases is obvious. One man delivers so well that he cannot be killed; the other is all pretense, failed pretense, a just object of scorn. One is courageous; the other, cowardly. The vow not to return might in some settings be prompted by despair and shame, but it is always, even when undertaken in despair, conceived as a testing of courage. But courage does not seamlessly mesh with the substance of the vow. Courage may refuse to end in glorious defeat even though it is meant to. It is equally capable of securing victory, and while its special grandness as a virtue owes something to its contemptuous disregard of safety, it ends being a remarkably effective way to gain it, often in spite of itself.

Great courage tends to expose its beneficiaries to envy as well as to awe and gratitude. Success in battle cannot be counted on to excuse the vow without more. The Cheyenne still worry about the effect of the vow, enough to discuss it. But they are filled with goodwill toward Two Twists. They fear that he will be so punctilious about experiencing any shame attributable to his "failure" that he will continually seek danger until he fulfills the letter of the vow. In the end this is an easy case because of the particular virtue that causes the failure of the vow. It turns out that an exception is more readily made for returnees who qualify as heroes. Nonetheless, the vow to die itself demands a certain homage, which is paid in the form of small embarrassments by those who do the welcoming and fairly major ones by the returning hero.

Two Twists gets much more generous treatment than the equally successful Aristodemus gets after Plataea. But there is an obvious reason for the difference. Aristodemus had to prove himself not to be the coward he had shown himself at Thermopylae. He starts out with his accounts very much in the red, discredited as a man of honor. Two Twists is healthily in the black. Other differences figure in this too. The Plains Indians had formal rituals for fixing to die in battle.[10] They were not all that infrequently undertaken, and presumably the people were fairly used to warriors coming back after having vowed not to. They may even have developed techniques for dealing with this kind of successful failure, which the Greeks had to handle on the fly because they had no such formal rituals. Indeed, Aristodemus' "vow" not to return may have been no more explicitly made than Lazarus'. For all we know, his reckless death-seeking fighting style raised the vow by necessary implication, just as the same was raised by Lazarus' sickness and death. Each, however, is held to some kind of account for the expectations of permanent departure they raised in others.

Fixing to die is not sure of its genre, oscillating as it can by merest circumstance between comedy and tragedy, farce and epic. It can even indulge in melodrama. Most fixing to die in battle means taking the offensive. Aristodemus, Two Twists, and Yokota must charge, hurl themselves forward into the fray. Suppose, however, an equally suicidal but passive form of fixing to die in which the actor seeks enemy fire so as not to quail before it. This type of display is in some ways more remarkable because it gains no psychological advantage from working oneself up into berserk fury. The rebel yell makes no sense if all you mean to do is sit on a horse and get shot at. Such is the style of Lieutenant Brayle in Ambrose Bierce's short story "Killed at Resaca." Like Aristodemus, Brayle means to live down an imputation of cowardice. His case differs in that there is no evidence that he was cowardly, just some malicious gossip originated by a rival for his fiancée's hand, but which she credits enough to wish for firm proof of its falsehood. None of his fellow soldiers understand his motive; he keeps his counsel. They read his behavior, which is otherwise perfect, as being "vain of his courage," his "one most objectionable and unsoldierly quality."[11] He means to die, this being the only way he can unambiguously prove his courage, but the passive way of seeking it requires that he keep coming back as he waits his turn for the bullet that has his name on it. He thus generates no awkwardness, only a kind of wonderment half mixed of respect and dismay. Brayle's fixing to die is an entirely private affair, and so there are no formal farewells to prompt the awkwardnesses generated in the other cases, nor would there have been any shame in his not getting killed; there is only a sick sense of waste, by both blue and gray, when it finally happens.

18

Concluding Postscript

WHAT BUSINESS DO I HAVE showing up for a postscript? I took my leave in the last chapter. I am like Scalp Cane unable to follow through on his vow not to return, or like an overeager guest who wears out his modest welcome but finally departs, only to your horror to return two minutes later to claim his forgotten umbrella. But a few concluding remarks are in order.

This meditation on the mystery of courage takes a middle ground. I mistrust the philosophic tradition that seeks to link courage too closely with reason, thereby reducing courage to prudence's handmaid; that tradition tends to make courage more a matter of judging and evaluating than of doing. I also doubt the virtue in undervaluing the courage driven by fear of shame relative to that motivated for virtue's sake alone. The standard is too strict, too ungenerous. The fact that courage's psychology remains a mystery to the manifestly courageous suggests that we should be more modest about setting forth theories of courage that would deny it to Doc, to Beowulf, to the heroes of the sagas, and also to the average soldier who charges ahead assisted, but only in part, by his tot of rum.

Philosophers tend to take as the purest example of courage the old Socrates as he awaits his punishment and faces death with complete equanimity. But they forget the Socrates whom no one would mess with physically, Socrates the soldier, the man of honor; the young Socrates was child to the old man. Though those who lived after Socrates can rightly honor him for the way he died, his moral authority during his lifetime was just as much a function of the courage he showed on the field of battle as of the skills he showed in conversation and disputation. Those sidelong glances he gave as he strutted loftily about town would have looked pretty silly coming from a physical coward.

But I would not be too generous in conferring courage either. Those ignorant of danger, whether because of stupidity, insensibility, or madness, are not courageous. One must appreciate the danger at stake, even if that appreciation does not prompt fear. And then courage is too valuable to grant it to everyone who succeeds at a task that it took some marshaling of will to do. There must be danger and hardship to overcome, real danger and hardship, publicly discernible, properly appreciated. We should not declare every achievement that demanded great commitments of labor, energy, and devotion a matter of courage. Most self-realization is not about courage, nor do all the obstacles that stand in our way require courage in their overcoming.

To return to a point made in the Introduction, courage, more than any other virtue, figures centrally in the stories we love best. We are treated to a steady diet of thick accounts of courageous people and courageous deeds, in both the aggressive style and the defensive style of endurance. We know roughly what courage is, because we so desperately seek it and admire it and love to hear it told about. But then we aren't always sure when *we* have it, even those fortunates who are clearly blessed with it. Our sincerest modesty comes when we have to judge the quality and quantity of our own courage. Our fear, our self-doubt make us suspect we just got lucky when we managed to do okay; but we have no great confidence we will do very well when the dragon comes again. Yes, there are those people of blessed disposition, confident that they will not run, no matter what, but they are rare. And it is not only types like these confident souls who elicit our awe and wonder; so do those average souls who come through in the crunch, unless finally too much is demanded of them for too long. The courage of average people forces us to make a personal accounting; it makes a powerful demand on us to conform and sets us to fearing that we might not be up to it.

There has been a recent spate of books and movies that look with great nostalgia on World War II, written by or directed by those who did not fight, who now in their middle age, when it is very safe for them to indulge this kind of wistfulness, think it vaguely amiss that that they missed out on war. Most of my social class in the United States (myself included) bought substitutes for the only war we were eligible to fight in and would no doubt do so again. So when in middle age I come at last to believe that a nation builds up a moral treasury of merit by the sacrifices of its people in war and I begin to worry, like those ancient moralists, that we grow fat, lazy, and contemptible amidst our plenty, I don't have a leg to stand on to make that claim. My father could; he fought; but he is too wise to make it.

I took the title of this book from Abner Small, Civil War soldier, who was puzzled by what he called the mystery of bravery, which for him meant that courage and cowardice seemed divorced from character and will. Men were heroes or cowards "in spite of themselves." For Small, the mystery is one of the relation between character and action; there was no predictability as to who would play what role. Some larger sardonic power, it seemed, assigned men roles in battle at random. Robert Burdette, who introduced this book, was mystified too, but on other grounds. He doubted that even the sardonic power Himself could tell who was playing what role when they were playing it: "But who are the cowards? And how do we distinguish them from the heroes. How does God tell?" These are troubled observations from two men looking back on what became the defining experience in their lives, and their experience also coincided with the defining experience in the life of their nation. So we can pardon the exaggerated tone, for there is great truth in their exaggeration.

I will give the last words to Mr. Small.[1] He is so good with them. It is after the debacle at Fredericksburg. The men know themselves defeated, but are relieved finally to be allowed the warmth of fires again after three days of battle.

> I went down the line of my regiment, fewer than half its men surviving, weary and dirty, their clothes torn and muddy, knapsacks rent, canteens battered, hands and faces daubed with muck and splotched with powder. There were pale faces and faces flushed, anxious and expectant faces, many that I had scanned three days before; the same, yet changed. There was something in the

expression, the attitude of those men, that awed me. An uprush of emotion blinded and choked me as I turned away.

By courtesy of the enemy they are allowed to take in some of their dead. Then Fredericksburg is left behind in haunting images that evoke (and are worthy of) Dante, Milton, and the Bible:

> Night closed in, and a gusty wind and pelting rain swept over the scene of battle, and under cover of the turbulent dark we obeyed orders to make ready in silence to move. Then we marched unmolested back to the pontoon bridges, that we had crossed three days before, and back across the bridges, muffled now, to the east side of the river. The whole army was spirited away. The field was left to the enemy and the storm.

NOTES

BIBLIOGRAPHY

INDEX

Notes

For full citations of the works mentioned here, see the Bibliography.

1. Introduction

1. Burdette, 97–108.
2. There is much conflicting evidence in the literature regarding the extent to which types like the good coward were sheltered and succored by the men or treated with coldness and hostility. One important variable is length of time in the line; the longer the men have been exposed to combat the more tolerant they are of desertion, cracking up, and giving way; see, e.g., Stouffer, 114, 141 (World War II studies); the extent to which men were willing to think someone was a psychiatric casualty rather than a coward depended on how hard he tried "to overcome the withdrawal tendencies engendered by intense fear . . . they were expected to try to put up a struggle to carry on despite their fear" (200); see also Manning, 82.
3. On "nice tries" see Miller, "Near Misses" 11–12.
4. With Geach who rejects the idea of any virtue assisting bad action, contrast A. Smith, *Theory of Moral Sentiments* 241; von Wright, 148, 153; Hare, 155; see also Foote, 15–16.
5. Sassoon, *Fox-Hunting Man* 256; see also Chapter 12, note 17.
6. MacIntyre links caring to courage: "If someone says that he cares for some individual, community, or cause, but is unwilling to risk harm or danger on his, her, or its own behalf, he puts in question the genuineness of his care and concern. Courage . . . has its role in human life because of this connection with care and concern"; *After Virtue* 192.
7. Aquinas, 2.2 Q123 A2.
8. Boswell, 5 April 1775, 609.
9. See Geach's defense of courage against its "depreciation" in academic circles (150), the main depreciator being R. M. Hare; see Hare, 149, 155.
10. See Plato, *Republic* 4.429c–430c; see also the less obscure but ultimately dissatisfying account in *Protagoras* 359b–360e, and below, Chapter 3, note 10.
11. See variously Pears, Urmson, Duff, and Ross, among others.
12. From a private in the 5th Wisconsin, quoted in Keegan, *Mask of Command* 210.
13. See Brandt and the discussion by Wallace, 60–63.
14. Boswell, 10 April 1778, 926–927.
15. See Pericles' anxiety on this score; Thucydides, 2.35.
16. See, variously, Casey, Wallace, Walton, and Yearley.
17. See, e.g., Aquinas, 2.2 Q123 A1.

18. On the historical moment when Reason became tendentiously allied with clerical and state-building interests see Cheyette.

19. Cicero, 1.78; Montaigne, 3.10, p. 1158.

20. Plato, *Phaedo* 68d; see also *Republic* 6.486b.

21. Shakespeare, *Richard II* I.ii.33–34.

22. See, e.g., Freedman regarding origin myths that impute prior cowardice to Catalonian peasants so as to justify their subordination.

23. Not all these soldier memoirists are "nature's children" with regard to their writing skills. Quite a few were writers who happened to have been soldiers; others aspired to be writers, but for many, especially the Civil War and Vietnam War memoirists, soldiering bore a causal connection to writing.

24. See Clover, "Maiden Warriors"; Miller, "Choosing the Avenger"; Hasluck, 223–224; Whitaker, 151.

2. Aristodemus, or Cowardice Redeemed

1. Similarly see the case of Othryades reported by Herodotus (1.82), the sole Spartan survivor of a battle against the Argives. After stripping the bodies of the Argives, he killed himself for the shame of having survived his companions.

2. Graves, 98.

3. The Penguin translator obscures the explicitness with which rushing forward in fury means leaving the phalanx line and thus breaking ranks.

4. Aristotle, *Ethics* 3.7.1115b25.

5. Ibid., 3.8.1117a5.

6. In the phalanx the hoplites stood tight together in ranks. Each man's left was protected by his own shield, his right by the shield of the man next to him. The main weapon was a spear, eight to nine feet long. The front rank was backed by as many as seven more.

7. Montaigne, 3.3, p. 926; see also Thucydides, 5.69–70: the Argives advanced "with great violence and fury, while the Spartans came on slowly to the music of many flute-players in their ranks. This custom of theirs . . . is designed to make them keep in step and move forward steadily without breaking their ranks, as large armies often do when they are just about to join battle."

8. On the folly of leaving the line see Lazenby, 95, 103.

9. Homer, *Iliad* 2.243–277.

10. "In battle individual hoplites raised on a diet of Homer no doubt balanced fear with ideals of heroic glory when they sang the paean"; Wheeler, 123.

11. Fourth- and fifth-century statements that approvingly express the uncompromising, risk-seeking, self-sacrificing style are readily found; see Dover, 162–163: "I cannot prove my willingness to sacrifice my life except by actually sacrificing it; and if I do that I can be forgiven all else." He qualifies this statement by citing the case of Posidonius and Aristodemus, which he takes as showing that "the degree of freedom from pressure in choosing to sacrifice oneself could be regarded as relative

to merit." But which way does that cut? That the presumptively honorable are held to a lower standard relative to the norms of death-seeking fearlessness in battle? The case shows that indeed there were degrees of freedom, but exactly which way they cut varied according to the politics of the situation.

12. Recall too that Plato found the perfect courage he granted to philosophers to be motivated by what the Spartans alleged to be the very defect in Aristodemus' courage: the desire to die. Plato would have Socrates argue, no doubt, that Aristodemus was dying for shame; the philosopher dies to escape the importunities the body makes upon the soul, Aristodemus to escape the defect of soul that produced his moral failure. But that would be unfair to Aristodemus, who simply lives in shame; disgrace, not fear of disgrace, is his lot. Both he and the philosopher are very similarly lamenting their present miserable state.

13. Plutarch, *Life of Cleomenes* chap. 9.

14. Aristotle, *Ethics* 3.8.1116b1.

15. "In a divisional assault—one by the book—one regiment is kept in reserve, two are committed in the attack. In each of the attacking regiments, one battalion is in reserve; in each battalion, one company is in reserve, and in each of the two assaulting companies one platoon is in reserve. Assuming rifle-company combat strength of 125 men, you come up with 1,500 men moving forward against the enemy out of a division of 13,000 men"; quoted in Smoler, 42.

3. Tim O'Brien and Laches

1. Small, 70.

2. The only other canonical philosopher I know of who distinguished himself as a soldier is Ludwig Wittgenstein, who received Austria's equivalent of the Victoria Cross and Medal of Honor—the Gold Medal for Valor—on the Italian front in World War I; Gilbert, 433.

3. O'Brien, *If I Die* 22.

4. The two toughest Norse saga heroes were not blond. One, Egil, was black-haired before growing gray and bald quite early; the other, Skarphedin, had chestnut-colored hair. Neither was good-looking.

5. Dostoyevsky, 1.3.

6. It is not quite true that charges cannot look foolish if they fail. Suppose five minutes after a failed suicidal charge by one of your men you take the position because the enemy was obliterated by its own friendly fire? See Miller, "Near Misses" 10–11.

7. Middleton and Rowley, 4.1.162–164.

8. The Greek phalanx style of fighting required no special technical skills. One pressed forward in ranks pushing with the shield and stabbing with one's spear. So the virtues of learning the art of fighting in armor turn out to be (1) the general merits of learning and personal cultivation and (2) developing skills for fighting

when the lines are broken. Nicias favors instruction for both these reasons; Laches thinks it a waste of time as proved by the fact that the Spartans don't bother with it and that the fencing masters often make fools of themselves at crunch time in battle (*Laches* 182a-184c).

9. *Laches* 189b; see also 181b.

10. *Laches* 199e. In later dialogues Socrates seems to accept the gist of Nicias' knowledge-based definition of courage ("courage is the knowledge of the grounds of hope and fear"; *Laches* 195a, 196d), which he was not yet willing to endorse in *Laches*; see *Republic* 4.429c–430c and Fortenbaugh, 64–66.

11. Johansen, who raced cars, undoubtedly knew a thing or two about twin-cammed engines too, but that is another matter. On cross-class disgust see Miller, *Anatomy of Disgust* chaps. 9–10.

12. Most recently: "I have written some of this before, but I must write it again. I was a coward. I went to Vietnam"; "The Vietnam in Me" 48; also *The Things They Carried* 63: "I was a coward. I went to war."

13. See Goffman, "Normal Appearances," in *Relations in Public* 283–309.

14. See Yearley, 114–115. Yearley's sophisticated treatment of courage, developed after O'Brien articulated his theory, agrees with him on the point that it is a special feature of courage that it be self-aware. Courage must always, in his view, involve assessments of the propriety of its motive and the value of the ends sought; without such awareness the actions are at best a semblance of courage. Contrast benevolence, he says, which finds itself compromised by self-awareness. See also Casey, 65: "The brave man is conscious of his virtue, and confronts his destiny with a certain style." Casey seems, I think, to be confusing the hero in the classical epic style with the person of courage who may or may not have a sense of his own courage. I am skeptical that such self-consciousness is a *sine qua non* of courage; see the cases of Doc and Lorenzo discussed in the text.

15. See Aquinas, 2.2 Q129 A5; Aristotle, *Ethics* 4.3; Hume, *Enquiry* sec. 7.

16. See Urmson, "Saints and Heroes" 203.

17. Rorty, "Faces of Courage" 303.

18. Sherman, 886–887.

19. In a seminar in which we read *If I Die*, all but one of the eighteen students felt that any theory of courage that excluded Doc, as O'Brien portrayed him, damned the theory.

20. As time erased the intrusiveness of some of the more annoying warts of these men, O'Brien grew more generous toward them. In *The Things They Carried* (first published in 1987), he grants the grunts an inner life, one of fear and anxiety, made all the more difficult to endure by norms preventing articulation of those inner states: "They were afraid of dying but they were even more afraid to show it . . . They endured . . . It was not courage exactly; the object was not valor. Rather, they were too frightened to be cowards" (19, 21).

21. J. Glenn Gray (111) would classify such people as occasional cowards; in a strange way his classification, though superficially uncharitable, is more optimistic about courageous possibility than O'Brien's theory of doing well on average. It assumes

that cowardice is a mere lapse rather than a necessary concession to the unrelenting demands of modern warfare.

4. Courageous Disposition

1. See Fortenbaugh, 63–64; Aristotle says: "Socrates thought that courage is a kind of knowledge"; *Ethics* 3.8.1116b5. This underestimates the complexity of the Socratic account, which in any event never really settles on a single theory of courage. See also MacIntyre, *Short History of Ethics* 22: "We do not wish to know what courage is, we wish to be courageous."

2. Aristotle, *Ethics* 2.3.1104b9.

3. See Pears for a detailed treatment of fear's precise role in Aristotle's discussion of courage. Pears argues that the fear that is present does not need to be overcome by self-control, for fear contributes to the action by being part of the process by which the goal is weighed against the costs of achieving it; that is, fear works into the equation of whether the action is worth the effort or whether it would be merely rash or stupid to pursue it (180–181). That fear is a medial fear, obeying the rule of the mean, and is apparently part of practical wisdom itself. Pears must develop an intricate and ingenious argument to make his case, and even he doubts whether, ultimately, Aristotle's text can support it; see also Duff, who tries a different route to save Aristotle's man of virtue from sinking to "mere" self-command.

4. Aristotle, *Ethics* 7.1–2.

5. Ibid., 7.5.1148b28.

6. Ibid., 7.1.1145a26.

7. Ibid., 2.4.1105b1.

8. Ibid., 2.2.1104b1.

9. Ibid., 2.6.1106b21; thus "the man who faces and fears (or similarly feels confident about) the right things for the right reason and in the right way and at the right time is courageous" (3.7.1115b18–20).

10. Getting a fix on practical wisdom is no easy matter either. See, e.g., Nussbaum's extended discussion, chaps. 10–12; and Urmson, "Aristotle's Doctrine of the Mean" 162–163.

11. See, e.g., Wallace, 62–63; Walton, 25; Yearley, 80–83; and Urmson, "Aristotle's Doctrine of the Mean" 162. But compare Rorty, "Two Faces of Courage" 307, who rightly criticizes the easy linkage of courage and practical wisdom. She argues that practical wisdom is too generalized an attitude to be of much help in encouraging those little actions that start the process of doing what you have to do in situations demanding courage.

12. We, however, also train to handle emergencies, hoping to make what we have to do in them routine. A good portion of the training for obtaining a pilot's license is devoted to emergency procedures, which one practices again and again; moreover, there are checklists that are supposed to be ready at hand to walk one through the procedures in the event that one's wits might fail. Aristotle knew too that in

emergencies practical reason must give way to the pure automaticity of the habitual virtue; see Fortenbaugh, 71–72.

13. Aristotle, *Politics* 3.4.1277b22: "For a man would be thought a coward if he had no more courage than a courageous woman."

14. See, e.g., Schwartz, Snidman, and Kagan.

15. The experiments are described in J. A. Gray, 35–52, and their results have not been invalidated; see also Konner, 218.

16. Aristotle, *Ethics* 3.6.1115a30–34; if this passage makes courage look like a matter of fearlessness, then compare 3.7.1115b13: "The courageous man ... will fear what it is natural for man to fear, but he will face it in the right way and as principle directs for the sake of what is right and honorable." We can reconcile the passages by understanding that facing death in the right way is to face it *as if* fearless.

17. Ibid., 3.6.1115a34.

18. Ibid., 3.7.1115b23.

19. Montaigne, 2.1, p. 378.

20. Manning, 10–11.

21. E.g., Crisp, 119.

22. Marshall, 182.

23. Hume, "Of Suicide" 580.

24. Blackford, 268–269.

25. Sassoon, *Infantry Officer* 46.

26. Ford, 303. Not just fictional characters: "I just can't face it, sir; it's the noise and those shells; I just can't face it any more"; a man to his officer in Normandy, 1944, in Watney, 209.

27. Mark VII, 49.

28. Manchester, 124–125. Contempt for not engaging the enemy frontally is for the most part a Western attitude; see Hanson, 9–18. The steppes warriors fought from horseback with bows at a distance, eschewed direct hand-to-hand fighting, and cut down the enemy after they had been put to flight or surrendered; see Keegan, *History of Warfare* 213–214, 332, 387–388.

29. On the horrors and special fears of being shelled see also the sources quoted in Winter, 116–120 (World War I); Ellis, 69–71 (World War II); also Holmes, 232–233; and Moran, 68–69.

30. Sledge, 63. Sledge's memoir has rightly received glowing reviews as one of the finest performances in the war-memoir genre; see Keegan, *Battle for History* 62; and Paul Fussell's introduction to the Oxford University Press edition of Sledge's memoir, xi–xx. Sledge's book and Abner Small's memoir belong in the canon of American literature alongside Grant's justly praised *Memoirs*.

31. Sledge, 69.

32. Ibid., 74.

33. Ibid.

34. Studies on military psychology confirmed that the rate of mental breakdown was much higher for those subjected to shelling than to other types of weaponry; see the works cited in Dean, 43.

35. Manchester, 124, 129.
36. See Ellis, 113–114; Shay, 128.
37. Graves, 96.
38. On not ducking cannonballs at Waterloo see Keegan, *Face of Battle* 179–180. See also Linderman, 140; and the consistently uncharitable Lord Moran, 52, who finds ducking a sign of "morbid alertness."
39. Crisp, 12; also see Fussell, *Doing Battle* 5.
40. Caputo, 93.
41. Aristotle, *Ethics* 3.6.1115a20.
42. See Dean's discussion of war and psychiatry, 26–45, with particular reference to the politics of post-traumatic stress disorder, demonstrating that the same symptoms were also frequent in the Civil War. On the history and politics of shell shock in World War I see Bourke. The recent trilogy by Pat Barker has dramatized many of these issues.
43. Owen, "S. I. W." ll. 12–16, in *Collected Poems* 74.
44. See, e.g., Richards, 199; Chapman, 60.
45. Jünger, 4.
46. Bagnall, 160.
47. Aristotle, *Rhetoric* 1389b25–35.
48. Graves, 171–172; see also Sassoon, *Infantry Officer* 26.
49. Hysterical symptoms of any sort appeared to be more common in World War I than in World War II; see Bourke, 109–113; Grinker and Spiegel, 104.
50. Appel and Beebe, 1470; the authors add that line officers were emphatic that "most men . . . were ineffective after one hundred and eighty or even one hundred and forty days." See Dean, 37.
51. Swank and Marchand, 238.
52. Swank and Marchand, 244; see also Winter, 138–139 (World War I). For powerful accounts of the conditions that ate away the souls of the soldiers, see Dean, 46–69 (Civil War); Ellis, 246–255 (World War II); and Holmes, 204–269, who establish in greater detail the points I am presenting.
53. Appel and Beebe, 1471.
54. Burdette, 207; also quoted in Linderman, 250.
55. From Elisha Paxton, 58; quoted in Linderman, 250.
56. Bagnall, 160.
57. Moran, x. Lord Moran served as a medical officer in World War I and as Churchill's physician in World War II.
58. Hume, *Enquiry* sec. 7, p. 88.
59. See Bourke, 117–122.
60. Nussbaum (333) argues that Aristotle concedes "that such extreme bad luck [as in Priam's case] *could* dislodge a good person from full *eudaimonia* [happiness, well-being]. But he reminds us that a person of good character and practical wisdom will often be able to resist this damage, finding a way to act nobly even in circumstances of adversity . . . Finally, Aristotle feels it important to stress that a person of good and stable character will not act diametrically against character just because

of continued misfortune; the stability of character will stand between him and really *bad* action." Though this view shows Aristotle willing to make some small accommodation to bad luck and misfortune it is still much too demanding a standard to be of much solace to those who faced the unrelenting demands of the trenches.

61. Owen, "S. I. W." pt. III.

62. See also Majdalany, 102, 130, 148, for an extended bitter exploration of the metaphor.

63. O'Brien, *The Things They Carried* 43-44.

64. Ibid., 44.

65. Ibid., 263.

5. Courage and Scarcity

1. *Senjinkun* [Field service regulations] (Tokyo: Army Ministry, 1941), chap. 2, sec. 8; quoted in Cook and Cook, 264.

2. See the grim accounts of group suicides on Saipan and Okinawa; Cook and Cook, 264, 281-292, 354-372.

3. See the accounts of Yamauchi Takeo and Kojima Kiyofumi, ibid., 281-292, 373-382.

4. Account of Miyagi Kikuko, ibid., 361.

5. Herr, 66.

6. There is the fanaticism that involves excess quantities of deeds we find admirable in small doses (charging a bunker), and then there is the fanaticism that generates actions we do not find praiseworthy in any quantity (killing your child so that she can go to heaven).

7. U.S. Senate, *Medal of Honor Recipients* 705.

8. Ibid., 622-623.

9. On American soldiers' significantly more virulent hatred of the Japanese than of the Germans see the questionnaire evidence assembled in Stouffer, 158; see generally Dower, *War without Mercy*.

10. Montaigne, 2.7, p. 429. Problems of local abundance or scarcity of courage also led to differentials in awards within an army depending on the war or theater within a war. Guy Chapman (266) complains that actions that would have passed for superhuman medal-winning performances in the colonial wars were just so much routine on the western front and hence went unrecognized there.

11. Cook and Cook, 289.

12. I do not need to buy into the rightly and roundly criticized distinction between shame and guilt cultures to make the claim that the pressure for conformity may be greater in one culture than in another. Dower has shown that fear of shame was not enough to suppress grumbling and graffiti in Japan during the war; shame gained a considerable assist from propaganda and government suppression of dissent, to say nothing of the gruesome lot that the government told its citizens awaited them at the hands of the enemy if taken alive, which, given the knowl-

edge of their own practices in China, probably rang true; *Japan in War and Peace* 101–154.

13. See Edwards' original and provocative essay.

14. Keegan, *History of Warfare* 9: "Cossacks, in short, were cruel to the weak and cowardly in the face of the brave."

15. See Urmson, "Saints and Heroes," for a useful discussion of duty and beyond the call of duty.

16. Origen, "Exhortation to Martyrdom" chap. 2, drawing from Romans 8:18; see also *Martyrdom of St. Polycarp* 1.3: "They despised the tortures of this world, in one hour buying themselves an exemption from the eternal fire." The cost-benefit calculation comes out more readily in favor of martyrdom if the future reward is certain, considerable, and not postponed too long after death; otherwise the calculation gets more iffy.

17. See, e.g., Clement of Alexandria, "On Spiritual Perfection" chap. 66; Gibbon's classic discussion, also citing church councils refusing the title of martyr to those who courted martyrdom, chap. 16 n. 95; and Aquinas, 2.2 Q124 A1, reply to objection 3 (a man ought not give another an occasion to act unjustly). *The Martyrdom of St. Polycarp* mocks a certain Quintus, a volunteer, who turns cowardly in the arena; the account takes care to show that Polycarp was not a volunteer (1.5); see Perkins, 30–31.

18. Thucydides, 2.39.

19. Du Picq, 63.

20. Dixon, 199; discussed also in Elster, *Alchemies* 148. Kojima Kiyofumi, for instance, is completely unapologetic about having helped write leaflets urging Japanese surrender; Cook and Cook, 381.

21. Bloch, 166; see also Ellis, 352: "Courage was commonplace, self-sacrifice the norm."

22. Reported in Manchester, 393–394.

23. U.S. Senate, *Medal of Honor Recipients* 1.

24. Thucydides, 4.40. For the view that it is the good who die see Moran, 115–117.

25. Fussell, *Doing Battle* 145. See also Bourke detailing the process after World War I by which all soldiers who had died (except those executed after a court-martial) became heroes (247–249).

26. Watney, 204.

27. Thucydides, 2.42.

6. "I Have a Wife and Pigs"

1. Aristotle, *Ethics* 3.9; see Yearley, 116.

2. Small, 186.

3. Aristotle, *Ethics* 3.6.1115a13–16.

4. Graves, 75–76.

5. Bowlby, 18.

6. Ibid., 51, 58.

7. Ibid., 127.

8. Ibid.

9. See, e.g., Wiley, *Life of Billy Yank* 87–90, citing cases of mass panic in which troops "were insensible to shame or sarcasm" (88); also idem, *Life of Johnny Reb* 86–88. Southern American dueling practice allowed that a man did not have to answer the note of "one that had been publicly disgraced without resenting it," in other words, a shameless man; see Wilson, chap. 2, p. 3, in Williams, 94.

10. Cited in Winter, 30.

11. In honor cultures cowardice and shamelessness in men were perfectly congruent.

12. The proverb is attributed to Thomas Fuller (early eighteenth century) in Regan, 73; I have not been able to track it down; however, the same proverbial expression appears in John Wilmot's "A Satire against Reason and Mankind" (1676): "All men would be cowards if they durst," l. 158.

13. Mark VII, 115; Crisp, 119.

14. In 1928 the British abolished capital punishment for sleeping on post, disobedience, and striking an officer; in 1930 it was abolished for cowardice and leaving a post without orders. The death penalty was, however, retained for mutiny and treachery; see Babington, 209–212.

15. J. G. Gray, 114.

16. See Huie.

17. Watney, 192.

18. Crisp, 12.

19. Why fight kicks in rather than flight is also inscrutable to science; Elster, *Alchemies* 3, uses it as an example of a psychological mechanism that is characterized by a core indeterminacy as to which of several causal chains will be triggered; see J. A. Gray, 195: "It makes better sense to imagine a single fight/flight mechanism which receives information about all punishments, and then issues commands *either* for fight *or* for flight depending on the total stimulus context."

20. See Keegan, *Face of Battle* 166, citing Hediger's well-known studies of flight distance in animals. The image of the fighting mouse was available for instruction to motivate people to be courageous in spite of their fear or the odds against them. See Plutarch, "Sayings of Spartans," Agesilaus no. 9, p. 110.

21. Graves, 131; Graves's courage and competence are noted by one of the men of his company who wrote his own memoir; see Richards, 109, 129.

22. Small, 185.

23. Caputo, 91.

24. Ford, 556.

25. Small, 185.

26. Moore and Galloway, 282.

27. Manning, 214; see also the description of emotional synesthesia in Caputo, 294.

28. Keegan, *Face of Battle* 20.

29. Small, 185.

30. Matthew 6:1–6.
31. Burdette, 108.

7. Shoot the Stragglers and the Problem of Retreat

1. 10 USCS §899 (1997), art. 99.
2. On crowds and armies see Keegan, *Face of Battle* 174–176.
3. See Bowra, 83; Keegan and Holmes, 53. See also Lawrence, 383–384: "Victory always undid an Arab force, so we were no longer a raiding party, but a stumbling baggage caravan, loaded to breaking point."
4. See Aristotle, *Ethics* 5.2.1130a18, 5.9.1137a20; *Rhetoric* 2.6.1383b20; Plato, *Laws* 12.944e. See also Polybius on capital offenses in the Roman army, 6.37–38.
5. See United States v. Gross 17 (1968) USCMA 610; 38 CMR 408.
6. United States v. Smith (1953) 3 USCMA 25, 11 CMR 25; United States v. Brown (1953) 3 USCMA 98, 11 CMR 98; United States v. McCormick (1953) 3 USCMA 361, 12 CMR 117.
7. 10 USCS §886 (AWOL).
8. United States v. Sperland (1952) 5 CMR 89. See 10 USCS §885 (desertion).
9. Small, 112.
10. Winthrop, 624, quoted in Sperland, 92. Winthrop is discussing the provisions as they appear in the U.S. Army's Articles of War, which provisions were later codified in the statute being glossed in the Sperland case and here.
11. See Samuel, 599–601; Barker, 1.16.
12. See too Hobbes, 2.21: "When Armies fight, there is on one side, or both, a running away; yet when they do it not out of treachery, but fear, they are not esteemed to do it unjustly, but dishonorably."
13. Montaigne, 1.54, p. 349.
14. See Eksteins, 226, on the excremental leitmotif in World War I memoirs and literature.
15. The American Model Penal Code (§2.09, comment 2) is concerned to make sure the actor's "cowardice" doesn't excuse him but not by going so far as to demand that "heroism be the standard of legality."
16. In the French army, however, as late as the Great War, a man selected by lot from each company of a badly failed regiment would be executed; see Horne, 64. Such an occasion forms the substance of Cobb's novel, *Paths of Glory*.
17. Kitto, 88.
18. Cited in Lazenby, 95. Given that hoplite battle involved a pressing of one force against the other, the shield was also an offensive weapon.
19. Hanson, 63.
20. Dooley, 46–47.
21. Ibid., 37–38.
22. *Battle of Maldon* ll. 186–196.

23. Retreat en masse in war raised different issues from solitary retreat in feud. Some warrior cultures were untroubled by retreat in battle. The horse people of the steppes for all their ferocity quickly retreated from battles they found harder going than they expected. Keegan claims that the Mongol hordes fought to win and quite unheroically; "eschewal of heroic display was, indeed, almost a nomad rule"; *History of Warfare* 213.

24. Homer, *Iliad* 11.544 ff.

25. Ibid., 17.100 ff.

26. When Menelaus attacks, he attacks with the "daring of a mosquito, which though constantly brushed away from a man's skin still insists on biting him for the pleasure of human blood"; *Iliad* 17.571. Even bugs provide heroic example, but on offense, not defense.

27. See also *Iliad* 21.544 ff., in which the temptations of cowardly flight are presented. Agenor, after deliberating whether to flee Achilles in the open or flee by getting lost in battle, decides Achilles will run him down in either case, so he might as well go forward. Just maybe Achilles' guardian deity will be sleeping.

28. *Egil's Saga* chap. 83.

29. An outlaw's dependents become charges on the local district. Sam may be motivated less by pity than by reluctance to bear the material costs of killing Hrafnkel.

30. *Hrafnkel's Saga* chap. 13.

31. See discussion in Miller, *Bloodtaking* 198–202.

32. Stewart's assertion that it is "only with the Renaissance that the idea appeared that one who fought valiantly (but survived) might preserve his honor even in defeat" (33) is an overstatement and insufficiently attentive to the accommodations that even fairly uncompromising codes of honor allowed for excuse, backing off, and backing down. Consider, for instance, the ransom agreements of medieval warfare in which one pledged on one's still intact honor to pay one's captor if he spared one's life. The politics of honor was always more complex than "Give me victory or give me death."

33. Plato, *Symposium* 221b.

34. From Strong, 123–125; quoted in Linderman, 69.

35. See Geach, 161.

36. See Linderman, 20, 159–160.

8. Offense, Defense, and Rescue

1. Scott, letter 6, p. 56.

2. The case has recently been argued for the primacy of defense in the early stages of human development, the reality being man the hunted rather than man the hunter; see Ehrenreich. But once we are into the discursive world of courage, man has already constructed a self-serving ideal of himself as predator, mostly of other men (and women). The ideology of courage puts offense first.

3. See too La Rochefoucauld, no. 252: "Humility is often only feigned submissiveness adopted so as to dominate others."

4. O'Brien, *If I Die* 135.

5. See Dixon on General Methuen, 57–60; see Caputo, 12, 61.

6. McDonough, 30, 108.

7. See Linderman's chapter "Sword and Shovel" 134–155.

8. See Ker, 5, who noted that the great theme of medieval heroic literature is the "defense of a narrow place against odds."

9. The Old Norse word for "narrow pass" is used to indicate not only a mountain pass but also the anus and vagina; see "Ale-Hood's Story." Says Broddi to Gudmund: "How do you expect to defend Clearwater Pass [*skarð*] so that I can't get through with my men if you can't even defend that little pass [*skarð*] between your thighs, as nasty rumor has it?" (my translation); on the failure of Old Norse to distinguish at the lexical level between anus and vagina, see Clover, "Regardless of Sex" 378.

10. See Miller, *Bloodtaking* 301.

11. Keegan, *Face of Battle* 302; see du Picq, 123–124, 146.

12. Keegan, *Face of Battle* 165. Not just humans. Animal studies show that stately lions and less imposing damsel flies recognize that possession confers some kind of title; Krebs and Davies, 157. Though the attacker must concede to the defender the superior moral claim to his territory, the human attacker at least assumes a greater force to inspire fear, which force du Picq, 123–124, sees as a moral force (suggesting the sense of morale but not completely).

13. Grant, 543, 580, 701–702.

14. Small, 70–71.

15. See LeDoux generally.

16. See Bourke, 109–113; Grinker and Spiegel, 104.

17. O'Brien, *Going After Cacciato* 150; also idem, *The Things They Carried* 21. Casey, 39–42, assumes that the courageous person inhabits his body in a particularly agreeable way. That is perhaps the case with the epic hero, but not with those soldiers whose courage meant that they constantly warred against their own bodies.

18. Caputo, 223.

19. U.S. Senate, *Medal of Honor Recipients* 517–518.

20. Graves, 155–156; Richards, 129.

21. Tawney, 14.

22. Hiram Sturdy, quoted in Bourke, 80.

23. Moore and Galloway, 159.

24. Grinker and Spiegel, 57–58.

25. Marshall, 50–63.

26. See the quite devastating attack on Marshall's implausible numbers by Smoler, who suggests Marshall failed to distinguish troops held in reserve from those at the sharp end, or, worse, that he simply made up the numbers.

27. Marshall, 59.

28. Ibid., 71, 78–79.

29. Ibid., 71; communication from Yale Kamisar; see also Walzer's discussion of the reluctance of soldiers to shoot at enemy who appear vulnerably human, as when they are defecating, eating, looking silly, or just smelling the flowers (138–143).

30. An Act for the Better Government of the Navy (1800), sec. 1, arts. 4–6.

31. See Winthrop, 623 n. 26.

32. Purely predatory raiders—Cossacks, steppe horsemen, Vikings—felt no need to construe their attacks as anything other than opportunistic. Presumably, however, aggressive moves within their communities had to be accompanied by some justifying gloss.

33. See Tversky and Kahneman.

34. See Polybius, 3.89.

35. See *The Martyrdoms of Saints Perpetua and Felicitas* and *The Martyrs of Lyons*.

36. See Aquinas, 2.2 Q123 A 6, reply to objection 1. One endures, it seems, because one has no better option; if one had more power, one would attack: endurance usually "implies that one is being attacked by a stronger person, whereas aggression denotes that one is attacking as though one were the stronger party." Endurance also implies long duration, "whereas aggression is consistent with sudden movements." The different rhythms of attack and defense make defense more arduous. See also Yearley's detailed discussion of Aquinas' transformation of courage from a preservative virtue into patience, an inclinational virtue, in which "courage ceases to exhibit any of its distinctive marks" (143); preservative virtues like courage and perseverance get their name from counteracting the forces that would undo inclinational virtues, like benevolence and generosity.

37. Perpetua records a dream she has the day before she is to be led to meet the beasts in the amphitheater. She sees herself in the arena, where she must fight an Egyptian of "vicious appearance." "My clothes," she says, "were stripped off, and suddenly I was a man." *The Martyrdoms of Saints Perpetua and Felicitas* 8.10. Her own image of courage, masculine in the active style of combat, forces her to reembody herself as a male wrestler, as an athlete. The transformation of herself into a male triggers a series of other transformations: passion becomes action, defeat becomes victory, and death immortality.

38. Aquinas is troubled enough to feel it necessary to explain the propriety of calling martyrs warriors so that the martyrs can participate in the conventional glory of martial courage; see 2.2 Q123 A 5, reply to objection 1. See also Perkins' lucid discussion of the early Christian martyrs (32, 104–123).

39. F. Fox, 36; quoted in Eksteins, 163.

40. Owen, "Mental Cases," l. 2, p. 69; Dean, 43.

41. *Saving Private Ryan* (1998).

42. The most decorated British soldier in the Great War was a stretcher-bearer; Holmes, 197.

43. Cited in Winter, 196.

44. See Watkins, 35.

45. Small, 71. In the Civil War, ration carrying, like rescue, could be floated as a cover for cowardice. One Wisconsin soldier wrote home to his parents in De Pere to set

the record straight about a local officer: "That story about Lawton's being so brave was all a hoax, as soon as the battle commenced he was seen making for the river about as fast as his legs would carry him. When asked where he was going he replied 'that he was going down to the river to *draw rations*, so that the boys could have something to eat as soon as they were done fighting.' Very thoughtful, wasn't he"; Newton, 19–20.

46. Tawney, 14–15.

47. Manning, 154.

48. Dunn, 51.

49. See Horne, 181–183. British stretcher-bearers in World War I were drawn from the ranks of the unit's musicians; Richards, 11; likewise in the Civil War; Burdette, 21.

50. Mark VII, 90.

51. For holding the plasma bag up see the Medal of Honor citations for Robert Eugene Bush, Desmond Doss, and John Harlan Willis (World War II) and Lawrence Joel (Vietnam); U.S. Senate, *Medal of Honor Recipients* 509–510, 538–539, 715. On the targeting of medics by the enemy see Moore and Galloway, 85; for the extraordinary bravery of medics see ibid., 99, 104, 137.

52. See Mowat, 228–229: "those who remained under sustained . . . fire could partially armour themselves with the apathy of the half-dead; but those [stretcher-bearers] had to come and go, knowing the searing repetition of brief escape followed by a new immersion in the bath of terror."

53. Graves, 132.

54. Keegan, *Face of Battle* 300.

55. Des Pres, 136.

56. The crusty S. L. A. Marshall attests his own commitment to rescue narratives by concluding *Men against Fire* with the story of a daring rescue under fire of a corpse (201–202).

57. See Mark VII, 176, 185–186; Richards, 143; Graves, 344–345.

58. Caputo, 223.

59. Vera Brittain, 264, makes a similar comparison: "The Man of Sorrows . . . after all knew—or believed—that He was God."

60. Manning, 80; J. G. Gray, 90, sees friendship differ from comradeship in that "friends do not seek to lose their identity, as comrades and erotic lovers do."

61. Quoted in Winter, 180.

62. See the story of James Young with a bullet lodged in his brain getting back after two days to his own lines in Moore and Galloway, 299, 318–322; and the account of Jack P. Smith that if not true would be unbelievable as fiction.

9. Man the Chicken

1. Compare Adam Smith's account of the savage who is unpitying, cruel, cunning, unloving, but possessed with total self-command regarding pain; *Theory of Moral Sentiments* 205–207.

2. On feral humans, unsocialized and fearful, see Malson.
3. See Bloomfield, 59–60; Miller, "Gluttony" 93–94.
4. Thackeray, *Vanity Fair* chap. 30.
5. See Herdt. Pericles took roughly the same position; Thucydides, 2.39–40.
6. See Pears, 178.
7. Manning, 22.
8. Damasio, 264.
9. Judges 7:3–7.
10. Homer, *Iliad* 11.37.
11. R. L. Fox, 231; Plutarch, *Life of Cleomenes* chap. 9, p. 78.
12. Homer, *Iliad* 4.420–421.
13. Ibid., 20.261–262.
14. See examples cited by Lazenby, 91; also du Picq, 44–46.
15. Bowra, 78; see also the moving desperation in the letters of Geoffrey Thurlow, who sees himself as windy, cowardly, and admits his fears openly to Vera Brittain and her brother; Bishop and Bostridge, 220, 270–273, 281, 286, etc.
16. Thus the Spaniards, having been outnumbered 500 to 1, admit, after the fact, that they urinated in fear before taking the Inca emperor Atabalipa captive; see Pizarro, 179–180. Note too that Hamlet's self-accusations of cowardice are made in the interrogatory style of someone who does not quite accept the truth of the self-accusation, and then he makes such accusations to himself only in soliloquy; see, e.g., "oh what a rogue . . ." II.ii.533–573.
17. Du Picq, 48, 94–95.
18. Ibid., 36.
19. Montecuccoli, 82, 92.
20. On cowardly horses see Keegan, *Face of Battle* 95, 159; for Hannibal's cowardly elephants see Polybius, 1.39, 15.12.
21. See Elster's insightful discussions of bootstrapping, willing what cannot be willed, and faking; *Sour Grapes* 44–60, 71–77.
22. Montecuccoli, 133–134.
23. O'Brien, *If I Die* 76.
24. A late Sung commentator (thirteenth century) on Sun Tzu's treatise also counsels the wise use of vices: let the cautious defend, use the avaricious and stupid in situations that suit them (5.23).
25. La Rochefoucauld, no. 114; also 115.
26. *Beowulf* II. 2179–80; Old English *slean*, modern English *slay*, could mean "strike" as well as "kill by striking"; in either case drinking bouts were risky affairs.
27. Hume, *Enquiry* sec. 7, p. 88, who takes the example from Longinus' treatise *On the Sublime*.
28. That Mel Gibson in the *Lethal Weapon* movies and Bruce Willis in the various incarnations of *Die Hard* also adopt this style does not change its racial marking; they are doing homage to the black style, not to Beowulf and Diomedes.
29. Bloch, 163. The thought that he was as much a threat to his opponent as the opponent to him came as an epiphany to U. S. Grant (165): "It occurred to me at once

that Harris had been as much afraid of me as I had been of him. This was a view of the question I had never taken before; but it was one I never forgot afterwards."

30. This is the view of threat advanced by Schelling, 35–43.

31. See Krebs and Davies, 78, for a photo of a Brazilian toad with two large eye-shaped spots on its hindquarters: "Many predators show avoidance responses to patterns resembling eyes."

32. Homer, *Iliad* 23.272–286; the Greeks apparently were of two minds on the effectiveness of nonplaying as a strategy for honor preservation. With Achilles compare Xenophon (*Memorabilia* 3.7.1), who expresses the view that a man is a contemptible creature if, having it in him to excel in sport, he declines to compete; cited in Dover, 231.

33. Burdette, 107.

34. The account is taken from Krebs and Davies reporting the work of Rohwer and Rohwer.

35. Some people have threateningness thrust upon them, sometimes by physiognomy and by skin color, sometimes by their numbers or by being out of place; they must continually cultivate strategies of alleviating the anxiety they cause. Thus the cultivated styles of servility in slaves, and thus too the history of strict laws against combination and assembly of the lower orders.

36. Wolff, 77.

37. See Keegan and Holmes, 19.

38. La Rochefoucauld, no. 219.

39. Polybius, 10.3; Genghis Khan kept himself well rearward too. The contrast with Alexander the Great couldn't be greater; for a discussion of when it became acceptable for generals to stay to the rear and not have their courage blamed, see Keegan, *Mask of Command* 118–123.

40. Manchester, 304.

41. See also Holmes, 321–323.

42. See Ashworth; Axelrod, 73–87.

43. Sorley, 236; also noted in Eksteins, 105. Note that Sorley recasts the parable so as to have the Good Samaritan passing by, which in Sorley's setting makes perfect sense, for to stop is to do harm.

44. Mark VII, 95.

45. Burdette, 102.

46. See Bourke's account of malingering and shirking in both military and industrial settings during the Great War period (76–123).

47. O'Brien, *If I Die* 146.

10. Praised Be Rashness

1. Aristotle, *Ethics* 2.6.1106b24–1107a7.

2. Justice, like courage, does not do very well with the theory of the mean either; see Urmson, "Aristotle's Doctrine of the Mean" 164–166.

3. Aristotle, *Ethics* 2.7.1107b2–3.

4. See Pears; Ross, 204–207; Urmson, "Aristotle's Doctrine of the Mean"; and Duff. Urmson suggests, following up on Ross, that the opposite of being overwhelmed by fear—cowardice—is not properly feeling confident but rather being underwhelmed by fear, that is, fearlessness, insensibility. The virtuous middle on this fear–fearlessness axis then belongs to courage. Rashness, according to Urmson, is the excessive extreme of a second triad, with timidity being the corresponding vice of deficiency and a proper sense of caution occupying the virtuous middle:

   Excessive caution (timidity)—caution—rashness

   Cowardice—courage—fearlessness (insensibility)

   This view suggests that cowardice, as an excessive response to fear, should be distinguished from something we call timidity, a more particularized kind of risk aversion that may or may not actually involve fear. For a brief overview of some aspects of Pears's important discussion see above, Chapter 4, note 3.

5. Aristotle seems to make room for proper fearlessness, as in Socrates' fearless retreat at Delium and the manner in which he faced his death.

6. Aristotle, *Ethics* 3.7.1115b29–34.

7. Sherman, 363.

8. Aquinas, 2.1 Q45 A4; Yearley, 122–123; J. G. Gray, 106; Laches takes a slightly different line; he supposes that it is cowards who are likely to become rash, not that the rash are cowards; Plato, *Laches* 184b.

9. Some may dispute whether a pure fake is a semblance at all and not just a vice; see Yearley, 19–20.

10. Aristotle does not exhaust the list of semblances; fanaticism seems to qualify, hardness, toughness, as well as those kinds of behavior that evidence what we call chutzpah and nerve.

11. Note that we rank thrill-seeking activities according to their dignity. Mountain climbing and space flight rank high, bungee-jumping pretty low, skydiving and white-water rafting a little higher. The ranking does not correlate necessarily with the level of risk, but with the amount of preparation, training, commitment, and, strangely, it seems, with whether one is going up or coming down.

12. He, R. J. Pinney, also denied the men their rum rations; see Sassoon, *Infantry Officer* 122, where Pinney appears under the name Whincop; Dunn, 319. See also Dixon's black-humored account of the British commanders in the Boer War who insisted the troops be "given no training in the 'cowardly' art of building defensive positions or head cover" (55).

13. Graves, 132–133.

14. Purists among mountain climbers already lament the commercialization of Everest expeditions, but the mountain continues to exact a hard toll nonetheless; see Krakauer, 24–29.

15. See Wallace, 80.

16. Yearley, 127.

17. Ibid., 114.

18. In Cicero's view (1.80) it is courage itself that allows one to make use of one's intelligence and wisdom for the task at hand. Aquinas, too, would offer as his most general definition of fortitude the capacity to keep to reason's dictates under fearful conditions; 2.1 Q61 A2.

19. See Schelling, 37; see also the discussions of the game of chicken in Elster, *Sour Grapes* 28–29; idem, *Ulysses and the Sirens* 121–123.

20. Callan, 523.

21. Johnson, *Rambler* no. 25 (12 June 1750).

22. Graves, 247.

23. United States v. Second Lieutenant Herman G. Sallee 10 CMR 376 (1953).

24. O'Brien, *If I Die* 85–87.

25. The warrior ethic of aggressive courage continued to make prudence difficult well into the twentieth century; see Dixon's account of military stupidity, a good portion of which he attributes to avoiding the appearance of cowardice.

26. Shakespeare, *Troilus and Cressida* I.iii.197–200.

27. *Grettir's Saga* chap. 15.

28. See Falk, 115: "Prudence . . . throughout the ancient world, was not yet the cheap commodity which it is with us; and the price of virtue varies with the market."

29. Homer, *Odyssey* 17.232–237 (enduring the insults of a vulgar beggar). On the theme of the linkage of *sapientia* and *fortitudo* see Curtius, 170–180; also Kaske.

30. See *Battle of Maldon* ll. 140–142. The senses of *fród* ranged from skill in specialized tasks, to prudence in counsel, to the general wisdom associated with old age, to a general epithet for being old.

31. Montaigne, 1.6, p. 26.

32. Sun Tzu, 1.17–20. On the very different understanding of retreat and deceit by the steppe horsemen and other Eastern styles of war see generally Keegan, *History of Warfare*; and above, Chapter 7, note 23.

33. Adam Smith goes so far as to suggest that deceit and dissimulation are necessary by-products of the courage of uncivilized cultures in which peace is so precarious that a premium is put on hiding all revelation of one's inner states; *Theory of Moral Sentiments* 208.

34. *Gisli's Saga* chap. 7.

35. Cruelty has an ambivalent relation with courage and cowardice. Montaigne gives voice to the common sentiment that cowardice is the mother of cruelty (2.27, pp. 787–789). See also Linderman, noting a Civil War soldier's observation that the cowardly were cruel to prisoners, the brave kind (238). Yet there is also a competing view that cruelty is closely connected with some kinds of courage. Thus the Machiavellian position that it is better to have the cold heart to do what is necessary now, though cruel, in the interest of securing advantage for a good end. In some kinds of raiding and scavenging cultures—Vikings, Cossacks, various steppe peoples—the inability to kill unarmed women and children might mark one as soft. The Viking Olvir got the gently mocking nickname "Babies' Man" because "he did not catch babies on his spearpoint as was the Viking practice" (*Landnámabók* S 379).

36. Genesis 32:24–28 (wrestling the angel); 28:18, 29:10 (rock-lifting); 33.3 (craven gestures of submission to Esau).
37. See Montaigne 1.5, p. 22, for the Roman view of Greek and Punic cunning.
38. Ibid.; see also Dover, 170: "those defeated by guile in war would vilify the successful enemy as cowardly, although they would not have hesitated to use the same degree of guile if the opportunity had presented itself."

11. *Stupidity, Skill, and Shame*

1. See Ellsworth.
2. See also Brittain, 313: "What a pity it is . . . that outstanding heroism seems so often to be associated with such unmitigated limitations! How seldom it is that this type of courage goes with an imaginative heart, a sensitive, intelligent mind!"
3. The folk belief is of ancient origin. The saturnine and melancholic disposition has long been associated with the contemplative and meditative; see Delumeau, 173–175. These folk beliefs have been supported scientifically; the depressed really do see things the way they are; see Alloy and Abramson; Taylor and Brown.
4. Nietzsche notes the Greek suspicion of hope as "blind and deceitful"; *Daybreak* no. 38.
5. On the breakdown during the Peloponnesian War of earlier understandings that prisoners were to be ransomed rather than slaughtered see Ober, 18.
6. Owen, "Insensibility"; Caputo, 122.
7. Aristotle, *Ethics* 3.8.1117a8. Sassoon makes a similar comparison when he contrasts unfavorably his own revenge-based heroics and blind bravado with the man motivated more by duty, "who did everything that was asked of him as a matter of course"; *Fox Hunting Man* 305.
8. Aristotle, *Ethics* 3.8.1117a15.
9. Not surprisingly, the confident soldier on average does better than the diffident one; see Stouffer, 3–58.
10. From the diary of Charles Wainwright, 2 July 1863; quoted in McPherson, 39.
11. Herr, 66.
12. I have been more generous than philosophers generally have been regarding what qualifies as courage because I am willing to let more mental states inform courage than a strict Aristotelian view would allow. I still have required that there be a real danger, or a rationally sustainable belief in the presence of real danger. The phobic who finally pets a beagle gets praised not for his courage, but for his climbing back into averageness. Those who would be inclined to think of the phobic beagle petter as courageous have left themselves no room to give any depth to the praise they would confer on someone who performed objectively courageous deeds.
13. Aristotle, *Ethics* 3.8.1116a17.
14. Ibid., 3.8.1116b15.
15. Gajdusek, 49.
16. Montaigne, 2.27, p. 791.

17. Ibid., 1.31, pp. 237–238.
18. The reference is to Vonnegut, "Harrison Bergeron."
19. See the apt examples assembled by Linderman, 68–72; for examples of chivalric refusal to take unfair advantage in ancient chariot warfare see Keegan, *History of Warfare* 173. A rationalist countertradition of ancient pedigree counsels the wisdom of taking any benefit that deceit, surprise, fortune, or wit may offer; see, e.g., Sun Tzu.
20. Eksteins, 165.
21. Aristotle, *Ethics* 3.8.1116b2.
22. See primarily Hunt, who is followed also by Yearley, 115, 125.
23. See Chapter 1, above; Plato, *Phaedo* 68d.
24. The Spartan view remained a viable one through the centuries. See, e.g., La Rochefoucauld, no. 213; Mandeville, 209: "The great Art then to make Man Courageous, is first to make him own this Principle of Valour within, and afterwards to inspire him with as much Horror against Shame, as Nature has given him against Death."
25. Aristotle admits the necessity of shame in the educative process, but once it has done its work in molding the disposition to do virtue for virtue's sake, it should bow out; *Ethics* 4.9.1128b17–29; see Burnyeat, 78–79.
26. In his funeral oration Pericles reformulates the epic style of individualized honor into communal honor, in which a citizen's standing is determined by his contribution to the communal stock of honor; Thucydides, 2.34–46.
27. The theory of small-group cohesion as the motivating force that keeps soldiers performing and not running has been variously criticized. One view is that small-group cohesion could just as well motivate the group to desert together as to advance together; see McPherson, 89–91; Bloch, 166.
28. Stouffer cites a soldier: "I was scared if I fell behind, but never dropped out. Always felt safer when I was up with the company" (144).
29. Gajdusek, 41.
30. Manning, 149.
31. See discussion by Horne, 181–183; for a firsthand account of the special miseries and courage of ration bearers see Mark VII, 137–141; see also Bloch, 164–165 (dispatch runners).
32. Raymond Jubert, quoted in Horne, 182. Compare, however, the contrary experiences of fighter pilots who found the lonely pitting of themselves against another solitary man in a machine one of the few settings modern warfare allowed for performances in the ancient heroic style; see Hynes, 85–92. Moreover, solitude provided them relief from being responsible for the safety of the men they would have had in their crews had they been bomber pilots; see Stouffer, 405.
33. Macmillan, 89–90.
34. What is the effect if the eyes are not those of your own people but those of the enemy? Imagine being the only person in a small town who speaks out in a public meeting against burning the local witch. All eyes are on you and are trying their best to shame you into conformity with their views, which to your mind would only be coercing you into cowardice and injustice. You are alone in your resolve,

despite all the eyes. But then the martyr amidst jeering enemies might find her resolve strengthened by their presence; the temptations to abandon her cause might rather be greater when alone in solitary confinement. See the discussion of shame's "being seen" requirement in Taylor, 57–68.

35. On supererogation see Urmson, "Saints and Heroes"; also Walton, 20–24, 181.
36. See Holmes on volunteering for service in a forlorn hope in the Peninsular Wars (303–304).
37. On the competition of saints for humility and self-mortification see Miller, *Anatomy of Disgust* 157–161; and *Humiliation* 146–148.
38. Levi, *Survival in Auschwitz* 119; Lorenzo's sad end is told in *Moments of Reprieve* 147–160.
39. But I worry that this account has his decency nearly lapsing into what some might consider obliviousness and stupidity rather than simple goodness.
40. See the discussion of courageous caring in Tec; also Todorov, 17–18, 71–90.

12. The Shape and Style of Courage

1. On the compensatory gestures we make because we feel it is impermissible to be disgusted by ugliness and obesity even as we are disgusted by it see Miller, *Anatomy of Disgust* 200–205.
2. The fat are barely allowed their grief. The nastiest observation I know of comes from Jane Austen concerning fat Mrs. Musgrove's grief for her dead son (*Persuasion* chap. 8): "A large bulky figure has as good a right to be in deep affliction as the most graceful set of limbs in the world. But, fair or not fair, there are unbecoming conjunctions, which reason will patronize in vain,—which taste cannot tolerate,—which ridicule will seize."
3. Downs, 118.
4. Shakespeare, *Hamlet* V.ii.290; see Harold Jenkins' spirited attempt in his edition of *Hamlet* (568–569) to save Hamlet from corpulence. He may be right, but there is so much wishful thinking motivating the gloss that I think that the shape of Hamlet's body must remain indeterminate.
5. Shakespeare, *Henry IV, Part I* II.iv.227, 452; II.ii.109; and variously in I.iv.
6. The process of distinguishing oneself from the poor has undergone some change now that white suburban kids adopt styles originated by inner-city black kids; but the aim is less to look poor (which is still perfectly avoided) than to look tough; the hope is that with the clothing of the poor will come their most salient virtues: toughness and cool; see generally Bourdieu, *Distinction*.
7. Manchester, 276–278.
8. Fussell, *Doing Battle* 115–119.
9. Ginzburg, 93.
10. Améry, 38; see Nietzsche's views of pain sensitivities varying by class, race, and level of civilization; *Genealogy of Morals* 2.7. For class variation in stress symptoms in World War I see Bourke, 109–113.

11. Mark VII, 34, 172–173.

12. Small, 38.

13. Bowlby, 170; Manchester, 124, 149, 173; Grettir, however, a saga hero of enormous arm strength, had a small penis; *Grettir's Saga* chap. 75.

14. Mark VII, 18–19.

15. Marriage and fatherhood were also felt to vary inversely with courage, if only because such people were expected to keep their heads down and not take unnecessary risks, even if they did not go as far as Mr. Probert in defense of his wife and pigs.

16. See U.S. Senate, *Medal of Honor Recipients* 560.

17. Graves, 233. In addition to Sassoon's *Memoirs of an Infantry Officer* see Graves's extended discussion of Sassoon's adventures in *Goodbye to All That* and Dunn, 329. Sassoon single-handedly took an enemy trench and then, according to Graves, sat down in it to read a book of verse.

18. Egil and David were warriors as well as poets, but some cultures considered poets warriors by virtue of their power to curse and damage an enemy with malediction independent of their skill in arms; see Tambiah.

19. Fussell, *The Great War* 9. It soon became apparent that shortness was better suited to trench warfare than height. Not only did it improve one's odds against snipers, but living in burrows, dens, and dugouts was less uncomfortable; see Bourke, 171–180.

20. McPherson, 8; see, e.g., Blackford, 14.

21. Moran, 21, 164–166; compare the brief discussion by Sassoon, *Fox-Hunting Man* 296.

22. Actually the unspoken import of the phrase was spoken, though it is quoted less often: "It is only wonderful that we should be able to make so much out of them afterwards"; see Keegan, *Mask of Command* 126–127.

23. McDonough, 63.

24. Holmes, 50.

25. Yet the diasporan stereotype is a tough one to beat; it survived the reputation of Jews as boxers in early nineteenth-century England and in the United States of the 1930s and will no doubt weather the Sabra assault as well. On Jewish boxers playing the role of enforcers and thugs in early nineteenth-century England see Herzog, 332–339.

26. Homer, *Iliad* 1.348–360, 9.114–656.

27. Eisenhower (4.2349) in a letter to Ernie Pyle.

28. Buber-Neumann, 5.

29. Ginzburg, 296.

30. A. Smith, *Theory of Moral Sentiments* 205.

31. Donat, 237; quoted in Des Pres, 146.

32. Brittain, 398.

33. Hersey, 36; there are equally quiet acceptances of indescribable brutality from the Holocaust; see, e.g., eyewitness Hermann Graebe's report of the dignified behavior of the Jews shot en masse in the killing pits at Dubno; Graebe memorandum printed in Chief of Counsel, *Nazi Conspiracy and Aggression* 5.696–699.

34. See Manning's portrait of Weeper Smart (145 ff.); compare, however, Rachman, 305, discussing evidence that the most distinguishing trait of decorated bomb disposers was health; they were the ones who never complained of illness.

35. See, e.g., the memoirs of private soldiers Watkins (Civil War) and Harris (Peninsular campaign), who continually complain of the miseries of war but never evince fear of battle. To their minds, battle often appears as a welcome distraction from their general physical discomfort.

13. The Emotional Terrain: Fear, Hope, Despair

1. Tomkins, 520.

2. Without the emotions the world would be stale and flat; for disgust reenchanting the world see Miller, *Anatomy of Disgust* 175–177. See too Casey's insightful discussion on the pervasiveness of fear and its relation to sexual desire (54–55).

3. Bechara; Damasio, 212–222.

4. Konner, 215.

5. Nietzsche, *Daybreak* no. 551.

6. Mandeville, Remark R, 219.

7. Matthew 26:39; also Mark 14:36; Luke 22:42.

8. Origen, chap. 29.

9. See Mandeville, 215; for the remark of Vanini, see *Historiarum Galliae ab Excessu Henrici IV* (Toulouse, 1643), 209.

10. Aquinas, 2.2 Q19 A11.

11. See the seventeenth- and eighteenth-century sources quoted by Delumeau, 410–411. Nietzsche reproduces a text attributed to Tertullian on the delights of watching the damned writhe in hell; see *Genealogy of Morals* 1.15. But what if the damned you are watching include your children or parents?

12. Aquinas, Supp. Q99 A1, reply to objection 4.

13. Ibid., 2.2 Q19 A5, A11.

14. Milton's Satan suspected God enjoyed slavish and programmed devotion; see *Paradise Lost* 6.165–170.

15. Once Satan musters his forces, however, he provides the occasion for angels loyal to God to show courage when they quit his camp; see Milton's depiction of Abdiel, *Paradise Lost* 5.804–907.

16. See Elster, *Alchemies* 233, 274–275, drawing the distinction between visceral fear and fear as referencing a certain complex of beliefs and desires; see the discussion by Gordon, 65–85.

17. Berridge's work reveals that the same dopamine systems that figure in reward and pleasure also are stimulated in aversive behavior, linking powerfully fear and desire, aversion and wanting; Berridge and Robinson, 348–349. The linkage between metaphors of combat and sexuality might be more deeply motivated than we ever thought.

18. See Aquinas: "there are various fears according to the various objects of fear"; 2.1 Q42 A4, reply to objection 1. More than fifty years ago the Canadian experimental psychologist Donald Hebb, following Aquinas, argued that fear's psychology could vary greatly depending on what elicited it. Contrast, he says, the great intrusion of aural stimulation needed to make sounds frighten little children with the lack of visual stimulation that makes the dark so terrifying to them (274); see also Frijda, 197–198. Recently the neuroscientist Joseph LeDoux has localized fear to a particular brain system, in which the amygdala plays the central role. He identifies two different pathways: one bypasses the cortex and produces hasty mobilization; the other makes finer distinctions, but to do so it must pass through the cortex before reaching the amygdala and is slower (LeDoux, 16, 163–165). Compare Berridge, who argues that fear comprises multiple subcomponents within a larger emotive system. The arrangements of subcomponents can be called up in an almost infinitely variable set of patterns. Even the same thing can be feared differently at different times. Berridge's view seems better able to account for the richness and variety of our fear experiences.

19. See the data assembled by Tomkins, 547.

20. See Rorty, "Fearing Death" 204.

21. The frighteningness/dangerousness distinction would seem to map on to LeDoux's distinction of a fast-acting but not very discriminating thalamo-amygdala circuit and the more discriminating detour through the cortex were it not that frighteningness itself seems to have important cognitive features; see above, note 18.

22. Stouffer, 233–235.

23. See also the discussion of the varying ability of certain emotions to be experienced vicariously, which though not the same thing as contagion may assist it; Miller, *Anatomy of Disgust* 194–196; Harré, 200–204; Hatfield, 155–156. Notice that to catch fear we do not need to know any of the underlying facts that caused the other's fear; we need only notice that the other is afraid. Contrast anger, which we cannot feel on behalf of another until we know the justice of his cause; see A. Smith, *Theory of Moral Sentiments* 34–36. Compare, further, love, which is only mildly contagious. If someone loves us we might reciprocate, but that hardly qualifies as an epidemic; the disease model doesn't work; we don't catch love so much as generate it to reciprocate the kindness of having received it. Moreover, if you see me in love with X you are no more likely to love X for that reason than to think me a fool or lucky as the case may be. Nor are you any more likely to love Y because I love X. The love bug seems to be highly personal and idiosyncratic.

24. Marshall, 145–146; even these falsely triggered panics suggest they are not a result necessarily processed by LeDoux's short direct pathway, but are based rather on a false interpretation of events; see above, note 18.

25. Caputo, 289–290.

26. Chandler, 297.

27. Levi, *Survival in Auschwitz* 73.

28. Sledge, 80.

29. Aristotle, *Rhetoric* 2.5.1383a32–35.
30. Liebling, 44.
31. Herr, 15.
32. Marshall, 148.
33. Hatfield discusses emotional contagion largely in terms of mimicry and feedback and thus fails to distinguish consistently between "catching" (mimicry in spite of oneself) and the conscious "according" of sentiments to the proper demands of a particular setting.
34. Grant, 205.
35. Cobb, 35.
36. On the issues here Milgram is the obligatory source.
37. We also have the sorry history of the crowd and the levels of brutality human combination can bring in so-called "authentic rites" of violence.
38. Sledge, 185.
39. See Rozin and Fallon, 32.
40. Mark VII, 54.
41. Aristotle, *Ethics* 3.6.1115a10; Aquinas, 2.1 Q41 A1. Pears notes an impoverishment of a definition of fear that is tied too closely to hope (174–175).
42. Aristotle, *Rhetoric* 2.5.1383a5–7; Aquinas, 2.1 Q41 A2.
43. Brittain, 447.
44. Bagnall, 216.
45. Quoted in Stouffer, 189.
46. Is fear felt simultaneously with despair or does it alternate with it from moment to moment? Cognitive appraisal theorists of the emotions would prefer oscillation; other theorists argue for the reality of blended emotions. Contrast, e.g., Smith and Ellsworth with Plutchik.
47. See above, Chapter 10, note 13.
48. Aquinas, 2.1 Q40 A8, reply to objection 3.
49. Ibid., reply to objection 1.
50. See R. L. Fox, 233, 235.
51. See Winter, 178; Holmes, 267–268.
52. Ford, 544.
53. Bloch, 133.
54. Keegan, *Face of Battle* 197, suggests that men may even seek to die bunched: "Can it be that, in extremes of fear, men will not only press together for protection . . . but actually fall together to the ground in heaps?"
55. Evans, 47.
56. A very large share (70 percent) of American soldiers sampled in World War II said prayer helped them when the going got tough more than any other thoughts that served to manage their fears. Officers ranked prayer second to not letting the men down; Stouffer, 174–180. The authors clearly were disappointed the evidence did not refute the canting about no atheists in the foxhole. But they get their digs in, somewhat unfairly, by suggesting the prayerful to be of cowardly inclination and by further suggesting that it may have been prayer that made them that way: "The data

could be said to indicate . . . that those men actually found prayer most helpful who needed it most. On the other hand, prayer, it might be said, could not in fact have been too helpful to them, as they remained the most frightened men . . . On purely statistical grounds, one could not rule out the possibility that . . . the men who found combat more frightening did so partly because of their reliance on prayer."

57. Moore and Galloway, 286–287.

58. For an excellent discussion of the convergence of cursing and prayer see Kerrigan, 125–139; for soldier comments on curses as prayers, see Manning, 174; and especially Richards, who consistently and comically uses the word "prayer" to mean "curse," 30, 157, esp. 195.

59. Wolff, 103. Also see Stouffer, 172–178; Linderman, 159; Holmes, 241–242; Cloete, 158.

60. McDonough, 15.

61. Herr, 91.

62. Wolff, 89.

63. Bao Ninh, 31.

64. Sledge, 227.

65. See Orwell, "A Hanging" 1.45, in which a man being led to his hanging takes care to step aside to avoid a puddle.

66. Stouffer, 397–398; Grinker and Spiegel, 27, 29–30, 34.

67. Mason, 271.

68. See the examples in Holmes, 38–39.

69. Du Picq, 121; T. E. Lawrence (140–141) cites the same example when he notes that four Arabs could stop a dozen Turks, but a company of trained Turks could handle a thousand Arabs.

14. The Emotional Terrain: Disgust, Anger, Relief

1. Caputo, 4; compare the horrific grotesquerie of the sight greeting Siegfried Sassoon, *Infantry Officer* 148: "floating on the surface of the flooded trench was the mask of a human face which had detached itself from the skull." See Blackford's description of Jeb Stuart's men vomiting over their pommels ("ecstasies of protest" he decorously called it) on the way to their first battle at Bull Run as their path led them through an outdoor surgery with its piles of amputated limbs (28).

2. Sharing space with big, bold rats is a constant refrain of Great War memoirs; they induced nausea and vomiting in Guy Chapman (29, 114) until he became hardened to their presence. It is a rat that provides the subject for one of the most memorable poems of the Great War; see the "droll rat" of "cosmopolitan sympathies" in Isaac Rosenberg's "Break of Day in the Trenches."

3. Blunden, 131.

4. Evans, 51.

5. Cloete, 237; see also Leonard Thompson's description of the bottom of the trench as "springy like a mattress because of all the bodies underneath"; Blythe, 40.

6. E.g., Moore and Galloway, 235.

7. See Des Pres's chapter "Excremental Assault."

8. Levi, *Survival in Auschwitz* 62.

9. Mark VII, 156–157.

10. Sledge, 278.

11. Ibid., 260.

12. Ibid., 288.

13. Sassoon, *Infantry Officer* 24.

14. Leonard Thompson in Blythe, 40; also quoted in Fussell, *The Great War* 88.

15. Sledge, 253.

16. Brittain, 166; also 375: "a regular baptism of blood and pus."

17. Cook and Cook, 356–357; see also the letters of Cornelia Hancock, 14–15 (Civil War) and the unrelentingly depressing accounts in Luard (World War I).

18. Kipling, *Epitaphs of the War 1914–1918*, ll. 55–58, p. 387.

19. Aristotle, *Ethics* 3.8.1116b24.

20. See, e.g., A. Smith, *Theory of Moral Sentiments* 240; Mandeville, 202; Casey, 55–56.

21. Anger/fear is not the only apt pairing. In the interpsychic domain anger pairs up with guilt; see Gibbard, 138–146. The person causing anger will experience guilt to the extent that the other's anger is justified. Gibbard's pairing, however, assumes a pacified public order in which we need not fear revenge from those we wrong. Instead our fear is attenuated to some weak form of revenge upon ourselves—guilt—which like fear might well lead us to make gestures of submission to the other.

22. Mandeville, 216.

23. Aristotle, *Rhetoric* 2.2.1378b1–9.

24. For Adam Smith, the self-command of fear is always admirable, but that of anger may not be. Those who control their anger may be up to no good or are just cowardly; *Theory of Moral Sentiments* 240–241.

25. Caputo, 294.

26. Both fear and anger affect heart rate in the same way. Fear, however, leads to lowered finger temperatures, anger to higher; see Ekman, Levenson, and Friesen; also Levenson, 24–25.

27. Manning, 214.

28. The rear is also where panics originate; on confusion and demoralization in the rear areas as opposed to forward areas see Grant, 232; du Picq, 66 n. 3, 90; Sherman, 204, 897; Watkins, 107–108; Keegan, *Face of Battle* 173 (panic among French at Waterloo starts in rear ranks); on mutinies beginning in rear areas see Holmes, 44.

29. McDonough, 158–159.

30. See, e.g., Crisp, 102.

31. Lawrence, 314.

32. See O'Brien's description of pulling oneself together after the cessation of total terror; *The Things They Carried* 18–19 and in *If I Die* 147, quoted above, Chapter 3.

33. See Solomon and Corbit.

34. Elster (*Nuts and Bolts* 64 n. 4) observes that the word "relief" does rather lazy service to describe three distinct feelings: "when a disaster just misses us, when a probable disaster fails to materialize and when an unpleasant state of affairs ceases to obtain." When it is good things we miss out on rather than disasters that we avoid, language makes finer distinctions: thus we have "regret," "disappointment," and "grief" to describe the negative feelings for which the single word "relief" does service on the positive side. The formal insight has a certain ingenious attractiveness to it, but I am not sure that the relief that we experience when a probable disaster fails to materialize isn't a subset of the relief we feel when an unpleasant state of affairs has ceased to obtain. The fear felt for probable disaster is itself an unpleasant state of affairs.

35. Marshall, 144–145, 194–195.

15. *Courage and Chastity*

1. Thus the male religious communities that consciously distance themselves from martial physicality; thus too diasporan rabbinical Judaism; see Boyarin.
2. Dover, 165; see Winkler, 47.
3. In Plato's *Timaeus* (90e) cowardly men are reincarnated as women; note, too, Hobbes's term "feminine courage" (2.21) to refer to men cowardly in battle.
4. Homer, *Iliad* 8.157–159.
5. *Laxdaela Saga* chap. 49.
6. O'Brien, *If I Die* 54.
7. In Albanian and Balkan feud, when women become avengers they must dress as men and swear to remain virgins. (Jeanne d'Arc plays by these rules too.) Only then can they bear the avenger's rifle; see, e.g., Whitaker. And several millennia earlier, but not far away as the crow flies, Hecuba is transformed into a dog for taking revenge; Euripides, *Hecuba* 1265–73.
8. As with the Icelanders so too the Greeks; see Winkler, 47: "Not to display bravery . . . lays a man open to symbolic demotion from the ranks of the brave/manly to the opposite class of women."
9. *Egil's Saga* chap. 85.
10. *Hrafnkel's Saga* chap. 17. See Clover's discussion of the proverb in "Regardless of Sex" 384–385. If the older a man gets the more a sissy he is, so too the younger a boy is the more a sissy he is. Even the toughest future warrior got sent home crying by older boys, every now and then.
11. *Laxdaela Saga* chap. 35; see the discussion in Miller, *Bloodtaking* 354 n. 35.
12. Clover, "Regardless of Sex" 375; see also Meulengracht Sørensen.
13. See, e.g., the discussion in de Beauvoir, 21–24.
14. See, e.g., Remarque, 149; also Holmes, 209.
15. It has been shown that excess female mortality, in some early modern European demographic regimes, was more pronounced in early adolescence than in

childbearing years, mostly because young girls were more poorly nourished than young boys; see Johansson, 465.

16. In Malagasey male rights to the children of a marriage are confirmed by a myth that claims that the man shows greater bravery in childbirth than the woman. God asks a woman in the throes of childbirth whether she would wish the child dead so that she could live; she answers yes, but the man says he will die for the child, and God then nicks him with a knife on the throat, the Adam's apple being the scar, and assigns the baby to the father for his courage; see Feeley-Harnik; see also Delaney, 38–39.

17. See Black-Michaud, 78–79, 219 n.; Cunnison, 116–118.

18. Christine de Pizan, 1.22.1.

19. Linderman, 87–88.

20. On women's role in the white-feather campaigns see Gullace.

21. Freud, "Medusa's Head."

22. Havarðar Saga chap. 5; quoted in Clover, "Regardless of Sex" 383.

23. Thucydides, 3.74. The Corcyrean civil war is mostly famous for Thucydides' description of it as an especially depraved instance of a moral order turned upside down. But Thucydides does not include women's fighting as a sign of that moral inversion. He only gives them their honorable due.

24. Gisli's Saga chaps. 32, 34; Laxdaela Saga chap. 15.

25. The Norse were rather more accommodating than Mediterranean cultures on the issues of chastity and virginity. Women who were otherwise attractive were not damaged goods if not virgins at marriage, and though expected to be chaste once married, if they failed they were no more likely to be punished, if at all, than the men they were having sex with.

26. Montaigne, 2.7, p. 431.

27. Ibid., 1.33, p. 246.

28. Crisp, 84.

29. Hasluck, 231. On these issues see the two excellent collections on honor and shame in the Mediterranean by Peristiany and Gilmore. See especially Pitt-Rivers, 45–51; Bourdieu, 220–228; Campbell, 100–101, 269–274; Delaney; also Giovannini, 67–68.

30. Brown, 141.

31. See Hopkins, 1–30.

32. Brown, 73.

33. At the start of the century these novels focus on the course of true love, but in the second half, beginning with Anne Brontë's Tenant of Wildfell Hall, they move to escaping the misery of bad marriages.

34. Eliot, Mill on the Floss bk. 4, chap. 3; also bk. 5, chap. 2.

35. Stendhal, Scarlet and Black pt. 2, chaps. 8–12; Stendhal is the author most praised by Simone de Beauvoir for his depiction of woman "as a subject in her own right" (247). The recklessly courageous Milena, who died at Ravensbrück, was eulogized as a Stendhalian woman; Buber-Neumann, 52.

36. Whereas stories of self-realization for well-to-do women are cast as matters of courage, the same is generally not true for stories of self-realization for lower-status men. Thus, in various degrees, the tales of Julien Sorel, Balzac's Eugène Rastignac, Dickens' Pip, Dreiser's Clyde Griffiths, in which self-realization takes the ugly form of social climbing, are largely stories of failures in moral courage.

37. Mathilde wants Julien to show courage to have her, which courage is tested by forcing him to climb a ladder into her bedroom, thereby exposing him to easy discovery: "I wished to test your courage, I confess . . . you are even more fearless than I thought" (2.16). Compare de Beauvoir, who writes: "The ladder that Mathilde de la Môle sets against her windowsill is no mere theatrical prop: it is, in tangible form, her proud imprudence, her taste for the extraordinary, her provocative courage" (242).

38. On Nurse Cavell's death see Ryder, 221–223.

39. For descriptions of nurses under fire see Brittain, 313, 417; and Luard, 110, 195–244. Note, too, the tough endurance of those women who accompanied their men to war, sharing all the miseries of campaigning and much of its danger without any opportunity for the glories; see, e.g., Rifleman Harris' account (81–88) of the horrors faced by the wives of private soldiers on the retreat to Vigo in the Peninsular campaign, 1809.

40. Ginzburg, 388.

41. Todorov, 77; Bondy, 321; Karay, 294–295, 306, notes that differences between male and female endurance depended greatly on the local conditions within the camps; but there is also evidence that women endured starvation conditions better; see Skrjabina, 61–62, describing conditions in 1942 during the siege of Leningrad.

42. Ginzburg, 344–345; see also Bondy, 323–324; Holmes, 101–102.

43. cummings, 120–122; see also Karay, 306–307. Who had it worse, men or women, is ultimately unknowable; there is something tasteless in trying to rank levels of victimization at degree zero.

44. See Todorov, 77–78, making the claim for womanly caring in the camps and citing others in support.

45. Levi, *Survival in Auschwitz* 149–150.

46. Des Pres's book is an attempt to reclaim virtue if not heroism for the survivors.

47. See Clover, *Chain Saws* 21–64.

48. Stendhal, 2.8, p. 298.

16. Moral Courage and Civility

1. Sidgwick, 333 n. 3.

2. There is a sense in which all physical courage has a moral component to the extent that it is not cowardice, but that is another matter. There is also a moral component to physical courage in sports. That is much of the reason we admire some

athletes more than others. In addition to their strength, skill, and fitness, they bring a special attitude that gives them a moral edge; see Casey, 92–93. This is part of the reason why the boldness of rashness is not quite a vice, but a type of moral achievement. I would add that in the courage of endurance the moral and physical are also inextricably intermeshed.

3. Casey claims that the physical/moral courage distinction cannot bear any weight. For him, moral courage is physical because it cannot be imagined as "passionless . . . or entirely abstracted from our physical being." But that is too weak a physicality requirement to collapse the moral/physical distinction. It can bear some weight, as I try to show, so long as we don't load too much on it; see Casey, 39–42, 93.

4. See Tec, 154: rescuers tended to be characterized by their separateness, their individuality, independence, a matter-of-fact attitude toward rescue as a mere duty, and, interestingly, an unplanned beginning to rescue efforts. Such unplanned beginnings often take the form of simply being asked to help. Even this kind of courage, it appears, is often prompted by a desire to avoid embarrassment; at the precise moment of being asked, it may be easier to take on big risks than to refuse someone to his or her face.

5. See Timerman's chilling account.

6. Orwell, "As One Non-Combatant to Another (A Letter to 'Obadiah Hornbooke')," stanzas 5–6, in Collected Essays 2.300.

7. These parents incurred no physical risk in taking their position. This distinguishes them greatly from, say, gays, who despite their numbers still run real risks of beatings and death. In many settings coming out can still be included within conventional understandings of physical courage.

8. See Financial Times (London), 27 July 1982, sec. 1, p. 3; also Reuters North European Service, 29 July 1982.

9. Levi, The Drowned and the Saved 129.

10. I am not backing down from my earlier suggestion that it may be better for a weak guy to back away from the bully. The way I posed that problem had the weak guy gaining nothing unless he did reasonably well, which he stood no chance of doing. These men, the good coward and Améry, meet a modest "reasonably well" standard.

11. See Polybius, 1.11.

12. See Walzer, 13: "Strategy, like morality, is a language of justification. Every confused and cowardly commander describes his hesitations and panics as part of an elaborate plan; the strategic vocabulary is as available to him as it is to a competent commander. But that is not to say that its terms are meaningless."

13. Graves, 263; Sassoon, Infantry Officer 183–225.

14. Grant, 76, 164, also 36, 56.

15. See especially his derision of those officers who had the "moral courage to proclaim" physical disabilities to justify their incapacitation for field service in the Mexican War; Grant, 36.

16. See Keegan's assessment of Grant's physical and moral courage in Mask of Command 183, 202.

17. Grant, 44.

18. This hypothesis receives some small confirmation from T. E. Lawrence's noting that Arab tribesmen, whose culture was centered on bloodfeud and raiding, made no distinction between physical and moral forms of endurance (495).

19. Mandeville delights in standing the old adage on its head; in his view, private vices cause public prosperity. Smith and Hume argue rather that prosperity enables refinements and virtues that have no occasion to flourish in an impoverished, violent regime.

20. A. Smith, *Wealth of Nations* 787; see Berry.

21. Hume, "Of Refinement in the Arts" 274.

22. Dostoyevsky, 2.1, p. 53.

23. Mandeville, 219–220.

24. See Goffman, *Stigma* 2, for the righteous demand we make for a smooth-running social order; see also Miller, *Humiliation*, chaps. 1, 4.

17. Fixing to Die

1. For Yokota Yutaka's account see Cook and Cook, 306–313.

2. Ibid., 319, the account of Kozu Naoji.

3. On Greek suicide see van Hooff, 15, 234.

4. Not all failed aspirations subject the failure to derision. The prior reputation of the aspirer, the reasonableness of the aspiration relative to the aspirer's capacities make a difference. But in competitive honor cultures the aspiration to glory invites mockery unless the failure qualifies as a glorious one.

5. T. Browne, 1.21.

6. The account is in Llewellyn and Hoebel, 164.

7. See Rosaldo; also Miller, *Humiliation* 106–108.

8. Llewellyn and Hoebel, 2–4. Compare the account of Talal el Hareidhin's fatal charge against the Turks to avenge the butchered women and children of his village; Lawrence, 651–654.

9. Llewellyn and Hoebel, 315.

10. See Lowie, 331–333, for a discussion of the "crazy-dog-wishing-to-die" status.

11. Bierce, 134.

18. Concluding Postscript

1. Small, 69–70.

Bibliography

"Ale-Hood's Story." In *Hrafnkel's Saga and Other Stories*. Translated by Hermann Páls-son. Harmondsworth: Penguin, 1971, 82–93.

Alloy, Lauren B., and Lyn Y. Abramson. "Judgment of Contingency in Depressed and Nondepressed Students: Sadder but Wiser?" *Journal of Experimental Psychology: General* 108 (1979), 441–485.

Améry, Jean. *At the Mind's Limits: Contemplations by a Survivor of Auschwitz and Its Real-ities*. Translated by Sidney Rosenfeld and Stella P. Rosenfeld. 1976. New York: Schocken, 1986.

Appel, John W., and Gilbert W. Beebe. "Preventative Psychiatry: An Epidemiologic Approach." *Journal of the American Medical Association* 131 (1946), 1469–75.

Aquinas, Thomas. *Summa Theologiae*. Translated by Fathers of the English Dominican Province. New York: Benziger Brothers, 1947.

Aristotle. *The Ethics of Aristotle: The Nicomachean Ethics*. Translated by J. A. K. Thom-son. Rev. ed. Harmondsworth: Penguin, 1976.

——— *Politics*. Translated by Benjamin Jowett. In *The Complete Works of Aristotle*. Edited by Jonathan Barnes. Princeton: Princeton University Press, 1984. Vol. 2: 1986–2129.

——— *Rhetoric*. Translated by W. Rhys Roberts. In *The Complete Works of Aristotle*. Vol. 2: 2152–2269.

Ashworth, Tony. *Trench Warfare, 1914–1918: The Live and Let Live System*. New York: Holmes & Meier, 1980.

Axelrod, Robert. *The Evolution of Cooperation*. New York: Basic Books, 1984.

Babington, Anthony. *For the Sake of Example: Capital Courts-Martial, 1914–1920*. Lon-don: Leo Cooper, 1983.

Bagnall, Stephen. *The Attack*. London: Hamish Hamilton, 1947.

Bao Ninh. *The Sorrow of War: A Novel of North Vietnam*. Translated by Phan Thanh Hao. New York: Pantheon, 1995.

Barker, Robert. *Honor Military and Civill*. London, 1602.

Battle of Maldon. Edited by E. V. Gordon. New York: Appleton-Century-Crofts, 1966.

Bechara, Antoine, Hanna Damasio, Daniel Tranel, and Antonio R. Damasio. "Deciding Advantageously before Knowing the Advantageous Strategy." *Science* 275 (1997), 1293–95.

Beowulf. A Dual-Language Edition. Translated by Howell D. Chickering Jr. Garden City, N.Y.: Doubleday/Anchor, 1977.

Berridge, Kent C. "Pleasure, Pain, Desire, and Dread: Hidden Core Process of Emotion." In *Well-being: The Foundations of Hedonic Psychology*. Edited by D. Kahneman, E. Diener, and N. Schwarz. New York: Russell Sage Foundation, 1999, 525–557.

Berridge, Kent C., and Terry E. Robinson. "What Is the Role of Dopamine in Reward: Hedonic Impact, Reward Learning, or Incentive Salience?" *Brain Research Reviews* 28 (1998), 309–369.

Berry, Christopher J. "Adam Smith and the Virtues of Commerce." In *Virtue*. Edited by John W. Chapman and William A. Galston. *Nomos* vol. 34. New York: New York University Press, 1992, 69–88.

Bierce, Ambrose. "Killed at Resaca." In *Ambrose Bierce's Civil War*. Edited by William McCann. Chicago: Gateway, 1956, 133–141.

Bishop, Alan, and Mark Bostridge, eds. *Letters from a Lost Generation: The First World War Letters of Vera Brittain and Four Friends: Roland Leighton, Edward Brittain, Victor Richardson, Geoffrey Thurlow*. Boston: Northeastern University Press, 1998.

Blackford, William W. *War Years with Jeb Stuart*. New York: Scribner, 1945.

Black-Michaud, Jacob. *Cohesive Force*. 1975. Republished as *Feuding Societies*. Oxford: Basil Blackwell, 1980.

Bloch, Marc. *Memoirs of War, 1914–15*. Ithaca: Cornell University Press, 1980.

Bloomfield, Morton. *The Seven Deadly Sins*. Lansing: Michigan State University Press, 1952.

Blunden, Edmund. *Undertones of War*. 1928. Harmondsworth: Penguin, 1982.

Blythe, Ronald. *Akenfield: Portrait of an English Village*. London: Allen Lane, 1969.

Bondy, Ruth. "Women in Theresienstadt and the Family Camp in Birkenau." In *Women in the Holocaust*. Edited by Dalia Ofer and Lenore J. Weitzman. New Haven: Yale University Press, 1998, 310–326.

Boswell, James. *Life of Johnson*. Edited by R. W. Chapman, revised by J. D. Fleeman. Oxford: Oxford University Press, 1970.

Bourdieu, Pierre. *Distinction: A Social Critique of the Judgment of Taste*. Translated by Richard Nice. Cambridge, Mass.: Harvard University Press, 1984.

———— "The Sentiment of Honour in Kabyle Society." In Peristiany, *Honour and Shame* 191–242.

Bourke, Joanna. *Dismembering the Male: Men's Bodies, Britain, and the Great War*. Chicago: University of Chicago Press, 1996.

Bowlby, Alex. *Recollections of Rifleman Bowlby.* London: Leo Cooper, 1969.

Bowra, Cecil Maurice. *Memories: 1898–1939.* London: Weidenfeld & Nicolson, 1966.

Boyarin, Daniel. *Unheroic Conduct: The Rise of Heterosexuality and the Invention of the Jewish Man.* Berkeley: University of California Press, 1997.

Brandt, R. B. "Traits of Character: A Conceptual Analysis." *American Philosophical Quarterly* 7 (1970), 23–37.

Brittain, Vera. *Testament of Youth: An Autobiographical Study of the Years 1900–1925.* 1933. Harmondsworth: Penguin, 1989.

Brown, Peter. *The Body and Society: Men, Women, and Sexual Renunciation in Early Christianity.* New York: Columbia University Press, 1988.

Browne, Thomas. *Religio Medici.* 1643. In *Sir Thomas Browne: The Major Works.* Edited by C. A. Patrides. Harmondsworth: Penguin, 1977.

Buber-Neumann, Margarete. *Milena.* 1963. Translated by Ralph Mannheim. New York: Arcade, 1997.

Burdette, Robert J. *The Drums of the 47th.* Indianapolis: Bobbs-Merrill, 1914.

Burnyeat, M. F. "Aristotle on Learning to be Good." In Rorty, *Essays on Aristotle's Ethics* 69–92.

Callan, Eamonn. "Patience and Courage." *Philosophy* 68 (1993), 523–539.

Campbell, J. K. *Honour, Family, and Patronage: A Study of Institutions and Moral Values in a Greek Mountain Community.* Oxford: Oxford University Press, 1964.

Caputo, Philip. *A Rumor of War.* 1977. New York: H. Holt, 1996.

Casey, John. *Pagan Virtue: An Essay in Ethics.* Oxford: Clarendon Press, 1990.

Chandler, Raymond. *The Little Sister.* In *Later Novels and Other Writings.* New York: Library of America, 1995, 201–416.

Chapman, Guy. *A Passionate Prodigality.* 1933. New York: Holt, Rinehart, 1966.

Cheyette, Frederic. "The Invention of the State." In *Essays on Medieval Civilization.* Edited by Bede Karl Lackner and Kenneth Roy Philp. Austin: University of Texas Press, 1978, 143–178.

Chief of Counsel for the Prosecution of Axis Criminality. *Nazi Conspiracy and Aggression.* 8 vols. Washington, D.C.: U.S. Government Printing Office, 1946.

Christine de Pizan. *The Book of the City of Ladies.* Translated by Earl Jeffrey Richards. New York: Persea, 1982.

Cicero. *On Duties.* Edited and translated by M. T. Griffin and E. M. Atkins. Cambridge: Cambridge University Press, 1991.

Clement of Alexandria. "On Spiritual Perfection (*Stromateis*, VII)." Translated by John Ernest Leonard Oulton and Henry Chadwick. In *Alexandrian Christianity.* Edited by J. E. L. Oulton. Philadelphia: Westminster Press: 1954, 93–165.

Cloete, Stuart. *A Victorian Son: An Autobiography, 1897–1922*. London: Collins, 1972.

Clover, Carol. "Maiden Warriors and Other Sons." *Journal of English and Germanic Philology* 85 (1986), 35–49.

———— *Men, Women, and Chain Saws: Gender in the Modern Horror Film*. Princeton: Princeton University Press, 1992.

———— "Regardless of Sex: Men, Women, and Power in Early Northern Europe." *Speculum* 68 (1993), 363–388.

Cobb, Humphrey. *Paths of Glory*. New York: Viking, 1935.

Cook, Haruko Taya, and Theodore F. Cook, *Japan at War: An Oral History*. New York: New Press, 1992.

Crisp, Robert. *The Gods Were Neutral*. London: Frederick Muller, 1960.

cummings, e. e. *The Enormous Room*. 1922. New York: Liveright, 1978.

Cunnison, Ian G. *Baggara Arabs: Power and Lineage in a Sudanese Nomad Tribe*. Oxford: Clarendon Press, 1966.

Curtius, Ernst Robert. *European Literature and the Latin Middle Ages*. Translated by Willard R. Trask. New York: Pantheon, 1953.

Damasio, Antonio R. *Descartes' Error: Emotion, Reason, and the Human Brain*. New York: Putnam, 1994.

Dean, Eric T., Jr. *Shook over Hell: Post-Traumatic Stress, Vietnam, and the Civil War*. Cambridge, Mass.: Harvard University Press, 1997.

de Beauvoir, Simone. *The Second Sex*. 1949. Translated by H. M. Parshley. New York: Vintage, 1989.

Delaney, Carol. "Seeds of Honor, Fields of Shame." In Gilmore, *Honor and Shame* 35–48.

Delumeau, Jean. *Sin and Fear: The Emergence of Western Guilt Culture, 13th–18th Centuries*. Translated by Eric Nicholson. New York: St. Martin's Press, 1990.

Des Pres, Terrence. *The Survivor: An Anatomy of Life in the Death Camps*. New York: Oxford University Press, 1976.

Dixon, Norman. *On the Psychology of Military Incompetence*. London: Jonathan Cape, 1976.

Donat, Alexander. *The Holocaust Kingdom*. New York: Holt, Rinehart and Winston, 1965.

Dooley, John. *John Dooley, Confederate Soldier: His War Journal*. Edited by Joseph T. Durkin. Washington, D.C.: Georgetown University Press, 1945.

Dostoyevsky, Fyodor. *Notes from the Underground*. Translated by Jessie Coulson. Harmondsworth: Penguin, 1972.

Dover, K. J. *Greek Popular Morality in the Time of Plato and Aristotle*. Rev. ed. Indianapolis: Hackett, 1994.

Dower, John W. *Japan in War and Peace*. New York: New Press, 1993.

———— *War without Mercy: Race and Power in the Pacific War*. New York: Pantheon, 1986.

Downs, Frederick. *The Killing Zone: My Life in the Vietnam War*. New York: W. W. Norton, 1978.

Duff, Antony. "Aristotelian Courage." *Ratio* 29 (1987), 2–15.

Dunn, J. C. *The War the Infantry Knew, 1914–1919*. 1938. London: Abacus, 1994.

du Picq, Ardant. *Battle Studies: Ancient and Modern Battle*. 1880. Translated by John N. Greely and Robert C. Cotton. New York: Macmillan, 1921.

Edwards, Peter. "Honour, Shame, Humiliation and Modern Japan." In *Friendship East and West: Philosophical Perspectives*. Edited by Oliver Leamon. Surrey: Curzon, 1996, 32–155.

Egil's Saga. Translated by Hermann Pálsson and Paul Edwards. Harmondsworth: Penguin, 1976.

Ehrenreich, Barbara. *Blood Rites: Origins and History of the Passions of War*. New York: Metropolitan, 1997.

Eisenhower, Dwight D. *The Papers of Dwight David Eisenhower*. Edited by Alfred D. Chandler Jr. et al. 17 vols. to date. Baltimore: Johns Hopkins Press, 1970–.

Ekman, Paul, Robert W. Levenson, and Wallace V. Friesen. "Autonomic Nervous System Activity Distinguishes among Emotions." *Science* 221 (1983), 1208–10.

Eksteins, Modris. *Rites of Spring: The Great War and the Birth of the Modern Age*. New York: Doubleday/Anchor, 1990.

Ellis, John. *The Sharp End: The Fighting Man in World War II*. Rev. ed. London: Pimlico, 1990.

Ellsworth, Phoebe C. "Levels of Thought and Levels of Emotion." In *The Nature of Emotion*. Edited by Paul Ekman and Richard J. Davidson. New York: Oxford University Press, 1995, 192–196.

Elster, Jon. *Alchemies of the Mind: Rationality and the Emotions*. Cambridge: Cambridge University Press, 1999.

———— *Nuts and Bolts for the Social Sciences*. Cambridge: Cambridge University Press, 1989.

———— *Sour Grapes: Studies in the Subversion of Rationality*. Cambridge: Cambridge University Press, 1983.

———— *Ulysses and the Sirens: Studies in Rationality and Irrationality*. Rev. ed. Cambridge: Cambridge University Press, 1984.

Evans, M. St. Helier. *Going Across or with the 9th Welch in the Butterfly Division*. Edited by Frank Delamain. Newport, Mont.: R. H. Johns, 1952.

Falk, W. D. "Prudence, Temperance and Courage." In *Moral Concepts*. Edited by Joel Feinberg. New York: Oxford University Press, 1970, 114–119.

Feeley-Harnik, Gillian. "Childbirth and the Affiliation of Children in Northwestern Madagascar." *TALOHA: Revue du Musée d'Art et d'Archéologie, Antananarivo.* Vol. 13. Forthcoming.

Foote, Philippa. *Virtues and Vices*. Oxford: Basil Blackwell, 1978.

Ford, Ford Madox. *Parade's End*. A tetralogy: *Some Do Not . . .* (1924); *No More Parades* (1925); *A Man Could Stand Up* (1926); and *The Last Post* (1928). Harmondsworth: Penguin, 1982.

Fortenbaugh, W. W. *Aristotle on Emotion*. New York: Harper & Row, 1975.

Fox, Frank. *The British Army at War*. London: T. Fisher Unwin, 1917.

Fox, Robin Lane. *Alexander the Great*. London: Allen Lane, 1973.

Freedman, Paul. "Cowardice, Heroism and the Legendary Origins of Catalonia." *Past and Present* 121 (1988), 3–28.

Freud, Sigmund. "Medusa's Head." 1922. In *The Standard Edition of the Complete Psychological Works of Sigmund Freud*. Edited and translated by James Strachey. 24 vols. London: Hogarth Press, 1953–1974. Vol. 18: 273–274.

Frijda, Nico H. *The Emotions*. Cambridge: Cambridge University Press, 1986.

Fussell, Paul. *Doing Battle: The Making of a Skeptic*. Boston: Little, Brown, 1996.

———— *The Great War and Modern Memory*. Oxford: Oxford University Press, 1975.

Gajdusek, Robert E. *Resurrection: A War Journey*. Notre Dame, Ind.: University of Notre Dame Press, 1997.

Geach, Peter. *The Virtues: The Stanton Lectures, 1973–74*. Cambridge: Cambridge University Press, 1977.

Gibbard, Allan. *Wise Choices, Apt Feelings: A Theory of Normative Judgment*. Cambridge, Mass.: Harvard University Press, 1990.

Gibbon, Edward. *The Decline and Fall of the Roman Empire*. New York: Modern Library, 1932.

Gilbert, Martin. *The First World War: A Complete History*. New York: H. Holt, 1994.

Gilmore, David D., ed. *Honor and Shame and the Unity of the Mediterranean*. Washington, D.C.: American Anthropological Association, 1987.

Ginzburg, Eugenia Semyonovna. *Journey into the Whirlwind*. Translated by Paul Stevenson and Max Hayward. New York: Harcourt, Brace, 1967.

Giovannini, Maureen J. "Female Chastity Codes in the Circum-Mediterranean." In Gilmore, *Honor and Shame* 61–75.

Gisli's Saga. Translated by George Johnston as *The Saga of Gisli the Outlaw*. Toronto: University of Toronto Press, 1974.

Goffman, Erving. *Relations in Public*. New York: Basic Books, 1971.

———— *Stigma: Notes on the Management of Spoiled Identity*. New York: Simon and Schuster, 1963.

Gordon, Robert M. *The Structure of Emotions*. Cambridge: Cambridge University Press, 1987.

Grant, Ulysses S. *Personal Memoirs of U. S. Grant*. New York: Library of America, 1990.

Graves, Robert. *Good-bye to All That*. 1929. 2d ed. Garden City, N.Y.: Doubleday/ Anchor, 1957.

Gray, J. Glenn. *The Warriors: Reflections on Men in Battle*. New York: Harper and Row, 1967.

Gray, Jeffrey A. *The Psychology of Fear and Stress*. London: Weidenfeld and Nicolson, 1971.

Grettir's Saga. Translated by Denton Fox and Hermann Pálsson. Toronto: University of Toronto Press, 1974.

Grinker, Roy R., and John P. Spiegel. *Men under Stress*. Philadelphia: Blakiston, 1945.

Gullace, Nicolleta F. "White Feathers and Wounded Men: Female Patriotism and the Memory of the Great War." *Journal of British Studies* 36 (1997), 178–206.

Hancock, Cornelia. *South after Gettysburg: Letters of Cornelia Hancock from the Army of the Potomac, 1863–1865*. Edited by Henrietta Stratton Jaquette. Philadelphia: University of Pennsylvania Press, 1937.

Hanson, Victor Davis. *The Western Way of War: Infantry Battle in Classical Greece*. New York: Oxford University Press, 1990.

Hare, R. M. *Freedom and Reason*. Oxford: Clarendon Press, 1963.

Harré, Rom. "Embarrassment: A Conceptual Analysis." In *Shyness and Embarrassment*. Edited by W. Ray Crozier. Cambridge: Cambridge University Press, 1990, 181–204.

Harris, Benjamin. *The Recollections of Rifleman Harris*. Edited by Christopher Hibbert. London: Leo Cooper, 1970.

Hasluck, Margaret. *The Unwritten Law in Albania*. Cambridge: Cambridge University Press, 1954.

Hatfield, Elaine, John T. Cacioppo, and Richard L. Rapson. *Emotional Contagion*. Cambridge: Cambridge University Press, 1994.

Hebb, D. O. "On the Nature of Fear." *Psychological Review* 53 (1946), 259–276.

Herdt, Gilbert. "Sambia Nosebleeding Rites and Male Proximity to Women." In *Cultural Psychology: Essays on Comparative Human Development*. Edited by James W. Stigler, Richard A. Shweder, and Gilbert Herdt. Cambridge: Cambridge University Press, 1990, 366–400.

Herodotus. *The Histories*. Translated by Aubrey de Sélincourt. Revised by A. R. Burn. Harmondsworth: Penguin, 1972.

Herr, Michael. *Dispatches*. 1977. New York: Vintage, 1991.

Hersey, John. *Hiroshima*. 1946. New York: Vintage, 1989.

Herzog, Don. *Poisoning the Minds of the Lower Orders*. Princeton: Princeton University Press, 1998.

Hobbes, Thomas. *Leviathan*. New York: E. P. Dutton, 1914.

Holmes, Richard. *Acts of War: The Behavior of Men in Battle*. New York: Free Press, 1985.

Homer. *The Iliad*. Translated by Martin Hammond. Harmondsworth: Penguin, 1987.

Hopkins, Keith. *Death and Renewal*. Cambridge: Cambridge University Press, 1983.

Horne, Alistair. *The Price of Glory: Verdun 1916*. Harmondsworth: Penguin, 1964.

Hrafnkel's Saga. In *Hrafnkel's Saga and Other Stories*. Translated by Hermann Pálsson. Harmondsworth: Penguin, 1971, 35–71.

Huie, William Bradford. *The Execution of Private Slovik*. New York: New American Library, 1954.

Hume, David. *An Enquiry Concerning the Principles of Morals*. La Salle, Ill.: Open Court, 1966.

———— "Of Refinement in the Arts." In *Essays, Moral, Political, and Literary*. Edited by Eugene F. Miller. Indianapolis: Liberty Classics, 1987, 268–280.

———— "Of Suicide." In *Essays, Moral, Political, and Literary*, 577–589.

Hunt, Lester. "Courage and Principle." *Canadian Journal of Philosophy* 10 (1980), 281–293.

Hynes, Samuel. *The Soldiers' Tale: Bearing Witness to Modern War*. New York: Penguin, 1997.

Jenkins, Harold, ed. *Hamlet*. The Arden Shakespeare. New York: Methuen, 1982.

Johansson, Sheila Ryan. "Deferred Infanticide: Excess Female Mortality during Childhood." In *Infanticide*. Edited by Glenn Hausfater and Sarah B. Hrdy. New York: Aldine, 1984, 463–485.

Johnson, Samuel. *The Rambler*. Edited by W. J. Bate and Albrecht B. Strauss. Vols. 3–5 of *The Yale Edition of the Works of Samuel Johnson*. New Haven: Yale University Press, 1969.

Jünger, Ernst. *The Storm of Steel: From the Diary of a German Storm-Troop Officer on the Western Front*. Translated by Basil Creighton. London: Chatto and Windus, 1929.

Karay, Felicja. "Women in the Forced-Labor Camps." In *Women in the Holocaust*. Edited by Dalia Ofer and Lenore J. Weitzman. New Haven: Yale University Press, 1998, 285–309.

Kaske, Robert E. "*Sapientia et Fortitudo* as the Controlling Theme of *Beowulf*." *Studies in Philology* 55 (1958), 423–457.

Keegan, John. *The Battle for History: Re-fighting World War II*. New York: Vintage, 1996.

———— *The Face of Battle*. Harmondsworth: Penguin, 1976.

———— *A History of Warfare*. New York: Vintage, 1994.

———— *The Mask of Command*. Harmondsworth: Penguin, 1987.

Keegan, John, and Richard Holmes. *Soldiers: An Illustrated History of Men in Battle*. New York: Konecky and Konecky, 1985.

Ker, W. P. *Epic and Romance: Essays on Medieval Literature*. 2d ed. New York: Macmillan, 1908.

Kerrigan, John. *Revenge Tragedy: Aeschylus to Armageddon*. Oxford: Clarendon Press, 1996.

Kipling, Rudyard. *Rudyard Kipling's Verse*. Garden City, N.Y.: Doubleday, 1940.

Kitto, H. D. F. *The Greeks*. Harmondsworth: Penguin, 1951.

Konner, Melvin. *The Tangled Web: Biological Constraints on the Human Spirit*. New York: Holt, Rinehart and Winston, 1982.

Krebs, J. R., and N. B. Davies. *An Introduction to Behavioural Ecology*. 3d ed. Oxford: Blackwell, 1993.

Landnámabók. Edited by Jakob Benediktsson. Vol. 1: *Íslenzk Fornrit*. Reykjavik: Hið Íslenzka Fornritafélag, 1968.

La Rochefoucauld. *Maximes et réflexions diverses*. Edited by Jacques Truchet. Paris: Flammarion, 1977.

Lawrence, T. E. *Seven Pillars of Wisdom*. 1926. Harmondsworth: Penguin, 1962.

Laxdaela Saga. Translated by Magnus Magnusson and Hermann Pálsson. Harmondsworth: Penguin, 1969.

Lazenby, John. "The Killing Zone." In *Hoplites: The Classical Greek Battle Experience*. Edited by Victor Davis Hanson. London: Routledge, 1991, 87–109.

LeDoux, Joseph. *The Emotional Brain: The Mysterious Underpinnings of Emotional Life*. New York: Touchstone, 1996.

Levenson, Robert. "Autonomic Nervous System Differences among Emotions." *Psychological Science* 3 (1992), 23–27.

Levi, Primo. *The Drowned and the Saved*. Translated by Raymond Rosenthal. 1986. New York: Vintage, 1989.

———— *Moments of Reprieve*. Translated by Ruth Feldman. Harmondsworth: Penguin, 1987.

———— *Survival in Auschwitz*. Translated by Stuart Woolf. 1958. New York: Touchstone, 1996.

Liebling, A. J. "Paris Postscript: May-June 1940." In *Reporting World War II*. New York: Library of America, 1995. Vol. 1: 32–52.

Linderman, Gerald F. *Embattled Courage: The Experience of Combat in the American Civil War*. New York: Free Press, 1987.

Llewellyn, Karl, and E. Adamson Hoebel. *The Cheyenne Way*. Norman: University of Oklahoma Press, 1941.

Lowie, Robert H. *The Crow Indians*. New York: Farrar and Rinehart, 1935.

Luard, K. E. *Unknown Warriors: Extracts from the Letters of K. E. Luard, Nursing Sister in France, 1914–1918*. London: Chatto and Windus, 1930.

MacIntyre, Alasdair C. *After Virtue*. 2d ed. Notre Dame, Ind.: University of Notre Dame Press, 1984.

———— *A Short History of Ethics*. London: Routledge and Kegan Paul, 1967.

Macmillan, Harold. *Winds of Change: 1914–1939*. New York: Harper & Row, 1966.

Majdalany, Fred. *Patrol*. Boston: Houghton Mifflin, 1953.

Malson, Lucien. *Wolf Children and the Problem of Human Nature*. New York: New Left Books, 1972.

Manchester, William. *Goodbye, Darkness: A Memoir of the Pacific War*. 1980. New York: Dell, 1987.

Mandeville, Bernard. *The Fable of the Bees or Private Vices, Publick Benefits*. 1732. 6th ed. Edited by F. B. Kaye. 2 vols. 1924; reprint, Indianapolis: Liberty Press, 1988.

Manning, Frederic. *The Middle Parts of Fortune: Somme and Ancre, 1916*. First published anonymously in 1929, then in 1930 as *Her Privates We*. New York: St. Martin's Press, 1977.

Mark VII (Max Plowman). *A Subaltern on the Somme in 1916*. New York: Dutton, 1928.

Marshall, S. L. A. *Men against Fire: The Problem of Battle Command in Future War*. 1947. New York: Morrow, 1966.

The Martyrdom of St. Polycarp. In Musurillo, 2–21.

The Martyrdoms of Saints Perpetua and Felicitas. In Musurillo, 106–131.

The Martyrs of Lyons. In Musurillo, 62–85.

Mason, Robert. *Chickenhawk*. Harmondsworth: Penguin, 1983.

McDonough, James. *Platoon Leader*. Novato, Calif.: Presidio, 1985.

McPherson, James M. *For Cause and Comrades: Why Men Fought in the Civil War*. New York: Oxford University Press, 1997.

Meulengracht Sørensen, Preben. *The Unmanly Man: Concepts of Sexual Defamation in Early Northern Society*. Translated by Joan Turville-Petre. Odense: Odense University Press, 1983.

Middleton, Thomas, and William Rowley. *The Old Law*. Edited by Catherine M. Shaw. New York: Garland, 1982.

Milgram, Stanley. *Obedience to Authority*. New York: Harper & Row, 1974.

Miller, William Ian. *The Anatomy of Disgust*. Cambridge, Mass.: Harvard University Press, 1997.

—— *Bloodtaking and Peacemaking: Feud, Law, and Society in Saga Iceland*. Chicago: University of Chicago Press, 1990.

—— "Choosing the Avenger: Some Aspects of the Bloodfeud in Medieval Iceland and England." *Law and History Review* 1 (1983), 159–204.

—— "Gluttony." *Representations* 60 (1997), 92–112.

—— *Humiliation and Other Essays on Honor, Social Discomfort, and Violence*. Ithaca: Cornell University Press, 1993.

—— "Near Misses." *Michigan Quarterly Review* 38 (1999), 1–15.

Montaigne. *Michel de Montaigne: The Complete Essays*. Translated by M. A. Screech. Harmondsworth: Penguin, 1991.

Montecuccoli, Raimondo. *Concerning Battle*. Edited and translated by Thomas M. Barker. In *The Military Intellectual and Battle: Raimondo Montecuccoli and the Thirty Years' War*. Albany: SUNY Press, 1975.

Moore, Harold G., and Joseph L. Galloway. *We Were Soldiers Once . . . and Young—Ia Drang: The Battle That Changed the War in Vietnam*. New York: HarperCollins, 1993.

Moran, Lord. *The Anatomy of Courage*. London: Constable, 1946.

Mowat, Farley. *And No Birds Sang*. Toronto: McClelland and Stewart, 1979.

Musurillo, Herbert, ed. and trans. *The Acts of the Christian Martyrs*. Oxford: Clarendon Press, 1972.

Newton, James K. *A Wisconsin Boy in Dixie: The Selected Letters of James K. Newton*. Edited by Stephen E. Ambrose. Madison: University of Wisconsin Press, 1961.

Nietzsche, Friedrich. *Daybreak: Thoughts on the Prejudices of Morality*. Translated by R. J. Hollingdale. Cambridge: Cambridge University Press, 1982.

—— *On the Genealogy of Morals*. Translated by Walter Kaufmann and R. J. Hollingdale. New York: Vintage, 1967.

Njál's Saga. Translated by Magnus Magnusson and Hermann Pálsson. Baltimore: Penguin Books, 1960.

Nussbaum, Martha C. *The Fragility of Goodness: Luck and Ethics in Greek Tragedy and Philosophy*. Cambridge: Cambridge University Press, 1986.

Ober, Josiah. "Classical Greek Times." In *The Laws of War: Constraints on Warfare in the Western World*. Edited by Michael Howard et al. New Haven: Yale University Press, 1994, 12–26.

O'Brien, Tim. *Going After Cacciato*. 1978. New York: Dell, 1989.

———— *If I Die in a Combat Zone Box Me Up and Ship Me Home*. 1973. New York: Dell, 1987.

———— *The Things They Carried: A Work of Fiction*. Harmondsworth: Penguin, 1991.

———— "The Vietnam in Me." *New York Times Sunday Magazine*, 2 October 1994, 48 ff.

Origen. *Exhortation to Martyrdom*. Translated by John Ernest Leonard Oulton and Henry Chadwick. In *Alexandrian Christianity*. Edited by J. E. L. Oulton. Philadelphia: Westminster Press: 1954, 388–429.

Orwell, George. *The Collected Essays, Journalism, and Letters of George Orwell*. Edited by Sonia Orwell and Ian Angus. Vol. 1: *An Age Like This: 1920–1940*. Vol. 2: *My Country Right or Left: 1940–1943*. New York: Harcourt, Brace, 1968.

Owen, Wilfred. *The Collected Poems of Wilfred Owen*. Edited by C. Day Lewis. New York: New Directions, 1965.

Paxton, Elisha F. *The Civil War Letters of General Frank "Bull" Paxton, CSA, a Lieutenant of Lee and Jackson*. Hillsboro, Texas: Hill Junior College Press, 1978.

Pears, David. "Courage as a Mean." In Rorty, *Essays on Aristotle's Ethics* 171–187.

Peristiany, J. G., ed. *Honour and Shame: The Values of Mediterranean Society*. Chicago: University of Chicago Press, 1966.

Perkins, Judith. *The Suffering Self: Pain and Narrative Representation in the Early Christian Era*. London: Routledge, 1995.

Pitt-Rivers, Julian. "Honour and Social Status." In Peristiany, *Honour and Shame* 19–78.

Pizarro, Pedro. *Relation of the Discovery and Conquest of the Kingdoms of Peru*. Translated by Philip Ainsworth Means. New York: Cortes Society, 1921.

Plato. *Laches*. Translated by Benjamin Jowett. In the *Collected Dialogues of Plato*. Edited by Edith Hamilton and Huntington Cairns. Bollingen Series LXXI. New York: Pantheon, 1961, 123–144.

———— *Laws*. Translated by A. E. Taylor. In the *Collected Dialogues* 1225–1513.

———— *Phaedo*. Translated by Hugh Tredenick. In the *Collected Dialogues* 40–98.

———— *Protagoras*. Translated by W. K. C. Guthrie. In the *Collected Dialogues* 308–352.

———— *Republic*. Translated by Paul Shorey. In the *Collected Dialogues* 575–844.

———— *Symposium*. Translated by Michael Joyce. In the *Collected Dialogues* 526–574.

———— *Timaeus*. Translated by Benjamin Jowett. In the *Collected Dialogues* 1151–1211.

Plutarch. *Plutarch on Sparta*. Translated by Richard J. A. Talbert. Harmondsworth: Penguin, 1988.

Plutchik, Robert. *Emotion: A Psychoevolutionary Synthesis*. New York: Harper & Row, 1980.

Polybius. *The Rise of the Roman Empire*. Translated by Ian Scott-Kilvert. Harmondsworth: Penguin, 1979.

Rachman, S. J. *Fear and Courage*. 2d ed. New York: W. H. Freeman, 1990.

Regan, Geoffrey. *Fight or Flight*. New York: Avon, 1996.

Remarque, Erich Maria. *All Quiet on the Western Front*. 1928. Translated by A. W. Wheen. New York: Fawcett, 1975.

Richards, Frank. *Old Soldiers Never Die*. London: Faber and Faber, 1933.

Rohwer S. and F. C. Rohwer, "Status Signalling in Harris Sparrows." *Animal Behaviour* 26 (1978), 1012–22.

Rorty, Amélie O., ed. *Essays on Aristotle's Ethics*. Berkeley: University of California Press, 1980.

——— "The Faces of Courage." In A. O. Rorty, *Mind in Action: Essays in the Philosophy of Mind*. Boston: Beacon, 1988, 299–313.

——— "Fearing Death." In *Mind in Action* 197–211.

Rosaldo, Michelle. "The Shame of Headhunters and the Autonomy of Self." *Ethos* 11 (1983), 135–151.

Rosenberg, Isaac. *The Collected Works of Isaac Rosenberg*. Edited by I. M. Parsons. New York: Oxford University Press, 1979.

Ross, W. David. *Aristotle*. 5th ed. London: Methuen, 1949.

Rozin, Paul, and April E. Fallon. "A Perspective on Disgust." *Psychological Review* 94 (1987), 23–41.

Ryder, Rowland. *Edith Cavell*. New York: Stein and Day, 1975.

The Saga of the Jómsvíkings. Translated by Lee M. Hollander. Austin: University of Texas Press, 1955.

Samuel, E. *An Historical Account of the British Army and of the Law Military*. London: William Clowes, 1816.

Sassoon, Siegfried. *Memoirs of a Fox-Hunting Man*. London: Faber and Faber, 1928.

——— *Memoirs of an Infantry Officer*. London: Faber and Faber, 1930.

Schelling, Thomas C. *The Strategy of Conflict*. Cambridge, Mass.: Harvard University Press, 1960.

Schwartz, Carl E., Nancy Snidman, and Jerome Kagan. "Early Childhood Temperament as a Determinant of Externalizing Behavior in Adolescence." *Development and Psychopathology* 8 (1996), 527–538.

Scott, Walter. *Redgauntlet*. Oxford: Oxford University Press, 1985.

Shakespeare, William. *Shakespeare: The Complete Works*. Edited by Alfred Harbage et al. Baltimore: Penguin, 1969.

Shay, Jonathan. *Achilles in Vietnam: Combat Trauma and the Undoing of Character*. New York: Simon and Schuster, 1994.

Sherman, William Tecumseh. *Memoirs of General W. T. Sherman*. New York: Library of America, 1990.

Sidgwick, Henry. *The Methods of Ethics*. 7th ed. London: Macmillan, 1913.

Skrjabina, Elena. *Siege and Survival: The Odyssey of a Leningrader*. Carbondale: Southern Illinois University Press, 1971.

Sledge, E. B. *With the Old Breed at Peleliu and Okinawa*. 1981. New York: Oxford University Press, 1990.

Small, Abner. *The Road to Richmond*. Edited by Harold Adams Small. Berkeley: University of California Press, 1939.

Smith, Adam. *An Inquiry into the Nature and Causes of the Wealth of Nations*. Edited by R. H. Campbell and A. S. Skinner. Oxford: Clarendon Press, 1979.

—— *The Theory of Moral Sentiments*. Edited by D. D. Raphael and A. L. Macfie. Oxford: Clarendon Press, 1976.

Smith, Craig, and Phoebe C. Ellsworth. "Patterns of Cognitive Appraisal in Emotion." *Journal of Personality and Social Psychology* 48 (1985), 813–838.

Smith, Jack K. "Death in the Ia Drang Valley." In *Reporting Vietnam*. New York: Library of America, 1998. Vol. 1: 208–222.

Smoler, Frederic. "The Secret of the Soldiers Who Didn't Shoot." *American Heritage* 40, no. 2 (1989), 37–45.

Solomon, Richard L., and John D. Corbit. "An Opponent-Process Theory of Motivation." *Psychological Review* 81 (1974), 119–145.

Sorley, Charles Hamilton. *The Collected Letters of Charles Hamilton Sorley*. Edited by Jean Moorcroft Wilson. London: Cecil Woolf, 1990.

Stendhal. *Scarlet and Black*. Translated by Margaret R. B. Shaw. Harmondsworth: Penguin, 1953.

Stewart, Frank Henderson. *Honor*. Chicago: University of Chicago Press, 1994.

Stouffer, Samuel A., et al. *The American Soldier: Combat and Its Aftermath*. Vol. 2. Princeton: Princeton University Press, 1949.

Strong, Robert. *A Yankee Private's Civil War*. Edited by Ashley Halsey. Chicago: H. Regnery, 1961.

Sun Tzu. *The Art of War*. Translated by Samuel B. Griffith. Oxford: Oxford University Press, 1963.

Swank, Roy L., and Walter E. Marchand, "Combat Neuroses: Development of Combat Exhaustion." *Archives of Neurology and Psychiatry* 55 (1946), 236–247.

Tambiah, S. J. "The Magical Power of Words." *Man* 3 (1968), 175–208.

Tawney, R. H. *The Attack and Other Papers*. London: George Allen and Unwin, 1953.

Taylor, Gabriele. *Pride, Shame, and Guilt: Emotions of Self-Assessment*. Oxford: Clarendon Press, 1985.

Taylor, Shelley E., and Jonathan Brown. "Illusion and Well-Being: A Social Psychological Perspective on Mental Health." *Psychological Bulletin* 103 (1988), 193–210.

Tec, Nechama. *When Light Pierced the Darkness: Christian Rescue of Jews in Nazi-Occupied Poland*. New York: Oxford University Press, 1986.

Thucydides. *History of the Peloponnesian War*. Translated by Rex Warner. Rev. ed. Harmondsworth: Penguin, 1972.

Timerman, Jacobo. *Prisoner without a Name, Cell without a Number*. Translated by Toby Talbot. New York: Vintage, 1981.

Todorov, Tzvetan. *Facing the Extreme: Moral Life in the Concentration Camps*. Translated by Arthur Denner and Abigail Pollak. New York: H. Holt, 1996.

Tomkins, Silvan S. *Affect, Imagery, Consciousness*. Vol. 3: *The Negative Affects: Anger and Fear*. New York: Springer, 1991.

Tversky, Amos, and Daniel Kahneman. "The Framing of Decisions and the Rationality of Choice." *Science* 211 (1981), 453–458.

Urmson, J. O. "Aristotle's Doctrine of the Mean." In Rorty, *Essays on Aristotle's Ethics* 157–170.

——— "Saints and Heroes." In *Essays in Moral Philosophy*. Edited by A. I. Melden. Seattle: University of Washington Press, 1958, 198–216.

U.S. Senate, Committee on Veterans' Affairs. *Medal of Honor Recipients: 1863–1978*. Washington, D.C.: U.S. Government Printing Office, 1979.

van Hooff, Anton J. L. *From Autothanasia to Suicide: Self-killing in Classical Antiquity*. London: Routledge, 1990.

von Wright, Georg Henrik. *The Varieties of Goodness*. London: Routledge and Kegan Paul, 1963.

Wallace, James D. *Virtues and Vices*. Ithaca: Cornell University Press, 1978.

Walton, Douglas N. *Courage: A Philosophical Investigation*. Berkeley: University of California Press, 1986.

Walzer, Michael. *Just and Unjust Wars*. 2d ed. New York: Basic Books, 1992.

Watkins, Sam R. *Co. Aytch*. New York: Touchstone, 1997.

Watney, John. *The Enemy Within: A Personal Impression of the Invasion of Normandy 1944*. London: Hodder and Stoughton, 1946.

Wheeler, Everett L. "The General as Hoplite." In *Hoplites: The Classical Greek Battle Experience*. Edited by Victor Davis Hanson. London: Routledge, 1991, 121–170.

Whitaker, Ian. "'A Sack for Carrying Things': The Traditional Role of Women in Northern Albanian Society." *Anthropological Quarterly* 54 (1981), 146–156.

Wiley, Bell Irwin. *The Life of Billy Yank: The Common Soldier of the Union.* Indianapolis: Bobbs-Merrill, 1952.

———— *The Life of Johnny Reb: The Common Soldier of the Confederacy.* Baton Rouge: Louisiana State University Press, 1978.

Wilmot, John. *The Complete Poems of John Wilmot, Earl of Rochester.* Edited by David M. Vieth. New Haven: Yale University Press, 1968.

Wilson, John Lyde. *The Code of Honor: or Rules for the Government of Principals and Seconds in Duelling.* 1838; reprinted as an appendix in Jack K. Williams, *Dueling in the Old South.* College Station: Texas A&M University Press, 1980, 88–104.

Winkler, John. J. *The Constraints of Desire: The Anthropology of Sex and Gender in Ancient Greece.* London: Routledge, 1990.

Winter, Denis. *Death's Men: Soldiers of the Great War.* Harmondsworth: Penguin, 1979.

Winthrop, William. *Military Law and Precedents.* 2d ed. Washington, D.C.: U.S. Government Printing Office, 1920.

Wolff, Tobias. *In Pharaoh's Army: Memories of the Lost War.* New York: Vintage, 1994.

Yearley, Lee H. *Mencius and Aquinas: Theories of Virtue and Conceptions of Courage.* Albany: SUNY Press, 1990.

Index